Awakening Our Faith in the Future

Awakening Our Faith in the Future investigates the avenues for creating a new branch of psychology, a *transformative political psychology*. In the past, political psychology has focused directly on analysis and knowledge acquisition, rather than on interventions that transform self and culture. A *transformative* political psychology combines the best of traditional social science with the transformative intent of clinical psychology in order to create a new political culture.

Peter T. Dunlap suggests that while liberals focus intently outside of themselves on changing the world, those with psychological interests focus much more internally on changing themselves. In this book, he argues that by combining political liberalism and psychology, and encouraging psychologists to develop cultural learning practices based on ideas of self-knowledge, there is opportunity to transform our political culture.

Divided into five parts, this book explores:

- stories of political destiny
- questions of development
- opportunities for political development
- a speculative theory of cultural evolution
- practices of a political psychologist.

This scholarly text uses personal experiences and the stories of progressive political leaders as pathways for addressing political problems, making it ideal reading for professionals and students in the fields of both politics and psychology as well as for activists interested in the future of liberalism.

Peter T. Dunlap is a political and clinical psychologist working in private and political practice. Peter works with organizations and communities, using educational, healing, and community engagement learning practices. His research includes an investigation into the political development of progressive political leaders titled "Destiny as Capacity: The Transformation of Political Identity in Human Development".

Peter Dunlap has written a provocative and insightful critique of liberal approaches to psychology and demonstrated the need to vocationalize the work of changing political culture and to create transformative political psychologists, political educators and political sociologists who can both analyze and treat a sick society. Chocked full of important insights that will be of great interest to social change advocates as well as to social theorists, "Awakening Our Faith in the Future" makes a significant contribution to contemporary thought and should be read by anyone who has ever gone to or contemplated psychotherapy.

Rabbi Michael Lerner, Ph.D., Editor of Tikkun Magazine, Chair of the interfaith Network of Spiritual Progressives, and author of 11 books including *The Politics of Meaning* **and** *The Left Hand of God: Taking Back our Country from the Religious Right*

To write well about politics and psychology, you have to be able to keep them separate whilst at the same time underlining their interconnectedness. You need to balance what you know about individuals and what you know about societies and nations. You have to have a passion for your cause, and be able to temper that passion with rational argument and respect for divergent views. Peter Dunlap manages these paradoxes superbly well – as well as anyone writing in this area today – as he turns Jungian psychology sharply towards a radical image of its political destiny. He proposes that we co-create a completely new kind of political psychologist whose responsibility is to bring a private-life focus more deeply into the public world. In this beautifully written and challenging book, Dunlap has evolved a practical path for the integration of emotion and thought in the service of social justice by demonstrating a wide range of inspiring "learning practices" that activate creative and progressive political energies.

Andrew Samuels, Professor of Analytical Psychology, University of Essex, author of *The Political Psyche* **and** *Politics on the Couch: Citizenship and the Internal Life.*

Peter's book is animated by a brilliant vision for Progressive Politics, what *Habits of the Heart* would call a new moral ecology. The vision reflects how the masculine and feminine archetypes organically can weave a pattern that integrates the inner world of affect and image (psychology) with the outer world of power and conflicting values (politics). To cultivate a new moral ecology, he envisions a new vocation, a political psychologist, and a new vision for the polis, the psychological citizen. Peter's work suggests new models of leadership, and not only will inspire social scientists, political activists, and educators, but all of us who aspire to a new political culture in the United States and beyond.

Dean Elias, St. Mary's Professor in the doctoral programme in Educational Leadership and co-founder of the Praxis Tank for Progressives.

Awakening Our Faith in the Future

The Advent of Psychological Liberalism

Peter T. Dunlap

Routledge
Taylor & Francis Group

LONDON AND NEW YORK

First published 2008 by Routledge
27 Church Road, Hove, East Sussex BN3 2FA

Simultaneously published in the USA and Canada
by Routledge
270 Madison Avenue, New York, NY 10016

Routledge is an imprint of the Taylor & Francis Group, an Informa business

Typeset in Times by Garfield Morgan, Swansea, West Glamorgan
Printed and bound in Great Britain by TJ International Ltd, Padstow, Cornwall
Paperback cover design by Lisa Dynan

This publication has been produced with paper manufactured to strict
environmental standards and with pulp derived from sustainable forests.

British Library Cataloguing in Publication Data
A catalogue record for this book is available from the British Library

Library of Congress Cataloging-in-Publication Data
Dunlap, Peter T., 1957–
    Awakening our faith in the future : the advent of psychological liberalism /
Peter T. Dunlap.
        p. cm.
    Includes bibliographical references and index.
    ISBN 978-0-415-44505-4 (hardback) – ISBN 978-0-415-44506-1 (pbk.)
1. Liberalism–Psychological aspects. 2. Political psychology. 3. Political
development. I. Title.
    JC574.D86 2008
    320.51–dc22

                                                            2007039023

ISBN 978-0-415-44505-4 (hbk)
ISBN 978-0-415-44506-1 (pbk)

I dedicate this book to my parents,
Janet and John Dunlap.

They found each other, raised my siblings and me
while finding time to raise Cain in interesting times.

Through their passions
and between their love for politics and psychology,
I caught the scent of the future.

The whole future of the earth depends on awakening our faith in the future.
(Pierre Teilhard, 1963)

Contents

Illustrations

Figures

Tables

Acknowledgments

I owe thanks to many people. Most notably to my wife, Margaret, who suffered through the way this book is giving birth to me: thank you for your patience, your love, and care for our children. To my son, Trask, for his reminding me that the goal was to finish so as not to miss any more of his company. To my daughter Lauren, whose smile and face always make me happy.

I also extend my thanks to the Dunlap and related clans and to the liberal community that thrives within the Napa Valley. Our shared family and community history has been one of the most profound blessings of my life. Whether at the dinner table, Christmas caroling parties, or election meetings we found a way of coming together that is fun-loving while recognizing our responsibility for the future.

I feel a great deal of gratitude to my two mentors, whose objectivity has helped me to find solid ground underneath my feet. Stan McDaniel taught me how to think passionately and to always seek the most difficult questions, whether there were any answers around or not. Aftab Omer, at the Institute of Imaginal Studies, helped me find an orienting praxis which I'm making my way into the world.

More recently I have been blessed by my friendships with Dean Elias and Ken White of the Praxis Tank for Progressives. Their support, feedback, and willingness to engage in all sorts of wild conversations have helped loosen, free, and make comprehensible the guiding vision of this book.

I also have had the benefit of working with a number of political change groups, whose meetings and membership have had a great deal of influence over me in the last four years. It is to Sonoma County Conservation Action and Petaluma Tomorrow that I look for a vision of a sustainable future, smart and ethical politics, and the recognition that politics is not enough, but requires community making as well. It is to the Community Catalyst Corps that I look for the willingness to make politics increasingly personal, while keeping the focus on community engagement.

I owe a great deal of thanks to Andrew Samuels and John Beebe whose encouragement helped me to think of myself as a writer. Also, to Art

Warmoth who was the first teacher I knew who lived at the crack in our culture's fabric between politics and psychology. And, thanks to my brother David who helped me write and rewrite earlier parts of this book in my dissertation until I understood it well enough to be able to explain it.

Lastly, to the nine progressive political leaders who volunteered for my research, they taught me, anew, that politics is sacred.

I also want to acknowledge the design for the section dividers. This design is derived from the "Transactional" philosophy of professor Stan McDaniel. The symbol is entitled "the schema of continuity" and it refers to the way in which any function of a system is analogous to the system as a whole as implied by the saying, "as above, so below." I use this symbol to represent my efforts to integrate the personal and the cultural in the political change work that I do. This work has been deeply informed by Stan's teaching, for which I am grateful.

Permissions acknowledgements

Translation of "Das waren Tage Michelangelo's" by Joanna Macy and Anita Barrows. Copyright © 1996 by Anita Barrows and Joanna Macy and Anita Barrows. Originally published in *Rilke's book of hours: Love poems to God*. Reprinted by permission of the authors.

"Das waren Tage Michelangelo's / Once I read in foreign books", from RILKE'S BOOK OF HOURS: LOVE POEMS TO GOD by Rainer Maria Rilke, translated by Anita Barrows and Joanna Macy, copyright © 1996 by Anita Barrows and Joanna Macy. Used by permission of Riverhead Books, and imprint of Penguin Group (USA) Inc.

Part I

Stories of political destiny

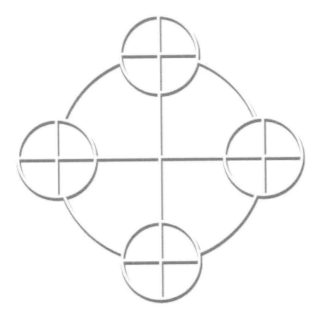

Chapter 1

The liberal's emotional body opens our faith in the future

Renewing liberalism by transforming political culture

Like many liberals I am frightened that our gluttonous appetite for material wealth is ruining the health of the planet. I am angry at the way this issue has been neglected and I am ashamed by my own participation in this abuse. I also feel anguish about our failures to be just and our struggle to use power accountably. All of this emotion, yes, I must be a liberal. We liberals feel a lot and often don't know quite what to do with these feelings, with the intensities evoked by the current crises in our culture, or with ourselves.

While I have too often felt helplessness about my own limits to respond to these crises, I have also sought out the company of others to help me direct these emotions toward new forms of social and political action. By joining with others the moral integrity intrinsic to liberalism comes alive and I feel more hopeful, determined, and capable. I am renewing myself and, with others, we are renewing liberalism.

Joining with others to renew ourselves and to engage our communities is a new approach to politics. Too often people become political in order to gain power and to control resources. Whether in the service of corrupt or humane values, the political identities they form focus too much on maintaining power and not on the opportunity to use power to support human development. When politics and human development become the motivating agenda new opportunities emerge. This is the current opportunity for liberalism.

The renewal of liberalism is taking place as individuals use political engagement not only to change political culture but also to change themselves, that is, to make human development the central focus of political activity and thus political culture. The idea that we can remake ourselves through our participation in politics is new and giving rise to a range of new types of political identities and political organizations.

For example, my own political identity is made up of my identification as a liberal and my forming myself into a *political psychologist*, the latter being a professional identity I am crafting to support my public participation. As a political psychologist I support groups to change the way they engage in politics by helping them become more responsive to the multiple crises in our culture. However, in order to accomplish this I am also helping them to attend to their membership. Here, the simultaneity of personal and cultural change is taking hold. Currently, I am working with several different political groups whose members are learning to channel emotions, as well as our imagination and thinking, into new practices of community engagement and into the development of their own political identities.

I will quickly describe three groups I am working with to give you a few initial images of the opportunities that I am finding. I offer these images not as solutions for you to take up, but, rather as examples of community engagement that I am finding currently available to all citizens. I know of literally dozens of other groups, and I suspect there are thousands, that are doing the work of developing what might be called a new "deep civility," that is, the work of activating a new level of political, psychological, and moral development for our times.

One group comprises members of two different political action committees, Petaluma Tomorrow and Sonoma County Conservation Action. These two groups have joined together to form a Know Your Neighbor project, which is focused on supporting citizens to turn out the "progressive" vote in their neighborhoods. This group is learning how to create a new type of precinct organization focused on inspiring and supporting a new generation of precinct workers to reclaim the sense of a neighborhood as a public space, each neighborhood being a center of community engagement.

This group is the most traditionally "political" group I have worked with so far. I find their commitment to renewing neighborhood participation in local politics inspiring, which helps me to find faith in myself, in others, and in the future. However, the members have predictable ambivalence regarding my idea that we are "liberals." Instead they self-identify as "progressives."

I find that this group and many others identify with progressivism to the exclusion of being liberal. This confuses me. While I think that the current use of the term progressivism simply means a form of what Harvard professor Michael Sandel calls "egalitarian liberalism," I have met with resistance when I use the word liberal to talk about my own or others' political identity (Sandel 1996: 11). I must respect their nomenclature and leave for another time the task of teasing apart their relationship to liberalism.

Another group I work with also identifies with the label progressive. They style themselves after Roosevelt's Civilian Conservation Corps and call themselves a new "Community Catalyst Corps" (CCC). Interestingly enough, they too have mixed feelings about liberalism.

Unlike the first group, the CCC approaches politics through a focus on education rather than on directly winning elections. In this group the focus is on developing practices that promotes leadership education. These practices activate leadership capacities in small groups. The stated goal of this group is to "transform" political culture through learning how to activate their own members' political development and that of other community leaders in Sonoma County, California.

A third group I work with is clearly focused on education. This group, the Praxis Tank for Progressives, based in Berkeley, California, has set out to change political culture through the development of salons, workshops, public presentations, research, and the publication of that research, which falls between the converging fields of politics, psychology, leadership, transformative learning, and organizational development. The participants in this group attend to their own political identities as part of the work of crafting new approaches to political engagement.

While each of these groups has a different focus, the first more traditionally political and the latter two more experimental, they are all committed to changing or transforming political culture. Additionally, these groups are all willing to try new approaches to realize this goal, as individuals and groups. These approaches are changing not only how we think and what we do, but they are also changing who we are as citizens. Each group and individual is willing to remake itself in the face of the failures of liberal politics over the last 40 years.

Each of these groups has established a willingness to experiment with new practices of community engagement and education, practices which I will refer to in the course of this writing as *learning practices*. These practices have emerged directly from the experiences of the group members, researchers in the social sciences, education, the field of leadership, and from the lives of current political leaders. The following list offers a sense of the breadth of influences informing our learning practices.

- the work of University of California at Berkeley professor George Lakoff, whose focus on identifying progressive values helps us attend to these values without overemphasizing the role of rational discourse in our communications to our communities
- the important works of the leaders of the new Religious Left such as Rabbi Michael Lerner and Reverend Jim Wallis with the goal of building bridges to and learning about the spiritual progressive community
- the new fields of leadership and transformative learning through the guidance and support of St. Mary's professor Dean Elias
- the research in the fields of individual development and cultural evolution as represented by the works of Harvard professor Robert Kegan, research psychologist Clare Graves, social theorist Ken Wilber, as well as my own research in the area of political development, with the goal of bridging psychology and politics
- The "healing practices" gleaned from psychotherapy. There is growing recognition that the successes of psychotherapy with people's private-

lives could support the greater transformation of political culture. This recognition comes from the seminal research and writing of British psychologist Andrew Samuels.

My own participation in these groups and development of learning practices is primarily influenced by Aftab Omer's Imaginal Transformation Praxis. Omer's distinct approach to "transformative practices . . . engenders the emergence of human capacities in a unique and connected way" (Omer 2006). Imaginal Transformation Praxis, as developed by Omer of the Institute of Imaginal Studies, a graduate school and research center, provides the foundation out of which my own work and this book arise.

What is liberalism?

In the context of this book, liberalism is not just a political idea or a specific political ideology; rather, liberalism is recognized first as a cultural impulse to bring to life new opportunities for human freedom, that is, to *liberalize*. However, the liberal urge toward this freedom is not simply freedom from oppressive social roles and institutions, it also reflects an awareness of responsibility. Second, liberalism means self-reflection leading to self-awareness, sacrifice, and learning how to contribute to our communities. It is this combination of meanings, "freedom from" and "responsibility for," that creates opportunities to renew liberalism that I discuss in this book.

This renewal requires that we change how we typically think about what it means to be a liberal. We need to understand it more broadly, by seeing it in a larger historical context in which the urge to liberalize culture, to create human freedom, takes place. This context will return attention to liberalism's original spirit, which is about finding freedom for the individual not only politically, but culturally, religiously, and psychologically.

In Western culture, the pursuit of freedom has many beginning points, depending on what one is trying to communicate. It is my purpose to identify the process through which liberalism developed as a cultural movement toward freedom, which has taken place over a period of many hundreds of years. Through this development, liberalism has supported the emergence of a new understanding of the individual. This individual is now understood to be: dignified, having religious and political freedoms, having the psychological capacity to be self-creating, and now thought to be capable of being a creator of culture.

Prior to the last five to eight hundred years the individual was not valued, had little dignity, and could be used, misused, and abused based on the desire to dominate, to be cruel, or simply on a callous whim. However, despite our current inhumanities, over the course of the last several hundred years, we have come to a new regard for the individual. This attention to the individual is the essence of liberalism.

Beginning in the twelfth century a new attitude toward the individual was exemplified by the legal idea of the writ of habeas corpus, which protected the individual from illegal search and seizure. This trend continued into the Renaissance where new images of a free individual, such as Michelangelo's *David*, helped people to see themselves in new ways that inspired dignity and creativity.

This liberal valuation of the individual did not stop with such artistic images but deepened considerably through the Reformation as Martin Luther challenged the traditional devaluation of people by asserting that we need not find our religiosity through the corruptions of the Catholic Church of his time, but we could establish a direct relationship to God.[1]

The cultural and religious freedom founded in these early centuries prepared society for a fuller penetration of liberalism into Western culture. Through the social discourse of the early modern period, the individual's value continued to rise. Extending past the aesthetic and religious vision of the individual, the Enlightenment philosophical discourse of Rationalism and Empiricism helped us to understand the role of the individual in creating new cultural knowledge through the emerging natural sciences.

These ideas of the individual culminated in the political discourse of laissez-faire liberalism which sought to protect the individual through a reformation of political institutions. Their success has been profound and too often minimized as we seek even more freedom and try to build even more humane institutions. However, in order to fulfill these aspirations the trajectory of liberalism must once again move forward. We must reestablish the spirit of liberalism beyond the confines of political liberalism.

While essential to the maintenance and growth of a modern age, the vision of political liberalism is incomplete. While focusing intently on the external social goal of progress, it has neglected the necessity of a parallel line of development: that is, the "internal" development of the person. While succeeding in creating "freedom from" much oppression, political liberalism has not known how to shape the individual into a being who could show necessary restraint in the midst of material freedom.

While we have created the initial material wealth that could support a free society, we have not created the concomitant individuality that could make use of and sustain these freedoms. In 1929 liberal political philosopher John Dewey identifies this need as the greatest problem of our time when he writes: "The problem of constructing a new individuality consonant with the objective conditions under which we live is the deepest problem of our times" (1929a: 32). Dewey responds to this problem by identifying the need to create "a new psychological and moral type" of individuality (1929a: 83). While relatively inchoate when compared to the task of building liberal political institutions, the need to create a new individuality has also been pursued for centuries.

Since its beginning, the liberalizing trend of culture has had a profound effect on individuals, supporting them to realize new levels of confidence, self-respect, and hope. In particular, the individual developed a sense of his or her own ability to change – and to change in a purposeful direction that included the value of service. For many centuries this inclination to "grow" was expressed through a range of different religious languages that emphasized the way in which the growth took place through a person's religiosity (Henderson 1984: 83). For example, regardless of what the Puritan movement has come to mean today, its original values focused on the promotion of self and social responsibility (Beebe 1995: 41–3). These ideas contained within them an understanding of the internal control that individuals would need to learn in order to create the type of world which would be able to sustain human freedom.

As time progressed this impulse to grow began to shed its overt religious expression and took on a new secular dimension, like the rest of Western culture, which began to be expressed psychologically, that is, in relation to the individual's capacity to develop, as distinct from their ability to be in a divine rapport with God (Henderson 1984: 83). The change from a religious to a psychological expression of the idea and experience of *individual development* took place over the course of the seventeenth through early nineteenth centuries in the lives of political leaders intent upon their own and their culture's transformation. They simultaneously focused internally on their own development as individuals and externally on ideas of "social progress." Their adoption of an increasingly psychological language is paralleled by the adoption of naturalistic and materialistic languages in the natural sciences and the language of political liberalism in government.

This transformation is apparent in the life of the American president John Adams, who brought a significant capacity to think psychologically to bear on the task of shaping his own political identity as well as on the task of shaping the identity of the country (Gellert 2001: 292). However, the psychological language that he was learning to speak did not carry much cultural weight: it did not help him to give the American character a self-reflective, psychological shape. Instead, the language of political liberalism dominated with its focus on *freedom from* and seeming disregard for *responsibility for*.

Fortunately, during the early nineteenth century the idea of "individual development" began to find its way into the political movements of that time. For example, in the women's suffrage movement the liberal religiosity or "spirituality" of the time found a psychological expression in the idea that political activism was rooted in the women's pursuit of "self-improvement." This marked a significant transformation of liberalism. Over the course of the nineteenth century interest in this psychological development grew and, like other liberalizing voices mentioned so far, eventually took on greater institutional form, such as in the eventual growth of developmental and clinical psychologies in the early twentieth century.

In this book I will reflect in more detail on this complex history of liberalism, primarily focusing on the emergence of this new "psychological consciousness" and its institutionalization in the form of what I will call "psychological liberalism." I juxtapose psychological liberalism with political liberalism and will be discussing the current opportunities to bring these two most recent voices of liberalism together within a new discourse, public philosophy, or what I will call a "public language" for the purpose of addressing the cultural ills of our time (Bellah *et al.* 1985: 334). Following this thought, I identify *political liberalism* as that force in our history that has built our major social and political institutions, such as our educational and legal systems, as well as the democratic instruments like the American Constitution and Bill of Rights. Political liberalism can be traced back to John Locke's seventeenth-century political philosophy, and continues to influence discourse to this day in its original form of libertarian liberalism (known today as "conservatism") and in increasingly more developed forms, such as in "egalitarian liberalism" – as represented in the current environmental and social justice movements (Sandel 1996: 11).

Similarly, I identify *psychological liberalism* as that more recent force in our history that turns the external focus of political liberalism inward, moving our gaze from "social progress" to "human development." The beginning of this latter form of liberalism can be traced to numerous sources that lead to its institutionalization in the social sciences.

In the last one hundred or more years these two liberalisms, political and psychological, have been too separate. Political liberalism has focused too intently on bringing about structural change and, while largely successful, has run into many limitations as political liberals have not succeeded in taking care of themselves, connecting to one another, or motivating a large enough political constituency. Similarly, psychological liberalism has made a profound positive contribution to Western culture. However, much of its energy, as directed by its increasing power in the institution of clinical psychology, has focused too intently on the private life of the individual, which has led to a fair-enough characterization of indulgence. In effect, psychology and its companion psychotherapy have supported human development while accidentally, at least, ignoring our cultural isolation and, at worst, exacerbating it.

Fortunately, this limitation of liberalism, its splintering into these two cultural voices or institutional forms, is being addressed by a new generation of citizens, who focus simultaneously on the need for external, structural change in the world of politics and internal change in the life of the individual person. This new bifocal attention has been described by numerous social scientists and activists, including Bill Moyer in his book *Doing Democracy* when he notes the limitations of political liberalism:

> Social movements have primarily focused on changing social systems and institutions to achieve their goals of a more peaceful, democratic, just, and sustainable world. However, there are many reasons why these goals cannot be achieved without equal attention to creating personal and cultural transformation – starting with activists ourselves.
>
> (Moyer 2001: 197)

Many individuals and groups are paying more attention to the divide between traditional approaches to social movements and traditional approaches to human development. In the groups that I work with we are creating *learning practices* that combine the community engagement practices of political liberalism with educational and healing practices developed in psychological liberalism. Through the use of these practices we are feeling less helpless, which is helping to renew our faith in liberalism, as both a political and psychological movement. These practices use the public focus of political liberalism to reshape the private focus of psychological liberalism into a new publically focused psychological liberalism.

Through this renewal I am remembering what it means to be a liberal and I am finding that I am proud of my liberal heritage. I am especially proud of the way liberalism does support us to face the current cultural crises of our time without losing faith in the future. Faith in social progress combined with faith in individual development offers new imagery that is awakening our faith in the future.

The unique contribution of psychological liberalism

The role of emotion in the activation of political energy

When facilitating a gathering of progressive activists I suggested a moment of silence for the Iraq war. One of the organizers of the group proclaimed that labor activist Joe Hill had said, "Don't mourn, organize!" While the positive sentiment of Hill's is clear, we have since learned a lot about the positive role of mourning. We have come to a much fuller understanding of the importance of emotions in all aspects of human life from our most private to public.

Drawing on over one hundred years of clinical and developmental research, psychological liberalism brings to political liberalism a willingness to work more directly with the emotions evoked by the current cultural crises. These crises, environmental degradation, social injustice, and the abuse of power, are not new, nor are the emotions they evoke new. However, what is new is the willingness I am finding in these social and political groups to attend directly to the fear, anguish, anger, and shame evoked by these crises. Furthermore, we are not attending to these emotions for the sake of endless "processing" or indulging in our private-life suffering (I find that political liberals' fear of such indulgence is both trustworthy and overblown). Rather than indulging our private lives, we are learning to attend to our emotions for the sake of activating a new level of "political energy" and a new political identity (Samuels 1993: 57–8).

This new political energy requires that we learn to direct emotional energy toward community engagement and not indulge in any reactive expression of it. Emotional reactivity or volatility is often simply a form of violence. Instead of withholding emotion and withdrawing into an indulgent private life or expressing it reactively, the task is to craft a new personal and public identity that uses emotions for what they are for, that is, to become more publicly responsible (Omer, 2005). This would require that we remake ourselves into a new type of citizen.

I believe that Dewey was on to something revolutionary when he called for a "new psychological and moral type" (1929a: 83). He recognized the interface between politics and psychology and saw the need to develop as a people. As a political psychologist, I see Dewey's call being answered by a new generation of citizen. This citizen is combining the values and wisdom of both political and psychological liberalism, which, in one group, the new CCC, has led to the following concrete mission statement: "To activate our political development for the purpose of transforming political culture."

British Jungian psychologist Andrew Samuels uses the term "political development" in a radically new way to refer to the way in which individuals can be said to develop politically (Samuels 1993: 53–61). Paralleling their emotional, cognitive, moral, and social development, Samuels asserts that individuals have an innate "political potential," which, when realized, fulfills a distinct psychological need: that is, the "psychological need to be political" (Samuels 2001: 30). According to Samuels, part of the realization of this psychological need requires that we learn to identify the way in which our private-life emotional suffering needs to be redirected outward, toward its political expression. Samuels argues that by redirecting emotions that are typically hidden like "self-disgust" and shame, a new "political energy" is released that currently lies at the root of a cultural level of depression (Samuels 1989: 196; 1993: 13–14, 57–8). Political development includes learning how to redirect cultural depression toward vital, concentrated public attention and action; again, not emotional reactivity, but emotion channeled effectively toward progressive change. Samuels takes Dewey's call one step further by identifying the way in which individuals can use their emotional experience to raise their political energy to activate their political development and to change political culture.

Throughout human history we have made substantial technical advances that, when supported by a corresponding level of psychological, political, and moral development of a people, has led to significant transformations of political culture. For example, the advent of modernity, when combined with the egalitarian values of the progressive movements of the nineteenth century, has led to a more humane form of political culture. While these transformations are not enough, it would truly be a jaded liberal who would not recognize women's suffrage, the abolition of slavery, and the farm and labor movements of that century as transformative. The flowerings of the social movements in the 1960s were born from these earlier progressive traditions, and even the failures of the 1960s do not take away from the significant political development of that time.

We are moving toward higher levels of individual development and cultural evolution. Specifically, by attending to our political development as individuals and groups we can continue and extend the progressive movements by transforming how politics is done, that is, we can transform political culture. Attending to our political development combines the interests of political and psychological liberalism. Political liberalism can be trusted to attend to the cultural crises and human suffering that stem from environmental degradation, a lack of social justice, and the misuse of power. Psychological liberalism can be trusted to forge people who are psychologically and morally able to respond to our cultural crises through their focus on human development. The two combined form a new public-psychological liberalism.

A new public-psychological liberalism is responding to the crises of our time. As the progressive movement embraces the convergence between political and psychological liberalism it will activate new levels of political development within individuals and groups. Achieving higher levels of political development will manifest through the acquisition of new capacities, which will help us become more responsive to the needs of our time.

Emergent capacities: generational attention, affect-freedom, and the capacity for destiny

Human beings respond to challenges by developing the capacities called for by their time. Whether we develop these capacities consciously or otherwise, we always try to cope, adapt, and sometimes we thrive. At this time in our history there are three such "emergent capacities," which have been activated by the perfect storm of the external crises like environmental degradation, social injustice, and the misuse of power, and the internal crises of psychological suffering, depression, self-disgust, and loneliness experienced in an alienated modern culture.

For the sake of this writing I define *emergent capacity* as a capacity that appears naturally in the development of a child, adolescent, adult, group, community, a people, or a culture. Accordingly, a capacity is said to be emergent when it is first being experienced and concretized by an individual, group, etc. Several quick examples will help establish a context for understanding the idea of emergence. Jean Piaget described how children gain reflective control over their bodily functions, and how such control is considered a reflective capacity that emerges. Or, a teen comes into the capacity for abstract operational thinking as an emergent capacity. Similarly, an adult may come into the capacity for insight or emotion regulation through psychotherapy; such a capacity would thus emerge quickly or slowly in their experience. Also, a group or community can become aware of its prejudices, thus activating the emergent capacity for increased moral experience. Lastly, a people or culture can differentiate new capacities, such as the way thinking and sensing became sources of trustworthy experience during the seventeenth century in Western culture that led to the Enlightenment. Similarly we can speak of the differentiation of moral experience in Western culture during the progressive social justice movements of the nineteenth and twentieth centuries as an emergent phenomenon.

In all, whatever nascent potential lies within personal development or cultural evolution could become active and emerge as a realized capacity. Here, the idea of emergent capacity will tie in with the idea of "cultural leadership" and political development (Omer 2005). For it is through "cultural leaders" that emergent capacities first appear and it is through their political development as leaders that people are exposed to higher levels of evolution. For example, at any time we are exposed to a range of emergent capacities that may or may not take hold of or be embodied by a people. If the task of changing political culture requires adopting those emergent capacities that would be most helpful to us, supporting us to respond to our current cultural crises, then, in order to identify the direction from which these capacities would emerge, we would look to where we have the greatest difficulty, the greatest need. Once we identify a greatest need, we would be able to find the inclinations, the emergent efforts, and the nascent capacities arising to respond to that need. Let's apply this line of thinking to make it concrete.

As far as I can tell one of our greatest difficulties lies in sustaining our generation's attention on the cultural crises of our time. Accordingly, it would only make sense that we are trying to do something about this: that is, we are trying to learn how to focus our generation's attention on these crises. Of course this is what is happening! And, we can work to make this process more conscious, more active. I speak of this turning passive into active as an awakening of our capacity for *generational attention*. Initially, generational attention is a capacity that is emerging at this time in human history. Generational attention emerges as individuals and groups learn to actively recognize, attend to, and engage the issues of their times. While this capacity would form at some level of awareness in any age, our current awareness of the process creates an opportunity to form our generation's attention more consciously and more actively.

Generational attention has cognitive and affective dimensions, which support understanding, emotional attentiveness, and community engagement.[2] Further, it is one of three capacities that I have identified that are emerging in response to the political, psychological, and moral necessities of our time. *Generational attention* is the first of these three capacities and the other two, *affect freedom* and the capacity for *destiny*, are nested within it. Accordingly, I will lay out my understanding of generational attention and how it functions before introducing the other two.

In part, generational attention is the capacity to reflect backwards into our history as a people and as a species in order to understand and to feel what it means to be a human being. We have not always needed this capacity. In previous ages the individual had the support of traditional cultural forms to maintain this connection to history and being human. It is only in the modern age that we have broken into such small forms of individual identity that we have lost sight of who we are as a people, where we have come from, and where we are going.

The emergence of generational attention is in response to the breakdown of previous traditional means of maintaining a connection to our shared past, present, and future. Since the modern breaking of ties that propelled us into the modern world, we have been too rootless. While such freedom has produced great gain, it has also produced profound suffering and shame-full actions. Responding to this suffering and our immorality as a people requires forming a new moral experience. Without some means of responding we are at risk of destroying the very world we cherish and depend upon. Whether on the political right or left, there is a growing consensus that we are a people at risk of losing, or have already lost, our moral compass. While once we could turn to a range of traditional institutions and other cultural forms to maintain a connection to our past and to provide moral guidance, we now are required to internalize such connective and moral functions.

Generational attention can be thought of as a psychological, political, and moral capacity that connects us to the consequences of our actions, but not just as individuals, also as a people. Numerous peace groups are learning to focus our generation's attention on being responsible for the past actions of our people as they sponsor "peace walks" to sites of war atrocities, sacred sites of other cultures, or other locations where our group memory must be activated. My cousin Louise is one such peace activist and her efforts in this direction have helped me to see the necessity of taking responsibility for the actions of our predecessors and to understand both the loss of and the importance of group memory.

Such group memory is also portrayed in popular culture in the bitter-sweet movie *Life as a House* (2001) in which actor Kevin Kline portrays a jaded architect who learns that he is dying of cancer and chooses to reconnect with his son to help ease the young man's own bitterness by asking him to help remodel the family home. While the painful reconnection between father and son is the central plot of the movie, there is a surprising twist at the end when the audience learns that the father's own father had been responsible for paralyzing a young woman in a car accident. Without verbal acknowledgement, at the end of the movie Kevin's son gives the refurbished house to the crippled woman, which pulls her and her family out of an impoverished living situation. Here the son finds his own generational attention to redeem his grandfather's shame and respond to his father's dying wish. Father and son embrace the family shame, truly a profound last gift between the two. This movie begins to offer concrete images about the nature of generational attention. Not only does the father seek redemption for his own actions, but for the actions of his father as well, and the son, who is largely innocent as an individual, joins in the family shame and redemption.

Similarly, in an American Indian culture there is a tradition that supports people to act with the understanding that the repercussions of that action will be felt for seven generations. This is a precursor to generational attention embedded in a healthy cultural practice which maintains a connection to the past while moving forward into the future. In the context of my own work as a political psychologist I am finding generational attention to be demonstrated as individuals and groups recognize, attend to, and engage with the issues of their time with an awareness of the psychological, political, and moral needs of their people. In this capacity, generational attention enables individuals and groups to understand a community's unique circumstances, heal a community's suffering, and activate a community's political energy.

Generational attention is both a cognitive and emotional or affective capacity which supports understanding, emotional attentiveness, and community engagement.[3] As a cognitive capacity it supports a coherent understanding of the history of a people in relation to their current and future developmental needs and moral obligations. In its emotional dimension, generational attention has nested within it the distinct capacity for *affect freedom*.

Affect freedom simply names the capacity to draw from a full range of the biological and psychosocial functions of our emotions for the purpose of determining moral experience and taking effective political action. Affect freedom is the capacity of individuals and groups to use their emotions for what they are actually for, that is, to allow people to:

- *assess* their own and their communities needs
- *connect* to one another for the purposes of conviviality and social and political action
- *motivate* and *direct* themselves and others for the purposes of learning, healing, and community engagement.

Restated, affect freedom is the capacity to experience and use a full range of emotion for the psychological, political, and moral needs of one's time.[4]

Generational attention also enables individuals, groups, and communities to focus their attention on the future. Such a future focus enables a generation to keep the cultural crises of their time in sight, which requires some foresight. However, generational attention is not simply about seeing the future or anticipating the best or worst outcome regarding political issues. While such foresight is valuable and a part of the cognitive dimension of generational attention, a more significant or neglected dimension is its ability to support the development of a felt sense of the future, which I refer to as the *capacity for destiny*.

For those individuals who are tuned in to the needs of their time, they are able to transform their passive experience of the future into an active capacity for destiny. Social psychologist Erik Erikson's work on this topic may be the best to date as he traces the way that Martin Luther, Thomas Jefferson, and Mahatma Gandhi were able to activate this capacity for destiny as their political identities became woven with the distinct needs of their people in a mutually transformative process.

In my own research I trace how the capacity for destiny is activated in current progressive political leaders. In that inquiry I learned how the route to transforming political culture draws from an individual their sensitivities, talents, and unique suffering in order to activate their capacity for destiny, which is nothing fancy. Destiny is simply a human capacity that emerges when the threads of a person's personal development intertwine with the evolutionary needs of their times. This intertwining of development and evolution transforms their passively lived experience of the future into an active shaping of that future, that is, the capacity for destiny.

Over the course of this book I return to the ideas of generational attention, affect freedom, and destiny as emergent capacities in order to show how they are appearing in Western culture, to examine how they function, and to identify the opportunities for individuals and groups to acquire these capacities. In order to respond to the needs of our time we will need to activate these capacities. Essential to this process is the willingness to attend to our experience of the future and to be willing to change that relationship. We need to relate to the future not as if it were some fearful or hopeful "thing" in the distance – out there somewhere – but rather we must find an experience of the future in the present moment (Omer 2005). My own experience of the future began to move in this embodied direction after I read, reread, and then read to others, over and over, the following poem by Marie Rainer Rilke:

You must give birth to your images
They are the future waiting to be born.
Fear not the strangeness you feel
The future must enter into you long before it happens
Just wait for the birth, for the hour of new clarity.
(Rilke 2007, italics added)

Following Rilke, we can change our relationship to the future as we attend to our bodies' experience, as we find the future in the presence of our bodies' fears, hopes, angers, shames, and anguish for what is happening to the world we live in, the world we will hopefully leave to our children with courage, humility, and with faith in the future.

The 2004 presidential debate offers two closed doors to the future

In order to move to a healthy future we must learn to attend to the way in which the future is present, immediately available in our bodily experience of Rilke's "strangeness" or Samuels' "self-disgust." By attending to these upsets we begin to shape the future. Following Samuels' transforming depression, self-disgust, or shame, directing anger toward political action gives the future its moral shape. For example, if we think that same-sex marriage is disgusting and if we act politically on our disgust, we work to pass legislation that defines marriage as being between a man and a women. This political path seems to be dominating the US. We seem to be a people who want to legislate the private-life conduct of its minorities. This is our current use of our moral experience. However, it need not be this way.

Alternatively, we could become a people whose experience of shame and self-disgust activates political energy to provide nutritional attention to children, or it could help us address issues of national and international poverty, or our anger and shame could be directed into raising mileage requirements and emissions standards. While all of these issues may seem to be more abstract – they aren't happening in my neighborhood – they could still become the focus of a new psychological and moral type. This would require changing the way liberals attend to their own emotional experience and the way liberal political leaders emotionally embody that message.

This may sound confusing, or too simple. However, it is neither confusing nor simple, it is just a difficult idea. It requires thinking about the need to change our relationship to the future. Bear with me as I explain and then I will offer a concrete example. If we could learn to use our emotions to create the future we want, we would need to have a different understanding of what the future actually is. We first need to recognize that the future is not an abstraction, it is not something we come to through thinking. Imagining or extrapolating possible futures by looking ahead can be useful as it can help us to keep in touch with both frightening threats to the future and inspiring opportunities. Such visioning or foresight too often gets mistaken for the full extent of our ability to contact the future. Fortunately, we not only can imagine scenarios about the future but we can also have a direct experience of the future. This is not to invite metaphysical gobbledygook about clairvoyance. Perhaps such capacities are possible, but

I am a simple man and have not experienced such visitations. Instead of anything fanciful I am suggesting that we already have a felt sense of the future through our emotions; and, this experience of the future varies from person to person and from ideology to ideology. In order for liberals to become more effective politically they will have to get this idea and see how it will enable them to change how they use their emotions and how they communicate to the public.

Whether we are a progressive, a neoconservative, or more mainstream Democrat or Republican we all have some sense of the future. On the right or the left the sense of the future may be determined by a range of common elements, including different ideological values, religious experience, cultural practices, and even different relationships to specific emotions. Each shade of the political spectrum twists these common elements into radically distinct personalities, political characters, or "political identities," which cause profoundly different felt senses of the future. For example, Julian Bond, former Atlanta legislator and former head of the NAACP, asserts that conservatives and liberals repress different emotions. Bond accuses conservatives of being shameless and liberals of being spineless, which he claims leads to the conservatives winning too many elections for, he says, "in the competition between the shameless and the spineless, the shameless win every time" (Cose 2002: 47).

As liberals we need to understand the way in which our felt-sense of the future works. I am concerned that we either ignore this felt-sense or underestimate its importance. In our focus on imagining the future, in picturing it rationally, we dwell too much on abstract political issues and not enough on our body's felt sense of the future. As a result we do not use our emotions, our body's source of knowledge about the future, as it is present now, to connect to and motivate the American people. Instead, we quietly use our emotions to assess the fearful and hopeful futures without sharing these feelings, even at times with ourselves. Instead we tell ourselves and others that our assessment is purely rational. Not only is this not enough, but it isn't factual.

Following Samuels, liberal political leaders could learn from what takes place in psychotherapy where therapists have learned that emotions of both the client and the therapist play a central role in the assessment and treatment process. The therapist is trained to use their emotions to help identify their clients' suffering and then support these people to identify their emotions, not just for the purposes of catharsis or any indulgence, but for the purpose of staying in touch with our experience and being able to communicate it effectively to others. This learning in psychotherapy, about the actual function of emotions, can be brought into a public light and used to help us understand what goes wrong in our efforts to help others to face the future. This is especially true in politics, where the culture's relationship to the future is modeled by our leaders. Let us look at how this works.

In the 2004 American presidential election, George Bush offered a stay-the-course attitude (which by late 2006 had become infamous in relation to the Iraq war, and by 2008 was challenged by almost every presidential candidate within both parties) that implied that the future is secure and that we do not need to do anything significantly different than what we are doing now. It is as if he were saying "things are fine," or if characterized sarcastically, "what, me worry?" Bush's stay-the-course strategy would have been adopted by the incumbent of any party: However, it particularly matches his personality and his "compassionate conservatism," which is about maintaining a small-town faith in an unchanging future. Bush clearly has an active capacity for generational attention; at least he is able to use its emotional dimension to connect to and motivate others. Unfortunately, his access to its ability to assess our current situation seems hobbled; he seems to live in a shameless denial of the future. As a result he communicates a vision of a safe future, when many of the rest of us experience the future as much less certain.

Comparatively, John Kerry argued for changes showing a greater sensitivity to the cultural crises of our time. His use of the emotional dimension of generational attention reveals an active use of its ability to assess the future. This capacity to assess is revealed in his emotional sensitivity. For example, he seems to experience the current threats to the environment fearfully. He also responds to the lack of social justice with anger; and he responds to the misuses of political power with contempt. These apparent responses suggest an active capacity for generational attention, at least in its use for assessment. However, while using his emotions to assess situations, he seems unable to use them in their other two aspects, that is, to connect and to motivate. In these latter respects his use of generational attention is muted; while he seems to feel a wide enough range of emotions, he keeps them to himself. He is a good liberal – his feelings don't show. Kerry is a well-contained politician who approached the cultural crises of our time, not as opportunities to display emotions, but as political issues to be discussed and argued for or against, strictly using rational means. Kerry rationalized his passions, much like Michael Dukakis who, in a 1988 presidential debate, responded to a question about what he would do if his wife were raped with a similar muted, rationalized expression. Dukakis was also a good liberal.

This muted emotionality is a liberal weakness. However, as Howard Dean discovered when the press attacked his display of emotions in the 2004 presidential primaries, there is a catch-22 involved. As Dean learned, the overt expression of emotions is also taboo in public, especially in politics. Kerry's relationship to his feelings reflects a standard liberal character trait; that is, liberals place rational discourse above passion and trust the future to reason. This is really different than conservatives, especially George Bush. While Kerry and other liberals use their generational attention within a very narrow band, to privately assess the world's crises, conservatives seem to skip this aspect of that capacity and focus on its other aspects: that is, they know how to use emotion to connect to people and to motivate them.

Bush's small town wrap-your-arms-around-your-neighbor is fully passionate and, perhaps, genuine. But, it is an untroubled passion, as Bond would note – appearing shameless. Bush acts much like a father would, offering his small children comfort; and many respond to Bush's soothing. Many people respond to Bush's own embodied hopefulness and get from it as much of the future as they need or want. People didn't want to struggle with Kerry's more complex, muted, and rationalized emotions. *They simply wanted a clear presence not a clear vision.* This difference, between presence and vision, is a central difference between Kerry's and Bush's characters, and perhaps between conservative and liberal characters – they each access different aspects of the capacity for generational attention. Do you see the dilemma this creates in our relationship to the future? Let us go back over this in a little more detail.

Unlike Kerry, Bush has an instinctive awareness that permeates his being, which can be seen when he speaks, such as when he says, "The American people know where I stand." This is not simply a reference to his stand on issues, but reflects something more significant, even literal. People can see him more clearly when he is standing in front of them. They see a man fully, though unreflectively, in his body; he is fully home behind his eyes. This is a severely limited, but genuine, form of affect freedom, which is, I repeat, the capacity to experience a full range of feeling in order to assess the psychological, political, and moral circumstances of one's time and to use those feelings to connect to others and to motivate oneself and others toward creative action. Bush's use of affect freedom reflects what social theorist Ken Wilber addresses when he says that conservatives exist at, embody, a healthy lower stage of development, while liberals exist at, embody, an unhealthy higher stage of development (Wilber 2000: 83–9). The conservatives are identified with a nationalistic mentality that focuses on taking care of your own in the immediate present and near future; and they are very good at this.

Comparatively, liberals aspire to a more egalitarian approach to leadership, one that accounts for the need to grow a model of government that offers justice for all and sharing the wealth of the world in the face of dwindling resources and increasing environmental degradation. The liberal's task is profoundly more complex as they must communicate with a wider range of emotions than they have yet learned to use. Thus they attempt to use rational argument to make up for their lack of ability to communicate a passionate shared vision.

Bush's access and use of emotion is in stark contrast to Kerry's disembodied, rationalized presence. Bush's capacity to be seen is a result of the subtle and successful development of what could be called his emotional body, or, what is called the human "affect system" (Nathanson 1992: 47). This development is particularly evident in his face and his speaking – they are fully congruent with one another. Bush's presence helps the American people to govern their own relationship to the future as well as their relationship to fear and shame, Bush models shamelessness and calm, which eases others' fears and shames. Bush's untroubled relationship to the future mollifies, but it does not lead.

Juxtapose Bush's easing of people's fear and shame in their relationship with the future with Kerry's own complex and ambivalent attitude toward the future. Which way would you rather feel? Do you want to feel good about yourself and the future, the way George does, or do you want to feel embarrassed, angry, and afraid about many things, including yourself and the future, the way John does? I can't feel the way George Bush does, but I don't want to feel the way John Kerry does. What a dilemma. Can we change the way we feel? Or can we find a way to feel the emotions that we do feel in such a way that others will find bearable? Can we make feeling like a liberal more palatable? This is the work of renewing liberalism. It begins with the liberal's body.

This book: foundations and intentions

This book is about the transformation of political culture. It connects new research in the areas of leadership, human emotions, and transformative psychotherapy to politics. This book applies Omer's Imaginal Transformation Praxis (ITP) to political development, political identity, and political culture. "ITP consists of concepts, principles, and practices that constitute an integrative approach to personal and cultural transformation. ITP has three distinct components:

1 Imaginal Process: an approach to transformative learning, understood as the emergence and cultivation of capacities by individuals, organizations, communities, and societies.
2 Imaginal Inquiry: a methodology for participatory research that weaves together both inquiry and transformation.
3 Cultural Leadership Praxis: a creative and collaborative approach to fostering cultural transformation within organizations, communities, and societies" (Omer 2006).

Omer conceptualizes a capacity as "a distinct dimension of human development and human evolution that delineates a specific potential for responding to a domain of life experience. For instance, the capacity for compassion responds to suffering, courage responds to danger, and faith responds to uncertainty" (Omer 2006).

ITP emphasizes the cultivation of the capacity for "reflexivity" which is emerging at this time in history. Reflexivity "refers to the distinctly human capacity for a self-aware presence that is integrative of the somatic, affective, and cognitive dimensions of experience." This capacity enables individuals and groups to transform their relatively passive ability for "self-reflection" into an *active* affect-informed capability for "reflexive participation" in community-making and the transformation of culture. "Each affect has a distinct capacity as its telos." Omer describes reflexive participation as "the practice of surrendering through creative action to the necessities, meanings, and possibilities inherent in the present moment."

The image of citizenship that emerges out of Omer's work necessitates a deeper level of self-awareness. When applied to liberalism, ITP implies a new focus on emotions, not as psychotherapy, but rather as the ground for cultural transformation through reflexive participation and cultural leadership. Omer suggests that "cultural leaders are able to transmute how they are personally affected by the culture into creative action that midwifes the future. The recognition and creative transgression of taboos and norms is at the heart of cultural leadership" (Omer 2005: 32).

This book is not about George Bush or John Kerry, or any of the current 2008 presidential candidates, nor is it about emotions *per se*. This book is about liberal's responsibility for the future. By learning to work reflexively with their emotional experience, in organizations and communities, liberals can focus the attention of all of the current generations on changing political culture. More specifically it is about learning how to help liberals to develop their power to the point where they can raise the political center of the world up a notch. Following Albert Einstein's own image, liberals have the opportunity to step into a new stage of human development (Gellert 2001: 297). From this new stage, liberal or progressive cultural leaders will augment their rationally oriented cognitive and moral development with a newly acquired level of emotional development: that is, they will be able to use emotions not only to assess psychological, political, and moral realities but they will also be able to use emotions to connect to and to motivate a new constituency and a new social movement.

Once a new use of emotion is activated, progressives will be in a better position to embody a more developed political presence, and become what social psychologist Erik Erikson calls a "numinous model" who guides us into the best possible future (Erikson 1982: 70). A numinous role model is someone who has a bead on reality, on the truth, in a way that draws others' interest. They may have difficult things to say – global warming is going to affect all of our lives in the next 20 years – but they can say it from an embodied presence that helps others to find the courage to be interested in and act on this truth. An effective numinous role model will embody emotions from within a new political identity that can help people bear the real fears, shames, angers, and the disgust that is to be expected when confronted with a modern culture careening toward an unguided future. Learning to bear more difficult, complex feelings is one of the primary tasks of a new progressive political identity, which Kerry could not offer.

A good psychotherapist helps their clients bear and direct the difficult feelings that may be at the root of depression or anxiety. A good leader does the same, but on a different scale. A good psychotherapist helps a client face the difficulties of life, find faith in the future while taking informed action in the present – however hopeful or limited that future might be for a given person's life situation. A good leader helps us face the future and find the necessary courage, regardless of what has to be faced.

George Bush seems to have little awareness of the fearful futures that we liberals can see appearing more each day; he wants emissions standards to be set voluntarily, not by law. He does not offer an active relationship to the future. While John Kerry, or most other democrats, progressive or otherwise, clearly sees more of the same futures I see, he does not offer an embodied presence that I would follow. I want to see the liberal leadership find a way of helping us establish a more active relationship with the future through a more embodied liberalism.

In this book I bring together politics and psychology into what Samuels calls a "new hybrid language" that will help us cultivate a more active relationship with the future: one that is based on progressive values but expresses those values from within a new embodied progressive/liberal political identity that does not revert to an abstracted, overly rational viewing of political culture (Samuels 2001: 13). Articulating and embodying such a new progressive identity responds to Dewey's call and parallels Mahatma Gandhi's recognition that it takes a change in identity to change political culture, which he expressed when he said "you must be the change you wish to see in the world" (Gandhi 2007).

In this book I will assert that this new liberal political identity is currently emerging from between the current institutional forms of politics and psychology. I will discuss how it is the job of a new type of political psychologist to develop cultural "learning practices" that would support this emerging new liberal identity. I will also argue for the development of a new branch of psychology, a "transformative political psychology," whose purpose it would be to support the development of a distinct line of social science research for the purposes of creating a new vocation, that of the *transformative political psychologist*.

Currently political psychology is a subfield of political science and successfully contributes to the social sciences through the application of psychological thinking to questions about what motivates leaders, constituents, and how groups form political identities. While this research supports a growing psychological awareness in academia and in culture, practitioners of this field do not bring a transformative intent to their research. Using traditional research methodologies, the current field of political psychology is primarily about analysis and knowledge acquisition and not about transformative intervention.

The image of a transformative political psychology that this book is about focuses on the opportunity to bring into politics the transformative intent that originates in clinical psychology, that is, psychological liberalism. However, unlike the private-life transformations of psychotherapy, a transformative political psychology would focus on activating the emergent capacities necessary to bring about the transformation of our political identities in our public life.

Samuels articulated the possibility of using the successes of clinical psychology in politics in *The Political Psyche* (1993). In that book he writes about the opportunity and necessity of learning how to do some form of "political therapy" with culture (Samuels 1993: 55). While the image of political therapy may be too problematic given the associations of therapy with individuals' private lives, some forms of cultural practices are already being used in numerous settings to bring about the transformation of our public lives. Following this intent, this book is written to help identify a new field of transformative political psychology as well as a new type of transformative political psychologist who would be able to:

- develop their own political identity by engaging the political culture of groups and communities in a way that activates a range of emergent capacities including generational attention, affect freedom, and the capacity for destiny
- use these capacities to articulate and embody a new, active relationship to the future, while connecting to and motivating others to participate
- support groups and communities to develop their own learning practices that support their political development and the emergence of a new political culture, based more on both tradition and egalitarian values
- engage in research projects for the purpose of answering the questions identified as crucial to the political development of our time.

Chapter 2

Transforming the felt-sense of the future into the capacity for destiny

> The whole future of the earth depends on awakening our faith in the future.
>
> (Teilhard 1963)

A brief history of our relationship to the future

Our difficulty in having a healthy relationship to the future is not new. Historically, we Westerners have related to the future through the fearful lens of religions. While premodern religions provided us with a rudimentary experience of meaning and community, they often do so through oppressive means that evoke guilt and fear. The upside of this oppression is how it supports the individual to learn to control and direct emotional impulsivity. However, the oppressiveness of culture also limits our development as its control is too authoritarian, imposed from the outside. Such "original oppression" is a central function of many premodern religions and does not provide opportunities for the individual to internalize a moral structure and learn to be self-monitoring and autonomous.[1]

Over the last few hundred years many have moved past the belief that our religion is the only one and that our fearful submission to it preserves our future. As a result, we have shifted our fear of damnation in an after-life to our hopes for material success in this life. While an improvement, this next stage of development is highly individualistic, too focused on getting for myself, my family, my nation in the short-run at the expense of building a shared human future.

Alternatively, there is the advent of liberalism, both political and psycho-logical, which turns attention away from the guilt-laden, fearful-religious and selfish-individualistic toward social progress and human development, respectively. The advent of these liberalisms promises and delivers a new relationship to the future. However, this new relationship is still very new; in fact, it hasn't really come together yet. One of the things that could help it come together is a common language, one that brings all the liberalisms together. This new language might begin through a single word that holds our new relationship to the future.

Finding a hope for the future in the right word

My hope for the future lies in the capacity for human beings to continually adapt, develop, or evolve. When faced with opportunity, we transform ourselves. While we cannot go outside of the range of our fate – the apple doesn't fall too far from the tree – when faced with necessity we make ourselves anew. In the last few hundred years Westerners have been forced to leave a premodern world governed by beneficial and oppressive traditions and enter into a modern world that lacks such community structure. It is hard to capture the profound change this has caused. The best metaphor I can imagine may be too simple, but it helps to express both the intensity of the birth of modernity and our current predicament. It is as if we have been shot from a cannon into a new world. While I don't think we have landed yet, we clearly have started the descent. As we fall, we have the opportunity to take in the landscape and try to figure out where we want to land. Unlike Icarus, our wings are still intact and, as a result, we still have some choice regarding our destination. However, the sun is getting hotter, and the risks of environmental degradation, the profound lack of social justice, and the struggles for power within and between nations, corporations, and local communities are all issues that require our attention. Without focusing our generation's willing attention, our wings will burn, our descent will accelerate and, we could, after all, burn up and plummet like Icarus.

In order to avoid this steeper fall we must face the necessities of these moral crises and make ourselves anew. Following Dewey's call for a new psychological and moral identity, we must remake ourselves to catch up with the radical changes in the material world brought about by the advent of modernity. We need to find the moral and psychological wherewithal to address the conditions in which we find ourselves.

In order to form this new identity we can apply what we have learned from psychology over the last one hundred or more years. In particular I am referring to our capacity to reflect on our past for the purpose of gaining insight into our present and supporting us in determining our future direction. This is the capacity for generational attention. While this capacity has been most successfully applied to the private lives of individuals through psychotherapy, it can also be applied to the life of a people. Accordingly, we can begin to imagine at least one aspect of a new psychological and moral type.

Stated simply, for the moment, a new identity would have the capacity to reflect on the past, personally and culturally, in order to choose future actions, not simply continuing to have a passive relationship with the future. Put in another way, we can use a growing "psychological conscious-ness" to form ourselves into that type of identity which would be capable of responding to personal and cultural crises. Following Gandhi, we can become the change we wish to see in the world.

For many already engaged in the struggle to address the issues that I've named, the work is primarily political. The visions of the progressive move-ment exemplify these efforts and are simply to be acclaimed and supported. However, as I argued in the introduction, political change is not enough. We must also make significant psychological changes that will change us into the type of people who would be able to stand behind the high level of moral conduct extolled by the progressive ideology. Political change sup-ports changes in the social structure and psychological change will support changes in our moral identity. The latter is required to weather the regressive assaults that a new level of moral development would provoke.

In order to combine liberal politics with this interest in creating a new psychological and moral identity we must address the limitations of our current identity. While I discuss both the strengths and limitations of the liberal identity in some detail in this book, for the moment I draw attention to what I find to be a crucial difficulty of this identity – one that I will address in depth and from numerous angles – that is, the liberal's inability to offer a cohesive and inspirational image of the future.

The liberal political identity does not lack a vision of the future, it simply has no way to get from here to there. The approach taken to the future by liberals emphasizes the political issues stated above. Liberals seem particularly clear on these issues, and their capacity to back their grasp of these issues with scientific research may be unsurpassed. However, as the Bush administration has proven beyond a doubt, relevant political issues and even sound science can too easily be set aside. In fact, it might be fair to say that liberals are overly identified with both political issues and the science behind these issues. Their relationship to both issues and science reveals an over-dependence on rational means, which I will be discussing in some depth.

Instead of depending on rational arguments and the hope that people will recognize and vote for their economic interests, liberals need to come to a better understanding of the way the future emerges, comes out of the experience of a people. Such an understanding would be based on a flexible awareness that is able to tap into the imagination of the people and activate images of the future that are commensurate with the crises we face and would provide the necessary glue that would allow us to bind ourselves to one another in a new level of moral and civic collaboration.

Accordingly, we not only need to be able to have the sense that some-thing is amiss in our relationship with the environment, in our understand-ing and application of the principle of justice to social disparities, and in our relationship with power, but we also have to have a sense of direction, a sense of a possible future. While many futures have been offered – some utopian, some apocalyptic – they have not sufficiently taken hold of the imagination. In *Individualism Old and New*, Dewey notes the way in which the modern world has left us without sufficient images of the future to hold our imaginations and to bind us together with a common purpose:

> The significant thing is that the loyalties which once held individuals, which gave them support, direction, and unity of outlook on life, have well-nigh disappeared. In consequence, individuals are confused and bewildered. It would be difficult to find in history an epoch as lacking in solid and assured objects of belief and approved ends as is the present . . . Individuals vibrate between a past that is intellectually too empty to give satisfaction and a present that is too diversely crowded and chaotic to afford balance or direction to ideas and emotions.
>
> (Dewey 1929a: 52–3)

We are not able to direct our generation's attention toward the realities of our falling; we have passed the apex of our ascent and are at that moment where we see the world fairly clearly, things are moving in slow motion, and we are beginning to feel the pull of gravity. Our stomachs may be first to feel the pull earthward; the future first comes to us in this bodily way while our eyes are still on the distant landscape.

Approached naively, the future may seem like indigestion, perhaps a mild form of anxiety; approached consciously, the future evokes fear, which can activate courage and determination. This conscious approach to the future is well expressed by Rilke's poem, cited in Chapter 1, in which the future appears as a present "image" or a present "strangeness." As Rilke notes: "The future must enter into you long before it happens" (2007).

The liberal incorporation of some of the sciences into their articulation of political issues is necessary, powerful, and not enough. The ideas and scenarios of possible futures viewed through a few of the sciences and politics are not enough. What is needed is more than these rational thoughts. In fact, the word future is – by itself – insufficient to capture the imagination of a people. The word future implies too much multiplicity, there are too many choices, there are too many ideas about the future, too many possibilities. Too many of us would like to weigh in with what we think. I'm doing just that now.

Instead of scenarios or rational thought we need something different, or more: we need to feel the future in our bellies and be able to transform the naive indigestion into a moral indignation and an image of a new identity, including a felt experience that can be shared and could catalyze a generation's attention. To do this we will need George Bush's capacity for embodiment, but fully integrated into the moral, disembodied experience of John Kerry. Like Rilke's experience of the power of a felt image of the future, we need a felt experience of the future. I know this felt experience exists. I have watched it be activated during times of distress when someone rises up and is able to direct the attention of their generation.

The troubled, fanciful, and shameful idea of destiny

Martin Luther King embodied the capacity to direct a generation's attention. However, his life, his work, and his sacrifice have almost become an extreme caricature. For some he is still the ultimate sacrificing hero; for others his sacrifice was too great to imagine following, his footsteps too big. Still others complain that he usurped the spotlight, which has disempowered the rest of us by occluding the numerous other cultural leaders of that time who made sacrifices that we could more likely follow. Perhaps the sacrifices of John and Robert Kennedy, of Martin Luther King or Malcom-X, are too frightening for us to want to be like them. What is needed is a greater awareness of what it is they did to become cultural leaders. With this awareness we would be more able to become cultural leaders ourselves and to help others to do the same. Again, there is no word for this power they held. Yet we witness their accomplishments.

In my own research with progressive political leaders, I asked them to tell me the stories that galvanized their political identities. These stories helped me to see what it is they did to become leaders in their community. In the course of two group meetings, which I will share more about in the next chapter and later in the book, I helped them tell the stories of how they formed their political identities and the effect that these new identities had on their lives and on the lives of their supporters and constituents. These stories helped me to piece together an understanding of the process through which liberal political identities form and become consequential.

These leaders have a felt experience of the future that is not simply an idea about the future or a rational analysis of the political wrongs in their communities – they felt the "strangeness" of the future. In fact, based on our shared experiences during the research meetings, I came to see that they had developed a distinct human capacity that enabled them to become political leaders. In the course of the research, I became aware of how the progressive leaders I had gathered had activated the human *capacity for destiny*, and it is this capacity that enabled them to move themselves and their generation's attention toward the political necessities of their time.

Hopefully, what I am offering is not just another idea, much less a silly idea, but a small step in reworking our language, telling a new story, or telling the old story in a different way. Perhaps I am making a small sound that is part of a new way of speaking that many of us have intuited is necessary, is possible, is a response to necessity within the range of our fate, holds our destiny. Between the fate and the necessity of our falling, having been shot from a cannon a few hundred years or more ago, as we fall we will have the opportunity to pursue our destiny. In this book I will attempt to tell a story of our relationship to the future to show our opportunity to transform our diverse, chaotic, and fearful experience of the future into the capacity for destiny. However, the word destiny may seem troubled, vague, fanciful, or shameful, depending on what your experience with that word has been. You may associate the word with traditional religious doctrines that expect us to sacrifice in this life in order to reserve a birth for ourselves in the after-life. Following this belief, the pursuit of destiny simply requires watching our "Ps and Qs" in this life. Yet, for many of us this has not been enough.

Despite religion's essential focus on a public morality, on bringing people together, its overly simple formulation of life's purpose is frustrating. Additionally, the tragic moral failures of religious institutions have narrowed many people's ability to access them as a source of guidance. Given the species' difficulty with forming moral institutions, the moral failings of religious institutions are not too surprising. However, this leads to an unfortunate result: we too easily confuse the forward-looking and moral function of religion with the historical and current failures of its institutions. Accordingly, if we associate the idea of destiny with these failures, then the word destiny becomes too troubled to use. What if we break this association or at least hold it at bay for the sake of reviving a powerful new use for this old word?

For some the idea of destiny is not so troubled as it is foolish or fanciful. In the last few generations, the retreat from the public institutions of religion has led to a rise in a more privately lived spirituality. While the growth of such a spiritual life has been healthy, the solace and sanity of many, it has not fostered a clear public consensus or sense of mutual purpose that is needed to activate a people's moral clarity. People connect to spirit separately, but not to each other, as the root of religion, "religio," means "to bind again" (Partridge 1959: 354). Accordingly, in the context of the diverse spiritualities many enjoy, the idea of destiny splinters in too many directions, means too many things, many of which have been dismissed as quackery, "new-agey," especially in the face of their failure – or disinterest – in forming a public consensus. This diversity may, in fact, leave the word without meaning, vague. What if we set these associations aside as well?

For others, the idea of destiny simply evokes shame. As an American I associate destiny with "manifest destiny" and the westward expansion of the nineteenth century that led to the murder of native peoples, war against the sovereign nation of Mexico, and the immoral enslavement, rape, and murder of Africans. It is clear to me that we Americans have conducted ourselves in such severely problematic ways that I suspect we have partially lost the capacity to feel shame. Aftab Omer associates this "shame numbness" with our own traumatic history of leaving our traditional homelands and coming to the "new world" (Omer 2003: 37–40). Perhaps part of our resistance to the word destiny is linked to this repressed shame. I'll be talking about the importance of shame, its true value as a means for determining moral experience, in this book.

I suspect other nations have their shames that get repressed when leaders attempt to focus their people's attention in a specific direction. This is when the idea of destiny gets abused. Didn't Adolph Hitler use some similar word or idea as he incited the German people into embodying and acting on a violent tribalism? It would seem that turning toward the future as a group, that is, consolidating a generation's attention, seems to risk this confusion of leadership with madness. No wonder the word destiny evokes ambivalence.

For whatever reason, inviting conversations about destiny requires attending to the risks of confusing leadership and madness. Whether thought to be too troubled, foolish/vague, or simply shameful, the idea of destiny retains little of its potential to evoke a shared relationship to the future. As a result we may have lost a key way of speaking about, a way of sharing, even a way of thinking about the future. We may have lost the capacity to move together toward the future. If, as Pierre Teilhard extols, we must find our faith in the future, then we have lost a great deal with the loss of the word destiny.

If we are to redeem this loss we can begin by simply reviewing the actual meaning of the word destiny. When destiny is considered, it is most often simply conceived of as being related to fate. However, following the New Shorter Oxford Standard Dictionary, destiny can be distinguished from fate in that it is something that can be pursued (Brown 1973: 648). Whereas fate is defined as that which has been "preordained," "fixed," "sealed," or even "doomed," destiny is defined as "the power or agency that predetermines events" (Brown 1973: 922). While the idea of "predetermination" implies inflexibility, it can also be imagined simply as the source of decision. Fate is determined, destiny determines. To be actively involved in destiny is to be engaged with the power that chooses.

Destiny is not passively received like fate, it is actively pursued. As a capacity, it moves a person from a passive to an active relationship with creating their own identity and engaging the world with that identity. Existential psychologist Rollo May claims that we can "engage" our destiny and through that engagement find our freedom (May 1981: 90).

As I've described, perhaps the word destiny has too much baggage and we need to look for other words to express the essentially active relationship with the future that we need. To regain that experience, that brilliant moment when we know what to do next, as persons and as a people, we might be able to use words like synchronicity, vision, or the complex idea of prescience, perhaps. It could also be that we do not need any such words, though I've already claimed otherwise. What I suspect is that, as a people, we are at risk of neglecting the future and we need a "language" that speaks to this neglect. In this moment I am drawing on University of California at Berkeley professor Robert Bellah *et al.*'s (1985) book *Habits of the Heart*. In this significant book Bellah refreshes the word "language" in much the way I hope to awaken the word destiny. Bellah defined language in a wonderfully broad way in order to be able to talk about how people form their identities around "languages" as "modes of moral discourse" (Bellah *et al.* 1985: 334). As a result of Bellah's creative expansion of our understanding of language it has become more possible to talk about moral experience. Paralleling Bellah, I hope to use the word destiny to change our relationship to the future.

By bringing destiny back into our language we will be able actively to pursue the future and not passively accept fate. As Omer says we "repress the future." Usually we think of repression as something we do with our troubled past. However, Omer's evocative idea helps us to consider that we can also repress the future. If we are to overcome this repression, this block, we need to account for our mixed relationship to the future, both currently and historically.

From fear and selfishness to progress, development, and the capacity for destiny

As I've suggested, fear of damnation in the after-life has helped people and communities to gain control over their emotional impulsivity, but represents a very limited relationship to the future in which we simply seek to gain approval and avoid punishment, which can be compared to Lawrence Kohlberg's (1981) stage of individual moral development in which the child's focus is on being a good boy and avoiding being a bad boy. The release of individual initiative that is so core to the new modern identity is also a release of the guilt and fear of the premodern good girl/bad girl identity. With the release of excessive guilt, individual possibility opens and with it a wild sense of imagination and hope is released. Unfortunately, or inevitably, it also unleashed a troubling sense of "What can I get for me?"

As a result, we replaced a troubled and fearful sense of waiting until later to be rewarded with the troubled sense of seeing how much we could get now, which certainly changed our relationship with the future. Instead of experiencing the future as a fearful time of judgment in hopes of gaining a berth in the boat crossing the river Styx, the experience of the future became a chance to fulfill one's personal or nationalistic impulses in the material world. Unfortunately, this attitude toward the future has not solved enough human problems. The invisible hand of human enterprise lacks much awareness of the value of holding hands with others in reciprocity.

Fortunately, there is another attitude toward the future, one that is drawn from the image of social progress. This image attempts to evoke some experience of destiny by reconciling what is problematic about previous attitudes toward the future. This reconciliation takes place through the power of the image of progress to focus our attention on our moral obligation to both treat this world with respect (i.e., environmental sustainability) and to treat all human beings as equals (i.e., social justice). This image supports an internal approach to maintaining control over emotional impulsivity, in which we hold back acting impulsively in order to create a shared future and not simply out of a fear of retribution, thus offering an alternative route to moral experience other than through fear and guilt. Similarly, the image of social progress could balance the short-sighted selfishness of the "me-first" attitude because of what the individual can gain though cooperation. Let's look a little closer at this idea of social progress.

The desire for social progress has a longstanding history that can easily be traced back into the earliest ideas and hopes for the modern age. This idea is focused on the belief that we can gain new experiences of the world and institute these experiences through the use of social learning practices. Whether in our political relations or in education, the idea of social progress has been, and continues to be, a substantial alternative to the religious tribalisms that would limit learning, especially limit the learning of any people we wish to subjugate, such as women, an underclass, or minorities.

Social progress is also an alternative to the excessive individualism of the modern age. Instead of the attitude of the rugged individual that can be characterized as "*I* did it myself, why should *I* help anyone else?" the attitude of social progress asserts that we are all in this together. While any togetherness can also become excessive, even oppressive, the assertion that we have a shared future powerfully directs our attention. Unfortunately, the idea of social progress has yet to bear the fruit needed to consolidate a shared experience of destiny encouraging us to pursue a sustainable and just world. In fact, there is evidence that too many people are reacting against that idea as they associate it with the significant moral failures of the twentieth century:

> There is a wide spread feeling that the promise of the modern era is slipping away from us. A movement of enlightenment and liberation that was to have freed us from superstition and tyranny has led in the twentieth century to a world in which ideological fanaticism and political oppression have reached extremes unknown in previous history. Science, which was to have unlocked the bounties of nature, has given us the power to destroy all life on the earth. Progress, modernity's master idea, seems less compelling when it appears that it may be progress into the abyss.
>
> (Bellah *et al.* 1985: 277)[2]

There is appropriate doubt about whether the idea of social progress has the legs to carry us past these earlier problematic attitudes toward the future and into a less fearful and more responsible attitude. Instead of finding strength in this idea we seem to largely agitate within the individualistic, short-sighted attitude toward the future. Or, we regress and experience an upsurge in the earlier hell and damnation attitude that leads to forms of tribal warfare with those of different religious or secular fundamentalisms, ethnicities, or simply different gang colors.

Clearly, the idea of progress is not enough. Perhaps, with support, it could be resuscitated, but not without a clearer understanding of its limitations. Fortunately, there is at least one other idea that is used to focus attention more effectively on the future. This idea too has its own relationship with destiny. This is the idea that we, as persons and as a people, develop.

Besides social progress, our relationship with the future has also been governed by the idea of human development. This idea is relatively new in human history, traceable in Western culture to the seventeenth century, but not supported by sufficient institutional structures until the nineteenth century. However, more often than not this idea is applied to individual people and not to whole peoples.

As individuals we, especially children and adolescents, are thought to develop. However, in the last few decades greater attention has been focused on adult development. The social psychologist Erik Erikson went so far as to extend the traditional stages of child and adolescent developmental to include stages of adult development that proceed from young adulthood to elderhood. Despite these advancements, the idea of development has still been largely viewed as a psychological phenomenon, as in the narrow idea of a psychology of the individual. For reasons I will discuss, the narrowly conceived notion of individual development has been further hampered by the way that clinical psychology has focused on the private-life suffering of individuals. Between their focus on private-life experience, developmental and clinical psychologies themselves may fail to evoke a powerful enough experience of the future; they don't have enough access to an active experience of our capacity for destiny.

What hasn't been considered enough is the possibility that as individuals we develop only as far as we as a people have developed; and to the extent that we participate in a larger process of cultural evolution, we join others and develop together. This idea has the potential to become a focal point upon which proponents of the two divergent ideas of social progress and human development could come together.

I want to locate a new understanding of destiny within the idea that our personal development takes place within a range determined by the current processes of cultural evolution, and that social progress and individual development are two faces of the same process of human transformation. Destiny is a capacity that focuses individual and generational attention. By evoking an experience of this capacity in people, a shared experience of the future is awakened. In this context, destiny is not a particular future, it is not your or my idea of the future. Rather, it is a capacity that, when active, transforms our experience of the future – in each moment – into the capacity to actively pursue a shared experience of meaning or purpose.

I am using the word destiny to awaken our relationship to the future. The future can be passively accepted or actively pursued. I have come to understand that both as people and as a people we have the capacity for destiny. Further, this capacity is activated as people find a personal relationship to a larger group, to their people, in support of both social progress and individual development.

Addressing powerlessness as a matter of the separation of self and world in order to found a new image of the individual in community

In the face of current social challenges we have too often felt powerless to respond. However, the intensity or extent of our powerlessness may be a vestige of the twentieth century, reflecting the modern individual's unfortunate, necessary, and now obsolete isolation. Because of the embedded strength of what I have come to think of as the "original oppression" of culture, it seems that it was necessary for the individual to break away and form such an isolated identity. However, despite the trumpeted up strength of rugged individualism, isolation seems to have led to a certain apathy and passivity. I am coming to suspect that this apathy is rooted in a historical deprecation of the healthy way in which emotions function to connect people to each other, to a shared image of the future, and to mutual action.

In order to use emotions more for what they are intended we need to see how they have previously functioned and how they currently function. So far I've suggested that the institution of the family and social and religious institutions have used fear and guilt to control emotional impulsivity in the child and the citizen. At more developed stages the original oppression of these cultural institutions is challenged by an individual whose relationship to emotional impulsivity is governed not by a fear of the future (i.e., eternal damnation) but by the desire for individual gain. This led, necessarily, to the individual cutting themselves off from the previous obligatory function of emotion, but at a great cost, which we have been sorting out for the last two hundred or more years. This sorting has required us to reflect on our extreme individualism, which many find very troubling. John Dewey reflects on this dissatisfaction when he writes (I repeat):

> Individuals vibrate between a past that is intellectually too empty to give satisfaction and a present that is too diversely crowded and chaotic to afford balance or direction to ideas and emotions.
>
> (Dewey 1929a: 52–3)

We can no longer simply use guilt and fear to control emotional impulsivity; the idea of eternal damnation is simply, in Dewey's words, "intellectually too empty." Nor can we continue to narrowly pursue individual or
nationalistic goals to the exclusion of an understanding of our impact on
others and on the future. Such constriction has led to chaos, to a profound
experience of having no common direction for shared emotions.

We have founded two forms of liberalism, political and psychological, that
would seem to offer alternative means for controlling impulsivity through
distinct ideas about the future, that is, social progress and individual development. While each of these dimensions of development has helped direct
common emotion, the divide between the two has created a gulf in our
experience between the public and the private, as neither social progress nor
private-life individual development has garnered a strong enough mandate to
move the culture/species forward. The division within liberalism, between its
public–political side and its private–psychological side, can be addressed.

In the twenty-first century we have the opportunity to overcome some
portion of the division in our lives between the public and private by
deepening our awareness of the limits of the hyper-autonomous individual
and reclaiming the healthy functioning of emotions, in order to provide a
guiding image of the individual in community. Finding and exploring such
an image is no simple matter. It requires recognizing what individuals
uniquely bring to their community, giving them room to explore their own
development, helping them attach emotionally to their communities, while
maintaining a focus on the needs of the whole. Balancing individual and
community needs is one way of expressing the central purposes and mys-
teries of modern culture. This purpose has guided the last several hundred
years of modern cultural experimentation and has led to both hope and
despair.

The modern experiment with integrating individuality back into community can move forward. However, many of us have the experience that
time is short and new efforts must be made to account for the immediate
risks to people, to our culture, and to the earth. Fortunately, the new
thinking and new practices that are necessary do not need to be imagined
from scratch. Much of the work has already been done. Now is a time for
synthesis and action. We need to act on the opportunities that existing work
offers. Almost all fields of inquiry and all human institutions have some
awareness of the gap between current circumstances and our inability to
respond to them. Whether in commerce, religion, education, science, politics, the arts, or the family, we are becoming increasingly aware of this gap
and the need for all of us to act, separately or together, to bridge it – to
respond to the challenges of life as we find it.

Unfortunately, awareness of this gap too often leads to despair as we
cannot imagine any force rising up to respond to the growing severity of
our situation. However, as I briefly noted earlier in this chapter, such

despair may simply be a function of our failure to recognize the distinct role we are capable of playing and to imagine what capabilities we could bring to our community in attempts to address this human crisis. Further, as I also noted before, it may be that this inability to recognize our place, our destiny, may be due to the false separation in our culture's language between the world situation and our own response to that situation.

In this light I will briefly describe how I have attempted to become the change I wish to see in the world, that is, I wish to show how one person can look at his own life and begin naturally identifying a role for himself in the activation of a humane future. In the following section I describe a way that I have come to think about myself that has addressed my own chronic powerlessness and awakened in me a nascent capacity for destiny. In the next chapter I will follow this thread by introducing to you the nine progressive political leaders I met during my research and show how they too have found the path through which they have turned their passive experience of the future into an active capacity for destiny.

My life: reconciling political and psychological liberalism

I was born into a family with significant privileges. We were landowners and drew on two family legacies whose roots went back to the settling of the Napa Valley by Northern Europeans in the mid-1800s. As part of this legacy, my great-, great-grandfather, Nathan Coombs, founded the town of Napa and represented it in one of California's first state legislatures. Following Nathan, numerous Dunlap and Coombs predecessors had taken part in politics. This is a family story, expressing the joy and exultation of privileged lives. The land was ours, and the future chronicles of the community built on it were partly ours to write. Whereas George Steiner claims that Shakespeare could "'hear' inside a word or phrase the history of its future echos," we were raised to believe that we heard inside the future needs of the Napa Valley and the state of California (Steiner 1976: 4). Whether out of arrogance, service, truth, or all three, we believed we had the ability and responsibility to lead.

I remember my father's story of his grandfather, Dave Dunlap, who had been the sheriff of Napa and whose difficulty capturing notorious stage-coach robbers earned him the nickname "no catch-em Dave." The way the story goes, grandfather Dunlap finally caught one of these robbers and hoped for vindication in the local paper. However, instead he found the headlines to read, "No catch-em Dave – 'cept once!" This story was a family favorite, often repeated.

The family story also includes my great-grandfather, Frank Coombs, who was the ambassador to Japan around 1896. His story is more inchoate, and lives through the Japanese ceramics and art in my parents', uncles', and aunts' homes. I sometimes wonder under what circumstance this bounty or booty was garnered. The Coombs were conservative Republicans, and my great-grandfather sought to limit Japanese immigration and was opposed to their right to vote.

The potential shame does not stop there. We were pioneers in the early 1800s who followed the creed of manifest destiny. While not all immigrants participated in the subjugation and murder of native peoples and Africans, most or all turned a blind eye to these brutalities. While we were once persecuted and oppressed for our religious beliefs and lower social status in continental Europe, we now had the upper hand and used it to perpetrate brutal wars against the Spanish colonies and the sovereign nation of Mexico. However, as my cousin Louise's activism expresses, there is a growing awareness of the need to account for these atrocities.

My father is a descendant of the family's political legacy. He was a fourth generation state senator. However, he was the first liberal Democrat after three generations of conservative Republicans. During my father's tenure in the legislature I remember being in parades with my dad, handing out matchboxes with his picture at the Veterans Home in Yountville. I remember roller skating in the halls of the state Capitol, and later bringing a girlfriend to see the Capitol – a memory that includes kissing her in my dad's Capitol office when he was in the legislative chambers.

As a legislator, my father fought for coastal access rights for Californians. He sponsored the Farm Labor Rights bill of the 1970s that supported the human rights of migrant farm workers, and he authored a range of legislation – one banning fluorocarbons in aerosol spray cans, and another requiring the state to divest its pension funds of stock in any company doing business with apartheid South Africa. These last two bills were among the first of their kind in the nation. As may be apparent, I am very proud of my father's accomplishments as a political liberal. I intended to continue the family legacy in the Napa Valley, following my father's footsteps into politics. I participated in numerous campaigns, including my own election as president of my junior high school; and in 1972 I started a George McGovern for President club at that school. However, by age 20, my ambitious intentions stalled. Something was missing.

I remember the moment when my political identity seriously cracked and started to collapse. I was reading an article posted on a bulletin board at Sonoma State University about how topsoil from the plains states was being washed down the Colorado River, and, the article contended, unless we did something to stop this loss, the agricultural capacity of these states would deteriorate significantly within the next 20 years. I felt compelled, standing there, to *do something*, to take part in preventing such a tragic environmental catastrophe. Yet, I remained immobilized, feeling nervous and guilty. I had been raised to recognize this as a crisis to which I needed to respond. However, my own suffering in my private life left me with little to give.

At that moment, I felt ashamed. I questioned my value as a Dunlap, and believed I had failed the family. I believed that I was in part responsible for the ongoing environmental degradation of our time, and especially responsible for taking a leadership role in its restoration. As a child and teen, I had participated in many political efforts to protect our natural lands, efforts which contributed to my sense of well-being and fulfillment. I had felt the family's legacy alive in my own budding political identity. However, at that moment, I had no contribution to make. In fact, I stopped believing that I was part of the solution. I was led to a drama of failure as a way of containing my shame. It was too much to bear and I used negative, self-critical thoughts about my limitations in order to sever my politicalness from my identity. I moved away from the bulletin board within a new, though narrowed, identity. I no longer had an ancestral figure ahead on the trail for me to follow, nor did I have a sense of belonging to a community. I turned my back on politics and did not seriously engage for more than two decades. I continued to express my political beliefs through simple, private tasks like voting and recycling. However, I stopped experiencing myself as someone with a public/political capacity to influence change. That was more than half my lifetime ago. I have now lived more years since than I had lived up to that moment in front of the bulletin board. I am now 50. It has taken me much of the last three decades to see that the political identity that I had hoped for was incomplete. I too easily sought my father's approval and did so by trying to emulate him. But, I missed the significant contribution to my family that my mother had made.

Over the course of the 1950s, 1960s, and 1970s, my mother sought to help herself, our family, and others with the psychological suffering that stemmed from the modern world, especially as it manifest in the inflated, traumatized, avoidant years after World War II. My mother sought out psychotherapy for herself, my father, our family, and carried the values of psychological liberalism into our community. In my own life I have had a hard time acknowledging her contribution. In my overidentification with my too often absent, though heroic, father, I devalued my mother, who was with my brother and sisters and me each day. Yet, it was her copy of *The Portable Jung* and other psychology books that I turned to when my life and my overidentification with political liberalism began to crack.

Turning aside from my father's path and embracing my mother's wisdom, I spent the next 20 years as a student of psychology and philosophy. This period has helped me to understand how giving up on being political was a necessary failure. With the help of my mother's psychological liberalism, I am now reframing my story as one of opportunity for transformation. In a sense, I am back at the ending-beginning point over 20 years ago, but seeing (for the first time) how to tell a different story. In this new story I see how the attempts I made in my youth to form an adult political identity, within the Dunlap/Coombs tradition, were thwarted by my private-life flaws. These flaws forced me to let go of the nascent political identity that had once sustained, guided, and provided my life with a sense of meaning and purpose. And, when I sought out help for my suffering I found such help in the form of psychotherapy.

My therapy brought relief and insight and helped me make important changes in my life. Yet, it felt incomplete. I was semi-conscious of the way that my family legacy and father's political calling was hunting me, sniping at me with images of who I had hoped to be. However, it was not just my own lost destiny that was limiting my therapy experience. It was that therapy itself was not focusing on the larger issues of the modern world, including my separation from both family history and community connection and responsibility, and my obligation to both. Therapy didn't help me connect back to the world. For some reason, this loss never became a significant focus of my therapy; I do not think I knew how to bring it out with my therapists. My emotions were interpreted primarily as a function of a painful private life, and not as an inability to find political expression for the complex combinations of emotions that I felt. The source of my shame was still blocked from me; the complex emotions resulting from the loss of my sense of family destiny were addressed primarily in traditional psychotherapeutic terms. I see now that my need to express my felt-sense of social justice and my starved desire for a human community were as important psychologically as any private, individualized symptoms.

Because of this schism between my own "private" experience of psychotherapy and my larger public interests, I could not forge a link to give direction to my aspirations.[3] While I had experienced the best that both political and psychological liberalism had to offer, I still felt powerless to become the self that I thought I was meant to be. However, this is where I suspected that my task was to find within my experience something unique that I had to contribute to the task of continuing to liberalize our culture. In order to do this I needed to find and establish an identity that expressed who I experienced myself to be.

This identity turned out to be neither the political leader that my father was (political liberalism) nor a psychotherapist that my mother aspired to be ("private-psychological" liberalism), rather it was some hybrid between the two, what I refer to as a political psychologist based in a new form of liberalism, a "public-psychological" liberalism.

As I have come to envision it, the purpose of this new "public-psychological" liberalism is to respond to the three wounds of modern culture I have identified through my own suffering and subsequent research. These are: first, in modern culture people do not feel like they contribute to the public good, which leads to feeling isolated; second, this isolation restricts people's ability to use the public function of their emotions; third, the loss of these first two leads to the loss of their own felt sense of the future, their capacity for destiny.

Through an image of myself as a political psychologist I began to restore my experience of the future. In this image I have found a way of bringing myself into the public light, thus enabling me to practice using my emotional experience publically, which helps ease my isolation. This vision of my future, my own rudimentary connection to destiny, has increased my experience of vitality – all directed toward the restoration of my own public-community identity as a citizen. This has returned me to my own roots, to the shame I had felt for abandoning the progressive/liberal identity I had been born into.

As a political psychologist I bring together my father's and mother's liberalisms and become curious about the contribution I could make to the transformation of political culture. Based on what I had learned in my own life experiences I chose to turn attention back to the political liberalism of my father to see what it is that a political psychologist could offer to these citizens. More specifically, I began to wonder what it is about progressive leaders that enables them to maintain their public identity and how this ties into their experience of the future.

In the next chapter I present part of my own research with progressive leaders in order to use their stories to show: how political liberals are able to transform their experience of the future into a capacity for destiny; and how, with the slightest aid from psychological liberalism (my facilitation), their capacity for destiny intensifies, which implies the opportunity for an integrated liberalism, focused on both personal and cultural transformation. By telling the stories of my research participants I can begin to fill out the abstractness of this idea of embodying destiny. Whether identified as progressives or liberals, these leaders are working the tradition of political liberalism. Their overt focus on changing the structural dimensions of society is both their gift and their bane. Accordingly, my task here becomes one of balancing an analysis of the strengths and limitations of their focus with an analysis of the strengths and limitations of psychological liberalism. Through this balanced analysis images of what an integrated liberalism would look like, focused on both individual development and cultural evolution, begin to appear.

Chapter 3

Stories of political destiny

Learning practices: truth, caring, and accountability

As a clinical and political psychologist, as a citizen as well, I have cultivated a personal relationship to my community that I use to establish what is true about my experience. This approach is a form of "learning practice," a truth practice. This practice has allowed me to reflect on my sensitivities, talents, my life circumstances, my moral shortcomings, and my distinct suffering. Through this practice I come to know, to have some experience of, what it is that I necessarily must contribute to my community. I have a sense of myself, my purpose, my destiny. While really more of a capacity than a sense, destiny definitely has a bodily dimension to it, a felt sense that brings with it an experience of truth.

As I learned to cultivate a truth practice, I added two other practices. In addition to truth telling, I began overtly focusing on being accountable to the truths about myself I was uncovering and learning to care for myself in the face of my suffering and the limits of my moral integrity. In turn I apply these practices in both my private and public life, as a member of my family, community, and both a clinical and political psychologist. Through these practices I am developing an experience of knowing what I have to give, which has enabled me to make this contribution more consciously and more actively. I suspect that my experience is common. Once we know what we have to contribute we begin to transform our experience of the future into an activated capacity for destiny.

Thought of in this way, the idea of destiny becomes less problematic and more common, common both in the sense of usual and in the sense of shared. A common destiny invites an active contribution by each of us. I found this common destiny to be an active experience of progressive political leaders. In my research with these leaders I discovered how a person's passive experience of the future is transformed into an active capacity for destiny. I learned how these leaders wrestle with their own sensitivities, suffering, and talents and, when faced with the necessities of their time, choose to become active shapers of events – leaders – rather than continuing to be passive victims of these same circumstances.

The time I spent with these leaders changed my life and helped me gain a new respect for what I can bring to the world. I too could draw on my sensitivities to shape capabilities that I could use in my community. My experience with them left me feeling more hope than I had previously known. This hope grows from within an emerging image of myself as a contributing citizen, as a clinical and political psychologist. It has helped me to bear the grief, shame, and fear that this world has evoked in me and to not let those feelings consolidate into despair. And I'm learning to use these practices to transform the despair that I do experience.

As these emotions began moving more freely, I felt more confident and less desperate. Realizing the connection between despair, repressed emotion, and lack of individual purpose has awakened in me a suspicion that the separation between the objective circumstances of the world and our experience of our own capabilities to respond to these circumstances is a problematic artifact that emerged simultaneously with the individualism of the modern era. What if the circumstances of the world and our capacity to respond to these circumstances are more intimately linked than we have thought? What if we naturally develop the ability to respond to the necessities of our time? What if our ability to respond is artificially hobbled by the way our history and our language has separated the ideas of social progress and individual development?[1]

If we do naturally respond to the crises of the world then we could likely find evidence for such a response; we could find individuals who actually do become agents for political change. Carl Jung offered the following description of the way in which individuals become agents of transformation for their time:

> Social, political, and religious conditions affect the collective unconscious in the sense that all those factors which are suppressed by the prevailing views or attitudes in the life of a society gradually accumulate in the collective unconscious and activate its contents. Certain individuals gifted with particularly strong intuition then become aware of the changes going on in it and translate these changes into communicable ideas. The new ideas spread rapidly because parallel changes have been taking place in the unconscious of other people. There's a general readiness to accept the new ideas, although on the other hand they often meet with violent resistance . . . if the translation of the unconscious into a *communicable language* proves successful, it has a redeeming effect. The driving forces locked up in the unconscious are catalyzed into consciousness and form a new source of power, which may, however, unleash a dangerous enthusiasm.
>
> (Jung 1919: 314–15, emphasis added)

While intriguing and somewhat abstract, Jung's vision can be grounded in the immediate experience of cultural leaders who tap into the unconscious through a capacity to know and to language a future; these leaders are able to activate the capacity for destiny. While this capacity has existed in human history in rudimentary forms since our beginning, there is evidence that we have crossed a developmental or evolutionary threshold that is enabling us to activate it more broadly. While at one time it was the domain of extraordinary individuals who manifest unique abilities to catalyze the transformations of culture, such abilities may be becoming more common and can be found within the experience of more citizens of good conscience, such as in the stories of the progressive leaders.

Through the stories of progressive political leaders we can demystify what has seemed miraculous about the abilities of great leaders to transform culture. Such a capacity is not reserved for exceptional individuals, but can be activated, and is being activated at all levels of social and political organization. Based on these leaders' stories we can begin to identify the capacity for destiny that is emerging into our awareness at this time in human history and the opportunities to intensify it through the confluence between political and psychological liberalism.

My research with progressive political leaders

In my research, "Destiny as Capacity: The Transformation of Political Identity in Human Development," I focus attention on the role of shame in the formation and maintenance of progressive political leaders' political identities. The result of this research describes the way in which openness to necessary shame transforms these leaders' "experience of the future" into a "capacity for destiny" (Dunlap 2003). Through their attending to the necessities of their times, these leaders activate destiny as an emergent human capacity.

Prior to going on it is best to offer a brief description of shame. Shame is first of all a biological response of a mammal. It is an aversion response that shifts an animal's interest – also a biological event – away from something that the environment says is shameful (Nathanson 1992: 153–62). In humans the shame response has a range of intensity that begins with mild embarrassment and extends all the way to humiliation. For the child, the biology of shame is one of the last affects to develop and becomes active as the child begins to turn toward awareness of their psychosocial environment.

While receiving much bad press, due to the misuses of shame such as when a child is shamed, shame functions for both the child and the citizen to shape their moral experience. Accordingly, despite its bad reputation and our disinclination to think positively about it, moral experience is dependent on healthy shame. This becomes all the more clear from the stories of the participants in my research. In their lives they have embraced necessary shame to form their own sense of moral necessity, which has activated their capacity for destiny.

Prior to my research, I had already been working with the concept of destiny, sensing that progressive leaders had some experience of the future that, if I could understand it, could teach me how to turn a passive experience of the future into an active desire to shape it. I hoped that I might then find a way to spark such an active pursuit of the future in other citizens. However, I had yet to grasp the idea that destiny could actually be conceived of as a human capacity. That learning came through the research.

As I prepared to explore the political identities of progressive political leaders, I was directed by my mentor and dissertation advisor, Aftab Omer, to focus my topic on exploring the shame experience of these leaders. Omer's own research had already identified how distinct emotions or "affects," the biological basis of emotions, could be transmuted into distinct capacities. At first I resisted Omer's guidance for me to incorporate shame into my research topic. Like many Americans, I simply was not that interested in shame (in fact, given its interest-abating function, it turns out that it is quite difficult to be interested in shame). However, I came around to be curious about the possible connection between shame and destiny in their relationship to the formation of political identities. This led to the following research question: "What is the relationship between a political leader's experience of the future, shame, and the realization of a political identity?" With this question in mind I formed the following research hypothesis: "Attending to shame is likely to intensify the experience of the future, which may have a transforming effect on the leader's political identity."

During my meetings with progressive leaders in the Summer and Fall of 2002 I guided them through a group process that focused broadly on their psychological experience of being in politics. In particular, I paid attention to their emotional experience and on finding out what activated their capacity to engage their communities politically.

Through an exploration of their political identities I learned many things relevant to this writing. I found that progressive political leaders yearn to share with others a genuineness they came to call their "authentic face," a face surfacing here and there in their day to day living, but usually submerged. Their experience of the authentic face is fragmented. Authenticity is restricted by what I came to call their various "political wounds." I had insight into the existence of these "political wounds," suffered at the interface between their private and public identities, and found that it was a common theme of this group. Chief among these wounds is the restricted range of affect, demonstrated by their masking of their personal/emotional experience in public. This leads to an ambivalent relationship to emotion itself (which is part of what keeps their authentic face submerged). While they feel ambivalence toward emotions generally, they feel a strong aversion to the possible value of their shame, but are nevertheless guided in their political intelligence by it. By means of this intelligence, progressive political leaders establish their moral integrity, transforming their private identity into an expanded political identity that is responsive to the needs of their communities.

I will draw on my learning from this research throughout this writing. Particularly important will be a fuller exploration of the role of emotion in the lives of progressive leaders, especially their current ambivalence to emotions. However, in this chapter, I focus on two things I learned from this research. First, I learned that these progressive leaders had gone through some form of a transformative experience that had catalyzed their experience of the future into a capacity for destiny which resulted in the formation of their political identities. Second, I learned that, when given the opportunity to reflect psychologically on their political experiences and identities, an intensification of their capacity for destiny can be noticed, which helped them to clarify the value of their political identities, intensifying the strength of these identities, and extending their faith in themselves, in each other, and in the progressive social movement.

Stories of destiny revealing a liberal social attitude

Most of the progressive leaders in my research told coming-of-age moments in their relationship to politics during which they faced a potentially shameful experience and were able to transform this experience into a heightened sense of public duty, which included a sense of responsibility, an increased sense of purpose, an experience of having a say in what happens in their communities, of belonging and participating in something larger than themselves, and of having found their calling.

Sandy's story

Sandy, an elected official, remembered being elected as part of a platform that supported the commercial development of land in a congested area of town. She took this stance because she confidently thought that the issue of traffic could readily be addressed. Upon review of the evidence after being elected, Sandy reversed her position and cast the deciding vote to kill the development project. As a result of her decision she faced the wrath of upset land speculators, who had financially supported her campaign. She described this as a horrible, humbling experience that helped her to forge her moral resolve to do the right thing and as a coming-of-age moment of her political identity.

Harry's story

Harry described being arrested at a peace demonstration as part of his emerging political identities. Harry said: "For me getting arrested . . . really, I started my dream to be [an elected official], because I was going to have some power. I was going to empower myself through politics, because I was going to be a decision maker." Later Harry did run for elected office and won. His manner of speaking in the group reflected the confidence of a leader who understands he has power and that he needs to use this power to motivate others. His speaking included a rhetorical flourish that suggested his experience of being a part of something larger, including when he spoke of how "we" were much closer to the types of political change that he deemed necessary – thus promoting hope – but also when he noted that it would still take sacrifice – thus acknowledging the hard work ahead.

Harry's arrest activated his experience that his voice mattered. What began as an experience of needing to demonstrate because of a threat to his community, that is, his "experience of the future," was transformed into a "capacity for destiny," in which he had the experience that his voice and actions mattered. He faced the choice of either staying passive and experiencing the future as something beyond his control or becoming active and thus embracing his destiny as an active agent for the good of his community. By facing the world Harry continues to pull himself – and now others – forward to face the necessities of their community.

Diane's story

Diane also experienced a coming-of-age moment when she was arrested at a demonstration. She is a long-time activist and leader in the peace movement. Her Jewish ancestry is prevalent in her story. Like Sandy and Harry, Diane expressed a sense of the rightness of her activism, including being in touch with something larger. She offered a wonderful image when she described the first time she was arrested and put in jail for protesting. She said, "I felt the first time that I was put in jail my family who died in the concentration camp were really applauding me." For Diane, the larger identity that comes through her is her own heritage and its mantle, which she wears with passion. The Holocaust is driving her activism. The scars of such evil are part of what gives birth to Diane's social conscience and guides it, sending her dead relatives to inspire her future actions.

Diane's coming-of-age moment turned the typically shameful experience of incarceration into one of exultation, which reminded me of Martin Luther King's statement to his fellow activists prior to a demonstration: "If he puts you in jail, you go into that jail and transform it from a dungeon of shame to a haven of freedom and dignity" (King: MPI video). In this statement we see Dr. King anticipating the experience of shame that comes from violating cultural taboos and showing the way to redeem what Omer calls the "cultural traumas" that would have us forget the real shame of slavery and its legacy (Omer 2005: 37–40).

In Diane's story, we see her "creatively transgress" the cultural taboo and bear its shame, only to transform that experience into a new-found capacity for activism, a capacity for the active pursuit of the future, a capacity for destiny.

Sandy, Harry, and Diane's stories all express moments of facing necessity, Sandy's facing a change of heart, Diane and Harry going to jail. In all three stories an experience of a "larger self" gives them a buoyancy – even a moral buoyancy – as they have challenged the status quo and formed an experience of right and wrong based upon their emotional experience and its connection to broader moral principles. Here, the shame experienced when facing a cultural taboo is redirected by an experience of morality that changes the person into someone willing to bear such taboos in the face of the moral needs of a community. By demonstrating and being arrested Diane defied the moral etiquette of that time. She went to jail and, like Reverend King, turned a potential experience of shame into a moral victory complete with an exalted moment of fulfilled destiny as she was applauded by her ancestors. She finds moral authority and destiny linked to this political action.

In Sandy, Harry, and Diane's stories we see how they willingly face what I have come to call "necessary shame," that is, shame that reflects back to us the moral needs of our time. Attending to necessary shame transforms their political identity, thus releasing their capacity for destiny. Their experience of the future moves from being passively experienced to being actively sought.

In these stories we see the emergence of the capacity for destiny, but not, per se, with any distinct psychological dimension. These stories do not show much reflection by the leaders on their own psychological development. No particular psychological insight is revealed about the influence of their political experience on their personal development. In one way or another, their experience simply reflects a "liberal" social attitude, which is a manifestation of political liberalism. Accordingly, the activation of their capacity for destiny seems no different than what we might imagine happens for other liberal leaders throughout human history: that is, they experience a need and find the resources to fulfill that need. As Erik Erikson notes, they "mobilize capacities" that their time calls forward (1958: 15).

How psychological liberalism intensifies stories of destiny

At the beginning of the second, and last, research meeting I fed back to my research participants the observations and insights from the first meeting. I interpreted their stories as examples of the way that progressive political leaders can be open to necessary shame and have this provide them with a moral sensitivity, a facing necessity that evokes the capacity for destiny, personal and collective. While they were resistant to hearing that there was any positive role for shame, reflecting my own original attitude toward shame, their interest heightened as I spoke about the way their sacrifices brought new meanings into their communities. In effect, I offered them a psychological interpretation about their political identity, its history and its function. This interpretation marked a meeting point between their politicalness and my psychological consciousness, a meeting between political and psychological liberalism.

Once introduced to my psychological consciousness, the group adapted quite quickly to its potential use and began working with my interpretation: it opened their own significant psychological capacity. My intervention launched the group into a new round of storytelling, which activated a transformative experience within the group. I think of these next stories as psychologically driven tales of destiny because of how the participants used the group to reflect on their political experience psychologically. This is evident in the difference between the stories told in the group on the first day and those told on the second.

In these psychologically driven stories, the participants search for psychological implications that have bearing on their own personal and political development. The process of sharing these stories evolved into an interactive process that they used to explore new reaches for my ideas within their own experience. These new stories included a courageous introspective quality that intensified the group's intimacy, as members used the group for a personal exploration of their political identities. This exploration included a passionate immediacy that fueled an awakening of mutual purpose. Here is the first "psychologically" driven story of destiny.

Sandy's story

When Sandy listened to my interpretation of her story, that is, its coming-of-age and activating-destiny qualities, her tone shifted and became quietly passionate. Linking up her difficult decision-making process and the hate it evoked in former supporters, Sandy then reflected psychologically on the way her political identity had broken free and carried her in ways she had not expected. She said:

> My life has unfolded for me in a way that I have not had to push anything, it's just been there, I've been able to be a part of it, and participate and give it more energy. I have not had to create my platform or create my persona. I have been me and I feel very strongly about it.

Next she reflected on the Rilke poem I had cited to the group, which I repeat here:

> You must give birth to your images
> They are the future waiting to be born.
> Fear not the strangeness you feel
> The future must enter into you long before it happens
> Just wait for the birth, for the hour of new clarity.
>
> (Rilke 2007)

Sandy added

> This [poem] is exactly what I've been living and I am enjoying life so much through that. The images that I give birth to . . . are coming out of me . . . are just coming out of me [emphatically spoken] it's incredible. And I'm so glad you are all a part of it, because you are a part of it and that's why it's so cool [expressed in a warm, vibrant manner]!

Sandy's comments were immediately followed by another elected official, Irene, who said: "I feel the same way, I'm doing exactly what I'm supposed to be doing."

Frank's story

Frank followed Sandy, connecting my description of necessary shame to his problematic shame of his own power and his shame for wanting to be more powerful. He said: "Somehow I internalized along the way the dynamic, that power is bad . . . I know in my own mind there is a struggle between power and shame." While trapped in this cultural taboo against power, Frank also notes the freedom that can come from this experience:

> So there's this attraction/repulsion when I feel powerful. I felt guilty and it's also what I like best about myself. And it has to do with being tied into my emotions, and my passion. When I do that, that's when I really feel alive. And at the same time there's that sense of shame that often accompanies that. It has to do with leading, with sensuality, it has to do with succeeding.

At this point Frank's insightfulness seems to be carrying him into an excited, vibrant place. I comment on this by saying, "You seem like you're almost vibrating." At this moment I am bringing in psychological reflection, which is immediately supported by the rest of the group with excited, supportive sounds that spark Frank to pursue the opening in himself.

Like Alice going down the rabbit hole, Frank begins talking about his "tremendous temper" as a child, the harm he did with it and the way it left him afraid of his power. He asks, "What am I to do? What will I destroy if I realize how I'm powerful?" I responded by saying, "And what would I create?" which Frank emphatically repeats and goes on to link this to a fear of success. At this point Diane joins in and asserts her own sophisticated psychological perspective, commenting that she thinks Frank is angry. She wonders what he's angry about, and speaking "as Frank" she says: "Oh, my God, I'm going to unleash this power, I'm going to unleash my anger at them. Oh, my God the anger is going to come out. It might not be treated well by society."

In this dramatic moment, Diane's fantasy of Frank's internal dialogue links up anger, power, and shame in an image of someone who holds back because of the risk of being cast out by society because of one's convictions, anger, and power. At this point, Frank turns his exploration more directly toward his childhood and makes a connection between anger and how it is linked to a sense of justice. He says:

> I think it's all jumbled up with the anger. I can remember instances when I was a child when anger caused sort of an indignant reaction about something . . . someone else was getting hurt, bullies in my neighborhood they hurt people. I still feel that anger now coming back. I would just get so angry, and I'd cry and I'd . . . but, it [the anger] was about the injustice.

Like shame, Frank now has connected his anger to morality when he says the anger was about the injustice. As he speaks, his voice is of a man finding insight that releases the past. However, this is not simply a psychological healing of his personal history. In addition, it is a moment in the development of his political identity.

Pursuing this connection between anger, power, and destiny Frank tells another story, calling it "one of my great moments in my life," a moment when he was able to direct his anger. While working at a veterans' hospital he came across a man who was also employed there and was "one of the littlest, weasely-est assholes." Frank's spontaneous sharing of this caricature got all of us laughing. Frank said, "My sole outlet was ping-pong. And one day I played him ping-pong and I was absolutely incredible [group laughter]. And I can still remember that game." I responded by saying, "So this is a game of moral action?" to which Frank again emphatically repeated, "*this is a game of moral action* . . . I was completely in control, but I had this immense reservoir of energy, anger." Next, Frank becomes more impassioned and excited, in his continuing cascade into insight. He says, "It's getting in touch with that authentic self . . . to give us the power. And for me there is always the struggle between the shame of claiming that . . . and just letting it go."

Frank realized how wonderful it feels to let his power come through, how much energy there is in it for him. Later, he turns back to this experience and adds:

> This whole business about shame and power is very important. That tapped into something that's very helpful to me. It raises an issue in my own process again in a way that I want to hang onto and deal with it after meeting here. It has raised some issues in my own way of operating that I want to pay attention to again.

Frank's passionate and insightful connections fuel his desire to become more politically effective. His revisiting the game of ping pong, during which time he was able to direct his anger, suggests an intimate connection between shame, anger, and the activation of moral capacities such as fierceness. What is noteworthy is his use of the group, its growing psychological consciousness, and the group's subsequent pursuit of the direction he opened. This opening is immediately pursued by Abe.

Abe's story

Abe is a very self-effacing man who contributed to the group in many ways including his humor and his extreme sensitivity to shame. Shortly after Frank's sharing, Abe speaks in a frustrated, almost tearful, monotone manner, expressing confusion. He is frustrated with himself as a "math person," and out of touch with his feelings and wants to find a way of being more emotional, and speaking morally in a more open way. He says:

> I'm a math person . . . I have a hard time with touching my own emotions . . . I'm used to analyzing things . . . I can analyze public policy until the cows come home . . . but, I think I'm starting to struggle with this . . . "how to speak from" . . . we talked about this last time, how to speak from your morals. How you convince people that you're right and they're wrong?

At this point I, as facilitator, want to deepen the group into the grief I and many of the other participants seem to feel. I make a *psychological move* by mentioning to Abe that he seems to be brimming with feeling, to which he responds, "That's a good try." This humorous deflection of my inquiry into his feelings was the latest of several self-effacing deflections on Abe's part and brought riotous and prolonged laughter from the group, including my own embarrassed but satisfying laughter.

However, Abe's deflection did not distract the group from extending its growing psychological experience. The group was clearly beginning to feel and enjoy its psychological power, and so Abe was immediately met by his friend Harry who stepped in and kept the heat on by saying to Abe, "I do not think you give yourself enough credit for holding the emotional." Then to the rest of us he described how Abe is sought out to moderate many important public discussions that require finesse, diplomacy, and, by implication, emotional awareness. It is as if the group's natural psychological consciousness had been pent up and then released. Somehow the research provided a context to bring the strengths of political and psychological liberalism together.

Harry's support seems to encourage Abe, who turns the conversation back to Frank's theme of the relationship of power, sensuality, and shame. However, Abe misheard Frank. Where Frank had connected power, shame, and sensuality, Abe curiously replaces the word "sensuality" with the word "sexuality." What followed was wonderful and suggests the importance of passion or Eros as a force of sensuality, sexuality within an expanding group intimacy. Abe starts by describing the satisfaction of moderating and the art of it. He likes having power but uses it lightly. He then turns to Frank and says:

> And one thing that you mentioned, sexuality in regards to power. And obviously the guilt and shame [group chuckle], you've got everything going right there. This is a terribly weird thing to say but, I've never felt sexier in my life than in the last couple of years. It's a shameful thing to say but . . . You know when you're moderating and have people's attention. There is a certain part of all of us in political life that loves the attention. At least for me, I acknowledge it, I love it. And I love public speaking, I love it. It's very empowering and I do not know, you're right you have to sort of let yourself go. Letting go feels wonderful . . . is not that a . . . to let yourself have the power, let yourself be the focus.

This conversation takes hold of the group, as Diane says, "I think everyone should feel sexy, I mean I think life would be more enjoyable." She is followed by Harry who says, "Good politics is masturbatory and a lot of politicians go, 'god damn sex is great!'" which brought more riotous laughter.

In this sequence Abe brought the group back into the territory of passion first explored by Frank, and the group is clearly eager to follow. Harry's comment brings in a ribald awareness of the passionate connection between sexual pleasure and political power. He continues to playfully exhort this connection. "If you do it, if you do it, if you do it right [group laughter], you share and you do it so that everybody is along and everybody's getting off."

You get off on politics done right and you get off on sex done right. Harry then refers the group back to Irene's story of getting a standing ovation when she offered a measured, effective response to a time she was verbally attacked at a public meeting. Harry said, "The applause that you got was an orgy response. It was a communal response, you know a response like 'she fuck'en told him!'"

Abe's satisfying experience of leadership has a clear erotic quality that carries over into the group's play with sex and politics. However, he also expressed shame for the erotic satisfaction he gets from leading. Like Frank, Abe experienced a burst of embarrassed, joyful satisfaction at sharing this connection. In psychotherapy cultural taboos against talking about sexuality and sharing emotions are challenged, which releases an experience of healing, development, and empowerment. This reflects the emergence of the psychological consciousness in relation to people's private-life experience. When the psychological consciousness is used to challenge the same cultural taboos in relation to the political identities of progressive leaders, an analogous release is experienced, which is a result of the emergence of a whole liberalism, political and psychological liberalism conjoined.

In the group experience, Frank and Abe are exploring the application of a psychologically oriented group process on their political identities. The group readily joins in and a joyful, passionate, and even erotic energy is released in the group. However, unlike group process focused on our private life, this process is activating the personal nature of our political experience. In the next story notice the change Dave goes through as a result of the group's growing psychological consciousness.

Dave's story

Dave is sophisticated and compassionate, though his emotions are somewhat muted. His story begins prior to Frank's passionate, vulnerable sharing. I go back to his experience before Frank's powerful deepening of the group's psychological experience and then I will skip ahead to revisit Dave's experience after the deepening. The change in his experience and being is significant. Prior to Frank's poignant sharing, Dave reflects on the theme of shame that I had introduced:

> The shame I carry around some days is that I'm not fully doing what I've come here to do. I'm falling short or holding back and not really kicking myself. Sometimes complacency, I get comfortable, stop letting myself feel the suffering of other people. But some of it is just that I'm not clear enough yet. When I go back, everything in my life has prepared me for this work. I've been given every opportunity, every advantage. The world is training me to do something, to serve something.

When I was reviewing the transcripts of this meeting I did not at first notice anything in particular about Dave's statement. In this first statement Dave expresses his shame, but his "training" holds little excitement, joy, or Eros. It is somber, determined. He has been trained by the world for "something" that is not clear. This frustrates him. Yet, within a few minutes Frank and then Abe have brought Eros back in through psychological reflection, by talking vulnerably and then about how sexy power feels. Immediately following Abe in the conversation described above, Dave is able to say:

> What I notice is, that there's a part of me that wants to glom on and hold people's attention, especially females' attention, which is probably about me been left in the crib too long [group laughter]. There's another part of me that particularly emerges when I'm facilitating, holding a space for a group of people to work together. And, it's kind of selfless, because I feel something coming through me. Yes, it's sexy, but it's sexy in any different way.

Retrospectively, I noticed how Frank and Abe's vulnerability followed by the release of the group's erotic feelings seems to have influenced Dave's way of speaking. Abe seems to have infused Dave with his own eroticism. Dave's passion begins to rise. He is playful and vulnerable, expressing desire for the attention of women and a humbling, humorous psychological interpretation of that. His increased excitement is palpable. He finishes with, "It's the power of something larger. And I align myself with it whenever I'm trying to serve. And that is more like my real self." With the help of the group's rising psychologicalness Dave did find a passionate, humble way of speaking, which he joyously and excitedly will serve. Dave has joined in the group's building psychological passion and the group does not stop there.

Elizabeth's story

In this last story, Elizabeth takes the group's growing intimacy and psychological consciousness and ups the ante. She is a young woman who had recently been elected to a position of responsibility in her community. Speaking of emotional abuse suffered in her own childhood and of her ability to successfully work through the issue in her private life, Elizabeth told the following story. She said, "I had to work through that issue and have really succeeded in . . . [working it through]." However, as her story unfolded, Elizabeth expressed her feelings of shame for not doing more publicly about child abuse. She said, "I realized I was not the only victim . . . I failed other young children who were probably taken by these people."

I responded to her vulnerability by saying, "What's here now?" to which she responded, "Well, I'm just sort of shaky inside and sweaty [and then she laughs]." Elizabeth is vulnerably sharing something deeply personal, but not necessarily something about her private identity. She is sharing her shame for not being more of an advocate for children. In fact, she describes feeling that her political identity interferes with her obligation to become more of a child advocate. She shares one side of an internal dialogue that tells her, "OK, you should really do this, protect other people, you really need to protect other people." The other side responds, completing the dialogue, "And you cannot do that publicly because of your political life, you have to be very careful."

After sharing her feeling of shame for not doing more, Elizabeth describes a dream she had as a kid, which is linked to the abuse she experienced. The dream woke her up in the middle of the night. She did not want to face the pain (represented by the dream memory) but did, working through the original abuse. As she tells of the dream and the pain she shifts it toward her political identity until it is incorporated. Her telling of the dream addresses how she has resolved the original abuse, but some suffering lingers. It is becoming clear that she now needs attention for healing her more public part saying, "But I think it's more painful not to take that step and being afraid because you're in politics too."

At this point she has opened both her mostly healed private wound and her still shameful political wound to the group. In turn, the group responds with an outpouring of support for her political identity, moving to reassure her and affirm the integrity of this identity. Sandy says, "Elizabeth you do not realize just how much you do to protect the people." Gillian follows by saying to Elizabeth, "I see you as a role model. You may not be doing the one thing . . . [implying child abuse prevention]. I think you're doing more as a role model for more people. You need credit for that." Frank adds to all of this, "Be gracious with yourself and the feeling of needing to do something in that specific area. And do not feel guilty about that one area but be patient, that time may come."

The group's outpouring of support seems to have an immediate soothing effect on Elizabeth. The transformative effect is apparent as the group lovingly responds to her. She echoes this transformation toward the end of the meeting when she says:

> I feel like I'm being redeemed of maybe my birth . . . of trying to deal with issues that I really do not have control over . . . I feel as though maybe I have done the work I thought I had not done . . . it's like, one extra layer kind of dropped off my shoulder so I feel like I'm almost ridden myself of that box that I always look at and say, "oh my God . . . and look at and [usually] shut the box. Maybe I have dealt with it and just did not know I had, [maybe] I'm just dealing with it in different ways.

Commenting on the influence of sharing in the group, she adds, "Sometimes you have to expose yourself to hear what other people have to say and realize that you're moving in the right direction and you just did not realize it."

This is followed by Frank who repeats one of the statements I had derived from the first group meeting and had posted at the beginning of this meeting. He says, "Look at No. Three [posted on the wall on a sheet of paper] 'Turning toward shame enables the individual or group to face necessity, which releases the capacity for human destiny.'" Sandy says, "Ah ha." Frank adds, "Brilliant." And Abe says, "It works."

The active use of the group's transformative capacity

In Sandy, Harry, and Diane's stories, the capacity for destiny is overt. Their stories reveal the way in which facing necessary shame catalyzed their passive experience of the future into an active pursuit of their destiny. In the last few stories, Frank, Abe, Dave, and Elizabeth tell different tales based on my introduction of an overt psychological consciousness that seems to activate a level of passionate participation that itself takes the capacity for destiny across a developmental threshold, making it something the group could actively pursue.

In these second stories and in the group's interaction, we see the impact that psychological reflection has on their political identities, focused on events in their lives and past and present emotional responses to them. It is through this process of activating a psychological experience in relation to their political identities that something new begins to happen. In these stories we see a cascading experience of shared intimacy that ties the participants together, forging a bond. This bond begins with their shared political philosophies, but is intensified by the process of shared psychological reflection. Central to this reflection is the mutual experience of living a passionate life that requires moral action. Further, notice the way that individuals in the group began to see what the group could be used for; notice their increased interest and passion. For example, in Frank's process he is beginning to use the group to move toward his potential, he is in a living *moment of destiny* in this group. He is discovering a trajectory for his destiny in a cascading series of insights, happening in realtime, that link his past with an experience of passionate involvement, which includes reflecting on the potential role of emotions in public. In his story, anger and shame are linked to power and morality as insight carries him to deeper realizations of the import and purpose of these emotions.

Frank's insightfulness is not about a particular identification with a specific cause or realizing a specific identity; it is about releasing the repression that has bound up his anger, his power, and his moral fierceness. While not linked to a specific image of destiny, his released repression does have a directional or telic component, that is, the realization of both a therapeutic and transformative potential. Frank is finding transformation in the attention offered by this group experience. It is therapeutic in the sense that it is working at the interface of the historical face of the unconscious, that is, the failure of his family to support him to fully embody the moral potential of his emotional experience. It is transformative in the sense that it also prepares the way for the future by opening his potential vitality amongst a group of political peers; that is, this could be a coming-of-age moment for Frank who is coming into his own in full view of a group of peers.

The role that this opening provides Frank may be temporary. Without a sustaining practice that brings the political and the psychological together Frank may not be able to sustain such insights or move further toward their implied actions. I will address the need for such sustaining "learning practices" later in this writing. For the moment it is sufficient to note that to Frank his experience in the group does imply a new future. It does open him to possibility, which he expresses when he says (I repeat):

> This whole business about shame and power is very important. That tapped into something that's very helpful to me. It raises an issue in my own process again in a way that I want to hang onto and deal with it after meeting here. It has raised some issues in my own way of operating that I want to pay attention to again.

Frank's use of the group for this therapeutic, transformative experience is noted by others. Soon after he has completed his "work" Abe steps forward and in effect asks the group for time to work on his own experience of frustrated political identity. He too ends up in a vibrant, impassioned place as the group's potential to be used for healing and transformation becomes more apparent to its members.

Following Frank's lead, Abe has taken the group through his own story of frustration and ambivalence about power and ended up, once again, bringing out the group's passionate experience. In effect, Abe said to the group, "I like what you are able to do for Frank, can you do the same for me?" In fact, the group could and did. It begins with his frustration and self-criticalness, and ends in a bright, hopeful, and playful space. While I do not claim that Abe was fully transformed by this experience, it is clear that he experienced it as supportive, invigorating, and, once again, the group felt its oats as it learned more about supporting its members to pursue greater "affect freedom," as they shared a widening range of emotions as political potential.

This transformative capacity of the group was not easily recognized by Dave. His first comment about shame and destiny had a painful yearning quality. However, Abe's emotional sensitivity has awakened the group to its hidden potential. With his next comment, Dave dove in and playfully began to make use of that group capacity for himself. Plus, he extended the group back to the specific theme of destiny. Dave pulls together the group's experience of shared passion and the research theme of destiny when he says, "It's the power of something larger. And I align myself with it whenever I'm trying to serve. And that is more like my real self." Notice the parallel between Sandy's and Dave's experiences. Sandy had said, "My life has unfolded for me in a way that I have not had to push anything, it's just been there, I've been able to be a part of it, and participate and give it more energy." In both cases something larger is coming through that carries them as they participate in it.

The growing confidence in this group's psychological ability left many members thrilled and eager to continue the process. As Evelyn noted, she hopes the meetings could be monthly. Elizabeth similarly was grateful as she felt that she had been "redeemed of . . . my birth." She found redemption in the group's attention to the connection between her childhood abuse and her current political identity. Frank's exclamation of "brilliant" and Abe's comment that "it works" speaks of this unfolding transformative capacity that the group was realizing with minimal facilitation by me as I felt my way into facilitating as a new type of "political psychologist."

Identity as a bearer of socially emergent necessities

The theory of political identity that is emerging from this research closely follows Erikson's theory of "psychohistory," which conceives of individual identity as a meeting point between the biological and the social. At this meeting point the individual's process of identity formation links to an analogous process taking place in society, that is, individual identity contains socially emergent necessities. Accordingly, whatever is needed by society becomes part of a telic pressure on the individual. Following Jung's idea that sensitive individuals respond to this pressure by forming their identities around these future needs of society, cited at the beginning of this chapter, we can begin to conceive of the individuals in this research as having within their personalities those seeds of humanity's future that liberalism is capable of recognizing, embodying, and articulating. For example, Dave's statement that the "world is training him" may seem too animistic. However, it might also simply be true, echoing Erikson's understanding of political identity as something created by social need and individual "identity" elements (Erikson 1974: 20). This parallels Erikson's description of Martin Luther whose psychological crisis was only cured when he found a "cause" (Erikson 1958: 14).

Erikson follows Luther's life, showing how his personality formed around a severe social problem, and was quite neurotic until it found a solution to the social situation. He became a bridge for "a political and psychological vacuum which history had created" (Erikson 1958: 15).

Similarly, Dave's personality has formed around numerous progressive causes as he, like Martin Luther, is being forced to "mobilize capacities to see and say, to dream and plan, to design and construct, in new ways" (Erikson 1958: 15).

For Sandy, Dave, and the others who had the experience of having something larger come through, this is part of their capacity for destiny. Here destiny can be thought of as the perfect fit between social need and individual capacity. This idea was echoed many times in the group and parallels Rollo May's sense of destiny "speaking through us" and Joseph Jaworski's description of stepping into a larger purpose and being carried along (May 1981: 89; Jaworski 1996: 179). Also, May talks about "cooperating, engaging, and confronting" one's destiny (May 1981: 89). Sandy's story of changing her vote and bearing the embarrassment has elements of each of these.

Like Martin Luther's story, these coming-of-age stories describe ways that they each turned against a socially accepted value. This required them to form values independent of their society. Lawrence Kohlberg's (1981) theory of moral development describes how individuals move away from socially determined ideas of morality toward more universally experienced values or principles, even though, as we have seen, these higher values become quite difficult to embody and speak about. The shucking off of societal morality by necessity comes hard – even as adults we still react like children to the mythic force of cultural taboos. In the context of these activists' political identities, achieving a more mature awareness of the world around them brought about a sense of awakening, vitality, and authenticity or an emerging originality of being which transcends the present and ventures toward human destiny.

However, this process is not simply about exaltation. It is, perhaps, primarily about making necessary sacrifices. These sacrifices are required as necessary social actions. Frank makes these sacrifices as he bears painful introspection in front of the others in the group. Despite his significant political development, he is openly critical of himself. In the context of this group he is reaching deeper into his potential political identity, he is yearning for more. This reflects his desire to bear more political weight, and to bear – in the sense of giving birth – more of the possible future. Interestingly, Frank's painful introspection is reminiscent of San Francisco Jungian John Beebe's description of integrity as an experience of aspiring to a higher moral standard, previously lived, but since lost. Beebe describes integrity as "an old-fashioned value, in danger of being eclipsed or lost, in need of defense or restoration" (Beebe 1995: 7).

While Frank is painfully reflecting on what he experiences to be an internal lack of coherence or integrity, he is actually asserting a personal vision, his hope for greater integrity, and, in fact, his realization of that integrity through a vulnerable yearning that inspired the group's deepening engagement. This pensive hoping combines shame, morality, and an experience of personal yearning or imagined but not touched destiny.

In this chapter we have reviewed the stories of nine progressive political leaders. We have seen concrete examples of how they actively pursue a vision of their community's future based on their own experience of the risks of the future that they no longer passively experience but have transformed into the capacity for destiny. Here, destiny is being simplified and demystified. It need not be worried about as something problematically religious or new-agey; it need not be thought of as a shameful call to immoral tribal actions against other peoples. It is simply a human capacity to find within oneself a willingness and capability to engage in one's community and work for healthy change, that is, personal development and social progress. Also in this chapter we have seen what can happen when the simple strengths of psychological liberalism are taken outside of their typical function in helping therapeutically with people's private-life suffering and into the realm of helping with people's political identities.

Generalizability: extending the research toward the future

The goal of my research was simply to establish the possibility that attending to shame would transform the political identities of these leaders, catalyzing their capacity for destiny. By linking this to the idea that there is a psychological consciousness emerging at this time in human history, it can be imagined that the experience of these progressive leaders may exemplify a cutting edge of human development/evolution that would be possible to activate more consciously through extensions of this research.

The new psychological consciousness I am imagining could be harnessed to support individuals and groups to use their emotions "reflexively" to activate foundational and emergent human capacities. However, the activation of these capacities is not simply for the benefit of the progressive political agenda. Nor is it simply for the purpose of healing private lives. Instead it is for the activation of a new liberalism that focuses on both. When the progressive movement is combined with the new psychological consciousness, opportunities emerge that are helping us to respond to the crisis in human culture that necessitates that we make ourselves anew. Such a making requires that we do not only focus on the different ideas we have of what needs to be addressed in the future, but we must also come together and form a common experience of the future in order for the human capacity for destiny to become activated. Once active, the capacity for destiny will naturally generate distinct paths to the future that will unify the structural and moral needs of our time with the suffering, sensitivities, and talents that we each have and have to offer. This is a path of not only political leadership but cultural leadership as well.

Part II

Questions of development

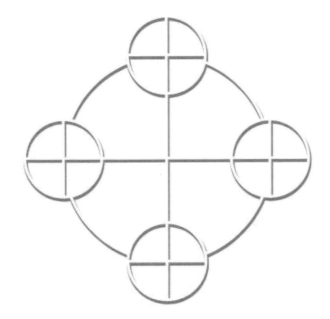

Chapter 4

From political to psychological liberalism

Freedom in psychological development

Religious liberalism: the roots of cultural evolution

In the context of this writing I have been using the idea of liberalism broadly to refer to the liberalization of Western culture. In Chapter 1 I briefly outlined a progression from the rise of a liberal culture during the Renaissance to an emerging psychological liberalism of our time. In this chapter I will go back over that history in more detail in order to show the developmental continuity of our history. Coming to see and know this continuity supports the emergence of the capacity for generational attention, which will help us focus all of our attention on renewing liberalism, for the sake of achieving greater human freedom.

Characteristic of the development of Western culture has been the identification of the increasing value of the individual and the importance of cultivating that value through the pursuit of human freedom. It is this broad movement that I look to as evidence of cultural evolution. However, I recognize this as a phase of differentiation requiring a reintegration of the individual into a range of community values that provide balance and further opportunities for differentiation.

Through differentiation and integration a process of cultural evolution is taking place and moving haltingly, but steadily, toward healthier personal and social relations. This is not to say that such evolution is assured or taking place in a moral manner. Unfortunately, civilizations always seem to come to an end, or at least crumble for a time, perhaps because of the limits of our moral experience. However, the trends of liberalism, including the recent advance of the progressive political movement over the last two hundred years, as well as the increased awareness we have of our own and others' humanity are hopeful signs. We can overcome the tribal zeal, both locally and globally, that continues to burst out and draw our short-term attention – such as has occurred in the first years of this new millennium, at least in American politics.

When we look from a larger historical frame, recent events mark a painful regression that we can stop. We can keep recent moral horrors from compromising the future by attending to and pursuing more actively a new psychological consciousness that has been emerging over the last several hundred years and is central to the liberalization of our culture. Over the course of modernity, the liberalizing of our social institutions, of our relations with one another, and of our very identity is evidence of this new psychological consciousness. Since the beginning, it has been people who have creatively adapted to the environment to bring us progress and development. However, it has only been in the last several hundred years that the importance of the individual has gained enough institutional attention to begin shifting all of us toward previously inaccessible levels of personal development and cultural evolution.

At first the liberalizing forces manifested in the cultural Renaissance of the fifteenth century, but soon were taken up in restricted but powerful forms in the religious transformations of the Reformation. Once manifested in religious institutions, it moved steadily toward the political. Central to this transformative process was Martin Luther's impact on European consciousness. He challenged the Catholic Church's authority by asserting that the individual could experience God directly, without the Church as an intermediary. Richard Tarnas, professor at the California Institute of Integral Studies, writes: "the fundamental question of the Reformation concerned the locus of religious authority . . . [which was located in] . . . the primacy of the individual's religious response . . . [and] . . . abetted the growth of political liberalism and individual rights (Tarnas 1991: 239–4). Despite Luther's pessimism about the opportunities for individual acts of will in the face of fate, he did assert the value and dignity of the individual (Erikson 1958: 215). Further, his assertion of individual religious authority led to "the modern mind's sense of the interiority of religious reality" (Tarnas 1991: 243). As I will be discussing, this interiority not only supported the rise of political liberalism, but also led to the identity of what I will call the "psychological person" as well.

The emergence of this personal religious experience or religiosity supports the emergence of a religious liberalism, which has increased our opportunities for social justice and human freedom. While its origins extend backwards to the Reformation and earlier, and while it has passed through many incarnations, religious liberalism continues to this day as an essential source of moral integrity. Most recently, the social forces of religious liberalism are trying to join with progressive politics leading to the potential for the emergence of a religious left. This effort is trying to consolidate anew the powers of religious liberalism. The new religious left is exemplified by the new evangelicalism of Jim Wallis and the radical Judaism of Michael Lerner. Their recent books *God's Politics* (Wallis 2005) and *The Left Hand of God* (Lerner 2006) are leading an effort to create a network of spiritual progressives to use religion to politicize progressive values. Similarly, there is a growing nondenominational political spirituality supported by Omer,

Joanna Macy, and other cultural leaders. Macy's work focuses attention on the role in political transformation of attending to individual and group despair. Omer's work focuses on developing psychologically aware cultural leaders through transformative learning practices within organizations and communities, which I will return to throughout this book.

The current joining of religious liberalism and progressivism is built upon a second wave of liberalism, that is, "political liberalism," which supported the extension of the liberalizing influence of modern culture through the formation of new educational and legal institutions. Following religious liberalism's emphasis on the value of the individual, political liberalism asserted that individuals have "natural rights," such as the right to decide where they will live and for whom they will work (Dewey 1929b: 4). Political liberalism helped consolidate a new idea of what I will call the "political individual," whose rights included a level of self-determination previously unavailable.

The success of political liberalism cannot be overestimated. Its doctrine of laissez-faire liberalism has dominated Western culture to such an extent that its tenants are now assumed within what Harvard professor Michael Sandel calls an unreflective "public philosophy" (Sandel 1996: 4). According to Sandel, this philosophy has a profound control over our culture that both aids and limits our thinking, actions, and even what we can talk about in regard to our current democracy. Understanding the value of historical political liberalism and its present limitations is one of the primary tasks of this book. Such understanding will help prepare us to grasp the importance of the way a new liberalism is rising up outside of the traditional institutions of political liberalism.

Passive reasoning and moral neutrality: the bane of the political liberal

Recent definitions of political liberalism include Patrick Garry's in *Liberalism and American Identity* (1992). Garry defines liberalism as "a belief in the freedom and dignity of the individual [and] a belief in the power and potential of individual" (1992: 34). From this conception liberalism can be seen as a philosophy that embodies a faith in the future based upon an individual who has "the power of reason and the capacity for virtue" (Garry 1992: 34–5). On this basis liberalism is optimistic.

Fred Kerlinger offers a parallel but broader social definition of liberalism in *Liberalism and Conservatism: The Nature and Structure of Social Attitudes*. He writes:

> Liberalism is a set of political, economic, religious, educational, and other social beliefs that emphasizes freedom of the individual, constitutional participatory government and democracy, the rule of law,

free negotiation, discussion and tolerance of different views, constructive social progress and change, egalitarianism and the rights of minorities, secular rationality and rational approaches to social problems, and progressive government action to remedy social deficiencies and to improve human welfare.

(Kerlinger, 1984: 15)

Kerlinger's definition does not reflect the original vision of liberalism which did not include his emphasis on minority rights and the use of "progressive government" to "remedy social deficiencies." These additions express a more recent account of egalitarian liberalism (Sandel 1996: 11).

What both egalitarian and the more truly original "libertarian" liberalism hold in common is a valuing of individual freedom and the use of rational means for the realization of that freedom. Whether egalitarian or libertarian, these political ideologies are rooted in the modern movement of liberalism, which uses ideology to connect the "past with the future by interpreting the past and using it to guide the future" (Garry 1992: 3).

The political liberal's moral neutrality

Over the course of the last few hundred years political liberalism has emerged as a voice of reasonableness. This reasonable voice includes a moral neutrality that has created the flexibility and tolerance needed in this modern age. However, the price for this flexibility has been high as it leads to moral relativity. Instead of expecting the deep civility and passionate involvement that is needed to articulate a community's moral experience, citizens are able to withdraw from public participation in the name of allowing each other to go their own way. For example, in the religious sphere, as political and religious liberals went their own way, we lost the use of a religious moral language to frame the crucial moral issues of the twentieth century. This left moral associations of God to the questions that interested a narrow Christian religiosity which focused on "individual and sexual morality" while abandoning "public justice" (Wallis 2005: 35). The framing of moral issues was/is left to people without moral timidity. Unfortunately, these "brave" souls have decided that who adults can and cannot marry is a moral issue worthy of our time. This moral regression continues to harm any effort to activate liberty in our culture.

The liberal's flexibility, their moral neutrality, warrants more attention

The view that liberalism holds the diversity needed in modern society is championed by John Rawls, author of *Political Liberalism* (1996). Rawls is acknowledged as one of the current defining voices of political liberalism. He asserts that the balance achieved by modern democracies lies in the way that political liberalism adopts a position of neutrality in the face of the competing values, views, and faiths of modern society. This stance is rooted in the manner in which political liberalism asserts that its idea of justice is not based on what is true but on what is "reasonable" (Rawls 1996: xxii). Here, reasonableness attempts to account for the irreconcilability of conflicting truth claims of different faiths in social institutions by not trying to discern which is right, but by asking how we can reasonably manage to live with these differences.

While this value-neutrality is to be acclaimed, it may not be sufficient to fulfill its goal of social progress. As I will show in Chapter 11, progressive leaders have taken this neutrality too far. They articulate a form of reasonableness divorced from the moral guidance of emotions like shame, which has infected their voice and restricted their "moral speaking." Clearly, Rawls's view of political liberalism has a problem.

Sandel recognizes this limit of political liberalism as he notes how the current political liberalism assumes that "government should be neutral toward the moral and religious views its citizens espouse" (Sandel 1996: 4). Sandel acknowledges Rawls as the current point man for this position when he writes: "According to John Rawls, a just society does not try to cultivate virtue or impose on its citizens any particular ends." Sandel articulates Rawls's position further when he adds:

> Since people disagree about the best way to live, government should not affirm in law any particular vision of the good life. Instead, it should provide a framework of rights that respects persons as free and independent selves, capable of choosing their own values and ends.
>
> (Sandel 1996: 4)

According to Sandel, political liberalism is fixed in this neutral stance as part of an unreflective public philosophy. Sandel defines public philosophy as "the political theory implicit in our practice, the assumptions about citizenship and freedom that inform our public life" (Sandel 1996: 4). This definition can be filled out a little further by reflecting on Bellah's description of public philosophy, as being made up of "languages" as "modes of moral discourse" (Bellah et al. 1985: 334).

Following Sandel and Bellah, we can speak about the need to create a new public philosophy as a new language of liberalism that can account for the political liberal's moral neutrality and resulting passivity. Sandel refers to the political liberal's philosophy as a "procedural republic," which he contrasts with the "republican" philosophy which argues that "liberty depends on sharing in self-government . . . [including] deliberating with fellow citizens about the common good and helping to shape the destiny of the political community" (Sandel 1996: 4–5). The republican philosophy offers an idea of freedom which necessitates "a politics that cultivates in citizens the *qualities of character* self-government requires." In contrast, Sandel writes: "the liberal vision of freedom lacks the civic resources to sustain self-government" (Sandel 1996: 6, emphasis added).

Sandel traces the problem of the liberal's vision of freedom to its roots in Immanuel Kant's philosophy of liberalism in which individuals are imagined to be so separate as to have such distinct "aims, interests, and conceptions of the good life" which then requires the agreement to live and let live and not to try to reconcile the different views and experiences about what the good life is made up of (Sandel 1996: 11). Given this philosophy, the difference it assumes, people are not expected to bother to work out their differences. Without some expectation of learning together, our experience of social, political, or moral obligation is reduced to the freedom to choose to participate or not to participate in creating the good life.

Bellah explores the different attitudes toward civic participation held by Americans and comes to conclusions that parallel Sandel's thinking. Both authors recognize the unintended consequence of the extreme images of individualism articulated by early liberals, from John Locke to Immanuel Kant. Unfortunately, liberalism does not invite reconciling debate, but accidentally invites the withdrawal of the citizenry into private lives.

When the last 40 years of American politics are taken into consideration, we can see how the conservative movement makes no bones about its social and moral agenda for politics and has successfully won over the minds of the public. Whether as a result of full agreement with their agenda, or simply not buying into the liberal's value-neutrality, or simply preferring Bush's morally innocent presence over Kerry's pensive neutrality, the American public has been more willing to follow Sandel's advice and to take up the "republican," public philosophy and to debate the "aims, interests, and conceptions of the good life."

As a result political liberalism has lost significant ground as conservatives have continually been able to define political discourse in terms of those issues that they identify as moral. Whether it be issues of gay marriage, flag burning, immigration, or war with other countries, conservatives have not been encumbered by the liberals' fear of moralizing. As a result, issues dear to liberals such as environmental protection, poverty, minority rights, and education have had to take a back seat. In order for the liberals' political agenda to move forward, they need to reconsider the extent to which they continue to think that our individuality makes us so different that we should not assert our moral experience in the course of political discourse. Is it true that we are so different that we cannot cooperate and form collaborative images of the good life? Isn't this differentiation without integration? The liberal's unreflective public philosophy must be questioned.

Following Sandel, this questioning could lead liberals to show up and engage in forms of public discourse that are not value neutral, but recognize our ability to work together. Following both Sandel and Bellah this could lead to new ideas about the nature of the individual and its capability to form a new public philosophy. Following Dewey this could lead, as well, to the formation of a new psychological and moral type, one not so based on the Enlightenment's idea of isolated independence and rationality.

Toward a new, more complex, liberalism

This reconsideration of the liberal's value neutrality is already taking place. For example, Lakoff challenges political liberalism by asserting that the liberal's rational approach to politics is the "bane of liberalism" (public lecture, 25 March 2005). He notes how conservatives are smart enough to avoid this trap as their approach to politics recognizes and uses an understanding that the individual is not motivated by rational means. They have successfully challenged this defining feature of liberalism by recognizing that there is something more than rational motivation, something psychological.

According to Lakoff, conservatives are able to "frame" political issues in terms that appeal to the "unconscious conceptual systems" that influence the American public's underlying political process. They recognize – to some limited extent – an underlying psychological dimension to individual experience (Lakoff 1996: 224). This idea that conservatives are tapping into a psychological dimension of human motivation suggests that, in fact, they might be more psychological. This is a troubling thought, especially for me as a liberal psychologist. When I consider that conservatives are working from a more complex, psychological way of thinking, I feel ashamed of myself as both a liberal and a psychologist. Samuels identifies this possibility when he writes: "It would be tragic if the most psychologically minded politicians were to turn out to be conservative leaders" (Samuels 2001: 19).

The idea that there are psychological factors which govern our personal and political process is new to those liberals who continue to hold out for the possibility that, given enough time, people will recognize and vote for the social positions that would help them out the most. However, this understanding of the irrational "frames," unreflective philosophies, or unconscious patterns is not so new to social scientists. For example, in *The Party of Eros* (1972), Richard King identifies several thinkers who want to link the future of liberal politics to a greater understanding of the psychological and irrational nature of human beings. He references the work of Paul Goodman who sought to identify a new "radicalism . . . rooted in man's psychobiological nature" (King 1972: 42).

Similarly, King draws on Lionel Trilling's goal of reconstructing "'the liberal imagination' in order to allow a degree of complexity and sense of the tragic to replace a rather mindless optimism about man" (King 1972: 45). Instead of the shallow optimism of the political individual, Trilling found hope in the attention offered to the depth of human experience recognized by Freud who gave "voice to the tragic and the complex in the human situation with which superficial liberalism and social engineering are unable to cope" (King 1972: 45–6). And it is exactly here that a transition from political to psychological liberalism becomes possible.

Once the original liberal's fantasy of the unencumbered self, independent to the point of isolation, is challenged, once we understand the complex relationships between individuals, both in terms of the irrational factors that limit cooperation and in terms of the irrational factors that lead to growth, we begin to factor in a more complex, psychological understanding of human nature. When looked at in terms of the evolution of culture we can see liberalism emerging from the religious, to the political, and now to the psychological. When political and psychological liberalism meet something new begins to happen.

Psychological liberalism – the current and future direction for cultural evolution

In addition to the voice of political and religious liberalism there is a new, distinctly psychological voice, and it is emerging naturally within the culture as we work to try to understand what has been happening to us over the few thousand years of our species' accelerated development, especially the last several hundred years. While awareness of our psychological nature has been used to manipulate the electorate and foster a passive consumerism, there is evidence that attention to our more complex psychological nature could also allow for conversations that transform political culture, activating a deeper understanding of our moral responsibilities to one another.

In anticipation of much of the content of this book, I will trace the emergence of this most recent psychological voice to show how it has appeared and why we can look to its further emergence for hope for the future. In the last two centuries the limitations of political liberalism, its overly rational, moral neutrality, have led to a passive citizenry and to the "me-first" attitude of the newly differentiated political individual. Fortunately, the resulting social alienation has given rise to a third form of liberalism, what I am calling psychological liberalism.

Whether as a result of the acute moral dilemmas identified by the progressive movements of the nineteenth century (women's suffrage, the abolition of slavery, the farm and labor movements) or the growing awareness of the people's psychological suffering from that same century (as identified and expressed through American transcendentalism and European existentialism and, eventually, clinical psychology), many cultural leaders became aware that neither religious nor political freedom would be sufficient to address the full range of human suffering and human possibility. This awareness arose as a result of a combination of factors including a new awareness of our personhood, which gave rise to the new identity of what I will call a "psychological person."

Over the last two hundred years the awareness of our personal suffering is a new manifestation of a psychological consciousness which has supported the emergence of social institutions, including the social sciences and particularly the discipline of psychology. These institutions have attempted – and succeeded in part – to relieve the widespread suffering associated with the new modern world. These institutions and the complexities of the times have supported the new psychological person to develop a range of unique capacities. Author Henry Sidgwick describes how these capacities are, in part, the result of the current philosophy, which itself fosters and is influenced by our growing psychological consciousness.

> We are growing year by year more introspective and self conscious. The current philosophy leads us to a close, patient, and impartial observation and analysis of our mental processes. We more and more say and write what we actually do think and feel, and not what we intend to think or should desire to feel.
>
> (Steiner 1976: 18)

Sidgwick's emphasis on self-awareness can be expressed in more detail in order to round out an initial idea of what I mean when I assert that we are becoming more psychological. Initially, I think of our growing psychological consciousness as an increasing awareness of the value of ourselves as persons. However, this growing psychological self-awareness is also beginning to include the following:

- An awareness of the way we are shaped by our history, both as people and as a people, and how a psychological focus on that history helps us to create the future.
- An awareness of the psychological dynamics that play out and govern our lives, that is, in our relationships within our private and public lives. Awareness of these dynamics and the influence of history on them support conscious choices that increase our intra- and interpersonal effectiveness, again, both in our private and public relations.
- An awareness-in-use of how our cognitive and emotional experience supports our ability to assess personal and cultural circumstances, to motivate and direct ourselves toward necessary action in the world, and to connect to others in these actions.

The emerging reflexive psychological consciousness draws on our growing understanding of how our personal and cultural life histories influence our current identity. What is becoming apparent is the opportunity that our psychological consciousness provides to understand our history as human beings and to use this understanding to more actively engage our possible futures, that is, to become self-creating.

Through a range of forms, the new psychological consciousness is being institutionalized as a new form of liberalism, psychological liberalism. Institutions like developmental and clinical psychologies support our awareness of the developmental process, thus giving us the opportunity to engage that process consciously, that is, they support us to be self-creating. While political liberalism also supported self-creation, its image of the self-made man has led to unintended but chronic selfishness. In the last two hundred years a growing awareness of the limits of the self-made man's independence has helped us extend the idea of self-creation to include women, children, minorities, and the underclasses.

In effect we are learning to extend the idea of self-creation to our entire community. Since the 1970s, and the first pictures of planet Earth in 1968 from the Apollo 8 spaceship, the idea of creating community has itself been expanded to mean creating an Earth community. The process of self-creation that is taking place works at both ends of this spectrum – self and community – through creative action taking place simultaneously at personal and cultural levels of experience. This process is essentially psychological, not exclusively, but essentially.

The transformation from the self-made man to the self-creating community represents a balance point between political and psychological liberalism. Here, psychological liberalism is not associated simply with psychotherapy. In the context of this writing, psychological liberalism is understood to draw from the strengths of the psychotherapy project: not for the purpose of overtly easing people's private-life suffering, but rather to help us develop effective public lives that are integrated with the extreme autonomy currently associated with the modern individual.

Despite the benefits of autonomy, the rugged individualism of political liberalism too often struggles with feelings of powerlessness in the face of the overwhelming size of the modern world. Dewey, Bellah, Omer, Robert Kegan, and many other cultural leaders speak of being "in over our heads," which is helping us to recognize the need to form a new psychological and moral type (Kegan 1994). There is a growing consensus that the task in front of us is just that, forming a new identity.

If such a psychological and moral identity is forming we might find evidence for it in popular culture. Such evidence is readily found in the media in at least two forms: first, in television shows that portray the new psychological consciousness in characters and their relations; second, in press reports evidencing resistance to such a psychological consciousness.

Is our culture becoming more psychological?

There are numerous examples in popular culture and in politics that at least imply my thesis that we are becoming more psychological. For example, going back into the 1970s, the popular American sit-com *The Bob Newhart*

Show depicted the life of a self-conscious, kind, almost bumbling, psychiatrist whose psychotherapy practice, clients, and private-life friendships introduced into the culture the values of psychological liberalism. This show was followed by other popular culture uses of the introspective self-reflection offered by psychotherapy such as in the movie *Terms of Endearment*, which showed how a psychotherapist could help a father and son deal with the tragic loss of a brother and son while also showing a rigid mother's inability to move toward introspection and thus her inability to find healing or forgiveness.

The integration of an introspective, somewhat passive, psychological consciousness into popular culture may be best represented by the recent television show *The Sopranos* in which we can see a confrontation between a modern rugged individualism and an emerging, though weaker, psychological liberalism. In that show a Mafioso boss, Tony Soprano, discusses both his family and his professional work with his psychotherapist, Dr. Jennifer Melfi. Scenes of the psychotherapy sessions are juxtaposed with scenes of family bliss and strife along with scenes of murder. This is startlingly different than the gangster movies of two generations ago that glorified and villainized the lives of Al Capone and other cultural antiheros.

The story of the relationship between Tony and Dr. Melfi is filled with irony on many levels that reveals the brittle weakness of Tony's rugged individualism and the ineffectualness of Dr. Melfi's introverted psychological liberalism, especially when it is limited to the private practice office of psychotherapy. Their relationship marks an interesting dilemma that currently lives between a modern individualism and a passive, private psychological liberalism. This dilemma is also reflected in Mathew Arnold's poem: "Wandering between two worlds, one dead, the other powerless to be born" (Bellah *et al.* 1985: 277). Watch how this plays out on this show.

While we would want the character of Dr. Melfi to be in a significant position of power, perhaps enough to challenge the moral development of her client, her effectiveness is quite limited which is portrayed when Tony has her followed by one of his thugs. The situation gets out of control revealing the limitations of each "type" when the thug loses control of his own resentments and emotional impulsivity and, acting as a plain clothes cop, pulls the therapist and her date over at night on a dark street.

This scene is classic as Dr. Melfi and her mild mannered date, both representing the ineffectualness of psychological liberalism once it is caught outside of the private practice office, assert their naive faith in justice and are indignant when the thug begins to play the bully. As a result of their arrogant naivety the man is beaten and sulks his way out of Dr. Melfi's life, which is a source of sadness for her. Tony Soprano is furious that this has taken place, but he does employ people who do not have the moral guidance that controls emotional impulsivity. This story becomes a failure for both. The moral I draw from this story is that as long as psychological

liberals place too much faith in a private-life process of personal development, they will remain the butt of jokes about their prissy fantasy of
changing the world one person at a time through psychotherapy. What is
needed is an active public-psychological liberalism.

There is also the unusual show *Deadwood*, which portrays a late nineteenth century American gold town in which the characters engage in
sophisticated Shakespearian-like dialogs and soliloquies that reveal levels of
psychological introspection and relationship subtly made congruent with
the despair, greed, and crude life of such a town.

Lastly, for I am not that much of a television watcher, there is the recent
show *Lost*, in which scenes go back and forth between castaways from a
plane wreck who are trapped on an island with one another. Individual
vignettes from each character's life prior to the fateful plane ride reveal
their history, plus help build an understanding of why they act the way they
do with one another in their real-time relationships on the island. Interestingly enough, this show also builds on some sense of a shared destiny, as
the different life stories overlap in too coincidental or synchronous ways.
However, even the implied destiny is constantly thwarted, as the accidentalness of life continually interrupts the hoped for but improbable possibility
of a shared, meaningful future.

The success of these shows reveals a cultural appetite for psychological
awareness in characters and interpersonal relations. They embody a new
cultural value that asserts the importance of self-reflection, emotional
awareness, and insight into the way in which the past shapes the present but
does not control the future, leaving some room for faith in change.

While these media examples are only anecdotal, there is other corro-
borating evidence that psychological experience is growing and becoming a
source of cultural power. For example, Lakoff manages to bring psychological thinking into the culture from the side door. His "cognitive science"
analysis of the root metaphors governing conservative and liberal ideologies
identifies images of the "strict father" and the "nurturant parent" (Lakoff
1996: 108). While on the surface Lakoff's research is not overtly psychological, his idea of "unconscious conceptual systems" actually addresses the
psychological nature of motivation (Lakoff 1996: 224). As a result of his
sleight-of-hand approach to including the psychological in the cultural
debate, Lakoff captures our growing interest in the psychological while
accounting for our simultaneous fears of it through his indirection. As a
result he has experienced a rapid burst of popularity that has helped bring
the psychological and the political closer together. However, given the
power of these two forces he has also faced some resistance in relation to
his work, from both the left and the right. Following the resistance to
Lakoff will allow greater insight into the way that psychology is powerful.
It will also help us to understand the culture's general movement toward
psychological consciousness.

Is psychology a threat to our moral integrity?

Psychology's capacity to shed light on cultural problems seems to be provoking a fearful response from those who may experience it as a threat to their own power. Even psychology's ability to alleviate individual suffering has been ridiculed. For example, I was reading a newspaper column by conservative columnist George Will. He criticized the impact of psychotherapy on American culture over the last few decades, accusing it of undermining Americans' self-reliance, that is, undermining our image of ourselves as rugged individuals (Will 2005). He cited a book written by two psychologists, Christina Sommers and Sally Satel. I picked up their book, *One Nation Under Therapy*, and read how they see psychology fostering a doctrine of "therapism," in which people are regarded as "essentially weak, dependent, and never altogether responsible for what they do . . . this emphasis . . . induces a moral inertia" (Satel and Sommers 2005: 6).

There may be a shard of truth in this caricature of psychotherapy, not because it sees people as weak but rather, more accurately, because of psychotherapy's indulgence in, or at least overemphasis on, clients' private lives. However, I suspect that the attack on psychotherapy primarily reflects a fear of the ability of psychology to pry under the surface of our individual and cultural identities. While this fear may be most overtly expressed by social conservatives, like Will, Sommers, and Satel, I believe there is a general fear of the growing power of psychology to reveal personal and cultural truths. For example, this fear of the psychological is reflected in White House Chief of Staff Karl Rove's accusation that Democrats want to do therapy with terrorists. Notice how therapy is implicitly associated with indulgence and even being unpatriotic – does therapy really risk such collusion with evil? Is Rove tapping into a cultural vein of fear of becoming psychological in order to attack Democrats?

Had I thought that such attacks would only come from social conservatives, I would have been wrong. The attack on psychological knowledge is also propagated by Democrats, as Democratic Senator majority leader Harry Reid responds to Rove with his own disparagement of therapy. In part a response to Rove, but also a response to the claims that Lakoff had helped the Democrats refine their message to challenge George Bush's second term legislative agenda, Reid attacked psychology saying, "I'm not going to waste a lot of time sitting in a room talking about how my parents weren't good to me or something like that," Reid said firmly. "I'm not involved in any of that gimmickry" (Bai 2005: 71).

Reid's resistance to psychological thinking is troubling, and where there is resistance there is likely to be fear. Maybe Reid is only afraid of the Republicans continuing to control the public language, too easily painting Democrats as weak, this time by associating them with psychological vulnerability. Reid would have Democrats appear invulnerable. Here, there is a fear of the vulnerability that naturally comes with becoming psychological. Where there is fear there is some power being abused or simply lying idle, waiting to be used. In this case, there is psychological power that could be used in the service of truth and liberty.

I think that these attacks on psychology reveal that psychological thinking is on the rise. While some would argue for a culture war against our becoming more psychological, I argue that there has never been an age in more need of psychological insight than our current time. The gap between our world and our capacities may in fact be a gap in our psychology or our psychological consciousness between its external political uses and its internal personal uses. To respond to this gap we need to learn more about our psychology as individuals and as a people. Learning about our psychology could help address the powerlessness that has been the shadow of rugged individualism. Learning about our psychology could also help redefine the naive idea of the political individual, thus filling out a more complex psychological understanding of the psychological person that could become the basis for a new language of liberalism.

Direction of our growing psychological consciousness: foundational and emergent capacities

Assuming that our powerlessness has been a function of the artificial separation between our life circumstances and our ability to develop the capacities to respond to these circumstances, I have described my own life with the intent of showing how I am, simply, a response to my life, to our lives' circumstances. My unique sensitivities, talents, moral limitations, and suffering play a central role in the development of my abilities to respond to the world as I find it. In this I am far from unique. Each of us has sensitivities, talents, moral shortcomings, and distinct ways we suffer and each of us is a responder to the world. The idea that we are made in this way, as responders to the world, was clearly articulated by Eric Erikson whose theory of "psychohistorical" development focuses attention on the way in which history and identity are not separable, we are both a creation of our times and we create our times (Erikson 1968: 27; 1974: 12–30). Erikson developed this understanding of history through compelling psychological analyses of significant historical figures.

In his psychohistorical biographies of Martin Luther, Mahatma Gandhi, and Thomas Jefferson, Erikson describes the way in which these historical figures developed what he calls "identity" elements in response to their times (Erikson 1974: 23). If our identity is such a response, then it is imaginable that we could set about crafting ourselves to match the needs of our times. While Erikson's research focuses on noteworthy historical figures, it equally applies to each of us. Certainly, in the lives of my research participants we see the way that they found a vein of gold within their identities and have become responses to the world.

If Dewey's call for a new psychological and moral identity reflects his awareness that the needs of our time are distinctly "psychological" and "moral," and if we combine this idea with the concept that we are becoming more psychological, then we could seek out those psychological attributes or capacities that would help us to form into the identity that necessity requires we become at this time in our history. The idea that we can be so flexible, that we can shape ourselves into answers to the situations in our lives, implies a capacity for adaptation. However, to take it a step further, it also implies that, as human beings, we are capable of developing. Is there a link between our capacity to develop, as people, and our culture's ability to develop? As people we can develop, but as a people do we or can we evolve?

Psychology's contribution to the question: do we evolve as a people?

Through psychology we have learned about a number of different ways in which the individual can be said to develop. Over the last one hundred and more years a wide range of psychological research has identified the way in which individuals develop along several key "lines" (Wilber 2000: 43). These lines include: *psychosexual* development (Sigmund Freud); *psychosocial* development (Erik Erikson); *cognitive* development (Jean Piaget); *moral* development (Lawrence Kohlberg); along a line of the development of *care* (Carol Gilligan); the development of an individual *ego* (Jane Loevinger); and, more recently, *epistemological* development (Robert Kegan); and even more recently *emotional* and *social* development (Daniel Goleman).

Each of these theories of development foregrounds, if not isolates, the individual as the *subject* that develops. Most of these theories also identify specific stages of development that individuals are said to go through in a unidirectional or "invariant" manner. Further, each subsequent stage is thought to be more developed and to transcend but include the earlier stages.

Factors prohibiting psychology from contributing to questions about cultural evolution

Because of how psychology has evolved to focus primarily, if not strictly, on the individual, it has largely been left to other social sciences to answer questions about cultural evolution. This specialization within psychology reflects a number of problematic historical changes, which made it nearly impossible for the social sciences of the twentieth century to address urgent questions about cultural evolution. Psychology's abandonment of these questions particularly has impacted the emergence in the social sciences of interest in the unique role that the individual is capable of playing in that evolution. Through an examination of these changes in psychology it will be possible to refocus our attention on these questions.

In psychology, the idea of development was originally applied to the individual and to human culture, and was motivated by the assumption of the "psychic unity of mankind" (Lewellen 1983: 4). For example, first generation psychologists ranging from Wilhelm Wundt, Sigmund Freud, and Carl Jung in Europe to William James and John Dewey in America pursued this unified idea of humanity as they explored the connection between theories of individual development and theories of cultural evolution. However, despite the interest of first generation psychologists, and despite the second generation work of a few thinkers like Erikson, these subject matters ruptured one from the other leaving questions of individual development up to developmental and clinical psychologists and seemingly abandoning the question of cultural evolution all together. There are at least four reasons why psychology abandoned questions of cultural evolution.

First, the idea of development was used indiscriminately and led to many problematic ideas that reflected the cultural bias of the time. For example, in the nineteenth century scientific thinking was thought to represent the highest stage of human development. It was thought that scientific thinking, based on rationalism, would replace all superstitious beliefs and fears and usher in an age of continued progress that would right all of the world's wrongs and reduce or end human suffering (Polkinghorne 1983: 16–20). This myth of progress dominated Western thought and its limitations went largely unexamined. The suffering of indigenous peoples, women, children, the underclasses, and the decimation of the natural world was propagated by upper class white men living through the unreflective myths of progress and rugged individualism. The growing anger and shame for such immoral conduct have made these myths untenable and the idea that one culture could be more developed than any other easily dismissed.

Second, while first generation psychologists were actively using developmental theories to try to account for processes of personal development and cultural evolution, the gap between these subject matters or domains of experience was experienced as largely insurmountable. While theorists like Wilhelm Dilthey tried to conceive of a social science that could hold all of these subject matters, by imagining the "broadest possible context" for its practices of inquiry, the fact was that human experience in the new "modern" age was becoming too fragmented to be so contained within a single field of study (Polkinghorne 1983: 29). The experienced gap between the individual and society was too much for the imagination of most thinkers of the time. As Bellah notes, it was too much to bear for those simply living through it as well.

Third, according to Bellah's analysis of this period, instead of achieving Dilthey's unitive vision of a "human science," the social sciences formed along professionalized lines that emphasized distinct departments of learning each with their own subject matter and little or no centralizing influence (Bellah *et al.* 1985: 299). Also, rising from the misapplication of the natural science's model of sharply distinguished fields of inquiry to the social sciences, the growth of research institutions, the perceived needs of economic development, and the institutionalization of business, these "developments" spelled a decline in the "unity and ethical meaning of higher education" (Bellah *et al.* 1985: 299). "The early social sciences . . . were concerned with establishing professional specialties providing useful knowledge about an increasingly complex society" (Bellah *et al.* 1985: 299). However, this specialization has driven interest in asking larger moral and ethical questions to the side. Bellah notes how, as a result, "the early nineteenth-century 'man of learning' became the twentieth century corporate 'scientist'" (Bellah *et al.* 1985: 299).

Fourth, despite the misuse of developmental theory to perpetuate cultural bias, despite the difficulty holding a unitive experience of the modern world, and even though the social sciences splintered into desperate institutions, psychology could have maintained its own interest in cultural evolution as a subject matter for inquiry. However, psychology's turn toward the clinical needs of individuals suffering from the burdens of the new isolating modern identity sent them scurrying into the forest of an individualized "unconscious." They could not afford to sustain the bird's-eye view that maintained a connection between the personal and the collective. Despite Freud and Jung's broader comprehension of the unconscious, and their recognition of its phylogenetic richness, the need to address human suffering required a narrowing in order to shape a new paradigm that would allow for an internal dimension of human experience and suffering to be recognized at all.

Following Thomas Kuhn, scientific paradigms form as new, complex understandings of human experience, in this case our understanding of human nature, are narrowed, and made into conceptual tools that can immediately be put to use in culture (Kuhn 1970: 92–3, 109–10). The paradigmatic reduction that took place in psychological thinking had to account for the external focus of the modern politically liberalized individual. Accordingly, the more complex idea that we have an internal landscape, and that landscape had a collective, cultural dimension, had to be reduced to the simpler idea that the internal landscape was simply individual. Thus, second generation ego psychologists redirected attention away from the richer understandings of Freud and Jung toward the simpler idea of a personal unconscious, an idea that was more palatable and could slowly gain cultural acceptance against the externally focused politically liberal identities of the modern individual.

Individual development and cultural evolution were experienced as too different to be pursued within a coherent project of inquiry. Instead, institutional and cultural pressures were directing psychological research toward the study of individual pathology and clinical treatments for that pathology. While some theorists like Erikson continued to ask larger questions, even their work was mostly focused on the development of the new clinical side of the science of psychology.

In effect, institutional and cultural pressures restricted both the actions and the imaginations of psychological researchers, which kept them from continuing to engage the larger questions about the possible role of the individual in shaping themselves, through individual development, and of shaping culture, through an active engagement with processes of cultural evolution. These pressures made it impossible to maintain institutional awareness about the interwoven nature of individual and cultural identity. The difference between these subject matters was experienced as insurmountable.

However, it is important to remember that this paradigmatic narrowing went against the interest in cultural evolution that was widely shared by first generation psychologists. Many of these early thinkers maintained a high hope that psychology could be a science that supported a confluence between theories of personal development and cultural evolution. It was thought that such a joining would lead to greater awareness about the ways in which the individual and culture interacted to create more humane futures for humankind. Despite Freud's doubt about such an outcome and despite his assertion that irredeemable conflict was more the rule, numerous other thinkers, like John Dewey, found hope in their explorations of the relationship between the process of individual development and cultural evolution.

Despite these interests, individual development was not viewed within a coherent understanding of a process of cultural evolution. Instead, psychological inquiry closed the door on the full implications of human history and focused attention on the developmental process of the individual. Beginning anew at birth, following the strictures of Locke's political liberalism, they accepted the idea that individuals start life as a blank slate, that is, a tabula rasa (Wilber 2000: 87).

During the twentieth century these four historical factors limited inquiry into questions of cultural evolution by psychological researchers. The misuse of developmental theory governed by an unreflective use of the myth of progress, the gap experienced between the individual and culture, the processes of institutionalization that governed the formation of the social sciences, and the subsequent economic pressures that shaped a professionalizing field of developmental and clinical psychologies have conspired to limit the applicability of the idea of development to children and adolescents, and only in the late twentieth century did the idea of development finally extend to the private lives of adults. However, it did not significantly reach past the individual.

While the doubts about the myth of progress were healthy and led to questioning the validity and morality of that myth, and while the other factors limiting the applicability of developmental theory may also be thought of as historically necessary, their net effect has been to reduce consideration of the validity and applicability of a psychological concept of development to culture. As a result, psychological inquiry into the possibility that culture actually does evolve and what relationship the individual does or can have in relation to this process has been severely limited.

Fortunately, the chaste view of development used since the mid-twentieth century has begun to give way to broader considerations. In the last 40 years, greater recognition of adult development has expanded our understanding of the full developmental potential of the individual throughout the life cycle. However, even this initial expanded use of the idea of development has failed to grasp the extent to which it now seems that human beings are governed by developmental processes. Yet, developmental theorizing, research, and applications are on the rise. There is evidence of a resurgence of consideration of what could be called a psychology of culture as we are beginning to integrate the efforts of numerous social sciences back together. The original differentiating or divergent burst of the social sciences may be giving way to a phase of convergence and integration.

While nascent, this convergence is generating new social science languages that bring together theory and practice within a new understanding of cultural leadership. Omer's Imaginal Transformative Practice exemplifies this integration through its focus on leadership capacity, moral imagination, and personal and cultural transformation. This is resulting in a clear beginning to new forms of social science focused simultaneously on individual development and cultural evolution.

Through the work of Omer and other social scientists/cultural leaders it is possible to pursue more humane futures in which the role of the scientist includes politics and the role of the politician includes self- and other development. However, in order for this future to be realized, we need a more cohering understanding of the idea of "development," a task I take up in the next chapter.

Chapter 5

The variety of uses of the idea of development

As I noted in the last chapter, first generation psychologists applied the idea of development simultaneously to the individual and to human culture; but this integrative perspective was shortlived. These subject matters ruptured one from the other leaving questions of individual development up to developmental and clinical psychologists and leaving questions about cultural evolution up to other disciplines. The subsequent divorce between these subject matters has been inculcated in several generations of social science theory, which has limited exploration of an integrative perspective of human development.

In this section I will discuss the idea of human development, particularly the disparity between different uses of that concept. Drawing from social theorist Ken Wilber's synthesis of developmental models, it is possible to come to a fuller understanding of the difficulty we have had in the last two or more hundred years and begin to speak a new language of human development. The desire for a common language has been reawakened as theorists are trying to move past the differentiating energy of the mid-twentieth century to reintegrate psychological, social, and biological theories of human experience.

The idea of "development" has a long history applying widely to both individuals, societies, and even such abstract ideas as the "development of an economy." However, using Wilber's analysis of all of the different uses of the idea of development, a list of the criteria of development can now be articulated. According to Wilber, development can be said to be taking place as the following are observed to be increasing: complexity, differentiation and integration, organization, interiority (capacity for self-awareness), autonomy, objectivity, telos/directionality, which bring about a decrease in narcissism (Wilber 1995: 67–78).

In social sciences other than psychology, the idea of development is applied in a range of different ways. Initially, many nineteenth-century social scientists attempted to apply Charles Darwin's theories of natural selection and the implied idea of development to culture. While the idea of development began earlier than the work of Darwin, it is his work that captured the imagination of the scientific community and popular culture and could be said to represent a significant beginning for the view that humans develop.

Following Darwin, other nineteenth-century "evolutionists" such as Sir Henry Maine and Louis Henry Morgan applied the idea of development to culture (Lewellen 1983: 2–4). These cultural anthropologists began identifying stages of cultural evolution, such as the "hunter/gatherer," "horticulture," and "developed agriculture" stages, which, like first generation psychologists, followed the assumption of the "psychic unity of mankind" (Lewellen 1983: 2–4).

Other stage models in cultural anthropology associated cultural evolution with the rise of civilization, which they equate with repressive political controls based on physical force. The coercive power of the state was viewed as an evolutionary advance based on the role of increasing population and increasing class stratification (Lewellen 1983: 10).

In political science, the idea of "political development," which I will discuss in more depth in Chapter 8, is used in a wide range of ways, including being associated with the emergence of a nation-state committed to the idea of "civil liberty," "economic growth," the political behavior of "already developed societies," the ability to "mobilize power," and "administrative and legal development" (Pye 1966: 33–8; Orren and Skowronek 2004: 37).

In political anthropology, "political evolution" is associated with increasing "systemic differentiation," which emphasizes "classifications of different levels of sociocultural" experience rather than "factors that caused evolution to what from one level to another" (Lewellen 1983: 10).

Many of these social sciences are able to differentiate stages of cultural evolution from the past to the present. In this context, there are numerous stage models that incorporate developmental criteria like differentiation, complexity, and organization. However, the social sciences doing this work and the models they use seem to lose their evolutionary perspective and turn instead to the structural dimensions of modern cultures.

Certainly the risks of cross-cultural comparison are known. Most theories do not attempt to be unidirectional: they are vigilant around the risks of culture-centrism. Nevertheless, whether because of these fears or simply not having a culture of the future to observe, it would seem that few social sciences are imagining a cultural evolution of the future. I suspect that this may have to do with their neglect of the relationship between individual and culture. When this relationship is studied, when the individual's impact on cultural evolution is considered, a range of questions and new thinking about cultural evolution becomes possible.

Unfortunately, those political anthropologists who did attend to individuals seem to largely focus on their power relations. While they did recognize dimensions of the evolutionary process like "differentiation" and increased "complexity" in relation to power acquisition, they did not account for such dimensions of development as: increased self-awareness, autonomy, objectivity, telos, or decreased narcissism. These distinctly individual, and perhaps psychological, dimensions of development were not accounted for in most of the theories of development articulated in the social sciences outside of psychology.[1]

Even when individual development is considered in political anthropology, by Abner Cohen, issues of adolescent development are integrated into a view of the social order as rites of passage are recognized as opportunities for the social system to integrate the personality of new members into existing social lineages that "reaffirms its unity" (Lewellen 1983: 111). While Cohen does acknowledge individual development, he does not attempt to identify the individual's impact on society; the individual's ability to participate in or even to activate cultural evolution is not considered. This is quite different from the understanding developed by psychologist Erikson, who thoroughly addresses this impact.

Notice how these social theories work from a limited understanding of the individual. Unlike the psychological theories, these thinkers primarily focused on the social side of the equation. Again, the disparity between these psychological and social uses of the idea of development reflects a modern condition in which the culture has expanded so rapidly while the individual has ruptured from living in a community to living in a society, leaving even social scientists with little understanding of the connection or sense of personal agency in the face of these impersonal forces. As a result, theories have either had to leave out any clear image of the individual interacting with society, instead focusing strictly on the social or political dynamics of human systems, or they have had to retreat from the social world and imagine only the psychological and immediate influences of developmental process on the private lives of individuals.

The inability to maintain an understanding of the connection between the social and the individual reflects the way in which the modern world has overwhelmed the imagination of our best minds. However, we are beginning to recover from this beleaguered condition. We are beginning to bring these two disparate spheres of our fuller human experience back together.

Ken Wilber's four-quadrant approach to human development

Wilber is one social theorist who has steeped himself in both psychological and social theories of development. As a result of his research, Wilber began to notice that theories of development not only divide along the axis of the psychological and the social, but also along a second axis which I will describe shortly. Based on his observations, Wilber began organizing different theories based upon what aspect of development and evolution they were focusing on. What he came up with is a four-quadrant matrix that helps us to understand more completely the full complexity of the development and

Table 5.1 The four quadrants of human experience

	Interior	Exterior
Individual	**Upper-left – "I"** Interior–Individual Intentional Emotion, morals, personal identity, and religiosity Discerned through introspection and shared experience Freud, Jung	**Upper-right – "It"** Exterior–Individual Behavioral, physical, affect Discerned through observation Skinner
Collective	**Lower-left – "We"** Interior–Collective Cultural Values, attitudes, cultural norms, worldview, communication Discerned through interpretation, meaning Dilthey, Wundt	**Lower-right – "Its"** Exterior–Collective Social Social structural; geopolitical; economic infrastructures; business; electoral politics Discerned through observation Marx, systems theory

Source: Adapted from Ken Wilber's *A Theory of Everything* (2001: 51).

evolution process as it has been described over the course of human history. This matrix also helps us to see just how complicated development and evolution are and, perhaps, why it has been so hard for the human species to get its mind around it, much less to interact consciously with it.

In Wilber's four-quadrant model he identifies theorists and their theories on the basis of which quadrant they focus on (Wilber 2000: 64). These quadrants are divided along two axes, the first is the individual/sociocultural axis and the second is the internal/external axis. I will take each of these up in turn. Table 5.1 presents Wilber's four-quadrant view of human experience.

The individual/sociocultural axis

The top/bottom axis identifies a range of experience from the individual to the sociocultural. This axis accounts for the difference between the theories of individual development and social development or cultural evolution that I have already presented. The theories of individual development listed above belong to the top quadrants. The list of theories of social and cultural development belongs to the bottom quadrants. Following the train of thought of this book, my thesis regarding the split between political and individual orientations toward the future, between social progress and individual growth, is diagrammatically represented in Wilber's four-quadrant model by the vertical axis.

The internal/external axis

The left/right axis identifies the way that theorists vary in their approach to the subject matter of development and evolution. In relation to the individual, the right-hand quadrant represents those theorists who approach development "behaviorally," focusing their attention on observations of actions in an environment. They focus on what can be seen through looking from the outside, that is, their approach is *external*. This empirical approach was developed in psychology within the discipline of behaviorism as initiated by John Watson, B. F. Skinner, and others. This is in contrast to theorists who approached individual development through an exploration of unconscious motivation. Here, the primary means of inquiry is not observation, per se, but rather "interpretation," that is, through consideration of the meaning of human experience. This interpretive approach is typified by Sigmund Freud and the psychoanalytic methods (Wilber 1995: 126–7).

In sum, while psychoanalysis and behaviorism have been historically at odds with one another, we can view their difference in terms of the former focusing on the *interior* of the individual (i.e., unconscious motivation), while the latter focuses on the *exterior* of the individual human (i.e., human behavior). Wilber notes that understanding individual development requires both; one cannot be reduced to the other.

We can use Wilber's understanding of these different approaches toward individual development to attend to an analogous difference between culture and society, which Wilber identifies in terms of the difference between the bottom right and left quadrants. Like the upper-right, the *lower-right quadrant* focuses on what can be known through external observation, that is, through empirical observation. While the upper-right focuses on individual behavior, the lower-right focuses on the behavior of social systems. The social system includes observable phenomena such as voting and consumption patterns, scores on tests, employment statistics, etc. All of these can be observed without having to ask what they mean. The lower-right focuses on what things do, not what they mean (Wilber 1995: 127).

In comparison, the *lower-left quadrant* is the location of any theory that turns attention toward what collective phenomena *means*; accordingly, they focus on culture, not society. These theories explore through interpretation and attend to the "shared values," "common world-views," "symbolism, language, and discourse" of cultures (Wilber 1995: 124).

In order to distinguish these distinct approaches to collective phenomena, Wilber uses the analogy of being in a foreign country but not knowing the language to represent what lower-right (social) inquiry can do. While in a foreign country we can observe interactions between people, architecture, food, or anything else with some surface area. However, we cannot determine the meaning of such experiences through observation alone; instead we must ask questions and interpret the answers we get. Such questioning seeks the meaning of what we see and moves us into the lower-left quadrant.

Wilber uses this four-quadrant scheme as a tool of analysis, which he employs to show which quadrant(s) a given theorist's work falls into, that is, through which quadrant(s) a theorist views the world and through which quadrants a theorist looks for solutions to human problems. When viewed as a whole, these four quadrants bring together previous theories by accounting for a full range of human experience, that is, internal/external and individual/collective.

Wilber's four-quadrant model helps us understand the natural inclination of developmental thinking to fragment along longstanding experiential divides within human experience. Through his recognition of these divides we are able to begin imagining a fuller image of human experience and human development. The emergence of this image requires recognizing the extent to which inquiry into the lower-left quadrant, into culture, has been largely missing from the social sciences.

The absence of inquiry into cultural evolution

In addition to Wilber's synthetic approach to human development is the work of Robert Kegan who has synthesized the upper-left and upper-right quadrants within a single theory of individual development. In his book *The Evolving Self*, Kegan traces the history of the internal *motive* and the external *behavioral* approach to individual development, offering an effective conjoined language between the two that focuses on "meaning-making" (Kegan 1982: 1–12). Unfortunately, there is no such broadly understood synthesis in the social sciences approach to collective phenomena. In fact, according to Wilber, the social sciences have neglected the lower-left quadrant with most social theorists focusing on the "social" lower-right quadrant (Wilber 1995: 129–33).

As a result, consideration of processes of cultural evolution has been reduced to ideas articulated within the languages of the lower-right quadrant, which leaves collective phenomena to be studied primarily in terms of their external, structural, and behavioral dimensions. Without a social science language that binds the two lower quadrants, or at least releases the lower-left from bondage to the methodologies of the lower-right, it is difficult to imagine a connection between the individual and culture spheres. When culture is reduced to society no connection can be made between the internal human and the external. If any contact is made it is only in the realm of the external, such as in cultural anthropology where individual experience is often understood in terms of social roles and the use of force. In order to speak in a full way about being human, we need a cultural language that connects the internal-individual with the internal-cultural. Wilber explains that the focus of social science inquiry on the external conditions of society reflects the methodological bias of the scientific paradigm of positivism, originating in the mid-nineteenth century, which overvalues models of inquiry that focus on the external behavior of societies, while neglecting cultural phenomena such as "cultural norms," "values," and "attitudes," which are "internal" cultural phenomena (Wilber 1995: 123–4).

The positivist paradigm attempts to approach the subject matter of inquiry from a value-neutral perspective in order to maintain scientific objectivity. Unfortunately, this reduces explanations of cultural evolution to the external language of the lower-right quadrant that can only articulate vague ideas like "social progress." As a result it leaves hanging those questions about the relationship between cultural evolution and individual development.

As a result of both the neglect of culture and the institutional divisions between the sociopolitical, on the one side, and the psychological, on the other, it has been next to impossible to build an understanding of human development that encompasses both individual development and cultural evolution. As a result, the potency of the very idea of development is divided into two cultural languages, two different liberalisms: the externally focused language of social progress that is measured by the problematic methodologies of positivism and the internally focused language of individual development. As we are seeing, both languages avoid culture. No wonder we are not able to speak about cultural evolution. In Table 5.2 Wilber's four-quadrant model is adapted in order to show the under-differentiated condition of the lower-left quadrant.

In Table 5.2 I have identified the focus, state, limitation, and language of each quadrant in its relationship to having articulated and been directed by a clear understanding of human development. In the case of the cultural sphere, I reflect on its potential rather than its limitation. This reflects that sphere's current "dormant" state: that is, we currently do not have a social science language that articulates the development and evolution activities in which we would need to engage within the cultural sphere in order for the social sciences to be actively pursuing processes of human development.

In order to activate the cultural sphere, we can draw on Wilber's four-quadrant model of development and evolution to support the articulation of a new language that combines the upper quadrants' language of a private-psychological liberalism with the lower-right's language of political liberalism to create a language of a public-psychological liberalism. Following Samuels' interest, this synthesis will create a new hybrid language between the internal and the external and between the psychological and the political, which will give us a language that focuses simultaneously on the future created by both.

Table 5.2 The four quadrants of human experience, showing the under-differentiated condition of the lower-left quadrant

	Interior	*Exterior*
	Upper-left and upper-right	
	Successfully being activated by combination of *internal and external* approaches to individual development: psychotherapy, educational models of child, adolescent, and adult development. Ken Wilber and Robert Kegan providing successful new language of individual development.	
Individual	• **Focus:** individual development • **State:** active • **Limitation:** dominated by focus on individual's private-life growth and suffering • **Language:** *private-psychological liberalism* as expressed through developmental and clinical psychologies.	
	Lower-left: interior	**Lower-right: exterior**
	Not yet activated except in the nascent work of: Samuels, Omer, Wilber, Gebser	Successfully activated by numerous theories of social and political development.
Collective	• **Focus:** synthesis of ideas of "development" and "progress" • **State:** dormant • **Potential:** psychology of culture focused on psychological, political, and moral identity • **Language:** *public-psychological liberalism*, which synthesizes political and psychological liberalism through the language of "political development."	• **Focus:** social progress • **State:** active • **Limitation:** dominated by focus on social issues expressed in rational, value-neutral language • **Language:** *political liberalism.*

Source: Adapted from Ken Wilber's *A Theory of Everything* (2001: 51).

Wilber's research helps us to start to consider the relationship between processes of individual development and processes of cultural evolution. Further, his synthetic model of development supports a range of questions that helps us to begin to be curious about the possibility that we, as individuals, could have an impact on cultural evolution.

In the remainder of this chapter I will introduce Clare Graves' model of human development, emphasizing its use as a model of cultural evolution. Graves' model provides us with a language that accounts for the artificial separation between the individual and society as a distinct stage of human development and evolution. This model is particularly important as it will help us contextualize the dilemma of the separation of the two liberalisms.

A model of cultural evolution

Graves' model of cultural evolution may be the most important developmental theory of our time. For example, when compared with Robert Kegan's theories of adult development, Graves' model may lack significant specificity. Kegan's synthesis of the two major strands of theories of individual development, psychoanalytic and constructivist, is unsurpassed. However, Kegan's model has so far been difficult to translate into actionable thinking in social and political spheres; it seems somewhat locked into its individualized frame.

Comparatively, Graves' model is immediately applicable to the individual and to culture. However he accomplished it, Graves has stepped outside of the modern reification of the individual and overcome its extreme differentiation by reintegrating it into a larger process of cultural evolution. Central to Graves' model is the understanding that individual development recapitulates the course of cultural evolution. As I described in Chapter 4, this idea was pursued by many first generation psychologists like Wundt, Freud, Dewey, and Jung. However, despite the continued interest of Erikson, second generation psychologists became absorbed in their clinical work with individuals and could not sustain their generation's attention on this connection.

Fortunately, interest in the parallel between processes of development and evolution is on the rise.[2] When viewed historically, this theory goes back to Locke's time and was used by one of his primary rivals, Jean Rousseau, who also believed that individual development and human evolution are analogous.

Graves' theory received significant attention when it was first published in 1966 and was used in the reconciliation work in South Africa. Graves' model applies equally to the history of the species, the current state of a culture, a group, or an organization, to stages of child and adult development, as well as to the present moment of any given situation. In Table 5.3 I introduce my own stage model of political development and compare it to Graves' stages of development/evolution and several theories of individual development.

While paralleling theories of individual development, Graves goes beyond Loevinger, Kohlberg, Erikson, and Kegan's models and works the cultural implications of theories of development. He applies the idea of development to culture, including tying it to specific historical developments. However, prior to applying it to the analysis of modern culture, which I take up in Part IV, it is important to note two powerful dimensions of Graves' model that

will help us as we attempt to use it to identify the current developmental/
evolutionary tasks of the individual, groups, and the species.

The reciprocity between "us" and "me"

First, according to Graves, each subsequent stage of development/evolution
emphasizes either the importance of the individual or the communal whole.
Accordingly, in the original undifferentiated tribal stage animistic thinking
is surpassed as an individual's differentiating energy emerges through the
rise of egotistical energy manifest in the child's appearing egocentricism or
the culture's rising feudal society (Wilber 2001: 9). In turn this individual
energy can be reintegrated into a new more developed social order, as
exemplified by the rise of new nation states.

This pattern of individual differentiation followed by collective reintegration is one of the key contributions of Graves' model that will support
the understanding of our current developmental/evolutionary tasks. For
example, in Table 5.3, the stage represented by the "mythic order" is a
communal stage which is considered premodern. With the rise of modern
culture we see a differentiation of the function of the individual, as represented by Locke's "political individual." I have adapted Graves' model in
Figure 5.1 to reflect this "spiral" dimension of Graves' theory.

Graves' identification of this spiral dynamic in the developmental/
evolutionary process supports a range of theoretical interpretations that
offer significant hope for our current generation. For example, when viewed
from Graves' model, Freud's pessimistic assertion that the relationship
between the individual and culture is intrinsically conflictual may reflect his
failure to see outside of the "orange" meme of his time with its problematic
assertion of independence.

While others have identified this limitation of Freud's and presented
alternative views, Graves' perspective offers even more freedom as it also
draws on the scientific developments of the last 50 years and shows us a
developmental trajectory which we can apply to the modern task of
liberalism, inviting an integration of the external focus of political
liberalism and the internal focus on psychological liberalism.

Figure 5.1 reflects Graves' spiral motion moving from the collective to
the individual and back to the collective. Additionally, Figure 5.1 notes the
historical group for each stage up to those stages that have yet to gather
enough community to be described as a historical group, which are then
described in terms of an "emergent group." This figure also notes both the
identity and identity attitude of each stage of cultural evolution.

The unique acceptance of development: the second tier's task

According to Graves, the first six stages of development are referred to as
the "first tier" of development/evolution. People whose consciousness is

Table 5.3 Synthesis of models of individual development and cultural evolution

Dunlap's political development		Graves' cultural development	Kegan's epistemological development	Kohlberg's moral development	Fowler's religious development	Erikson's psychosocial development
Institutional form	Individual identity					
Universal liberalism	Religious citizen	Global perspective: sustainability			Despair to post-moral brotherhood	
Psychological liberalism	Psychological citizen (public)	Functional hierarchy: equality and natural degrees of ranking and excellence	5th Order	Morality of principles	Universalizing faith	Generativity vs. self-absorption
Psychological liberalism	Psychological person (private)	Sensitive self: pluralistic, anti-hierarchy, ecological sensitivity	4.5 Order	Moral relativity	Paradoxical-consolidative faith	Intimacy vs. isolation
Political liberalism	Political individual (egalitarian)	Sensitive self: pluralistic, anti-hierarchy, ecological sensitivity	4.5 Order	Moral relativity	Paradoxical-consolidative faith	Identity vs. role difference
Political liberalism	Political individual (libertarian)	Scientific achievement: rises from herd individualism, achievement	4th Order	Democratic contract	Individuative-reflective faith	Industry vs. inferiority

Initiative vs. guilt	Synthetic-conventional faith	Law and order Good/bad boy	3rd Order	Mythic order: rigid paternalistic social hierarchies, righteous order	Social roles	Religious liberalism
Autonomy vs. shame and doubt	Mythic-literal faith	Instrumental hedonism Punishment and obedience	2nd Order	Individual identity: powerful, egotistical, impulsive	Individual identity	Tribal liberalism
	Undifferentiated faith		1st Order	Magical-animistic: good/bad thinking	Group identity	Tribal liberalism
Trust vs. mistrust				Archaic instinctual: survival needs	Mammalian	Social hierarchy

Source: Adapted from http://www.clarewgraves.com/theory_content/compared/CGcomp1.htm, and as described by Lawrence Kohlberg in *The Philosophy of Moral Development* (1981: 344–7).

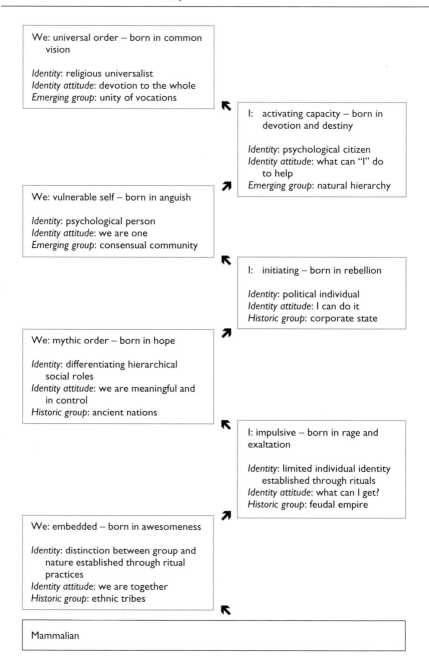

Figure 5.1 The rhythm of individual development and cultural evolution

Sources: Adapted from Don Beck and Christopher Cowan's *Spiral Dynamics* (2006), Ken Wilber's *A Theory of Everything* (2001), and with the invaluable help of Ken White.

developed to any of these first stages have difficulty in communicating with others at any of the other stages. The difficulty communicating across these developmental levels reflects many of the cultural crises of our time. An example will help express this difficulty. The current cultural war between religious fundamentalists who seek to undermine the teaching of evolutionary theory and the secular educational and legal system reflects the difficulty integrating the languages of what Beck and Cowan refer to as Graves' "blue" and "orange" memes. While creationism seems intellectually bankrupt to many secularists, the orange meme's adherence to ideas of natural selection, with its implied attribution of *accidentalness* to human *life*, seems morally bankrupt to the blue meme's values. As a result the blue meme continually attempts to adapt quasi-scientific thinking, such as "creative design," to challenge the orange meme's failure to account for the purposiveness of development/evolution.

While the secular courts are able to continually see through the blue meme's shallow attempts to bring purpose, and thus moral values, back into the educational system and thwart those efforts, the limits of secular humanism, neither the political liberalism of the orange meme nor the psychological liberalism of the green meme are known to fundamentalists. They grasp the modern failure to provide individuals with a cultural language that offers a sufficient account of purpose. As I discussed in Chapter 4, this once again reflects the moral neutrality of a political and a private-psychological liberalism that does not want to weigh in on questions of human purpose.

Because of the inability of these liberalisms to sufficiently account for human purpose, the culture is continually vulnerable to the regressive side of religions that correctly assert the need for there to be a collective sense of purpose. While the rise of a private-psychological liberalism has brought back into the culture some unifying images of common purpose, like the 1970s image of Earth as a single planet that we must share, this liberalism confuses equality with sameness and has asserted a model of political equality that does not sufficiently account for the actual developmental differences that currently exist within the species.

As a result of the current limits of liberalism to account for developmental differences, the lack of coordination between political and psychological liberalism, the regressive forces of religion, and the underlying impulsive violence of people continue to rise up and put the future at risk. This dilemma reflects that of the first tier where the real developmental differences of this tier are not treated as objects of reflective attention in either political or psychological institutions. Instead, the political institutions continue to maintain their focus on social progress, the lower-right quadrant, and the psychological institutions continue to focus on individual development, the upper-left quadrant. Accordingly, the task becomes focusing a generation's attention on creating public institutions that operate at the second tier of development, the yellow and turquoise meme, or what I will call a public-psychological liberalism, which is unique in its integration of the concepts of social progress and individual development and in its pursuit of learning practices that activate each. Here, awakening our faith in the future depends on this integration.

Chapter 6

From image to institution

Consciously activating development: methods and practices

Turning passively acquired attitudes into actively sought capacities

Through inquiry we have learned that individual identities are governed by processes of *development*. The idea that people can form personal identities, that they are *psychological* beings, and that their individual *psychological consciousness* develops, is the foundation of modern culture and has become the subject matter of the science of developmental psychology. As a result of advances in this field, people are learning to focus attention on their children's, other people's, and their own development. This focus on development has activated a nascent capacity for us to take conscious control over the processes of development.

The idea that we can, to some extent, control the process of development reflects a process of turning what is passively experienced into something that can be actively pursued. This process has been examined by developmental theorists such as Sigmund Freud who refers to the child's process of turning what was passively experienced into an activity-sought experience. Reflecting on Freud's idea, Erikson notes how this is happening at a cultural level as well (Erikson 1968: 28). Erikson identifies "psycho-historical" forces that are supporting the human species to gain control over developmental processes (Erikson 1968: 27; 1974: 12–30). How should we go about this process? What is the role of organized inquiry, that is, *science*, in this process?

The role of the individual in activating cultural evolution

By adapting the intent of learning how to consciously activate individual development and cultural evolution and by using a clear scientific method, we are learning how to participate in a historical process that is taking place on a large scale through which the species is differentiating the capacities needed to respond to the crises of our time.

Central to the process of the conscious activation of human development is the recognition of the increased value of the individual in Western culture. As a result of the growing awareness of the creative, religious, and political value of the person, the human species has leapt forward in hopeful, halting, and frightening ways. This process has brought some level of freedom to many people. However, it has also brought new forms of subjugation and domination. Potentially, all individuals are capable of participating in a process of conscious development; but historically too often it has been limited to exceptional individuals. These individuals are not only the chief beneficiaries of this process, but they have been the ones that bring into the lives of the rest of us the broader cultural benefits as well.

Central to the process through which cultures evolve is the *activating* role played by these exceptional individuals. In the interaction between these individuals and their culture a reciprocally activating process takes place, that is, culture activates the personal development of these leaders as they activate the potential cultural evolution of their time. In order to activate and use the influence that personal identities can have on the cultural evolution of their time, we can pursue the question: how does the historical formation of personal identities influence cultural evolution? Once a rudimentary understanding of this process is established, we will be in a better position to study the specifics of the cultural evolution of the last few hundred years and use that understanding to identify currently emergent capacities for both the individual and the culture. Once identified, the activation of these capacities becomes a subject of reflection for the social sciences as they have the opportunity to approach human development from a broader perspective, thus making active what has been passive.

From image to institution

Using the emerging hybrid language between politics and psychology, we can begin to see how the progressive political leaders from my research have had a direct experience of having an insight or revelatory *image* that has activated their capacity for destiny and thus brought about some joining of their personal and political identities. Through the activation of this identity they come to influence institutions, which enables them to change political culture.

Through this process of moving from revelatory image to changing institutions, these leaders exemplify the connection between processes of individual development and cultural evolution. However, we do not yet have the language to fully understand how this process takes place. As we develop this language we will be in a better position to connect these processes.

Between the individual and culture lies a creative potential that comes to life as the individual activates a distinct identity. This begins as a person's experience of the imagination – as an *image, intuition, insight, vision,* or *revelation* – is activated and leads to a change in their identity. Through the imagination the individual forms a new identity, which, in turn, influences the cultural evolution of their time.

According to Carl Jung, the unconscious is the source of both ordinary and transformative intuitions. Once or twice a passing vague thought about a friend has come to mind only to have that friend call in the next few minutes. Frequently I think about the ice cream in my freezer, only to find myself getting up and serving myself some. Sometimes we imagine the need for a new community park. We share that image with others, use it to motivate ourselves and our neighbors to labor and politic, and we bring the park into existence. In these contexts, we imagine the future, it appears as an image. This image implies a possible future; it is an image of destiny. Such images can be ordinary but delicious – ice cream – or exceptional – creating a park. Such images can be personal and/or they can be shared. An image might reflect a person's private-life impulses, suffering, or life trajectory, or it may represent the confluence of larger social events. Jung spoke of this latter circumstance when he wrote:

> We are living in what the Greeks called the **kairos** – the right moment – for a "metamorphosis of the gods," of the fundamental principles and symbols [we live by]. The peculiarity of our time, which is certainly not of our choosing, is the expression of the unconscious man within us who is changing.
>
> (Jung 1957b: 304)

The "right moment" is bigger than an individual, it is a time for the emergence of something larger but still human. If, in fact, we are living in the right moment of some nascent human wisdom then the guiding image might first come to an individual. Or, many people may get it simultaneously, in separate parts of the world, expressed through their own subjectivity seeking objectivity. In this case an image is emergent, which means it appears from somewhere (Jung's "unconscious" with a "Janus-face," one side looking back into history, the other toward the future) and suddenly or slowly gains access to our awareness and hopefully our actions – it brings the future (Jung 1939: 279).

Such numinous images challenge the image-bearer to intensify their personal relationship to the truth of the image, such as Harry's image of becoming a leader, which requires that they use their own experience to bring forth greater objectivity by binding personal and cultural realities. Let us take a look at this a little slower. Remember the terrific Rilke poem. Did I mention that I repeat it over and over?

You must give birth to your images
They are the future waiting to be born.
Fear not the strangeness you feel
The future must enter into you long before it happens
Just wait for the birth, for the hour of new clarity.

(Rilke 2007)

In this poem, the idea of "image" is associated with an experience of foreknowledge or foresight, but not in the traditional sense of an actual vision of the future, that is, an actual image based in seeing; rather, in this poem the image of the future is based in feeling, as in a strange feeling that enters into us and that we are responsible for birthing. Notice the more active opportunity and responsibility this bodily description gives us for the future. This represents a transition from passive vision to active feeling as the motivating link to the future. This experience of birthing the future also carries with it the sense of birthing new human futures, as expressed by Stephen Daedalus, the main character in James Joyce's *Portrait of the Artist as a Young Man*. Joyce ends the book with Daedalus proclaiming: "Within the smithy of my soul I create the uncreated future of my race" (Joyce 1916: 237). Joyce's beautiful phrasing describes with a poetic sense the accomplishment not only of the artist but also of so-called religio-political visionaries such as Martin Luther and Mahatma Gandhi. They used their personal experience to bring new objectivity into the world. Carl Jung offers a parallel description of this same identity formation process and how it leads to a "communicable language" in the quote I cite in Chapter 3 (p. 43). In his statement the individual becomes aware of the changes going on in the collective human experience and translates these changes into a communicable language (Jung 1919: 314–15).

Erikson's thinking about this creative relationship between the individual and the culture parallels Jung's thinking. Working his own sensitivities and talents, Erikson adds more depth about how this process impacts cultural leaders. Erikson describes how such leaders go through a process of "identity" formation in which they submit their personal identities to the collective forces of their time and, as a result, have some new piece of knowledge and leadership to bring to the world (Erikson 1958: 15). Through this process of identity formation the person activates what Erikson refers to as an "anticipated future" (Erikson 1968: 87).

Importantly, Erikson draws attention to the deeply conflictual nature of this process. Drawing on the wisdom of Freud, Erikson notes the intensity of suffering inherent in the relationship between the individual and the culture. However, unlike Freud who thought that the relationship between the individual and the culture was irredeemably conflictual, Erikson sees the way in which a person can establish an individual identity that remakes themselves and their culture; he finds hope in the relationship between the person and culture:

> Some young individuals will succumb to this crisis in all manner of neurotic, psychotic, or delinquent behavior; others will resolve it through participation in ideological movements passionately concerned with religion or politics, nature or art. Still others, although suffering and deviating dangerously through what appears to be a prolonged adolescence, eventually come to contribute an original bit to an emerging style of life: the very danger which they have sensed has forced them to mobilize capacities to see and say, to dream and plan, to design and construct, in new ways.
>
> (Erikson 1958: 14–15)

Implied by this citation is an additional idea that Jung is less explicit about but would wholly support. Erikson extends Jung's understanding of the way new ideas come into the culture to include the positive impact these ideas have on the carrier. Erikson notes how events "mobilize capacities," creating new personalities (Erikson 1958: 15). Here, we see a variety of shapes the person can take in response to the convergence of the process of identity formation and the wider fate of their social milieu. Erikson writes: "In the period between puberty and adulthood, the resources of tradition fuse with new inner resources to create something potentially new: a new person; and with this new person a new generation, and with that, a new era" (Erikson 1958: 20).

The possibility that a person can enter into a process of self-creation and use that process to bring into the world something new, mobilizing new capacities, may offer more than just the resolution of a conflict; it may identify the essentially developmental nature of conflict, or at least the developmental potential of conflict. For example, Jung describes conflict as potentially redemptive for both the person and the culture. Jung offers more specific thoughts about what it is that is experienced as redemptive when he writes:

> When a problem which is at bottom personal, and therefore apparently subjective, coincides with external events that contain the same psychological elements as the personal conflict, it is suddenly transformed into a general question embracing the whole of society. In this way a personal problem acquires a dignity it lacked hitherto, since the inner discord always has something humiliating and degrading about it.
>
> (Jung 1971: 80)

Paralleling Jung, Erikson also notes the redemptive nature of this process of identity formation when he discusses the life of Martin Luther. He speaks of the way Luther suffered from psychological symptoms that did not dissipate prior to his finding a solution that was personal and social. In a sense, Erikson notes how Luther found his personal cure by discovering a social cause: "Luther . . . at one time was a rather endangered young man, beset with a syndrome of conflicts . . . his solution roughly bridged a political and psychological vacuum which history had created in a significant portion of Western Christendom" (Erikson 1958: 15).

If we follow Jung, Erikson, and Joyce, we can begin to explore the images that are evoked in relation to this essentially creative and redemptive relationship between the person and the culture. In the poem I cited above, Rilke identified the body as the source of the future; while immediate and personal, Rilke also sees how the personal transforms the culture. Reflecting on the life of Michelangelo, Rilke formed the following poem:

Das waren Tage Michelangelo's

Once I read in foreign books
of the time of Michelangelo.
That was a man beyond measure – a giant –
who forgot what the immeasurable was.

He was the kind of man who turns
to bring forth the meaning of an age that wants to end.
He lifts its whole weight
and heaves it into the chasm of his heart.

The anguish and yearning of all those before him
become in his hands raw matter
for him to compress into one great work.

Only God escapes his will – a God
he loves with a high hatred
for being so out of reach.

(Barrows and Macy 1996: 71)

In his compelling phrasing Rilke identifies parts of the creative human process. These parts include: a relationship between creation (God), a creative spirit (Michelangelo), a limiting world in which creation is taking place (human history), a necessary failure to recognize this world's limits (forgetting that life cannot be measured), an emotional response to limits (hatred), and transcendence (the compression of suffering into "one great work").

Whether aesthetic (Michelangelo) or religio-political (Luther), or simply socio-political, there clearly is a distinct process through which the individual influences their culture's evolution. In this process the individuals themselves are also clearly transformed, mobilizing what Erikson refers to as "new capacities." However, could this process itself become an object of awareness? If we could reflect on this process and gain some degree of conscious control over it, what would be the result? Or is this process already becoming more conscious? And, if so, what evidence would we find in our cultural history?

The historical emergence of the subject and its role in founding an objective psychology

So far this discussion does not make any historical distinctions and might easily be imagined as applying to all of human history. There are numerous thinkers who have worked with similar ideas in an effort to identify how the process of birthing new ideas and identities originated for the human species. For example, F.M. Cornford pulls together much of the best thinking of his time about this transformative process in *From Religion to Philosophy* (1912). In this book Cornford draws on the anthropology of his day to imagine how individual identities were first differentiated in human history, and how these identities became a culture-shaping force. I will return to his work in Chapter 9.

Another good source is Julian Jaynes' book *The History of Consciousness in the Breakdown of the Bicameral Mind* (1976). Whether the reader accepts Jaynes' thesis regarding brain functioning, the author sets an interesting context for establishing how culture forms through an analysis of the role of ritual in differentiating individual identity.

Jung and his followers, like Joseph Campbell, also till this soil where ritual meets religion and both function to activate individuating and culture-forming energies in the human species. Jung offers an important insight in this area where individuality and culture meet as he notes that "subjectivity" is not opposed by "objectivity," but rather both work together. That is, the growth of the individual person contributes to the possible objective range of culture. According to Jung, as unique "subjects" (i.e., individuals) come into existence, as they become psychological creatures, that is, as they develop their uniqueness as subjects, they gain objectivity. Here, Jung turns on its head the modern notion that objectivity and subjectivity are opposed to one another. Instead, Jung asserts that they are both opposed to "collectivity." Jung locates this capacity of the subject to know objectivity within their psychology:

> Nowhere is the basic requirement so indispensable as in psychology that the observer should be adequate to his object, in a sense of being able to see not only subjectivity but also objectivity . . . The recognition and taking the heart of the subjective determination of knowledge . . . is

fulfilled only when the observer is sufficiently informed about the nature and scope of his own personality. He can, however, be sufficiently informed only when he has in large measure freed himself from the leveling influence of collective opinions and thereby arrived at a clear conception of his own individuality.

(Jung 1971: 9–10)

In this citation Jung extends our growing understanding of what it means to be psychological. This is paralleled by liberal philosopher John Dewey who, in *Experience and Nature* (1925), claims that the emergence of individual "subjective" experience marks a great gain for the species (Dewey 1925: 13).

Once there is a basic understanding of the process through which individuals come into existence, and once the culturally creative dimension of this is at least traced, as I have attempted to do here, it is possible to begin making subtler distinctions that might shed light on the current state of human history, including opportunities for shaping our culture that are unique to this time in history.

As I mentioned above, the capacity to become a source of the future for a culture, for one's people, may itself have gone through a metamorphosis over the last one or more hundred years giving us the opportunity to engage more actively in the creation of culture. One of the clearest ways that I have found of understanding this development has been through San Francisco Jungian Joseph Henderson's idea that a "psychological attitude" has recently emerged in human history that is significantly changing our capacity to objectively reflect on our experience of being human as it focuses our awareness on the psychological and developmental nature of human experience. The developmental process through which individual development influences cultural evolution is itself passing from being passively experienced to being consciously activated.

The emergence of the psychological attitude and the creation of personal identity

In *Cultural Attitudes in Psychological Perspective* (1984) Joseph Henderson describes four primary "cultural attitudes" and the role they play in the life of the individual and evolution of the culture. These attitudes include: social, aesthetic, religious, and philosophical. In this section I focus primarily on the role that religious and philosophical attitudes play in the formation of a fifth cultural attitude: the relatively recently developed "psychological attitude." However, it is worth following Henderson's analysis of both the social and aesthetic attitudes to show his depth of understanding of the historical formation of cultural attitudes.

According to Henderson, the *social attitude* "is concerned with maintaining the ethical code of the culture" and while resistant to change due to its embeddedness it is also a necessary part of our disposition, especially of the original "unconscious identification" it reflects upon and replaces (Henderson 1984: 17–18).

The *aesthetic attitude* focuses on "the unity of beauty and truth" (Henderson 1984: 45). He notes how this attitude is often reduced to "art for art's sake" as the social attitude of "utilitarianism" deprecates aesthetic experience, causing a retreat from mainstream culture by those governed by aesthetics. Henderson identifies this retreat in the attitudes of the Romantic and Victorian movement in the nineteenth century as the dominant philosophy of the day, utilitarianism, restricted awareness of the role of beauty in modern culture, reducing truth to whatever it takes to get things done. This oppression of aesthetics extends into the twentieth century and the aesthetic attitude became the refuge of many people, including social scientists who were unable to find purchase to influence the juggernaut of modern culture with its materialist values. For example, even the faculty of the Frankfurt School for Social Research that conceived of their research as a form of socially engaged action as "praxis" retreated into an aesthetic attitude when faced with the horrors of Nazi Germany (Jay 1973: 4; Marcus and Tarr 1984: 403).

Both in the context of the person and the institution, the aesthetic attitude can challenge overly concretized forms of the social attitude. As Henderson notes, this challenge takes place through the artist's willingness to encounter the unconscious and to bear new images to consciousness, thus closely following my earlier discussion of the function of image. However, the risk of the aesthetic attitude is that its host is not changed by the experience of the unconscious, per se, but settles for less in an effort to "organize it [the new image] so . . . to aestheticize it" (Henderson 1984: 51). This passivity of the aesthetic attitude can be juxtaposed to both the religious and psychological attitude.

According to Henderson, the *religious attitude* is the means through which a person can bring into their lives some substantial renewal that may also offer regeneration to their culture. According to Henderson, there are developmental levels of the religious attitude that need to be considered if its transformative dimension is to be activated. For example, Henderson distinguishes between the fully developed religious attitude and religious feeling. He notes how Freud was right to be suspicious of "infantile religious feeling" (Henderson 1984: 27). Drawing on Tillich, Henderson notes how religious feeling is not enough to activate a mature religious attitude. The religious feeling brings with it an unreflective "ecstasy," paralleling the original participation mystique of indigenous religions; but this does not become useful to a mature person or more evolved culture without reflection (Cornford 1912: 112; Henderson 1984: 28).

When combined with the "rational discourse" contributed by the *philo-sophical attitude*, the religious experience extends into a social realm that allows the individual to interact with the social realities of their time, the "kairos" which Tillich defines as "the time when a theologian [cultural leader] must speak to his own age" (Henderson 1984: 28). Distinguishing the religious attitude from the social attitude, Henderson argues that a mature religious attitude requires a time in which an individual must establish a personal relationship to their god: "a young person . . . is encouraged to experience the god by himself alone" (Henderson 1984: 28). Notice the parallel between Henderson's description and the purpose of the Reformation; the latter established the value of this personal connection to divinity.

While the lived experience of a religious symbol may evoke collective action in ecstasy – or persecuting zeal – there is a need to make that symbol personal, which is to say manifest in a person, lived by an individual. Thus, Luther, Gandhi, Rilke, Joyce, and Michelangelo all bore some of what Rilke describes as the "strangeness," that is, the embodied – but yet-birthed – future that enabled them to become the carriers of the kairos, the makers of the future of their time.

It is through making such symbols personal that people are able to become the carriers of the kairos, the makers of the future of their time. According to Henderson, the process through which religious symbols come to inform culture has gone through a transformation that has resulted in greater reflection on the personal dimension of the symbol, that is, the symbols themselves begin to have a more personal impact on the exceptional individuals who experience them. Accordingly, the symbol not only represents a birth of new meaning for the culture but, coming out of an "intensely personal experience," also provides new knowledge for the person. This brings a uniquely "psychological" dimension to the discovery process between consciousness and the unconscious, which Henderson refers to as a "scientific" or "psychological attitude" (Henderson 1984: 77).

Because of its newness, Henderson doubts that the psychological attitude can be given the same "epistemological authenticity" as the social, religious, aesthetic, or philosophical attitudes (Henderson 1984: 77). Yet, despite its newness, Henderson thinks that the psychological attitude is capable of helping people break free of unconscious identifications with other cultural attitudes, supporting greater objectivity. The cultural objectivity available through the realization of the psychological attitude is achieved as the contents of the unconscious, however worked by the other attitudes, are specifically applied to individuals. For example, Henderson distinguishes between a religious image and a psychological one. He notes that "in their religious form these images represent the incandescent experience of spiritual reality . . . or the experience of the immanent god in nature" (Henderson 1984: 83), whereas other images are more "developmentally alive" and, when viewed from the lens of the psychological attitude, they lend themselves to an "evolutionary" rather than a "creational" interpretation (Henderson 1984: 83).

This evolutionary interpretation comes to the person in the form of a powerful personal encounter with the unconscious, through which the unconscious is responding to the newly achieved level of individuation by the individual that previously was achieved by few – few are called – but seems to be becoming available to greater numbers of human beings.

When compared to the philosophical attitude, the psychological attitude provides a greater opportunity for personal transformation, and, as a result, may in turn have a unique impact on cultural transformation. While the philosophical attitude can transform religious feeling into rational discourse relevant to a person's time, it risks narrowing the person's access to the transformative nature of religious feeling, whereas through the psychological attitude a person can attend to the symbols of the unconscious more personally, thus bringing out of those symbols meanings particular to the person and their opportunities for transformation. In all, the psychological attitude creates a new surface area in human culture as it supports the emergence of personal experience that, when woven back into the other cultural attitudes, can unite them in a way that accelerates the process through which image (religious and aesthetic) transforms people (psychological) and transforms culture (social and philosophical).

When Henderson's idea of the newly emerging psychological attitude is tied back in with Jung's notion that personal issues can be redeemed when connected to social issues, and Erikson's assertion that through a process of identity formation individuals come to mobilize "new capacities" that serve their community, we can begin to imagine that at this time in human history the relationship between the individual and culture is becoming increasingly psychological. By implication we might attempt to speak about some not yet clearly understood but understandable process through which human development/evolution is accelerating.

From passive attitude to active capacity

The idea that there is a "psychological attitude" that has recently appeared on the evolutionary scene has significant implications for any effort to understand and activate cultural evolution. This psychological attitude may reflect the way in which individuals are more able to treat themselves as objects of awareness and form a joint personal-collective identity, that is, a "political identity," which could actively pursue both personal development and cultural evolution.

It is something to experience religious feeling; it is quite another to develop a religious attitude by reflecting rationally on the religious feeling, through the philosophical attitude, and have it intensify into a religious revelation about the nature of one's historical era. It is something else again to ground the revelatory experience psychologically, that is, to maintain a truly personal relationship to the religious experience.

The psychological attitude lies at the center of the modern transformation of consciousness and is intensifying and broadening out. As this attitude takes hold of people and culture something new begins to happen. People recognize its value and, rather than wait for revelation, for so few are called, people begin to seek out psychological experience. Such was the experience of the participants in my research: they actively pursued the psychological attitude I introduced in my telling of their stories and in my interventions in the group. Such seeking intensifies the breadth and depth of the psychological attitude. At the root of this intensification is a developmental process that Jean Piaget recognized in children when they are able to draw from previous experience to actively seek new experiences for exploration and growth rather than passively waiting for such experience. Erik Erikson's theory of identity formation also reflects this process of intensifying or consciously seeking out psychological experience.

According to Erikson, identity was once something that overtook you, but now it has something to quest after (Erikson 1968: 20). The experience of identity broadened out in the twentieth century with more people going through periods of identity confusion and reformation. This process reached a point of cultural crisis during which time the natural process of identity formation that adolescents go through became infused with this accelerating need to become psychological. The meeting of these two events created a crisis in culture that led to what we now refer to as the "identity crises" of the 1960s (Erikson 1968: 28). Pierre Teilhard similarly notes the transformative possibilities when human beings realize the extent to which they could consciously participate in their evolutionary process as the movement from "cosmos" to "cosmogenesis" (Teilhard 1963: 251).

Are we moving from a passive psychological consciousness expressed through aesthetic, religious, and political attitudes or forms of liberalism, to the psychological attitude? Will this lead from a private to a public psychological liberalism? If we are, will this shift our relationship with the capacity for destiny from being passively experienced to being actively sought? Or, is the capacity for destiny intensifying, that is, going through a metamorphosis due to the appearance of the psychological attitude?

The impact of the psychological attitude on the capacity for destiny

The confluence between the religious and philosophical attitudes provides individuals with the transformative power of religious feeling linked to a vision of the kairos, the current needs of their time. When activated within a uniquely personal experience, the religious and philosophical attitudes support the emergence of a psychological attitude. Here, Henderson's concept of the psychological attitude implies that the individual who achieves such an attitude has a unique relationship to the future. Henderson notes how the emergence of the psychological attitude establishes a relationship between the individual and the unconscious that activates future possibilities. Accordingly, a psychology that treats this relationship as its subject matter becomes a psychology about the future. Henderson makes this connection when he asserts that Jung's analytical psychology is the first "psychology of the future" (Henderson 1984: 95).

As a psychology, Jung's work implies that knowledge of the future can be realized by the individual or institution through the establishment of a direct relationship to the unconscious that draws on the "telic" nature of the unconscious, that is, its future orientation. Jung notes that the unconscious has a "Janus-face," one side turned back toward the past and the other toward the future. One of my favorite sections of Jung's writing places this idea in a grand context when he writes:

> If it were possible to personify the unconscious, we might think of it as a collective human being combining the characteristics of both sexes, transcending youth and age, birth and death, and, from having at its command a human experience of one or two million years, practically immortal. If such a being existed, it would be exalted above all temporal change; the present would mean neither more nor less to it than any year in the hundredth millennium before Christ; it would be a dreamer of age-old dreams and, owing to its limitless experience, an incomparable prognosticator. It would have lived countless times over again the life of the individual, the family, the tribe, and the nation, and it would possess a living sense of the rhythm of growth, flowering and decay.
>
> (Jung 1931: 349–50)

Jung's larger than life vision can easily be grounded in the immediate experience of cultural leaders who tap into the unconscious through a capacity to "know" the – or to "craft" a – future. In effect, we can say that the realization of the psychological attitude opens the individual to the opportunity to craft themselves in relation to their unique talents, sensitivities, suffering, and the needs of their time. As a result, the psychological attitude activates a new human capacity at this time in human history: a "capacity for destiny" emerges within a new relationship between the person and their culture.

The use of the capacity for destiny enables us to inhabit a "gathering place where we sit face to face around the fiery gifts of the unknown, without the densities of certainty, trusting that the river of imagination will find and carry us" (Omer 2005: 33).

Part III

Opportunities for political development

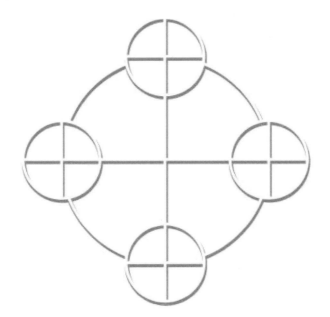

Chapter 7

Political development and emotion

The attitude that we can be active creators of our lives is primarily a product of psychological thinking focused on the individual spheres of human experience. Other social sciences seem to find little opportunity to discuss individual agency, particularly the possibility that we can be creators of culture. Collective theories of development focus on the externalities of the lower-right "social" quadrant and have largely ignored the lower-left "cultural" quadrant. Further, because of their methods of inquiry, the passive observation of visibly apparent behaviors taking place in social systems, there has been little place for individual agency. However, following my research with progressive activists and the fuller story I am telling about how the individual can play an active role in the creation of culture, it is possible and necessary to develop a fuller understanding of the cultural sphere. It is especially important to work out its connection to the individual sphere. Such a fuller theory is not only possible but already exists in nascent form in the multiple images surround the idea of "political development."

The idea of political development

Traditionally, the idea of political development has been articulated from within the field of political science, focusing entirely on the cultural and social spheres. I will review some of the uses of the term from those languages, recognizing that, as a political psychologist, I may be omitting or misrepresenting key aspects of the use of this term in the field of political science. However, I will take this risk for there is a great need to pursue a unified or synthetic theory of human experience and development.

In 1890, John Burgess founded the first department of political science at Columbia University. He associated political development with the "emergence of a nation-state committed to the idea of civil liberty" (Orren and Skowronek 2004: 37). Based upon this premise and after incorporating historical analysis that identified earlier developmental stages leading to the American Constitutions, Burgess determined that political development is

protection of the autonomy of individuals through
enshrined in fundamental laws" (Orren and Skowronek
...ce the extent to which political development is not associated
with the individual sphere, but is a social phenomenon.

Many of the uses of the idea of political development have been summarized by Lucian Pye in *Aspects of Political Development* (1966). When we overlay Pye's understanding of political development with Wilber's four quadrants, we can identify those uses of the term that fall within each of the lower quadrants. Most fall within the lower-right social quadrant such as those listed in Chapter 5 including: "economic growth;" the political behavior of "already developed societies;" the ability to "mobilize power;" and "administrative and legal development" (Pye 1966: 38–9).

However, contrary to Wilber's largely accurate assessment that the social sciences focus primarily on the lower-right quadrant, many of Pye's other descriptions of what it is that develops politically fall into the lower-left cultural quadrant such as his idea of "citizenship development;" "conventions" and "social norms;" "national self-respect, dignity in international affairs, post nation-state attitudes, spirit or attitude toward equality, mass participation and popular involvement in political activities" (Pye 1966: 38–9). In fact Pye recognizes the limitations of a strict lower-right focus when he writes: "[a] political development that focuses on institution building without also focusing on citizenship development is limited" (Pye 1966: 38–9).

In his book Pye identifies three major criteria for political development within political science including: *equity* by which he means, "law should be . . . universalistic . . . applicable to all . . . impersonal;" *capacity* which he associates with "effectiveness and efficiency in the execution of public policy [and] political leaders should be selected on the basis of capacity;" *differentiation* which means "functional specificity, integration of complex structures and processes" (Pye 1966: 48). These criteria match several of Wilber's and, given Pye's focus on sociocultural experience, it is not surprising that he does not identify other developmental criteria. His approach does not attempt to draw in a psychological dimension of political development, though his identification of "capacity" seems prescient.

Pye's idea of "institution building" can easily be linked with the successes of political liberalism, and his recognition of the need for an active approach to "citizenship development" can be linked with the need to institutionalize the growing psychological consciousness within a form capable of addressing such development. In order to actively pursue citizenship development we need to take the linkage of citizenship to development very seriously. The sociopolitical understandings of political development articulated so far are not enough. Pye intuited this direction when he wrote that the idea of political development is limited to the extent that it does not consider "other forms of development of the society," which could include the political development of the individual, an idea introduced by Andrew Samuels (Pye 1966: 43–8).

Resolving the gap between the person and culture through political development

The most promising idea that could connect the individual and cultural spheres is Andrew Samuels' idea of "political development" (1993: 53–61). Samuels' use of the term begins to immediately imply a connection between the individual and the culture, that is, his language works from the perspective of the individual and moves toward culture; if you will, his is an upper-left language with a lower-left directionality.

In *The Political Psyche* (1993), Samuels draws on the insights of depth psychology for the purpose of bridging the problematic divide between the personal and the cultural, the private and the public. Through both theory and practice Samuels uses his idea of political development to help us imagine how we could activate our own other's "political energy" (1993: 57). Samuels' psychological approach to politics directly takes up Pye's desire for us to attend to citizenship development. Samuels identifies the way in which individuals can be said to develop politically, implying the possibility of activating developmental potentials beyond the private life of individuals, beyond the narrow but important context of psychotherapy, and into a broader cultural context.[1] Samuels asks questions that imply a new upper- and lower-left quadrant language, for example: "What happens if we factor the political into our narratives of the psychological development of the person?" (1993: 53).

Samuels asserts that by exploring a person's political development we expand our understanding of a person to include their culture, society, economic/political system and environment. This challenges the boundary between what is personal and what is social (Samuels 1993: 55). He considers raising political process to the same level of psychological significance as sexuality, spirituality, morality, and aggression when he writes that "maybe [psychological] theory could be expanded so that a political channel could be postulated for the flow of libido, alongside biological, moral, and spiritual channels" (Samuels 1993: 57).

According to Samuels, through this factoring of the political into the psychological we would find "a political level of the psyche" which would allow us to think of "political processes as psyche speaking, and internal processes in terms of politics" (Samuels 1993: 56). This reorients traditional psychological thinking about development, disallowing any artificial separation between the public and private realms. By adding sociopolitical factors into our thinking about the development of the person we are able to consider the effect that political events have on an individual's development. Samuels refers to this as the "political history of the person" (1993: 53). By

, we can also discuss the repression of the person's or political energy" (Samuels 1993: 57).

new way of thinking about the individual's experience of politics, Samuels finds fresh questions for us to ask such as "what was the destiny of that repressed political energy?" (Samuels 1993: 58). Here, Samuels also finds the word destiny helpful as it supports us to consider the trajectory of political energy. Samuels' identification of "political potential" enables him to ask questions about the need for the individual to have avenues to express their political energy. He writes:

> If a culture does not allow a flowering of political potential to occur and express itself and the political self to flourish, then that culture loses one of the most productive avenues for personal growth and individuation. The individual loses out as well as the prospects for transformation and healing of psychopathology within political systems.
>
> (Samuels 1993: 58)

Notice the weaving of the languages of individual development and cultural evolution as Samuels speaks of the political energy of the individual and the psychopathology of political systems. This marks one beginning point for the "new hybrid language" between psychology and politics and between individual development and cultural evolution (Samuels 2001: 13). By speaking of the individual's "psychological need to be political," their capacity for "political energy," and the potential to activate their "political selfhood" through their political development, Samuels is radicalizing Pye's and other political psychologists' use of the term (Samuels 2001: 28–30).

The function of emotion in political development

One of the more exciting aspects of Samuels' exploration of the territory between politics and psychology is his connection between an individual's political development and their emotional suffering. Here, Samuels is well on the way to redeeming the extreme private-life focus of psychotherapy by identifying a public value of attending to our emotional experience. According to Samuels, part of the realization of this psychological need to be political requires that we learn to identify the way in which our private-life emotional suffering needs to be redirected outward, toward a political expression of this suffering. This marks a significant shift from a passive, private-psychological liberalism to an active, public-psychological liberalism. Samuels argues that by redirecting emotions that are typically hidden, like "self-disgust" and shame, a new "political energy" is released that currently lies at the root of a cultural level of depression (Samuels 1989: 194–6, 1993: 13–14).

Political development includes learning how to redirect cultural depression toward a vital, concentrated public attention and actions. Here the world we tend to think of as "inner," psychological, or even private is being actively connected to the "outer" world of politics. Through this description, Samuels is offering some initial use of the new hybrid language between political and psychological liberalism. He connects the development of the person with the coming out of themselves and into a world which includes – requires – some public, political action. In fact, this coming into the world turns out to be not only for the reduction of the symptoms of individuals, but to treat symptoms of our political culture, such as a cultural level of depression. Here, social progress (i.e., cultural evolution) meets personal growth (i.e., individual development) within the activation of political development.

Through his new language, Samuels is not only redeeming the privatized emotions of the individual, but he is also redeeming the emotional focus of psychotherapy. This sheds new light on Jung's statement that "when a problem which is at bottom personal . . . coincides with external events that contain the same psychological elements . . . the personal problem acquires a dignity it lacked hitherto, since the inner discord always has something humiliating and degrading about it" (Jung 1971: 80).

Jung's redemption of individual suffering is expanded and differentiated by Samuels as he specifies a political function to individual emotional suffering. Additionally, Samuels is redeeming the psychotherapy project as he begins to bring it back out toward the world, again imagining a public-psychological liberalism. In this new political context, psychotherapy can be seen as an institutional form that is successfully redirecting attention toward what I will be referring to as the transformative capacity of emotion.

A new understanding of emotion: the human affect system

In Chapter 4 I identified three criteria for being psychological: (a) an awareness of the way we are shaped by our personal and cultural history; (b) an awareness of the psychological dynamics that play out in our lives; (c) the healthy use of our thinking and emotions. The latter criterion is what I have referred to as the emergent capacity for *affect freedom*. I identified affect freedom as the ability to use emotions for what they are actually for, that is, to allow people to do four things: to *assess* their own and their communities' needs; to *connect* to one another for the purposes of conviviality and social and political action; and to *motivate* and direct themselves and others for the purposes of learning, healing, and community engagement. Restated, affect freedom is the capacity to experience and use a full range of emotion for the psychological, political, and moral needs of one's time.

This understanding of what could reasonably be called the objective use of affect draws from revolutionary research in "affect science" conducted by Silvan Tomkins at Stanford University in the 1950s. Tomkins' research has shed light on the objective function of emotions, primarily in our intrapsychic landscape. However, this emphasis of affect science has been extended by psychotherapists who also focus on its interpersonal functioning for the purpose of healing from trauma, as developed by Donald Nathanson, Susan Johnson, and Diana Fosha. Similarly, affect science is being used at the interface between individual development and cultural evolution in my own research into political development and in Omer's Imaginal Transformation Praxis.

The new perspective on the functioning of emotions is part of our growing psychological consciousness. It supports psychology's move away from the limits of a private and privileged psychotherapy towards a public psychology that supports wider growth and the evolution of culture. Understanding the history of this new theory of human emotions is crucial in any effort to integrate private and political/public identity.

The human affect system

Beginning in 1872 with Charles Darwin's publication of *The Expression of Emotions in Animals and Man*, we have been learning that our emotions are rooted in biological responses to the environment, to each other, and to ourselves. Darwin identified how emotions were not only cross-cultural but also cross-species, that is, invariant and universal (Fosha 2000: 18). Darwin viewed emotion as functioning in our daily life to help us respond to all situations quickly, without thought (Goleman 2003: 135). While Darwin's work informed psychology in a number of different ways, clinical psychology's understanding of the function of emotion was primarily influenced by Freud's psychoanalysis and by behaviorism. Unfortunately, neither of these approaches to human experience fully embraced or worked out the implications of Darwin's initial research.

Eighty years later Silvan Tomkins approached the study of emotions from a perspective that clearly pursues Darwin's original ethological approach and is critical of the two veins of psychology. Building on Darwin and other theorists, Tomkins expanded our understanding of the specific biological roots of human emotions in what he called the individual's "affect system." Drawing from Tomkins' work and that of other affect scientists it is possible to show the way that individuals can be understood in terms of the functioning and maturation of their affect systems.

The human affect system and its evolutionary significance

Like other systems within the human organism (the central nervous system, skeletal system, circulatory system, immune system, reproductive and digestive system), the affect system, and its related components, functions in a distinct way independent of, but related to, other functional systems. The affects are fixed patterns of emotional response that have identical features in the old and young alike and are universal to the species, as well as other mammals. The affects are rooted in the biological functioning of the limbic system, and are in a functional relationship with many other brain structures and other aspects of physiology (Scherer 1994: 172).

The affect system is thought to have an "evolutionary significance" in how it prepares an organism physiologically to respond to its environment, which is referred to as its capacity for "action readiness," "resource mobilization," and to "conserve resources" (Clark and Watson 1994: 131).

Tomkins' nine primary affects

According to Tomkins, the affect system is made up of nine primary affects. In Tomkins' theory, these nine affects can be divided into categories of positive, neutral, or negative affect (Nathanson 1992). Most of the affects have a range of intensity necessitating one word for low intensity and another word for high intensity. Table 7.1 lists Tomkin's nine primary affects.

Table 7.1 The nine affects (biological basis of emotion)

Negative	Positive	Neutral
Fear – terror	Interest – excitement	Surprise – startle
Distress – anguish – grief	Enjoyment – joy	
Anger – rage		
Embarrassment – shame		
Disgust		
Dissmell (related to contempt)		

Source: Adopted from Donald Nathanson's (1992) presentation of the work of Silvan Tomkins.

Affect, feeling, emotion, and mood

Affect theorist Donald Nathanson discusses the difference between the basic emotions and those that have more cultural variance as the difference between affect, feeling, emotion, and mood. While affect is a relatively brief "pattern of biological event" lasting between "a few hundreds of a second to a couple of seconds," feeling is an event where an organism becomes aware that they are having an affective response (Nathanson 1992: 49). According to Nathanson, "feeling implies the presence of higher order mechanisms or components that allow knowledge and understanding," whereas emotion is a movement from biology to psychology in the way in which affects intertwine with memory over the lifespan of the individual, and mood is the way in which "memories bring to current attention an unresolved problem from the past or the emotions hovering around a relationship we never managed to resolve" (Nathanson 1992: 50–51).

Nathanson draws an interesting conclusion from this distinction between affect and feelings when he writes that "people may be raised in a culture or an environment that denies the existence of certain feelings; and even when affect is triggered they may not feel it because the ability to perceive it has been extinguished" (Nathanson 1992: 50). Notice here the idea that culture can train individuals to ignore certain biological responses and, as a result, limit their capacity to be able to identify the way that they feel. Certainly psychotherapists run into this regularly in their clinical work. We notice patterns of specific affect repression like the repression of anger, grief, fear, or shame that may be linked to familial oppression or may be generational, race, or gender-related oppressions.

The cultural oppression of affect could make anger, grief, or fear taboo. In current American culture I suspect it is *shame* that is mostly actively repressed. Also, I suspect that cultures can also indulge in specific affects, such as the way American culture seems to be currently indulging in *contempt*. I have discussed the function of shame in American culture and in the formation of strong political identities at length in my dissertation research (Dunlap 2003).

Sites of affect

According to Nathanson, the face, circulatory system, and the voice are the primary sites of affect. The drawings in Figure 7.1 were developed by Gary Faigan (1990) in relation to the research of affect scientist Paul Ekman. According to Nathanson, the voice is modulated by affect in what seems like an infinite number of ways. In fact, he speculates that the voice may have evolved due to the power it brings to the expression of affect, playing a significant role in the survival of the species (Nathanson 1992: 54–65). In the circulatory system, the heart races and blood vessels constrict under the influence of different affects, thus preparing the organism for a range of actions, including the basic responses of fight or flight (Nathanson 1992: 54–65). While these are the three primary sites of action, there are numerous other sites, some as small as "the *erector pili* muscles attached to the hair root," which, when triggered by the affect fear, cause our hair to stand on end (Nathanson 1992: 54–65). Referring to the work of Tomkins, Nathanson summarizes affect theory:

> Affect, says Tomkins, makes good things better and bad things worse. Affect makes us care about different things in different ways. The reason that emotion is so important to a thinking being is that the affect controls or acts upon the way in which we use thought, just as it takes over or influences bodily actions at the sites specific for it.
>
> (Nathanson 1992: 59)

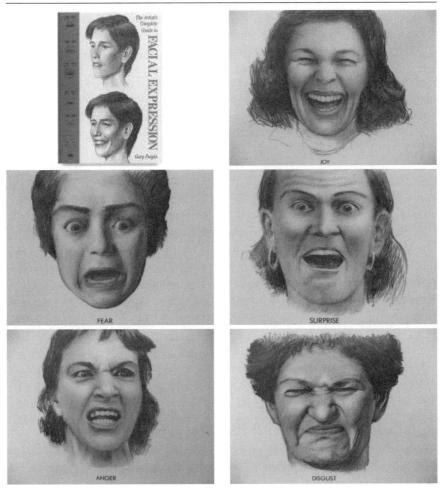

Figure 7.1 Displays of affect in the human face

Source: Gary Faigin (1990) *The Artist's Complete Guide to Facial Expressions*, New York: Watson-Guptill.

When affect theory is added to the equation we can rethink the traditional disparagement of the role of human emotions, which I suspect is a result of political liberalism's push toward individual independence. While it may have been necessary to deprecate emotion as part of our effort to break free of the oppressive social obligations of religion, it is now necessary to reclaim emotion in its objective functioning. Instead of being thought untrustworthy, emotion can be re-envisioned as a trustworthy link between the natural functioning of the body – its drives, sensations, and perceptions – and its sociopolitical environment. Notice the connection here to Samuels' treatment of emotions like self-disgust.

The interface between affect science and psychology is creating a hybrid language that could aid a wider scientific and cultural reconsideration and restoration of the role that emotions play in both individual development and cultural evolution. Like our rational and sensing capacities, affect can be viewed as a source of trustworthy, even objective, human experience and cultural knowledge.

If affect has been an objective source of knowledge since before the human species distinguished itself, then what role has it played in our cultural evolution? Could the affect system be said to develop? Answering these questions has provided me with a pivot point for my thinking about the future, which has helped me to imagine the role a political psychologist could play in changing political culture. My thinking in this area has been largely shaped by my education at the Institute of Imaginal Studies, where Aftab Omer has established a graduate school and research center anchored in ITP.

Affect dynamism in Aftab Omer's Imaginal Transformation Praxis

Earlier in this writing I identified "affect freedom" as a human capacity emerging at this time in history. My understanding of affect begins with the work of my mentor Omer, who introduced me to affect science and to his own unique understanding and approach to the use of affect for healing and capacity development at personal and cultural levels. By applying ITP it is possible to explore the questions posed at the end of the last section and to begin to more fully integrate the processes of individual development and cultural evolution.

Omer has created a theory and practice of personal and cultural transformation that has generated a unique understanding of the way affect "transmutes" into distinct human capacities. According to Omer, over the course of the last several hundred years human experience has been "privatized" and "colonized" through oppressive social and cultural conditions, which has had a fragmenting impact on the individual's ability to integrate their cognitive and affective experience. As I have just mentioned and will later go into more detail about, this fragmentation of cognition and affect can be traced to the shift from religious to political liberalism. At the earliest levels of the religious social role, culture triggers guilt and fear in order to control individuals through their affect system. At the level of the political person this control is rebelled against and Western culture represses emotions broadly as sources of trustworthy experience. At the beginning of modernity emotion is deprecation while thinking and sensing are privileged.

During the Enlightenment, affect was split off from cognition, relegating affect to an inferior "subjective" or "irrational" position. However, this "growth" has led to the modern alienation of the individual, or what Omer refers to as the "privatization of experience," during which affect becomes self-referential and its intrinsic ability to link individuals to the social world is broken. Responding from the position of a public-psychological liberalism, Omer has developed a range of transformative learning practices that he utilizes in organizational, community, and public contexts for the purpose of supporting individuals and groups to work with repressed affect and to rebuild the necessary social connections between individuals through working with affect and imagination. Accordingly, such practices bind the tension between the psychological and the cultural and between our private identities and our life as citizens.

Part of the basis of Omer's transformative practices lies in his rethinking the function of affect in human experience. According to Omer, the affect system responds to the environment and that "each affect has a distinct capacity as its telos" (Omer 2006). Through specific transformative practices individuals in communities and organizations are able to transmute specific affects into distinct capacities. Through mourning practices grief is transmuted into compassion; through intimacy practices fear is transmuted into courage; through conflict practices anger is transmuted into fierceness; through accountability practices shame is transmuted into integrity, dignity, and autonomy.

Omer's theory and practice of the relationship between affect and capacity marks a revolution in both psychology and other social sciences as he successfully uses an understanding of affect to extend the transformative value of the psychotherapy project into increasingly public practices. Recognizing the risks of indulging in affect found in some forms of psychotherapy, Omer writes, "the object is not to elevate affect over cognition, but to end their alienation" (Omer 1990: 45). Omer's recognition and development of the affect/capacity link may be the single most important practice that we have to work with to reconnect personal and cultural transformation. Through this linkage the human capacities intrinsic to leadership can be recognized to have their foundation in the individual's affect system and the cultural practices that shape that system. Accordingly, based on Omer's research and practices, we can answer both questions posed above. If affect is the basis of distinct capacities, then the affect system clearly develops; and as these capacities embolden cultural leadership, affect clearly plays a central role in the evolution of culture; specifically it shapes both individual and cultural identities.

Omer integrates affect awareness with a range of learning practices informed by practices of indigenous cultures; psychotherapeutic practices; practices of accountability that focus on social justice; and, other religious/spiritual practices that activate complex and integrative states of human consciousness. Through these practices, Omer works "liberate human experience from the interlocking shackles of psychological repression and social oppression."

Individuals and groups participating in these transformative learning practices are working to activate the foundational capacities identified by Omer as well as other emergent capacities, such as those I identified in my research. As a result of Omer's research and practices, people participating in the settings where he works become more able to respond to their own suffering, the suffering of those around them, and more responsive to the social ills of their communities. As they develop these capacities they are able to diminish the privatization and powerlessness associated with living in the modern world.

Summary and conclusion

I have argued that the institution of a private-psychological liberalism arose in response to the way that individuals became symptomatic in light of the breakdown of traditional communities and the intensifying of people's private-life suffering. I have argued that this private liberalism problematically focuses on the individual. As a result of many historical factors, including the need for several generations of psychologists to focus their creative attention on the individual's suffering, interest in questions and issues of cultural evolution waned within this institution and no language of a liberalism of the cultural sphere emerged.

Fortunately, psychology's overt attention to the suffering of the individual resulted in the current legacy of the psychological sciences, that is, a robust understanding of healthy development and pathology, which supported clinical treatments, and the understanding of child and adult development. This understanding provides the foundation for the current private-psychological liberalism with its focus on individual development.

Most recently, theoretical and technical advances in the social sciences are synthesizing this well-developed understanding of individual development with the less understood processes of cultural evolution. This synthesis is building a common language that is reuniting these twin dimensions of human experience – in theory and practice. This is where our growing understanding of the functions of emotions is helping us to be aware of our current human conditions, which is leading to the emergence of a public-psychological liberalism.

However, while Darwin was able to connect the range of human emotions to fixed action patterns in facial expressions, and while Tomkins and the new generation of affect scientists have extended our understanding of the affect system, they have not linked affect to a theory of human development; they do not seem to be speaking about affect development or the development of the human affect system. What seems to be missing is a recognition of the opportunity to ask questions about and attend to the relationship between affect and human development.

Nathanson notes how people's affective range can be repressed by their culture. Implied by the notion of affect repression is the idea of affect maturation. Following Omer, we are beginning to be able to speak about such a topic and its implications for both individual development and cultural evolution, specifically the way they connect within the idea of political development. In Table 7.2 I develop what I have come to think of as a rudimentary descriptive model of the relationship between cultural evolution and affect maturation. In Table 7.3 I view affect maturation as a distinct emergent capacity that I have been calling "affect freedom." These tables begin to tell the story of the history of affect maturation in Western culture, as well as introducing the possibility of viewing the last several hundred years in terms of the differentiation of thinking, sensing, and affect.

In order to pull all of the new voices presented in this and earlier chapters into a social science language of the future, I will present my own theory of political development. This theory describes in greater detail the way in which an image, as revelation, first occurs to a creative individual and then moves to encompass the lives of a few, then more, people. It also shows a bare-bones way of beginning to account for how revelation or new consciousness must move toward becoming institutionalized. Despite our native associations with the word institution, human freedom depends on our growing competence at processes of institutionalization.

Table 7.2 The relationship between cultural evolution and affect maturation

Identity and function of affect

Identity: Religious citizen
- Affect used to bridge unique individual identities, focus on binding differentiated capacities into effective vocational and organizational forms.
- Social sciences and social scientists bridge research domains. Integrative phase of inquiry.
- Collaboration across institutional lines bringing government, commerce, education, religion, and other institutions into effective relationship focused on cultural evolution.
- Private and public experiences are reunited within a public psychological liberalism.

Identity: Psychological citizen
- Affect becomes object of self-awareness that is actively transmuted into emergent capacities in the individual who is focused on identifying their role, destiny in activating cultural evolution.
- Emotion reassociated with moral authority but without externally focused locus.
- Emergent capacities gives rise to a "natural hierarchy" that focuses moral authority within the needs of the situation and the capacities of the individuals or groups involved.
- Individual difference and autonomy is viewed through a lens that focuses on serving human transformation.
- Social science research reconnects the separation between processes of individual development and cultural evolution.

Identity: Psychological person
- Emotion is an object of awareness that evokes new experiences of social bonds, communality without individual differentiation, "we are all one."
- Political correctness confuses equality with sameness.
- Private, diverse spiritualities activate individual religiosity.
- Psychotherapy renews value of private-life emotion, preparing the way for a public psychology.

Identity: Political individual
- Affect is disparaged in order to break individual from affect as social bonds.
- Individual autonomy replaces the authoritarian understanding of obligation.
- Autonomous individual suffers isolation from community, social alienation.
- Origin of the epidemic existential crises and pathologies of the individual.

Identity: Social role
- Guilt is institutionalized and used to contain the impulsivity of the child or feudal society.
- Affect connects people to each other through obligatory social and familial roles.
- Growing awareness of individual's distinct affective experience.

Identity: First individual
- Affect as impulsive assertion of individuality as will.
- Stories of temperamental gods/goddesses reflect the differentiation of individual conscious.
- Affect is fully embodied and not a subject of reflection.

Identity: Group
- Ritualization between mother and child shapes affect and identity (Erikson).
- Consciousness-shaping rituals create culture in the form of taboo and custom (Freud, Jung).
- No reflective awareness of affect.

Identity: Instinct
- Affects are instinctive forming display behaviors. Affect is used to assess threat and opportunity, to direct motivation, and to establish attachments or connections.

Table 7.3 Emergent capacities arise from psychopolitical necessities

↑ **Destiny** Identified in the late 1900s	A recognition of the confluence between individual and cultural transformation emerges through the work of: • Erik Erikson's idea of "psychohistory" (1967) • Carl Jung's theory of "individuation" (1939) • Aftab Omer's Imaginal Transformation Praxis (1990) • Peter Dunlap's theory of "destiny" as an emergent capacity (2003).
↑ **Generational attention** Identified in late 1800s	Emergence of understanding of the relativity of history, our capacity to participate in the creation of culture, and the role of affect in this creation through: • Wilhelm Dilthey's idea of "historical consciousness" (1880s)
↑ **Affect freedom** Emerges early 1800s	**Institutionalization of psychotherapy** • Sigmund Freud's (1930) assertion of humanity's passionate, irrational nature in *Civilization and its Discontents*. • Carl Jung (1927) uses archetype and affect to understand processes of individual and cultural differentiation. • Diana Fosha's (2000) explanation of the transformative power of affect in psychotherapy. **Scientific study of emotion** • Charles Darwin (1872) begins the scientific study of the function of emotion. • F.M. Cornford (1912) integrates affect and cultural evolution in *From Religion to Philosophy*. • Silvan Tomkins' (1950s) founding of "affect science" study of the biology of emotion. • Andrew Samuels' (1993, 2001) description of affect as objective response to politics, describes the political development of the individual. • Aftab Omer's (1990) thesis of affect dynamism as source of emergent capacities. **Revolution and reform** • Political use of emotion for moral development of Western culture: political and social reform movements starting in the late 1700s running through twentieth century.
↑ **Sensory freedom** Emerges late 1600s	John Locke's "empiricism" declares that the individual is self-determining and not obligated to feudal lords. This position is developed through the idea that we are born as a blank slate, sensory experience discovers natural laws, thinking and sensing are trustworthy, feelings are not to be trusted.
↑ **Reasoning freedom** Emerges early 1600s	Descartes' "rationalism." "I think therefore I'm free" defines rationalism. The individual has an immortal soul and can be a source of original thinking.
↑ **Religious freedom** Premodern	• Knowledge comes through revelation and is expressed in sacred texts, which supports rise of mythic order. The individual is not valued, nor can individual experience lead to valid knowledge.

Chapter 8

The rhythms of political development

> People generally do not know that a world view or theory will eventually become the social and moral functioning of people two generations later; what was only a world view at first develops into actions later.
>
> (Steiner 1920/1991)

Rhythms of political development: from image to identity to institution

The following is a model of the rhythms of political development. However, unlike psychological models of development, this model is not viewed as solely individual. Similarly, this model will not simply describe social or political phenomena. Instead, it will combine these dimensions of human experience in an effort to present a model that is all-quadrant. This approach parallels Lawrence Kohlberg's highest stage of moral development, stage six, which has been interpreted as requiring "discourse" between individuals for its activation. Gerhard Sonnert and Michael L. Commons write:

> Morality is no longer a property of individuals, as it is at earlier stages, but a property of the social enterprise of discourse. This leads to a novel politization of morality and, conversely, to a moralization of politics.
>
> (Sonnert and Commons 1994: 31–55)

Paralleling a theme of this book, these authors are reconnecting morality and politics, and identifying the way in which they are phenomena that develop. By following Kohlberg, I describe phases of political development and associate the emergence of higher states of development with the way in which new ideas, as new states of consciousness, are experienced by individuals who then find ways of bringing these states into the larger culture. I will speak about the way that liberalizing ideas, ways of being, or states of consciousness come to change individuals and then change political culture. Herein lies the connection between individual development and cultural evolution – they meet, for one, in our moral and political experience.

The descriptions of these phases of political development are meant to evoke insights regarding the way in which new states of consciousness first come to individuals as "images" or "revelations," and make their way toward greater differentiation and embodiment as new identities. In turn, these new identities can be further differentiated as they receive cultural support and are eventually established as cultural norms through the adoption of a range of supportive cultural practices – what I am calling "learning practices." During this last phase, the new identities shape private and public institutional forms in families, educational programs, commerce, or government. I refer to this as a process of moving from "image" to "identity" to "institution."

Like any good developmental model, this model is intended primarily as description. The phases of political development I have identified have been determined through experience. However, these phases are not yet fixed. Like all good science they are intended to be initial descriptions as hypotheses. Further research may reveal distinctions within or between phases as I have laid them out requiring revisions, additions, or subtractions to my model. These changes may be necessary because an all-quadrant idea of political development is relatively new. Accordingly, I request that the reader sits with my descriptions and attempts to formulate doubt, confusion, or disagreement as clarifying or challenging questions.

While I will be speaking in Chapter 9 about stages of the political development of liberalism (i.e., religious, political, private- and public-psychological), the phases I identify are part of the rhythm of the developmental process. These phases explicate the already differentiated rhythm between the esoteric and the exoteric phases of cultural evolution, to which I return in Chapters 9 and 10.

In this writing I will emphasize the phases of political development that take place in the lower-left quadrant. For the moment, enough has been said about the standard ideas of political development articulated in the lower-right quadrant. At its present level of maturation my model is divided into five phases:

1 *Imagining–embodying the future* (revelation and felt experience).
2 *Articulating the future* (thinking and private sharing).
3 *Practicing activating the future* (systematic community embodiment practices).
4 *Public speaking about the future* (using public discourse to shape a new moral conversation).
5 *Institutionalizing the future* (vocationalizing/professionalizing; establishing new institutional forms).

Phase One: imagining–embodying the future

The first phase of political development supports the imagining and embodying of possible and necessary human futures. These images lead to the formation of new psychological, political, and moral identities. Once established these identities become the foundation for new humane social structures. Imagining–embodying is a first step toward extending new individual identities into culture through later stages of identity formation, community practicing, forming a public language, and institutionalization.

Initially, exceptional and ordinary individuals have insights that change at least the way they think about themselves and the world. However, as these insights deepen toward revelatory experiences the new way of thinking brings with it a new way of being that changes both the individual and their time. Following Erikson we can speak of the birth of "a new person; and with this new person a new generation, and with that, a new era" (Erikson 1958: 20).

The transformation of individual and cultural identity begins at this stage with insight and moves toward deeper revelation which opens necessary futures through the imagination. In fact, revelation breaks through individual and cultural repressions of the imagination to create new thinking and experience as a function of what Henderson calls the religious and psychological attitude. "The repression of the imagination and the repression of the future co-arise" (Omer 2005).

While seemingly abstract or esoteric, the idea of identity formation has become quite concrete. Significant research has taken place in the area of "identity" formation including specific research into the formation of "political identities" (Dunlap 2003).

The formation of political identities

According to Erikson, through the formation of a political identity cultural leaders go through personal crises that enable them to reform their identities in ways unique to their time. For example, in *Young Man Luther* (1958) and *Gandhi's Truth* (1969), Erikson pinpoints the way Martin Luther and Gandhi had to wrestle with personal crises and, by resolving these crises in relationship to the contemporary issues of their time, were able to form political identities that renewed the human conscience of that time (Erikson 1958: 20). Erikson makes it clear that forming a political identity is not simply a rational process, but a deeply transformative process that shapes identity.

Erikson notes how Martin Luther faced a severe emotional crisis early in his life and how through that crisis he found within himself a vision of moral integrity that not only redeemed his suffering but found redemption for the corrupt European culture of his time within a new vision of

Christianity. His psychological symptoms did not dissipate prior to his finding a solution that was personal and social. Martin Luther challenged the corrupt Catholic Church's practice of selling redemption and articulated an understanding of our relationship to God that did not turn on the fear of condemnation nor the possibility of making up for moral transgression through bribery. Erikson notes how Luther found his cure by finding a social cause: "Luther . . . at one time was a rather endangered young man, beset with a syndrome of conflicts . . . his solution roughly bridged a political and psychological vacuum which history had created in a significant portion of Western Christendom" (Erikson 1958: 15). Through the formation of a religious identity, or in Henderson's language through the adoption of a new religious and philosophical attitude, Martin Luther changed the political culture of his time. His religious identity activated a political identity, and his religious and philosophical attitude activated the formation of a new social attitude.

In all, the formation of political identities marks the upper-quadrant activity that indicates political development. As increasingly developed political identities form, the entire developmental system (personal, social, religious) has the opportunity for greater political development. In order for activated political identities to influence culture, the new consciousness they embody must have some way of broadening out into the culture: that is, the new consciousness must be activated in increasingly wider social circles, an expanded public space. The cultivation of this new space requires a sharing of the insight to activate new thinking and a sharing of the revelation to activate new ways of being. This sharing begins within some newly formed community or within a transformation of an existing community.

Phase Two: articulating the future

Articulating a private language

At first the new consciousness is heavily influenced by its originator's own personal psychology, that is, their temperament, talents, and the ways that they have suffered and thrived. The new consciousness comes through the individual's affect system and political identity, which requires some engagement with others to mature. Through private speaking the idiosyncrasies that often accompany the original personal nature of the insight can be sorted out in order to embody the experience and to articulate, at first, a private language shared by a new community. This requires pursuing the emotional freedom as increased levels of affect freedom within a new community. Such a community provides the container in which learning practices can be adopted to support such maturation of its member's affect system and identities. Thus the revelation begins to be stretched to encompass the felt necessity and destiny of others. This is an initial move toward generalizability within the private language of a community of practitioners.

Following Erikson, the new person mobilizes new capacities that are direly needed by their time. As the new capacities become embodied by a community of practitioners, the revelatory experience begins to assert an influence on current human conditions. This could simply be in the form of a new political awareness, or something more complex such as a new community ethic. It certainly includes a new moral identity supported by maturation of the function of the affect shame within the individuals and group. Ideally, this is at first a private speaking, requiring conversation and opportunities to practice using emotions for what they are for at the level of the new consciousness through truth, caring, and accountability practices.

Good ideas, affective states, and new states of consciousness and identity need to be developed in order to separate out their naïve or inflated dimensions. Part of this work requires the creation of a protective "esoteric" environment. In such an environment the new idea/state of consciousness can be experimented with in order to determine its value to the practitioners, and in order to begin imagining its applicability outside of the esoteric setting, thus raising the obligation of increasing the generalizability of the new consciousness.

However, during this phase, questions of generalizability can be problematic and reflect fear or resistance to the new consciousness, as premature concerns with applicability can interfere with the emergence of the nascent experience or consciousness. Questions such as "How will this play in Kansas?" as often as not reflect an individual's natural struggle with their own process of development. It is one thing to grow as an individual, making modest changes in our world view, expanding our capacity for empathy, or simply having insight into our own histories, which have helped us to change current habits. Such personal growth is valuable, but it is not indicative of political development. It is an entirely different matter to attempt to embody a depth of consciousness that would address what Henderson refers to as the needs of one's time. This latter transformation requires going out on a limb and finding within oneself the type of identity, political or otherwise, that would contribute to a transformation of political culture.

This was accomplished in the early modern period by culture leaders like Descartes and Locke, who began embodying the political individual's new independence. They had to stretch beyond the controlling external authority of religious social roles. Similarly, as I will discuss in Part V, the progressive movement needs to move toward the developmental awareness of a public-psychological liberalism in order to overcome the political correctness of the psychological person that confuses equality with sameness.

When individuals within a community of practitioners prematurely focus on generalizability or applicability, they are likely to be experiencing fear. In my work with groups I have identified a number of fears, all of which can be understood in terms of normal fears of new experience, which I refer to as the "fear of not knowing."

The fear of not knowing

> There is wisdom in turning as often as possible from the familiar to the unfamiliar; it keeps the mind nimble, it kills prejudice, and it fosters humor.
>
> (Santayana 1968: 15)

It is easy to understand our fear of the unknown. While human beings are intrinsically curious, we also prefer to keep our peace of mind, the comfort that comes with certainty. Any time we go out on a limb we risk disturbing this equilibrium, which brings anxiety. In fact, stories that capture the imagination of generations are often told of heroic figures who have risked disturbing the peace by bringing some new experience to their community. Whether this new experience is evoked in art, science, politics, or religion, courageous individuals take their community and sometimes their age to the edge of not knowing.

When the task is to change political culture, the fear of the new threatens to limit the applicability of a new way of thinking or a new consciousness. This is a typical experience of relatively well developed people when they are confronted by a new political/cultural consciousness. Such individuals often do not understand what Einstein understood when he wrote that the problems of one stage of development cannot be resolved from within that stage of development (Gellert 2001: 297). Relatively well adjusted people may be inclined to think that they already embody sufficient awareness or identity and that necessary political change will primarily require some form of rational dialog through which they convince others to see the world and the world's problems in the way they do. They do not recognize the likelihood that they – themselves – will actually need to change, to develop into a higher stage of consciousness, in order to become the change the world needs.

People identified with the political individual or the private-life focused psychological person cannot be fully aware of the sense of responsibility that arises when the developmental scale of cultural evolution becomes the focus of a public-life focused psychological citizen. As a result they are unlikely to be able to consider the developmental scale upon which cultural evolution takes place that, once recognized, requires us to aspire to adopting a philosophical attitude which allows us to see ourselves within the context of cultural evolution.

This fear of the need to shift into a higher stage of consciousness has several manifestations that I have identified in my work with political change groups. These fears include: fear of loss of a clear identity; fear of a loss of power and of not belonging; fear of being marginalized, of losing touch, or of falsely imagining superiority (inflation). I will briefly address each of these in turn.

Fear of loss of a clear identity

The fear of new consciousness can also trigger an individual's fear of not having a clear identity from which to contribute to political change. The emergence of new ideas and new ways of being includes a necessary period of instability, that is, Erikson's stage of "identity moratorium" (Prager 1986: 31). Insight and revelation break apart traditional ways of thinking and being and lead to the need for private conversation during which time individuals attempt to find ways of speaking and relating that support the emergence of the new consciousness. This requires some tolerance for ambiguity, for not knowing, and a willingness to let go of known capabilities and identities to allow these to reform along yet to be determined lines without any certainty of one's power or place in the newly forming community or culture.

Fear of a loss of power and belonging

Every individual, whether they can acknowledge it or not, wants to be powerful and to have a place for their current talents to contribute to political change. While social change groups can draw from the current and potential strengths of every member, there is a need to adopt an attitude of what the Buddhists refer to as beginner's mind, or what the nineteenth-century poet John Keats referred to as "negative capability" (1817).

In the context of this phase of political development – articulating the future – "negative capability" requires individuals and groups to suspend a clear understanding of how change will take place, and what exactly they have to contribute, in order to welcome new ways of thinking and being. It is the cultivation of negative capability that enables individuals and groups to suspend rigid knowing, to set aside ideas about what they have to contribute or how they will belong in a newly forming group, and to allow room for new experience.

Fear of being marginalized, of losing touch, of falsely imagining superiority

Fear of new experience can also appear as individuals begin to understand or experience the new way of thinking and being and yet cannot imagine how they could ever communicate this newness to others. Here the fear of the new can manifest in a distinct worry of being marginalized as they cannot imagine communicating the new way of thinking and being to others. More than once I have had someone assert "How will this play in Kansas?", or "Liberals won't understand that," or "George Bush wouldn't see himself that way." These statements reflect a natural tendency to fear separation from others, even when such separation marks personal and cultural development. In particular, I suspect this fear represents the difficult transition from a collective stage of development to an individual stage, such as Graves' shift from either the "blue" to the "orange" meme or from the "green" to "yellow" meme. Being at the cutting edge of one's community to set out and create new knowledge is intrinsically frightening.

Such fears are important to consider for they raise legitimate concerns that require that we attend to the issues of generalizability. This attention can be focused through the following two questions:

1   "Are we heading in a direction that is too far outside of the culture?"
2   "Are we deluding ourselves and others by thinking that we are developing when we aren't?"

The fears I have described, as well as others, are in fact necessarily accounted for by pursuing the next several phases of development that require participants to "return" to the realm of culture, as we find it, and seek effective application of the new consciousness.

However, following esoteric traditions, there is a great benefit for culture for some communities to maintain esoteric traditions and not to actively return to culture. Whether Buddhist, Christian, or other, there are groups whose purpose is to maintain the wisdom traditions, without attempting – too actively – to focus on extending them. Nevertheless, the model of political development presented here notes the way in which there can be a path between the esoteric and the exoteric. Through the later phases of this model, wisdom can be more actively brought into culture without closing the door on the benefit of having a protected space in which new ideas are cultivated. For example, in the next phase of political development, practicing activating the future, new ideas/ways of being are supported in privacy, in their own community, in preparation for going public.

Phase Three: practicing activating the future

Learning practices and the formation of a new public imagination

At Phase Three private conversations within a community of practitioners have created enough hope and new experience to inspire individuals and small groups to begin to routinize the new consciousness through the adoption of specific learning practices. Initially, learning practices can be understood as those activities that build a shared experience of meaning.

They take place in both our public and private lives. These practices exist in community groups of all sorts, but also exist at the foundation of healthy families. Families engage in learning practices on a daily basis, including routines such as shared meals, reading before bed, or doing chores. Learning practices include activities that transmit human knowledge and capacities across generations, such as practices that maintain hygiene, tool use, public awareness, as well as artistic, musical, craft, and other capacities. Learning practices are also at the heart of the healthy activities of religious, political, and social service organizations. They bring people together across differences; they activate an experience of shared humanity.

When a new idea/state of consciousness has been activated through Phase One and Phase Two, then learning practices can be used to embody the new state of consciousness by people as a lived experience. Such practices are made up of patterns of activity implied by the new consciousness. These activities are engaged in by groups of individuals who are committed to extending the new consciousness into a range of activities: some daily – such as meditation, prayer, a new means of child rearing, or the work of a committed group of people working in a school district; others are repeated within cycles – such as weekly or bi-weekly psychotherapy, or volunteering in one's community to support social justice or environmental sustainability.

These activities can be based on truth, caring, and accountability learning practices that support the extension of the new consciousness into an initial semi-public context moving toward greater public awareness. These practices enable others to move from less developed states of consciousness to the new state and prepare the way for the next phase of development, that is, "public speaking." In combination with an initial experience of community, advocates of a new idea or state of consciousness will begin to imagine what form will be needed to extend their work into the public's imagination. In order to accomplish this, a group will need to address the prejudices that would interfere with the activation and maintenance of the new state of consciousness.

Addressing the prejudices of lower levels of political development

Crucial to this phase of development is a conversation within the community of practitioners about the interface between their emerging culture and the exoteric culture of their time. This conversation is deepened as the community of practitioners uses its experience of doing learning practices to learn about themselves and about their culture. At this phase, practices can be designed and used to anticipate the difficulties that a new type of practitioner will have in adapting their learning into a new, wider public imagination. These difficulties will likely reveal the prejudices embedded in both the current public imagination and language and the prejudices of the newly emerging community of practitioners. Ideally, the exposure of these prejudices is brought back into the learning practices themselves to help refine the applicability of the new consciousness. Exposure of and engagement with the prejudices of either the community of practitioners or the wider culture requires the advancement of more refined learning practices. This is where the learning practices must differentiate at least the following three types of practice: education, healing, and community engagement.

At this phase of political development the community of practitioners is learning to work directly with the larger community, experimentally, for the purpose of learning how to address the prejudices that restrict the public imagination and thus limit its political development. Here, educational learning practices are used to identify the prejudices that maintain a lower level of political development in both the community of practitioners and the larger community that they are beginning to encounter.

Once some *initial sense* of the prejudices restricting political development has been identified, the task of the community of practitioners is to attempt to find within their own experience the roots of these prejudices, which will be located within their psychological, political, and moral identifications and suffering, which I will discuss in Chapter 11 as their "political wounds." On the basis of this initial sense, the community of practitioners sets about developing a new type of learning practice that will both throw light onto the identifications and suffering underlying the prejudice and initiate the type of kind, firm attention that heals such conditions.

While it is likely that the community of practitioners will have previously made use of healing practices, such as in the initial development of a private language and beginning embodiment practices, it is also possible for a group to move through the first two phases without attending to its own or its members' identifications or suffering. However, once the group begins to move directly toward its culture, to create a new public imagination, it is unlikely that it will be able to successfully address the prejudices of lower stages of political development without initiating healing practices that attend to the identifications and suffering embedded in these lower stages. I address the specific prejudices I see limiting the political development of the current progressive movement in Chapter 13.

The difficulty of going public with effective embodiment practices

Sometimes new learning practices take place within a cultural tradition. For example, Eastern and Western esoteric religious traditions have numerous religious learning practices that engage the body (embodiment practices) – including meditation, yoga, and prayer – and substantially support the embodiment of higher states of consciousness. However, there is an inverse correlation between the extent of these practices and the extent to which they are able to move into public use. Such practices have been historically esoteric, and, despite current efforts, they have not become mainstreamed enough to sufficiently reshape the consciousness of Western culture. I suspect that this is because they have yet to be tailored to respond to the actual condition and suffering of our culture. This would require embodiment practices contained within a larger process of political development and not reduced to matters of personal health or a private-life spirituality. This challenge can be understood by viewing this phase of political development through the example of twentieth-century political liberalism.

Franklin Delano Roosevelt (FDR) supported a range of community engagement learning practices that activated a new public consciousness as part of his Civilian Conservation Corps. His work was an extension of the traditions of political liberalism, which reimagined the role that government could play in the consciousness of the American people. However, despite Lyndon Johnson's extension of FDR's community engagement learning practices, and the deep community engagement of the civil rights era, the liberal vision has yet to be effectively extended into a fuller public imagination. Such an extension would require a range of learning practices that could activate a sustainable liberal public imagination. FDR and Johnson's efforts extended well into the public sphere, and because of that might seem to belong to a later phase of political development. However, while they did capture the public imagination (to some extent), the actual vision or "image" of liberalism they acted on was neither well articulated enough nor supported by sufficient embodiment practices to transform the American consciousness.

The political liberalism of the twentieth century exemplifies a range of implicit/explicit political attitudes that have not fully been explored or embodied by the public's imagination, and certainly not articulated within a public language. For example, despite numerous efforts to extend humane images of how we could treat one another into institutional forms, liberals failed to negotiate effectively this phase of political development. The liberal failure to develop learning practices focused on political development within a community of practitioners limits our ability to bring the public on board with our vision.

Because the attitudes and practices implied by a new liberal consciousness may or may not be fully articulated in a public language, the strengths and/or limitations of the new consciousness may not have been worked out sufficiently prior to their going public. In fact, in some cases, the learning practices adopted can actually truncate the reach of the new consciousness.

At Phase Three numerous factors can either support or undermine the embodiment of the new consciousness by more individuals and more broadly through the culture. FDR's political liberalism could be considered too focused on external social progress, while the infusion into our culture of the practices of Eastern religious traditions may focus too internally on individual development. This divided image represents the split between political liberalism and the first step of psychological liberalism, that is, a private-psychological liberalism.

If embodiment practices focused on identifying prejudice and healing its underlying "political wounds" are successful enough, then the affective roots of the limitations of the political individual and the psychological person can be recognized. This would enable a new phase of the political development of liberalism to unfold, that is, an extension of effective learning practices into a new public imagination and public language. Accordingly, the work becomes active using the learning practices, developed by the community of practitioners, to address the cultural prejudices restricting greater access to a higher stage of political development. This requires engaging in the newly developed learning practices more broadly, and working to support their wide acceptance by fostering a new "public imagination" through the differentiation of a new public language.

Phase Four: public speaking about the future

Revelatory experience is first articulated in private speaking with others. Then it is embodied in community practices, and its trajectory is moving toward engaging with the kairos, that is, the spirit of the time. Engaging the spirit of a time takes place in our thoughts and in our actions with one another through the "languages" of our time, as "modes of moral discourse" (Bellah et al. 1985: 334).

The task at this phase of political development is to engage existing moral languages through discourse for the purpose of creating a conversation that transforms. As George Steiner writes: "the public crust of language must be riven. Only then shall the subconscious and anarchic core of private man find a voice" (Steiner 1976: 178). Through these new forms of discourse a public dialog is established that will begin to influence existing institutional forms. However, prior to such institution formation this dialog must shape a new public imagination.

During this phase, the new consciousness runs into issues of translation. No longer simply working within a community of practitioners, the advocates for the new consciousness must set about creating a new public imagination, which implies that it must influence from afar. To develop such influence, advocates for the new consciousness must assert a power over the imagination and language of a people. Assertion of such power is a challenge for the community of practitioners as they must test the truth of the new consciousness in increasingly complex and abstract ways. No longer does transmission of the new consciousness have the benefit of close proximity. What is successfully communicated through a combination of presence and articulation must now be communicated through articulation alone.

At this point religious or political traditions can impose specific social attitudes or beliefs that, as easily as not, limit the reach of the new state of consciousness. The test at this level is to work out a new language that allows the new consciousness to be transmitted through the new public imagination. Exposed in this process are the limitations of the community of practitioners as well as the limitations of the new consciousness. Here, the community of practitioners may have difficulty recognizing the actual effect of the new consciousness on them. There is an inclination, unintentionally, to simplify the change they have gone through and to express that change too hopefully, believing that it could be easily transmitted to others. For example, too often developmental changes are not experienced as developmental: that is, people may not realize the full extent of their own transformation and think their new experience can be communicated more easily than it actually can.

Issues of translation can be found in the twentieth century in the attitudes of both social scientists and political liberals, which I will describe in Part IV. The successes and failures of these two groups, as well as the distance between them, reflect the difficulty in extending the emerging psychological consciousness into modern culture.

Phase Five: institutionalizing the future

Through processes of embodying and articulating (privately and publicly), the new states of consciousness begin to broadly establish a new stage of human development and evolution. This requires that the "state" be institutionalized as a "stage," that is, to move the state to an institutional form – from image to identity to institution. So far I have discussed four phases to institutionalizing a new stage of human evolution. Through a people's political development, a new stage of cultural evolution moves from the esoteric experience of a few, based in shared practices of embodiment and articulation of that experience, toward the exoteric experience of a wider public, through the further articulation of the original revelatory experience in an increasing public language that activates a new public imagination.

The last phase of political development identified by this model is also the last step required for the fuller activation of a new stage of cultural evolution. This phase focuses in an increasingly overt way on forming the public institutions implied by the original revelation: that is, public institutions are formed that enable the new stage of cultural evolution to spread widely throughout the culture. One way of thinking about this last phase of political development is to view it as a process of "institutionalizing." However, this word has many associations that are not positive, which may reflect on our difficulty in embracing the tasks of this phase. However, the connotations of the word institutionalization do not match its denotations. While it connotes rigidity and even a degree of inhumanity, its denotative associations circle more around the positive need to be organized. While both conservatives and liberals may equally fear the abuses that come from past and existing institutions, there is good reason to view this fear as a reflection of past and current limitations of our ability to create humane institutional forms.

If we were simply to follow the thinking of anarchists, existentialists, or Freud, we would have to conclude that to be human is to fail to create humane institutions. However, it might be a better idea to follow Dewey and think that it could just as easily be that to be human is to create increasingly humane institutions. This would be especially true as we follow the trajectory of human political development through which the most humane images are being institutionalized over such long periods of time. Unfortunately, it may be too intimidating and disheartening for us to consider. Could it be that we are in a position to understand processes of political development such that we could gain some degree of conscious control over the process of institutionalization? This last phase of political development has just that intent, learning to actively pursue the possible transformative intent of processes of political development. I now subdivide this phase into two subphases.

Subphase One: vocationaling and professionalizing the new phase of political development

The first phase of institutionalizing a new stage of political development requires imagining services that could be performed by some form of a practitioner who could support the wider public embodiment of the new consciousness, in a psychological and moral form. This took place at the end of the nineteenth and early twentieth centuries in psychology with the emergence of the practice of psychoanalysis and the initiation of psycho-therapy as a vocation.

Subphase Two: coordinating vocational activities into new or renewed institutional forms

The second subphase requires pulling the earlier four phases forward, concretizing them into a distinct institutional form and/or integrating them within existing institutions. In Part V, I set out to apply this model of political development to the ideas in this book by showing ways in which these ideas can be institutionalized through a new type of transformative political psychology.

Summary and Conclusion

The idea of political development supports the formation of a coherent social science language that is both fully linked to the history of the social sciences and successfully integrates the previously differentiated concept of development, identified by Wilber and represented by his four-quadrant model. Currently this is leading to research opportunities as the idea of political development can become a focal point of social science research and political activism, thus bringing back together the culture's capacity for learning and changing as well as rejoining the roles of the scientist and the activist. Through its articulation as a social science language, the political development of a people can be more consciously and actively pursued. And, this is already taking place.

Central to political development is a clear recognition of the activities that would take place in the cultural sphere, which would bring the personal and the social together. As a result the different attitudes toward the future become reconcilable: "individual development" and "social progress" meet in political development. This confluence offers healing attention to the dichotomy between political and private-psychological liberalism.

As a result of the active pursuit of their political development, individuals and communities are coming into a range of new capabilities that enable them to focus on forming organizations that respond not only to their political and moral needs but also to the psychological and developmental needs of their communities. New organizations are emerging that combine the political, psychological, and moral interests of a community, thus changing the way people and groups relate to the future. Through these new organizations, people are finding a role for themselves that fits or accounts for their unique sensitivities, talents, and suffering, while maintaining a focus on community engagement. Thus, the idea of community engagement is itself broadening. We can engage in community-making without focusing obsessively on our own suffering; following Samuels, it becomes a source of our "political energy."

While a focus on suffering may be too overtly psychological – or even "therapeutic" – for most groups, a few groups are learning to focus attention on the suffering of their members. These groups are learning how to attend to suffering without getting bogged down in becoming some form of therapy group. They are finding ways of directing their suffering, again, toward community engagement.

Through whichever type of group or form of engagement, individuals and groups are finding a place for themselves as active members of their communities, which is helping them to experience a new hope or faith in the future. This faith in the future maintains the traditional liberal focus on individual achievement and on supporting the social progress of our communities, but it also now includes an overt interest in the psychological experience of individuals and groups. This interest reflects a general trend in Western culture in which people are becoming more psychological, and it is through this increasing psychologicalness that individuals are able to establish a creative relationship to culture, and thus become creators of culture.

The development of this new public-psychological liberalism extends traditional forms of political and private-psychological liberalism into a new stage of human development represented by a range of institutional forms governed by traditional and liberal values. In identifying this new stage of human development we will be able to draw on numerous developmental theorists and a range of social activists in order to begin imagining the "vocational" and "professional" identities that will be needed in order to use the new social science language that is emerging from numerous sources, including this book.

Prior to working out these new identities I will try an experiment. In Part IV I will see if I have developed the new language of a public-psychological liberalism sufficiently to establish it within the public imagination of you, the reader. Through this experiment I will be asserting this language as a Phase Four language to see what happens, what I can learn, and what I can contribute. However, I recognize that this experiment is limited: it does not really dive too deeply in its efforts to influence a public imagination. On that basis it represents some semi-public foray that extends beyond the Phase Three embodiment practices that are used by the political change groups I am involved with.

Part IV

A speculative theory of cultural evolution

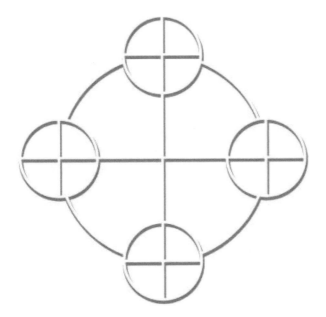

Chapter 9

A new story of liberalism

Summary and initiating a learning practice

So far in this book, we have been exploring the idea that our culture is becoming more psychological, that it develops or evolves. We are also examining the key role that the individual plays in this process of cultural evolution. Individuals can actively shape the cultural evolution of their time and in turn be shaped by their time. I call this the capacity for destiny, which was illustrated through the stories of progressive leaders in Part I. The idea of destiny, as a capacity, supports our recognition of the ways in which personal and cultural identities pull each other forward.

In Part II I turned to several significant theories of individual development and cultural evolution that support an emerging understanding of the reciprocity between personal development and cultural evolution. These theories culminate in Part III with my own understanding of political development, which begins to trace an overt line of development between these two. All of these theories support an emerging awareness of our opportunity to participate in cultural evolution. Following Graves, the emergence of this awareness indicates the stirrings of a transition from first-tier to second-tier awareness. Following Henderson, this awareness is understood to be an emerging psychological attitude.

Samuels also contributes to this emerging paradigm through his idea of political development, his understanding of the "psychological need to be political," and his grasp of the public function of emotion (Samuels 2001: 30). However, despite his interest in development, Samuels' approach is not overtly developmental. Instead, he implies a developmental trajectory for liberals, suggesting our need to draw on the wisdom of clinical psychology to establish practices of self-care for our political selves and our organizations.

Omer's Imaginal Transformation Praxis is developmental while consciously avoiding developmentalism. He offers the most promising opportunity to create culture by linking the continuing transmission of human capacities to learning practices of conflict, accountability, and intimacy.

To these thinkers, I add my own voice. I suggest that the emerging capacity for *generational attention* can support our efforts to gain a degree of conscious control over the future course of culture. Through my own growing generational attention, I have focused on the modern condition that separates our identity into public and private dimensions, which limits the twin champions of political and psychological liberalism. This focus specifically challenges and then combines the external, rational focus of political liberalism and the internal, alienated focus of the private-psychological liberalism. Viewing these liberalisms as stages in a developmental process, the capacity for generational attention activates images of a new, conjoined public-psychological liberalism.

Following my understanding of political development, I have identified the task of moving to a new image of a conjoined political and psychological liberalism. This requires the establishment of increasingly public learning practices, and the articulation of a hybrid public language of psychological liberalism. Through the articulation of this language, a new awareness is shifting the attention of a generation toward the necessity of a conjoined expression of social progress and individual development.

In the first three parts of this book I have attempted to speak about – and speak – this new language of liberalism. This language is being birthed from numerous sources, and has been brought into my life through the political liberalism of my father and the psychological liberalism of my mother. In at least one respect, the social sciences are playing a cultural leadership role, supporting the synthesis, use, and extension of this language. To fulfill their role, social scientists will need to re-evaluate and expand their understanding of human development. A fuller image of human development will enable social scientists to help all of us understand the relationship between the individual and culture. Although in time each person will have access to this capacity, the future of humanity depends on an adventurous group of cultural leaders achieving it – and quickly.

But how will cultural and political leaders achieve this new understanding? How can those leaders connect their stories with this new story of cultural evolution? These questions reflect the shift from Phases Three and Four of my model of political development, that is, between a story of cultural evolution that is understood by a few people with common practices (Phase Three) to a wider audience through written and spoken materials (Phase Four).

To begin testing my model to see if it was coherent enough and made sense of the experience of progressive leaders and others pursuing changes in political culture, I told the story of cultural evolution to a few members of two political change groups. I organized the presentation of this material as an educational learning practice. The intended learning outcome was the activation of the cognitive dimension of generational attention in the participants. In using the learning practice with my colleagues, we successfully engaged in Phase Three (activating the future) of the political development of the new language of liberalism. As I wrote in Chapter 8: "At Phase Three private conversations within a community of practitioners have created enough hope and new experience to . . . begin to imagine what form will be needed to extend their work into the public's imagination."

I initiated this phase by presenting this and the next chapter as a PowerPoint presentation and inviting informal conversation as we went. My intent was to test the extent to which I was successfully creating a new "public language" of liberalism through a story of cultural evolution. The measure of success would be if the learning practice helped the participants imagine new ways of changing political culture that included opportunities for their own participation. Another way of framing this might be: Could the participants experience a confluence between the ongoing development of their political identities and the story of cultural evolution? Would images of their own destiny spontaneously arise? If such images did arise I might expect that they would experience an increasingly clear sense of direction for changing political culture, a heightened sense of their individual agency and their group's agency and purpose, and ultimately an increase in the sheer enjoyment of each other's company. If successful, this learning practice would intensify their capacities for generational attention and destiny – however incrementally.

After this Phase Three presentation I asked the participants how they had been impacted and, in fact, they reported that they had been so moved. They did experience an excited clarity about the past and present of the evolution of Western culture and this extended into the sharing of spontaneous images of the opportunities for their own future participation, as individuals and as a group. Having succeeded as a Phase Three practice, I was encouraged to take the next step and to present the story as a Phase Four learning practice, that is, as a public language of the past, present, and future of cultural evolution.

In the next two chapters I will engage with you, the reader, in this Phase Four, without recourse to the Phase Three practices developed by the political change groups. Your response will help determine if I've developed enough theoretical material, and presented it adequately, to activate generational attention and destiny more broadly. If successful, this would indicate that I am articulating a language of a public-psychological liberalism. Framed more formally, in this chapter and the next I will tell the story of the evolution of Western culture, to discover if the telling activates the capacity for generational attention and destiny in its readers. Let's see what happens.

The story of the evolution of Western culture

In this chapter I will tell the story of the liberalization of culture in a new way by reworking its historical constituents. Central to this storytelling is an understanding that in order to find faith in the future we must speak a language that accounts for the political, moral, and psychological needs of a people. The historical analysis that follows is cursory at best, a first cut at using the language of a public-psychological liberalism that is emerging in this writing. I am certain that a more through analysis will reveal gaps in my thinking, such as my failure to recognize good work done in other fields that would carry significant weight in my analysis. For the moment, I plunge ahead knowing such critical feedback awaits, and that this rough beginning risks psychologizing history in problematic ways.

Nevertheless, such risk is necessary. I step ahead with the certainty that political history is the province of psychology, not just political science or the political psychology currently identified as a subfield of political science. In fact, here I will challenge all of us to consider the timidity of psychology's current, though fading, propensity to limit its inquiry to only the private-life histories of individuals. I suspect that time will show this timidity reflects psychology's brilliant but troubled youth, and not its future. Psychological thinking is needed in relation to all human history, in relation to our private-life sufferings and joys, as well as our most public and moral experiences with each other.

In this chapter and the next I will trace a continuous path of development from the beginning of Western culture to the present in order to activate the emergent capacity for generational attention. Through the development of this capacity, countless opportunities emerge for individuals to participate in cultural evolution. These opportunities will appear as we confront the prejudices that keep us in a passive relationship with cultural evolution.

As cultural evolution becomes a phenomenon we can more fully consider and discuss, our own relationship to it will also come into focus. This is simply the capacity for destiny. Using our sensitivities and talents, we come out of isolation and join the human community to celebrate joy and share suffering.

On the basis of the theories of development and evolution presented so far, I will combine images of the history of Western culture with theory and speculation to draw attention to the interior "cultural" dimension of the evolutionary process.[1] In the cultural realm, the external-social (lower-right) and the individual (upper-left and upper-right) domains meet and the meaning of human experience emerges from learning about our past, present, and future evolution. It is from the depths of the lower-left cultural domain that we can expect a cohering language of the future to sound.

Criteria for a theory of cultural evolution

As I have mentioned, Wilber's criteria for a theory of cultural evolution include: increased complexity; differentiation and integration; organization;

interiority (capacity for self-awareness); autonomy; objectivity; telos/ directionality; and decrease in narcissism (Wilber 1995: 67–78). In this chapter and the next I will emphasize the minimally understood "interior" dimension of cultural evolution. I associate this dimension with the emergence of a private-psychological liberalism, within which egalitarian values are the norm and an individual's subjectivity and emotional experience are highly valued. This is a crucial level of political development that many political liberals need to achieve. Through the writing of this book, I see more clearly the important role that expanding our internal experience during the last few centuries has played in our political development. However, I also realize that we need much more detailed criteria in relation to the cultural sphere if we are to create a new language of liberalism.

Below I present five criteria I will use to tell the story of the evolution of Western culture. These criteria fall into two types: evolutionary lines and rhythms. Wilber posits that evolutionary "lines" indicate what it is that develops. For example, cognitive, moral, or epistemological capacities can be said to be "lines" that develop. To these lines, I add "affect maturation," "ritual practices," and "linguistic development" as lines of development that need to be attended to in order to understand the cultural evolution of the West. The idea of evolutionary rhythms is my own idea, comprising: "turning passive into active" and "moving from esoteric ruptures to exoteric consolidations."

The description of political development offered in Chapter 8 is a further explication of the esoteric/exoteric evolutionary rhythm. Esoteric and exoteric ideas account for the rhythm of moving from an esoteric image to a new identity, to an exoteric institution. Similarly, in different parts of this book I have described the rhythm of moving from a passive relationship with a capacity to actively reflect on it and thus gain greater conscious control over it. This movement is a natural result of development. In sum, additional criteria for cultural evolution include:

1   *Developmental lines:*
    • affect maturation
    • ritual activities
    • linguistic activities.
2   *Developmental rhythms:*
    • collective to individual
    • turning passive into active
    • moving from esoteric ruptures to exoteric consolidation.

Through an examination of these criteria, the developmental continuity of Western culture becomes more apparent. As this continuity is excavated from our cultural history, an interesting path into the future appears.

Dewey's principle of continuity between the biological and cultural

During the mid to late eighteenth century, questions about humanity's place in nature abounded, particularly efforts to understand the human mind. Prior to the emergence of a new language of evolution, the mind was largely interpreted through a variety of theological lenses. Although the language of evolution did not immediately dominate public awareness, it profoundly influenced the creative thinking of that time. For example, Wilhelm Wundt posited that both the individual and human culture were essentially "goal-directed" (Buxton 1985: 25). William James, the father of American psychology, was deeply influenced by Wundt, Darwin, and others. He developed the idea of "adjustment" that combined an evolutionary and adaptive view of human experience that found faith in our movement toward the future (Buxton 1985: 122). However, unlike Wundt, James did not extend toward culture his primary interest in the individual, being drawn instead to the developmental issues of the upper quadrants.

James's student, John Dewey, extended this idea of "adjustment" beyond the individual, using *teleological* explanations to account for large-scale historical processes, describing them as essentially developmental processes. Dewey connected human history and culture to biological processes, using analogy and the articulation of the "postulate of continuity" (Dewey 1938: 23). Both Wundt and Dewey seem to be responding to Wilhelm Dilthey's desire to create the broadest possible context for the study of mental processes. Dewey expresses his breadth of perspective as follows:

> The adaptations made by inferior organisms, for example their effective and coordinated responses to stimuli, become teleological in man and therefore give occasion to thought. Reflection is an indirect response to the environment, and the element of indirection can itself become very great and very complicated. But it has its origin in biological adaptive behavior and the ultimate function of its cognitive aspect is a prospective control of the conditions of the environment.
>
> (Dewey 1931: 30)

Implicit in this last statement is Dewey's belief that scientific activity is developmentally continuous with other evolutionary adaptations. Accordingly, his assertion that "adaptations . . . become teleological in man" suggests that biological evolution is continuous with what I call "cultural" evolution.

The implications of Dewey's assertion are many, and cannot be discussed here adequately. However, it is noteworthy that Dewey's position is not supported by the current proponents of the social sciences, despite Dewey's founding role in humanism, and its influences on political liberalism, education, moral philosophy, and social psychology. However, British Aristotelian scholar F. M. Cornford took Dewey's "functionalism" and articulated a significantly more advanced theory of cultural evolution.

Cornford's identification of developmental continuity between ritual, religion, and philosophy

In his 1912 book, *From Religion to Philosophy*, British philosopher F. M. Cornford advances a particularly well-articulated description of the continuity of Western cultural evolution. More recent social theorists like Wilber offer a considerably more updated view of this history, and Wilber certainly acknowledges the continuity between the biological and the cultural and the teleological nature of human experience. However, Wilber does not effectively account for the continuity through the earliest stages of Western cultural evolution. As a result, Wilber seems predisposed to look outside of Western culture for the solutions to our current problems. I suspect this is linked to Wilber's inattention to the ongoing role of *ritual*, *affect*, and *language* in cultural evolution.

To address this gap in modern thinking, I turn to the dated but crucial work of Cornford. He traces a clear line of development from the earliest rituals of our predecessors through the religious, and then philosophical, languages of Western culture. He introduces into Western cultural history a social science language that reflects on the function of affect, particularly its moral function, at different stages in the development of Western culture. The continuity between rituals, religious languages, and philosophical languages and the maturation of affect may be the most important – and least understood – criteria of the internal cultural domain.

Cornford describes how the rituals of our earliest ancestors give rise to religion, which turns into philosophy through a process of *linguistic development*. An understanding of the impact of the differentiating and integrating forces of language can only arise from an understanding of how cultural rituals formed the first human identities, and gave rise to efforts to control nature. Initially, Cornford describes how the basic human identity rests in the group. However, this group does not experience itself with much distinctness, being embedded in nature. Cornford's view of this basic relationship parallels Graves' first stage of development, which is governed by the survival needs of the group. Students of Graves, Don Beck and Christopher Cowan have made a useful addition to this model by color coding it. This first stage is colored "beige" (Beck and Cowan 1996: 197).

At this earliest level of cultural evolution, individuals are submerged within a group identity that makes no distinctions between "self" and "other," or between group and nature. The first thoroughly affect-laden distinctions are made not among individual identities (that development comes much later), but between the tribal identity and nature. According to

Cornford, the group's first experience of itself as a distinct identity arises from an awesome and fearful experience of nature, specifically the way nature limits the group. These limits are experienced emotionally, and give rise to a sense of boundary, which is the first rudimentary moral experience. In Classical culture this moral experience is known as "moria" (Cornford 1912: vii). The experience of moria comes through the group as it engages in "mimetic dances" or rites (Cornford 1912: 76). These rites support the group, marking a turn from a passive instinctive relationship to nature to an active conscious relationship, and the beginning of the "purple" stage described by Graves.

Mimetic rites are repeated behaviors taking place within the human group that create a *reflective surface* as "collective representations" of the relationship between the group and nature (Cornford 1912: 43). These representations consist of group emotion and the rudiments of a group imagination. As the emotions and imagination are harnessed by the ritual activities, the group is able to assert a broader sense of control over its relationship with nature in the form of new cultural activities that activate both the physiology of the affect systems and the imagination.

What previously was a fixed pattern of instinctive interaction (display behaviors) becomes more flexible, expressed through a widening range of affective experiences initiated through ritual.[2] At this stage of development the only *internal* experience is that of the group in relation to nature – an experience that is, at least in part, disturbing. According to Cornford, a primary function of these rites is to work with the felt disturbance between the group and nature by channeling affect, body, and imagination into enthusiastic and ecstatic states of group and nature unity, thus breaking down the nascent separation it experienced between itself and nature.[3] Through these states the group is able to influence, in increasingly effective ways, the behaviors of individual bodies – at first only during the ritual, but eventually over wider time and space relations.

Following Jung and the interesting writing of Julian Jaynes, rituals infuse individual bodies with the group's spirit or "daemon" (Jung 1928: 42; Jaynes 1976: 140). Here, an "internal space" emerges that is the rudiment of an individual identity. The formation of such an identity requires the gradual internalization of the ritual activities as a social role. Initially, the group's daemon controls the affect systems and imagination of each body in the group. Ritual focuses on emotion because the identity of the group is largely within the affect system (Jung 1927: 154). Simply put, through ritual practices, tribal groups learn to direct the attention of their members toward work activities that support the life of the group.

As the human group's experience is differentiated, it uses ritual to make increasingly more refined classifications between nature and the human group. For example, Cornford notes an early developmental shift when the human group is able to more fully distinguish itself from other species and thus move beyond "totemism" (Cornford 1912: 56). This shift leads to a break in the group's consciousness between an emerging cognitive capacity and its imaginal and affective capacities. As the cognitive capacity is differentiated from the group's imagination and emotion, it connects to the human senses and forms the rudiments of naturalism and rationalism; whereas, through their imaginal and affective experience, a subgroup forms to maintain and extend the identity-rupturing esoteric function of culture, which leads to the formation of new and renewed identities. Examples of such subgroups include magical societies and their histories, which are developed further as esoteric religious traditions.

These two distinct capacities emerging from the group's experience reflect a new level of functioning through which the rhythm of esoteric identity ruptures and exoteric identity consolidation allows for cultural renewal. The emergence of rationally directed sensory experience supports an increase in control over nature by the human group; interestingly enough, this also leads to greater control over the human group itself. However, ritual and then esoteric religious practices continue to enable groups to use the imagination and affect to break apart existing identity structures and reconnect the human group to nature. Through such rituals we are able to re-experience the unity at the beginning and at the core of our identity. Through affect and imagination we birth new images, identities, and institutions.

Cornford traces the trajectory of the *cognitive and sensory capacities* up through the religions of Western culture, noting how it leads to the development of distinct human identities, whereupon individuals learn to manage their own affective experience. This differentiation of individual identity marks the beginning of a new level of internal experience, which Beck and Cowan describe, and the shift from the "purple" submergence of individuality to the "red" assertion of an impulsive individuality (Beck and Cowan 2006: 215).

The emergence of an internal experience of individuality goes through successive stages. Initially, mimetic rites activate imagination and affect in such a way that the group "personifies" the elemental forces of nature as "gods." Jung addresses the fusion of affect and imagination and the resulting personification as the gods when he writes:

> It is not the storms, not thunder and lightning, not rain and cloud that remain as images in the psyche, but the fantasies caused by the affects they arouse . . . these affects anthropomorphize the passion of nature, and the purely physical element becomes an angry god.
>
> (Jung 1927: 154–5)

Through ritual, members of the group come to identify with different realms of nature giving rise to totemism. As these personifications deepen, they evoke a rudimentary experience of "I" in which particular cultural leaders begin to be identified with the "daemon" of the ritual (Cornford 1912: 101). Through ritual, what Omer refers to as "imaginal structures" take on increasingly human form until they give rise to specific images of the "hero" and the "chief" (Cornford 1912: 104–7). In time, the personifications activated in ritual become social roles that individuals embody both during and in between rituals.

The stories of the Greek gods reflect the growing impulsive and interior experience of the individual. Over time, these stories take on an increasingly differentiated shape as the gods have to work out the complex identities and relationships that simultaneously are being differentiated by the human group. In these stories we hear accounts of the newly emerging individual identities. In time, the Greek tragedies become complex psychological and political representations of the individual and the group sorting out their affective and moral experience. Through these stories, the individual internalized the original tension of union and separateness that the group first enacted in its relationship with nature. As the culture evolves, the stories reflect an increasing level of individual identity. At first, the Greek gods have every human problem, and then begin to become more abstracted as their function transforms. Next, the gods retreat from the waters, forests, and cities to Mount Olympus, and later the mountain itself detaches from the earth.

These differentiations mark the change from language as story to language as religion. As the individual internalizes the ritual structure as a rudimentary ego structure, serving the same imagination- and affect-containing function as the ritual, ritual behaviors are replaced with religious doctrine. Here, the behavior-managing function of ritual gives over to doctrine which can manage affect and imagination with their newly differentiated identity without as much emphasis on the repeated behaviors of ritual and story (Cornford 1912: 118–19).

The stories of the gods themselves mark their own demise: "unfed by human emotion, and shedding his own inherent life, the Olympian god is doomed to perish of inanition" (Cornford 1912: 118). However, before the gods leave Apollo offers a brief summary of the history of their purpose. He identifies the way in which the stories of the gods led people to self-knowledge, particularly knowledge about "moria," that is, knowledge about knowing where our limits are. Cornford cites Apollo saying: "Know thyself and do not go too far" (Cornford 1912: 119).

As individuality becomes more differentiated, so the need for renewal intensifies. Renewal is pursued and maintained through the individual and group's imaginal and affective capacities. Through traditions stemming back to the mystery religions of Dionysus, affect and imagination have been kept alive as the tools of esoteric rupture and renewal. Through ritual, the tribes of Western culture achieved increasingly higher levels of cultural evolution. First, ritual has been used to hone the group's affective and imaginal experience in ways that begin to assert conscious control over its relationship with nature. This gives rise to the cognitive distinction-making, which supports the further differentiation of distinct human identities with their own internal experience of self-consciousness. In turn, affect and imagination continue to be harnessed to break through the increasingly complex individual and cultural identities, thus creating intense experiences of unity which renew the individual and human group.

Here, Cornford's identification of the renewing function of ritual connects to Chapter 6, where I discuss the role of the individual in bringing new images to culture. Cornford notes how new ideas come into culture through the consciousness of sensitive individuals or "mystics," who find a way of breaking with the cultural views of their time to bring new ideas and ways of being to culture. He writes: "All mystics have fled from the world to find their own souls, as Jesus went into the wilderness, and Buddha into the jungle" (Cornford 1912: 193). He cites several examples in which the mystery traditions, from the cults of Dionysus, to the Orphic traditions, to Pythagorean schools, continually challenged the rationalism of their time. He draws special attention to Heraclitus, who saw human language as the vehicle through which an individual could find their own sense of meaning and break free of the prejudicial rational thinking of their time, thus renewing the "common wisdom" (Cornford 1912: 192).

Religious liberalism: controlling affect and identity through fear, guilt, and meaning

With increased development interactions between individual and cultural identity, the affect system, imagination, human will, and language become more complex.

The function of emotion

As the emerging individual begins to differentiate from the group, impulsivity becomes an object of awareness inviting reflection. This reflection creates an internal awareness of the results of impulsivity, which evokes guilt and an increased interior experience of self-consciousness. At the level of culture, religious language is beginning to foster guilt, one of the affects in the shame family (Nathanson 1992: 144–5). Guilt functions as an increasing tool of social control. It becomes institutionalized as religious experience becomes codified and religious vocations and institutions emerge at higher levels of political development. This awareness leads to the "blue" level in Graves' scheme, and what I call "religious liberalism" (Beck and Cowan 2006: 229).

Emotion now connects minimally differentiated people (primarily lived as narrow social roles) to each other, to moral conduct, and to their community's chosen god. Emotion is the glue that connects people to moral restraint through the imposition of fear and guilt-evoking external authorities. While there is still little individual identity, emotion directs attention through religious doctrine. These controls are expressed through the distinct shapes of family and social roles. Guilt and fear keep attention focused on these roles, and deviation reflects negatively on subgroups, so that families are pressured to impose the social order on their members. Without more individual identity, emotion remains passively experienced, that is, it happens to you as an external superego-cultural force. The full potential of affect as a tool for self-development is only realized by a few leaders, artists, and religious mystics.

Differentiation of affect and imagination

Stated too simply, at this level of religious development the task is to contain the impulsive emotionality of the rudimentary individuality to create social structures that can broaden out the new experience of individuality, but within the confines of significantly more social control. This takes place as the mythic images evoked in the group by the individual become codified in religious practices that repress emotional impulsivity into a new religious order. The creation of this order requires that affect and imagination become more differentiated in relation to one another. As they have become teased apart from the imagination, the intensities of anger, fear, and other affects begin to be more regulated, as the group contains the emotional experience of the individual by managing what images the emotions evoke.

Because a fuller individual was just beginning to be formed out of raw emotionality and rudimentary individuality, people simply were not valued as sources of knowledge. While knowledge did come through individuals, it was thought that they were embodying a revelation from God or some other divine force. Given the rudimentary, undifferentiated nature of thought, when an individual did experience insight, it carried a numinosity that implied divine origin. There was little or no recognition of the role of the sensitive individual in bringing into the culture the unconscious potentialities of the group. Instead of a recognition of the function of the individual to manifest the group's unconscious wisdom and creativity, this energy was still held as "supernatural," and the intensity of revelation that lived through minimally differentiated affect systems did not help to identify this relationship. Besides, original thinking came through so few individuals that there was little consideration for individual origins of knowledge.

The expectation of certainty and its origin in original oppression

As individuals became more differentiated, they slowly became recognized as sources of cultural knowledge. However, at this religious level of development the individual rises up in the shadow of the mythic order. Leaders use religious language to direct cultural attention (unconscious generational attention?) through a paternalistic external authority. At this level, something can be said to be "true" only to the extent that it is beyond doubt. Without such certainty, doubt would arise, and doubt was too rattling. It may be hard for us moderns to imagine just how big a problem doubt posed. In the last few hundred years we have come to have so much faith in our individual experience that we can tolerate doubt. Yet, prior to the sixteenth century, few had consolidated a trustworthy individual identity, and doubt had a chilling effect. I suspect it evoked an intolerable fear, otherwise there would likely have been less pressure on knowledge claims to be certain.

Doubt brought individuals out of the collective power of the religious trance. It brought them down into the individual body with its individual fears. At this stage, the power of the group resided in the ability of language (as consolidations of ritual in symbol) to draw people together and give them a sense of group purpose. Doubt would break the trance. Tracing the way we came to control our fears offers us a better grasp on the intolerability of doubt, which will help us understand just how deep the mistrust of the individual goes. It cascades forward through religious, political, and into psychological stages of development. In fact, a general mistrust of the individual permeates our language and institutions to this day. Once identified, this mistrust can become an object of reflection, and a new direction for freedom can be found in a language that enables us to find our faith in the future.

The political developments of esoteric and exoteric Christianity

Through revelation, the numinosity of the unconscious comes through individuals who express it in religious languages, which break through the public languages of their time to allow cultural learning through new practices. These practices bring new levels of cultural evolution to a widening range of peoples through distinct patterns of political development. Specifically, these practices help form new individual identities, which are themselves functions of the relationship between individual affect systems and group will. Learning practices, as ritual, and new religious experience bring the affect systems of individuals together where a new esoteric group will is forged out of an interaction between necessity (nature) and destiny (potential).

As the affect systems of individuals differentiate, individual identity forms and the group's rudimentary experience of time begins to expand. Originally, the future is simply an experience of the raw affect of the natural world, which is not thought to be controllable. Up through Classical culture there is little sense of agency in relation to the natural world. Instead, thought is used to understand and accept the religious order of that world. While such acceptance has value, later religious developments began to offer the hope that the individual could have some impact on the world, have some choice.

One of my favorite descriptions of this birth of agency is in George Steiner's 1976 book *After Babel*, where he reflects on some subtle mutations of language occurring at the level of religious development, which catalyze a rudimentary experience of the individual as someone who could influence the future. In the following citation, notice how revelation uses language to shape affect and to change a people's relationship to future – not to "the future" but to future or what could be referred to as futurity. Steiner writes:

> [The Hebrew prophet's] uses of the future of the verb are tautological. The future is entirely present to him in the literal presentness of his speech-act. But at the same moment, and this is decisive, his enunciation of the future makes that future alterable . . . In ancient Judaism man's freedom is inherent in a complex logical-grammatical category of reversibility. The prophecy is authentic: what is foretold *must* be. But it *need* not be, for God is at liberty to non-corroborate His declared truths.
>
> (Steiner 1976: 146, 148)

In his book *The Fate of America*, Los Angeles Jungian Michael Gellert associates the emergence of a "personal god" with the Hebrew religion (Gellert 2001: 13). Here we connect the differentiated experience of such a god with the new experience of being "personal," which the prophet experiences and expresses in the mythic language of his time. This expression of personalness is first personified in the character of a god, but for the unconscious purpose of showing personalness as a new image of possibility to which we could all aspire. Notice the humanizing effect this has on the affect system, as fear of condemnation is replaced by the possibility of redemption. Here, shame and the experience of time are differentiated simultaneously, creating images of freedom.

Following my own understanding of political development, we trace this changeability of time ahead into Christianity, and begin to see in religious development the power to create "images" of a better world. Jesus extends the Judean assertion of individual agency into mythic images that calmed superstitious fears and gave people a new direction for their imagination to go, bringing emotional relief. Steiner identifies this in terms of a mutation of the time sense brought about by Jesus's revelations and carried into Western culture through the political development of esoteric Christianity. He writes: "We cannot recapture what may have been rapid or profound mutations in time-sense, in the grammars of temporal statements among the first Christians and initiates in the mystery religions" (Steiner 1976: 151).

This citation deepens Cornford's understanding of the function of esoteric religions as it connects affect, language, and the capacity of the imagination to engage futurity. We can also see more clearly the inspiration offered by Jesus's teachings. His images of futurity activated people's affect systems in new ways that greatly reduced the extent to which they were dominated by fear. The newly evoked joy, surprise, and excitement revealed new affective potentials of the human being within their individual capacity for agency – which, itself, would lead to the later capacity for destiny. While not discussed in the affect literature that I have read, it seems that Jesus's impact on the affect system evoked a greater capacity to love. What is the relationship between affect maturation and love?

At the core of these developments was the influence Jesus had on the people around him. Through his own affective presence he communicated the love and joy possible for human beings, even amidst intense suffering. In functioning as a cultural leader he initiated learning practices that likely activated the foundational capacities which are the telos to the affect system, such as: grief transmuting to compassion/grace, shame to humility/redemption; anger to fierceness/devotion; fear to courage/faith (A. Omer, personal communication, Spring 1999).

Through his own embodiment and use of learning practices, Jesus stepped his initiates through the first, second, third, and perhaps fourth stages of political development. However, as we can imagine, the institutionalization of his vision could not be accomplished through any practice that relied on his continued presence. The appropriate translations of Jesus's esoteric images and learning practices did not find a full expression in the exoteric institutional structure of the Church that emerged over the centuries since Jesus's death. Nevertheless, both his esoteric work and his growing exoteric influence on Western culture, expressed through a growing public language, supported a transformation of human consciousness that helped control and direct affect and shape personal and cultural identity. As this language became institutionalized, it reached more people and deepened its impact through the Middle Ages and to this day.

Through the political development of Christianity, Jesus's vision not only supported a rudimentary affect freedom as it helped people with fear, but it also inspired people to have a budding sense of their own value and agency as individuals, evoking hope for the future for themselves and their culture. Yet, much of this "humanistic" Christianity remained esoteric or nascent. The primary thrust of its exoteric institutional form was driven by the religious assertion of control over personal and cultural identity, and its language shaped the affect systems of the people accordingly. Through its increasingly powerful institutions, emotional impulsivity could be controlled by force. Through its images of the after-life and threats of eternal damnation, exoteric Christianity directed people's fear toward new levels of social cooperation. Additionally, social control was asserted by the public language of Christianity as it activated the latent potential of necessary shame, associated with the Christian's guilt, to guide right action.

Alas, the task of human development in the many centuries between the life and death of Jesus and the beginning of modernity was daunting. While the life-affirming dimensions of Jesus's teachings offered direction for affect and imagination, the institutionalization of those positive qualities was not wholly possible. Instead of the institutional forms we can now imagine through the humanistic values of psychological liberalism, the paternalistic institutions of the time established themselves through persuasion, force, and domination – all characteristics of control through external authority.

In addition to physical force, the manipulation of guilt and fear supported the formation of social roles that could easily be controlled through the Church's public language. However, part of the evolutionary power of the Christian mythic order was its recognition of the intrinsic dignity and value of the individual, as directly experienced in the esoteric rituals of the Christian initiates. This power did make its way into the exoteric language of Christianity through its doctrine of the immortality of the individual soul.

Unfortunately, the restrictive force used by the Church allowed little room for individuals to express this new dignity. This led to an internal contradiction that was expressed through a re-emergence of individuality. This time, however, instead of impulsivity came the directed attention realized at the level of political liberalism (associated with Graves' "orange" level; Beck and Cowan 2006: 244). At the level of political liberalism, the religious deprecation of the individual had to be addressed, which led to a significant compromise between the two developmental stages of religious liberalism and political liberalism. Within this compromise, the cultural language of the political liberal maintained the religious restrictions on the individual as a source of cultural knowledge.

The religious-political compromise: mutual distrust in the individual as a source of cultural knowledge

The Christian doctrines and practices steadied the affect system by separating it from the imagination. The imagination was directed away from all of its fearful superstitiousness and redirected toward the peaceful images of an after-life. As a result, the physical world was freed from an unbounded imagination that had "animated" it with a range of mythic, supernatural, fairy-tale-like beings that had been fusions of undifferentiated affect and imagination, generated by a culture's own group energies. While some view this as a tragic disenchantment of the world, there is reason to believe, given the resources of the time, that it was a developmental necessity.

Imagine the emotional struggle that people experienced as their thinking became more differentiated, paralleling the child's transformation from Piaget's stages of "preoperational" to "concrete operational" thinking (Piaget 1962: 218–21). As the imagination gave way to thinking, thinking itself was still imbued with a supra-individual level of group energy, as imagination, but was not recognized as such. Rather, it was believed that thought was a process analogous to perception through which an individual passively "perceived" externally existing or metaphysical "forms," such as Plato's forms. The experience of these "externally" existing forms must have carried much the same emotional charge as the personified images of gods. The intensity first connected to the gods transfers to the abstractions of thought. Once gods walked the earth; now thinking can discover "certain" foundations of that world. Both gods and timeless truths carry the numinosity of the group energy.

Because thinking was considered passive, and because individual experience was only gradually becoming known as trustworthy, thought could only be relied on to the extent that the individual did not interfere with the way the "perceptiveness" of thought came into the world. For an individual's experience to become a trusted source of cultural knowledge, it had to lay claim to being as valid a source of truth as the accepted, emotionally laden supernatural and metaphysical forms. Given the way in which religious doctrine helped to control fear, any shadow of doubt in the knowledge created by individuals undercut claims to validity, for doubt was equivalent to untruth. Accordingly, it became the task for several generations of philosophers and cultural leaders (at least until Kant's epistemological turn) to identify a way in which individual experience could be asserted as certain, beyond doubt.

At the level of political liberalism, the passivity of the individual in relation to the creation of knowledge continued, though significantly more differentiated. In the compromise between religious liberalism and political liberalism, individuals became known as a source of knowledge, but only to the extent that they held still, that is, accepted the limiting stance of only using thinking and sensing to apprehend passively a pre-existing world. This has since been referred to as the spectator theory of knowledge.

Political liberalism: rebelling against affect to find individual freedom

With the advent of political liberalism, individual identities begin to form in earnest, independent of family or social role. In Western culture this development was supported by the Christian belief that individuals have immortal souls, and the growing faith that they could become centers of creative action. Whether traced to the Renaissance, the Reformation, the Enlightenment, or the Industrial Revolution, over the last five to seven hundred years individuals have emerged full force as sources of unique creative experience.

However, the development of political liberalism led to a bifurcation of thinking and feeling that is not intrinsic to our nature – an overlooked source of some of the severe problems of modernity. While the public function of thinking and sensing had previously been separated from the esoteric function of affect and imagination, they still operate – however conflictually – within the same cultural system. At the level of political liberalism, the separation becomes significantly more calcified. In Eastern traditions, thinking and feeling do not suffer the same bifurcation (Goleman 2003: 134). In Western culture, the two are separated in order to create an autonomous individual. This compromise between religious and political development releases a fractured and alienated individual into the world as an independent agent – with fantastic and horrible results.

Thought and sensing became dominant social functions, supporting the development of the sciences during the Enlightenment, and raising the individual up as an independent source of cultural knowledge, but only as long as emotion was set aside. At this point, society begins to privilege thought and sensing even more, by associating emotion with delusion, bias, or problematic subjectivity. Even as we were still learning how to work with our emotions, the deprecation of emotion by the political individual made trusting them more difficult. This attack on our emotionality was politically motivated and may have been necessary, if we assume that individual agency needed to be released into the world at that time. The deprecation of emotion also supported the individual to break the authoritative religious feudal bonds that used the emotions to maintain oppressive social roles.

Graves recognized that developmental stages oscillated between consolidation of the group and individuals pulling out of the pack. My own understanding of political development describes the movement from revelatory image to identity to institution where the political individual's distrust of emotion can be interpreted as rebellion against religion's external control over the individual emotionality of the earlier stage. While emotion is indulged to found a new separate identity, exoteric religion oppressively controls the emotions of the new identity, and, in turn, the political individual abandons emotion in order to break free of that control.

The deprecation of emotion in cultural evolution is analogous to an adolescent's emotional distancing from the family as she finds her own way in the world. However, this break lingers to this day in our culture, as the political individual influences scientific theories about emotion and thinking. Emotion continues to be imagined as distorting, and thinking continues to be privilege – even though it has become impotent, cut off from its birthright connection to feeling as a source of assessment, motivation, and connection. Remember the image in Chapter 1 of John Kerry as a disembodied intellectual.

In the exoteric religion of the times, emotion had harnessed individuality by tying it to indentured servitude. For the political individual, thinking identifies the principle of freedom within the idea of autonomy, replacing the use of emotion to oppress. However, the price was steep, as the newly autonomous individuals lost touch with the capacity to make connections, which accounts (in part) for the last several centuries of community collapse, growing social alienation, and the epidemic of existential crises and pathologies of the individual that burst on to the scene in the mid- to late nineteenth century. This loss of community sets the stage for a return to community through a new egalitarian ethic. However, a fuller understanding of the complexities of the religious-political compromise will set the stage for the opportunities and limitations of our times.

The political individual's compromise: the quest for certainty and the mistrust of the individual

The struggle between the paternalistic Church and the rising tide of individuality led to a culture that values sensory experience over the human imagination as a source of data about the world, and thinking over feeling as a reliable integrator of that data. Where once the imagination was trapped in Christian images that had become hidebound idols, and emotion was wedded to oppressive cultural control expressed in feudal bonds, a new image of the individual and a new public language were needed to follow the developmental line of human freedom.

Political liberalism enabled individuals to come to be trusted as sources of valid cultural knowledge; and sensing and thinking opened the natural world for our exploration and manipulation. The new power asserted by the individual eased a wide range of the "original oppression" of culture represented by the Catholic Church. A further differentiation of sensing and thinking challenged oppressive cultural attitudes. At first, individual experience was supported by the freedom of the Renaissance and then by the religious liberalism of the Reformation, culminating in both the creativity of the Renaissance and the religious freedom of the Reformation. Martin Luther's assertion that individuals could determine their own religious experience through a direct encounter with divinity thrust individuals into the light of day as new centers of dignity requiring the recognition of cultural institutions. However, Luther also recognized the extreme limitations of the people of his day.

Luther saw how Christian doctrine bred idolatry which was used to manipulate superstitious fears. He doubted people's ability to rise above their fears and challenge the oppression of the Church. He doubted that the individual really could have any significant impact on culture. Unfortunately, this attitude also became inculcated into Protestantism, as he expressed doubt about whether individual acts of will could influence fate (Erikson 1958: 215). Given the undifferentiated state and emotional impulsivity of individuals, it would take quite a while to achieve our full potential as creators of culture.

Descartes learns how to bear doubt

At the beginning of the seventeenth century, René Descartes extended and reshaped Martin Luther's faith in the individual. Where Luther asserted that individuals need not find their religiosity through religious institutions, Descartes similarly asserted that people need not find truths about the world only through sacred texts, as the Scholastics had asserted. Individuals, Descartes claimed, could discern knowledge about the world through their own thinking. By developing his thinking capacity, Descartes activated his capacity for what I will call "reasoning freedom." This founded a new level of individual development characterized by Descartes' ability to sustain extended periods of time during which he turned his thinking, like a blade, on all assumptions of his time, including the very possibility of his own existence. This acute doubting represents a profound courage used by Descartes to clear new ground within himself, and can be represented by turning the phrase typically associated with him, "I think, therefore I am," into the phrase "I doubt, therefore I am." This is expressed by Descartes when he writes: "Am I not that very being who doubts of almost everything" (Beardsley 1960: 36). Descartes imagined that, since God was beyond doubt, his own doubting would reflect his own original thinking. From this "image" of God allowing him to doubt, Descartes sets himself free from the belief that no new thinking could come from the individual. Remembering that to doubt still carried a collective taboo, and was fraught with fearful experience, Descartes' ability to bear doubt and to pivot his thinking on the experience of doubt is itself an act of courage. Descartes established a new relationship with God. God allows the individual to doubt, and by doubting, individuals could become more of their own people and bring creative insight to culture.

Through a conversation with San Francisco Jungian John Beebe, I was able to deepen my own understanding of Descartes, linking thinking to freedom, which Beebe expressed as "I think, therefore I'm free" (John Beebe, personal communication, Spring 2007). However, following the valuing of doubt, Descarte' statement may best be spoken as, "I doubt, therefore I'm free." His freedom is to assert the connection between human fallibility and the ability to create culturally valid knowledge. Centuries after Descartes, Bentley and Dewey make this claim explicit when they write:

> We recognize that as observers we are human organisms, limited to the positions on the globe from which we make our observations, and we

accept this not as being a hindrance, but instead as a situation from which great gain may be secured.

(Bentley and Dewey 1960: 80)

While not overtly psychological, Descartes' claim required the immediate use of his own experience and, as a result, turned greater attention to the potential role of the individual in creating knowledge, and thus culture. Following Jung's understanding of how a communicable language emerges from the collective unconscious of a people, Descartes gave voice to the unconscious forces of his time and shaped his culture.

Descartes sought personal freedom through an application of Henderson's "religious attitude" (Henderson 1984: 27). Descartes' *Meditations* focused attention on the previous limits placed on individual thinking and, through a religious image of God recognizing his efforts, he saw a way for human thought to be considered objective, a reliable source of cultural knowledge. Descartes used his capacity for the religious attitude to focus on his own experience of thinking, which activated a new personal connection to the unconscious. Reflecting on God's perfection Descartes was able to image some portion of it transferring to him. He wrote:

Perhaps I am something more than I am supposing myself to be; perhaps all those perfections which I am attributing to God are in some fashion potentially in me, although they do not yet show themselves or issue in action. Indeed I am already aware that my knowledge increases, perfecting itself little by little.

(Beardsley 1960: 49)

Through these words we can see some of Descartes' process. He is clearly looking for a way of speaking that accounts for his own growing sense of agency. As he focuses on both God's perfection and his own growing perfected knowledge, we see the standard that the language of his time requires of him. We also see the emergence of a rudimentary internal space. While planted in the soil of rational process, which has come to mean anything but internal process, Descartes' thinking actually births an active psychological consciousness. Through his efforts, and those of others, the capacity for reasoning freedom emerges and becomes a focal point upon which individual, cultural, and archetypal energy could reciprocally focus their attention.

Descartes' philosophy supported the differentiation of reasoning freedom and gave rise to a new faith in thinking. This radicalized Western culture as the new rationalism supported a broad liberalization of culture. This instigation of reasoning freedom encouraged the activation of liberal experimentation, conversation, political organizing, and the emergence of new institutional forms. Because we have adapted to it, and even see its limitations, it may be hard to grasp the full impact that the new rationalism had on culture. In conjunction with British Empiricism, the two would lead to new human freedoms expressed in the cultural and scientific Enlightenment.

British empiricism and the broader movement of rationalism

The British empiricists extended Descartes' differentiation of reasoning freedom by focusing cultural attention on the experience of sensation. As a result, the human capacity to sense, what I will call "sensory freedom," also began to be viewed as a source of cultural knowledge. Thought and sensation emerged at this time in history as capacities that the culture drew out of the individual for the development of both. While previously differentiated to some extent in Classical culture, these new capacities became the workhorses of the emerging modern world. Prior to the growth of empiricism, the human senses had largely been considered suspect, only capable of identifying negligible "appearances" about an impermanent and untrustworthy natural world and not thought to be sources of knowledge.

The differentiation of both the person's rational and sensory capacities strengthened the emerging psychological consciousness and became part of the foundation for the cultural revolutions that gave rise to the new democratic social movements.

Francis Yockey links the philosophy of rationalism to the Western Enlightenment and its differentiation of both reason and empirical observation/experimentation. Through an appeal to rational means, human problems were approached as questions of science, answerable through an examination of their causal antecedents. Reason was viewed as the highest stage of human development, surpassing previous religious approaches to knowing and human relations (Polkinghorne 1983: 17). Through these capacities we learned to direct our problem-solving abilities toward the "external" material world. "This adaptation of reason to material problems causes all problems whatever to become mechanical . . . Rationalism regarded all spiritual values as its objects and proceeded to revalue them from the standpoint of 'reason'" (Yockey and Ulick 1962: 208–23).

Rationalism put ultimate trust in knowledge derived from rational and empirical means, usurping the previous use of customs and social roles. Further, given that emotion was the glue of customs and social roles, they were relegated to the "private" sphere of women and branded problematically "subjective." Rationalism also replaced trust in religious faith as a source of meaning, renewal, and solace in the face of the harsh realities of life in traditional human cultures. Anything not visible to immediate experience, anything mysterious or partially hidden, became suspect: "no more spirit, no more soul, no more God, no more Church and State. The two poles of thought are 'the individual' and 'humanity'. Anything separating them is 'irrational'" (Yockey and Ulick 1962: 208–23).

The disenchantment or demystification of religious doctrines brought about by rationalism was not a dispassionate effort to do away with superstition. Rather it reflected a radical impulse to free people from the intellectual and sociopolitical subjugation of the original oppression of culture. Christian theologian Paul Tillich offers a description of this early experience of reason:

> We must understand what this reason was. It was not [just] a calculating reason, which decides whether to do this or that, depending on which is more advantageous. Rather, it was a full, passionate, revolutionary emphasis on man's essential goodness in the name of the principle of justice.
>
> (Wilber 1995: 381)

The "revolutionary emphasis" combined reasoning and sensory freedom to found a new level of cultural awareness about the individual's capacity. As I have already discussed, social philosophers like John Locke used the new positive attitude toward the individual to begin shaping the idea of the political individual. However, this individual was defined using some understanding of psychology. Locke asserted that "psychological laws, based on human nature, are as truly natural as are any laws based on land and physical nature" (Dewey 1929b: 10). Using such psychological arguments Locke set out to revolutionize Western culture.

In effect, Locke politicizes the emerging psychological consciousness by asserting that people are more than their social roles, that they are autonomous political individuals, and have their own distinct experiences that are to be recognized in law. Yet, it can also be said that he psychologized this political individual, giving them power through a definition that went beyond social relations. About Locke and other early eighteenth-century liberals Dewey writes: "Their psychology was not in fact the product of impartial inquiry into human nature. It was rather a political weapon devised in the interest of breaking down the rigidity of dogmas and institutions that had lost their relevancy" (Dewey 1929b: 42). Locke's idea of the political individual is rooted in psychology both as a theory of knowledge and a theory of child development.

John Locke's politicization of the theory of child development

In Western culture, developmental thinking can be traced to the sociopolitical thought of the late 1600s. At this time social, political, and educational institutions were going through rapid changes. Almost all areas of life were subject to being politicized as the Enlightenment and beginnings of the Industrial Revolution created opportunities to challenge traditional cultural ideas and social roles – including the politicization of childhood.

The emergence of a merchant class and the need for increased numbers of workers in the cities led to the articulation of the idea of the political individual. John Locke presented an individual who existed independent of past relationships and social obligations (Dewey 1929b: 9–10). Like Gandhi, Locke sought to encourage people to become the change that was needed by the times. However, he did not simply think of what his political cause needed and then concoct a vision of an independent person. Rather, he sought to uncover the autonomous nature of being human. Locke's vision of the political individual did not articulate a new, underlying truth, rather it reflected/anticipated a necessary individualistic stage of development and evolution.

Locke's vision of independence did not apply only to adults, but extended to children as well. This extension may be political liberalism's first effort to create a psychological liberalism, materialized in Locke's articulation of a theory of child development. In Locke's time, children were considered simply smaller versions of adults. This belief, called "preformationism," may be the result of adults not investing too much attention in children due to high child mortality, or it may simply be adult egocentrism (Crane 1980: 5). Regardless, beginning in the late seventeenth and early eighteenth centuries, a new account of childhood development began to emerge. As part of that account, Locke argued that children come into the world as blank slates, "tabula rasa," and that they learn through the accumulation of experiences, linked together as associations (Crane 1980: 6). While Locke's rudimentary psychology did influence later psychological theorizing, it also supported his political agenda. By influencing how parents thought about children, Locke helped spawn a new generation of more independent children. Here, Locke's political liberalism is based on his "image" of the independent political individual, which found its way into the public's imagination and language.

In effect, Locke asserted a political agenda by inviting parents to raise children to become the change he wished to see in the world. Locke loosened family ties, which helped provide the next generations of workers – comparatively free from family and social ties. By supporting an image of the child as increasingly independent, Locke passed to parents the political goal of greater social independence, which gave rise to a new vision of individualism. Locke helped the parents of his time raise children who could become active determiners of cultural knowledge as they asserted their political rights and challenged traditional social institutions.

From the perspective of Wilber's four quadrants, Locke's psychology of the child begins in his political philosophy, which draws on the imagery of independence from social constraint, a lower-right quadrant image associated with freedom to choose where one lives and what sort of work one will engage in – that is, physical and social freedom. While articulated as a psychology of childhood, an upper-left perspective, the theories of child development of Locke and subsequent thinkers, even as recently as Sigmund Freud, did not include much direct attention to children.[4]

Locke's epistemology: a turn toward psychology

In addition to his theory of child development, Locke also developed a psychology of how we come to know the world. In effect he asked: Through what dimensions of our experience can we have a trustworthy experience about the external world? With this question, Locke built an epistemology (the study of how we know) based in the psychology of the person. According to Locke, we come to have knowledge through our sensory experience, from which our rational capacity builds associations into knowledge of the world. Interestingly, and unfortunately, his epistemology leaves out our emotional experience as a source of trustworthy experience.

Looking ahead to the understanding of emotions that emerges more recently (as we have seen through the work of Darwin, Tomkins, and Omer), emotions are not problematically subjective in the way Locke suspected or asserted. Despite human beings' mixed relationship to emotion, Locke was simply wrong about this. Nevertheless, his use of reasoning freedom and his articulation of sensory freedom, his deprecation of emotion, and his assertion of the independence of children all fueled his political goal of breaking individuals free from the social bonds that kept them locked into religious dogmatism. It would not be until at least a century later that emotion began to re-emerge, in a new understanding, as a source of personal and cultural knowledge within a public language. Nevertheless, Locke's political philosophy has come to be associated with the birth of the modern world and the rise of a political liberalism based in a rational view of the world that became the new Enlightenment.

Summary: liberalism and enlightenment

The philosophies of the Enlightenment asserted that the individual could be considered an independent source of knowledge (rationalism), that individual sensory experience could be trusted to discover truths about a manipulatable natural world (empiricism), and that individuals came into the world not locked into preordained social roles but with a blank slate, that they had "natural rights" to freely engage in "social contracts" (political liberalism). The emergence of new commercial centers provided opportunities for the individual to advance their social position (Dewey 1929b: 4). By defining the individual in these terms, an age of Enlightenment set itself against the original oppression of the individual and prepared the world for a new level of cultural evolution.

Notice the way the Enlightenment language of political liberalism established a "psychological" language as the foundation of this new level of political development. Locke founded political freedom in a psychological image. Locke's psychology was developed to generate an image of an emancipated individual; we were freed by a psychological "definition" or "description" of the individual. Over the course of subsequent generations, this "image" of the emancipated individual becomes institutionalized.

Locke's psychological description may represent the first political psychology or one possible beginning point for psychological liberalism. Regardless, the public language of political liberalism replaced previous doctrines that had little or no recognition of the value of the individual. However, the definition of Locke's new political individual was constrained by the imagination of the early liberals and their limited understanding of freedom. For these liberals, freedom was primarily a political concept and not so much psychological. Accordingly, their approach to freedom did not fully account for a simultaneous and necessary process of psychological development through which the person, as distinct from a political individual, had distinct responsibilities for directing their own experience reflexively, for the sake of developing as a human being.

Chapter 10

The advent of psychological liberalism

Introduction

Religious liberalism maintained control by denying the individual's capacity to create cultural knowledge. Yet, its images of an immortal individual soul created a tension that led to a rupture of emergent individuality. Even as the new political individual railed against external authority and made its way in a new world opened up by will, senses, and rationality, it could not fully come to trust itself. At the heart of freedom lay self-doubt. While Locke had enabled the individual to break free from cultural oppression, emotions had become suspect, and the new political individual lacked a trustworthy internal experience. However, despite his alienation from himself, the political individual found a route to a new stability, a balance between internal and external forces.

In the transition from traditionally determined social roles to autonomous individuality, clear roles have been replaced primarily by the new ideal of the political individual. Although this individual is largely externally focused and has no specific interiority, some inchoate internal experience begins to emerge in cultural leaders and others over the course of the eighteenth and nineteenth centuries.

This chapter builds a lower-left quadrant cultural language of this new interiority, and shows our difficulty integrating it into a public language, much less into public institutions. This task is made more difficult by the continued dominance of the lower-right quadrant language of political liberalism. The continued emphasis on social progress actually hinders the further development of liberalism, chronically turning away from interiority in favor of presenting change as a matter of external and structural changes.

Although political liberalism's vision of change is crucial to our future, you cannot get there from here by rational means alone. The political individual must accept their obligation to understand their own process of development. The political individual must take into consideration – turn toward – the need for a new "psychological person." The transition from the political individual to the psychological person parallels the transformation from the "orange" level to the "green" level in Clare Graves' model of cultural evolution. To explore this comparison, I will describe the functioning of what I call "psychological liberalism" and how emotion – particularly shame – functions in this form of liberalism. I will turn attention toward the transition from the political individual to the psychological person as a way of talking developmentally about recent processes of cultural evolution. Here, the linkage between Graves' model and my own is experimental.

Psychological liberalism: the return of emotion to shape group moral experience

A private-psychological liberalism emerges first in those cultural leaders capable of receiving its images. They articulated it through conversation with each other; embodied that stage of development; and tried to find a public language through which it could enter into the public's imagination. Through an exploration of the emergence of psychological liberalism, the continuity of the evolution of Western culture becomes more apparent. This continuity helps us to imagine a trajectory for resolving the current crisis of liberalism. In subsequent chapters, I follow this trajectory in relation to the current progressive political agenda and movement.

In Chapter 5, I described Graves' model of human development, which cycles between individual and collective stages through processes of differentiation and then integration. At the level of the psychological liberalism, the differentiation/independence of the political individual is integrated/sublimated within a new collectivity. However, unlike the impulsive individual chafing against the control asserted over it at the level of religious liberalism, the psychological person does not wrestle as intensely with containing emotional impulsivity. As long as there is a healthy religiosity providing an integrative meaning for raw emotion, impulsivity is contained. As a result, psychological liberalism does not use oppressive force to contain the fractures of the previous individual phase; it addresses only the political individual, the most recent individual phase.

Because of the broader and deeper ego strength of the political individual, psychological liberalism's task is to sublimate, not repress. In this case, what is sublimated is the shortsightedness and self-centeredness of the political individual, within new internal values of diversity and equality, not in domination or oppression. Psychological liberalism focuses attention on the importance of the collective, but not in supplication to an external authority.

Through the language of a private-psychological liberalism, emotions begin to come back to the fore, beginning, for one, with Charles Darwin's exploration of the biological and psychosocial function of affect. However, unlike his theory of natural selection, Darwin's interest in emotion did not significantly influence a public language; rather, it was a dormant seed we've more recently watered. It would not be until the appearance of psychoanalysis and the institution of psychotherapy that emotion re-entered the culture as part of a maturing public language and institutional form – and those developments did not influence culture widely until well into the twentieth century.

Although the public languages of the nineteenth century could not hold our current understanding of the function of emotion, a growing number of cultural leaders were awakening to the values that would be needed in an increasingly complex modern culture. These leaders were learning to live within complex egalitarian social bonds that recognized the internal experience of the human being, particularly the importance of dignity and the need to ease human suffering. This would deepen the culture's recognition of empathy and compassion as valued human capacities.

Religious liberalism had developed a healthy use of shame controls, shaping emotional impulsivity by evoking the need for social order and the recognition of social standards. However, this became dangerously oppressive, and the unhealthy manipulation of fear and guilt led to the challenge of political liberalism. Later, when the political individual went too far and asserted a shameless degree of independence – to the point of every-man-for-himself – a healthy use of shame was reinstated through psychological liberalism. This activated humility in the face of our failures to be more empathetic, given the suffering brought on by callousness.

For the psychological person, the healthy use of shame supplements and extends the religious person's recognition of the need for social standards by evoking necessary shame within the political individual. For the psychological person, shame awareness is not imposed from the outside as an external standard (as with religious social roles), but comes from the individual's growing awareness of an internal experience of shame. Awareness of the dignity of every human being activates necessary shame and grief in the face of widespread human suffering. Here we see Wilber's criteria of increasing interiority operating, as the political individual becomes complex enough to be shaped by egalitarian values and ideas without the force that had been required when religion met emotional impulsivity.

In its earliest manifestation, the empathy of the psychological person stops short of recognizing universal principles, a characteristic of later, more public development. It was not until human suffering boiled over into the middle classes at the end of the nineteenth century that the interior world of the individual gained a public language. Even then, the language of psychotherapy focused too intently on the private life of the psychological person.

Without some clear public moral language the nineteenth and twentieth centuries were pulled by unhealthy dimensions of both religion and politics as cultural oppression and an inflated individualism set the culture's course. Psychological values were not expressed with enough moral authority, and were lost in the morally neutral language of psychotherapy or a range of spiritual languages, emphasizing nonjudgmentalness. As time went on, however, more and more cultural leaders began to make the shift to psychological awareness, and to use this rudimentary psychological attitude.

The new psychological consciousness gave many of the cultural leaders inspirational experiences that helped them see growing fractures in the cultural sphere. These leaders sought to find a more public expression, but lacked a public language sufficient to express their psychological under-standing and head off the violence represented by the ongoing oppression of minorities, women, working people, and children. This violence was funded by the immoral divide in wealth brought about by the new material success of the culture. Instead, the language that did work its way into the public sphere was materialistic, with political liberalism barely able to keep up some rudimentary, but growing, idea of social progress. What was missing was the ability to bring into the public sphere the psychological attitude implied by the new private religiosity of the nineteenth-century cultural leaders.

Although the psychological attitude did not have the political weight to change culture to the extent needed, it did become a hidden or esoteric dimension of the political movements of the time. For example, the psychological attitude was part of women's suffrage movement of the early nineteenth century as they adopted the attitude of "self-improvement" into their public protest.

Difficulties the original liberal luminaries had in embodying the psychological attitude

Introduction

The distinction between the political individual and what I am calling the psychological person will, for the moment, roughly characterize the differ-ence between political and psychological liberalism. Both of these liberal-isms are born from the emerging psychological consciousness. However, psychological liberalism would cultivate the interiority necessary to embody a fuller expression of the psychological consciousness in the psychological attitude. Unfortunately, at the beginning of modernity, little institutional support for this attitude existed, and political liberalism ascended to a position of power in Western culture as the primary voice against the regressive efforts of unhealthy religions and other tyrannies. The images of political liberalism were the first to create a public language and gain institutional form. They united with more base human motivations rooted in the language of materialism to shape new social institutions.

The emerging financial institutions of the Enlightenment and early Industrial Revolution encouraged a confluence between the needs of a new merchant class for workers and the idea of freedom from prior social obligation. Locke's political psychology supported the lower classes – previously locked into indentured servitude – to think of themselves as free to choose their own employment, free from social customs that had forced them to work the same property, under the rule of the same landlords, for generations. Unfortunately, this freedom led to new forms of subjugation as an individual's freedom to choose was limited by the social conditions of the early Industrial Revolution.

Although the association of political liberalism with materialism aided the political power of each, there is every reason to believe that many of the liberal leaders of the day were also searching for a public language through which they could assert their own awareness of the religious dimension of the "images" that guided them. While their political images did lead to the development of effective political institutions, the religious/spiritual dimension of political liberalism found little institutional support. When combined, the religious and political liberalisms can support the emergence of the nascent psychological attitude. However, this "new" attitude could not be expressed or shared effectively through either the religious or political languages of the time, especially given the growing domination of the rational language of scientific materialism and its contempt for the "irrationality" of emotion and religion.

The tasks of cultural evolution faced by individuals holding a new egalitarian "religiosity" and liberal political perspective were daunting. Examples of this appear in the lives of the original liberal luminaries. I assume that many of the original liberal luminaries, such as John Locke, Adam Smith, and John Adams, experienced images of what they, as persons, were capable of becoming and of what we, as a people, are capable of becoming. In effect they found ways of foreshadowing Gandhi's wisdom: "you must be the change you wish to see in the world" (2007). While the most obvious application of their experience was toward the material and political world, their experience itself was also often religious and rooted in a new experience of personal freedom and public responsibility.

Many of the early liberals contained within their experience this exoteric/esoteric tension. Exoterically, the times called for political liberalism, which was readily expressible given other necessities like economic and material freedom. Esoterically, at least a few of them were also rooted in an experience of personal freedom through which the religious attitude was gaining a new "developmental" appendage as it began to manifest the psychological attitude. Through this attitude they experienced their own individuality in ways unique in human history. While primarily fueled by the newly differentiated functions of rational and sensory freedom, they also were having a more personal relationship with the unconscious, thus activating the emergent capacity for the psychological attitude. However, again this remained a hidden motivator for the most part. The founding of America exemplies this dilemma.

The esoteric underpinnings of the transformations of culture

The founding mothers and fathers of America drew on both faces of the psychological consciousness: the twin ideas of the new political individuality and a personal, egalitarian religiosity. The combining of exoteric and esoteric experience represents the two dimensions in which the psychological consciousness was manifesting in the emerging modern culture. The resulting image and reality of a new type of political individual coupled with personal religiosity led to the birth of a new type of nation state, based on democratic principles.

During this time, the exoteric political power of the Enlightenment was used to accelerate cultural evolution through a joining of materialistic and liberal languages. However, the transformations of culture were also supported by the less understood esoteric power of many cultural leaders' personal experience of their own religiosity, which accelerated their own (and others') psychological and political development. Political and religious liberalism gave birth to two faces of the new psychological consciousness. This led to numerous opportunities to advance human consciousness into more evolved states that support our deepening humanity.

However, keeping the new politics and the new religiosity together within the life of political or religious leaders was virtually impossible; their languages were simply at odds with one another. While numerous gifted individuals managed to create life works that reveal an uncommon depth of understanding of both of these spheres, articulating a fuller public language was beyond their capacities. Following my stages of political development, these leaders may or may not have had the "embodiment practices" (political development Phase Three) needed to maintain and extend the psychological attitude. Whether they had such practices or not, they did not extend to the next level of development: creating a public language that contained both their religious and political experience (political development Phase Four). Instead, only the language of the political individual gained a foothold in the public imagination, which suggests the extent to which the people were, at best, working the edge between the external authority of religious liberalism and the autonomy of political individuals.

In the absence of a public language to support the esoteric religiosity of these cultural leaders, only the emancipatory intent of political liberalism could rise into the general awareness. The ideas of freedom that the doctrines of political liberalism set loose in the world emphasized the individual's freedom from physical and social coercion. There were no complementary images of responsibility or restraint, needed to institution-alize the community-mindedness at the root of a more egalitarian liberalism that draws from the vision of a human dignity found in a personal reli-giosity. Without some institutional form of a psychological liberalism, political liberalism could not cultivate the interiority and integrity necessary to make healthy use of the freedoms it championed.

Whether through the lens of egalitarian or libertarian liberalism and their temperamental differences, our idea of freedom has a distinctly Jeffersonian feel, which Gellert claims is too narrow, lacking awareness of the role of effort and sacrifice – that is, the necessity of linking freedom to the cultivation of "integrity" (Gellert 2001: 291–3). Here the idea of integrity extends our understanding of freedom. As John Beebe notes, "to bring Christ's ideal of integrity into family, commercial, and political life would require a continuous effort" (1995: 43). In this context, freedom would require integrity, especially for the leaders of the new world.

John Adams and the struggle to activate psychological liberalism

Gellert compares the political philosophies of Thomas Jefferson and John Adams to accentuate the difference between freedom from and freedom with integrity. Adams doubted that people could maintain an awareness of the needs of the whole, while Jefferson had faith in "the will of the people" (if appropriately educated) to rise above individuality (Gellert 2001: 292). Adams believed that "personal integrity is the bridge that connects the psychological freedom attained by the individual with democratic freedom of society (Gellert 2001: 291–2). Citing historian Joseph Ellis, Gellert draws out the extent to which Adams recognized and embodied a rudimentary psychological attitude that could focus on freedom and sacrifice. Ellis writes: "Virtually all of [Adam's] political convictions, especially his most piercing political insights, derived from introspection, or what we would call psychology" (Gellert 2001: 292).

Following Ellis' understanding of Adams, Gellert writes: "Integrity was characterized by an honest effort to confront one's demons and at least keep them plainly in view and under a modicum of control" (Gellert 2001: 292). Clearly, Gellert is describing a man attending to his internal experi-ence, and doing the work necessary to create a psychological attitude. Adams' psychological orientation was prescient. Unfortunately, in the late eighteenth century he found no institution of the social sciences, no lan-guage of psychology, no clear embodiment practice or public language to draw upon to support his insight or propagate his personal psychological discipline.[1] Although Adams was aware of the difficulty of institutionaliz-ing his hard-won psychological experience into a form of psychological liberalism, he recognized this as the necessary task of the time.

Unfortunately, Jefferson's premature faith in the people predominated, building a strong culture of political liberalism that was an enormous step forward, but which also fostered the immoral excesses of the individual. Under the banner of freedom, destiny became manifest destiny and a degree of impulsivity joined with individual ingenuity to produce "unprecedented levels of social and economic inequality" and the oppression and genocide of whole peoples (Gellert 2001: 295).

Adams recognized the need to make a significant adjustment in order to align individual opportunity with the responsibilities of the person, which Ellis captures simply as the need for a "quasi-sacred devotion to the 'public'" (Gellert 2001: 295). Without a larger institutional shift in our relation to the public, societies tend toward what many social thinkers, including Jung and Dewey, have thought of as a mass-mindedness. Dewey reflects on this initial result of a new democracy:

> A peasantry and proletariat which has been released from . . . bondage will for a time have its revenge. Because there is no magic in democracy to confer immediately the power of critical discrimination upon the masses . . . who have taken their morality and their religion from an external authority above them . . . it does not follow that the ineptitude of the many is the creation of democracy.
>
> (Dewey 1929a: 28–9)

Dewey characterized the consciousness of a people in a way that fits neatly with Graves' description of the "external authority" of the "blue" level, and the difficulty shifting to the independence of the political individual.

Following Jung's and Dewey's concerns about the way in which the external developments of modernity have led to the domination of a mass-mind, we can look for a way to reconnect the tremendous value of the external focus of political liberalism to Adams' idea of developing integrity – as Gellert describes it, "an honest effort to confront one's demons and at least keep them plainly in view and under a modicum of control" (Gellert 2001: 292).[2]

What happened after the founding of America to the twin purposes of political and psychological liberalism? Certainly, the humanizing intent of political liberalism continued in the early and mid-nineteenth century projects of woman's suffrage and the abolition of slavery, and in the late nineteenth century in the farm and labor movements (Zinn 2005: 282). The focus on these necessary human freedoms shows the continued positive power of an externally focused political liberalism. It also seems likely that at least a few of the leaders in each of these movements grounded their motivation in a personal religiosity, thus uniting within themselves the tear in the psychological consciousness between political and psychological liberalism.

However, there was also a significant retreat from the inspiring vision of a new human community thought possible at the beginning of the American project. The seemingly necessary alliance between political liberalism and materialism was at odds with the vision of human possibility fostered by the new personal religiosity. This retreat shows itself in a new intellectual/spiritual battle that begins to take shape toward the beginning of the nineteenth century.

The deprecation of emotion in the life of the rugged individual

Between Locke and the early twentieth century lay more than two hundred years during which the task of liberalism became the further differentiation and consolidation of an independent political individual with its new capacities for reasoning and sensory freedom, expressed within the languages of liberalism and materialism. This development was primarily political, and the philosophy, political theory, and even the emerging natural and social sciences all worked to articulate the languages needed to sustain this advance. Here, the social milieu meets the scientific paradigm as they work together to create a new modern culture.

While science was succeeding in opening the new reaches of the natural world, and while there was an abundant, but naive, hope that the new political freedoms would lead to an equitable society, there was also a profound level of suffering that could not be languaged in the prevailing social milieu. This suffering became all the more intense as people had to learn to use their emotions in a radically different way. No longer did emotion simply tie people to communal obligation. Instead, we narrowed their functioning and tied them to the independence and short-sightedness of the rugged individualism. The values of individualism made it easier to turn a blind eye to the suffering of others.

To the extent that reasoning and sensory freedom became coins of the realm, emotion became, in part, associated with oppression. Concurrently, the ability to attend to emotional suffering was hobbled, replaced by a new callousness. Even when critiques of the rising industrial society were articulated in earnest in the mid-eighteenth century, by Karl Marx and others, attention to human suffering focused on the social dimensions of oppression, that is, the lack of social justice. While these social critiques offered alternative images of social and political organization, they still did not offer sufficient imagery regarding individual development, nor cultural evolution. These alternatives were virtually all expressed within a lower-right quadrant language. They did not account for the growing individual suffering that arose as the dominant language of materialism could not focus attention beyond creating opportunities for material wealth for the affluent and a growing middle class.

The absence of an internal awareness within the political individual kicked off a new level of reflection, manifested in a range of religious, philosophical, and personal thought/feeling that supported the emergence of the psychological attitude. However, there was still no language that could be used to attend to this suffering, experienced broadly throughout the culture, but largely unarticulated. Efforts were made to craft such a language, focused on an emerging interiority during the Romantic period, as people began to think that each person had a unique "creative destiny" (Baumeister 1986: 158). This nascent experience of individual destiny was embodied by a range of cultural leaders who contributed to the emerging egalitarian culture. Walt Whitman and William James exemplified different dimensions of this new individual identity.

William James and the conscious activation of the psychological attitude

In 1855, Walt Whitman expressed the emerging personal, psychological consciousness in the following poem:

> Observe the summer grass
> I celebrate myself
> And what I assume you shall assume,
> For every atom belonging to me as good belongs to you.
> I loaf and invite my soul,
> I lean and loafe at my ease . . .
> observing a spear of summer grass.
>   (quoted in Kaplin 1980: 187)

Whitman shows us a dimension of the new interiority that is not simply about suffering, but embraces the joy that can come with self-awareness. While not overtly religious, Whitman expresses a new personal spirituality in which he invites each person to participate. He shares this awareness and invites the people of his time to follow him into a new impassioned personal identity: one sensitive to the suffering of others; one that recognized an intimate connection between humans and nature; one delighted by a direct encounter with the world.

One woman responded to Whitman's writing with the following letter: "I read *Leaves of Grass*, and got new conceptions of the dignity and beauty of my own body and of the bodies of other people, and life became more valuable in consequence" (Kaplin 1980: 43). In this simple response we see the freedom on the other side of both the authoritarian control of religious liberalism and the isolation of political liberalism. Whitman's brilliance, his "images," shifted this woman's consciousness, evoking a new psychological attitude that she experienced as immediately freeing. Yet the freedom was not freedom from, rather, it was freedom in relation to, and it connected her to others and to a larger sense of what it means to be human.

In a similar vein, William James sought to form a distinct personal identity. He suffered through an extended adolescence and stayed open to the identity potentials that lay within him (and could be supported by his family's liberal lifestyle and upper-class standing). Suffering from physical pain and depression, bouncing between occupational interests, and spending time in Europe and South America, James fought off the risks of premature identity foreclosure to turn himself into a unique expression of his age, and became known as the father of American psychology. As I cited in Chapter 4, Erikson describes this act of staying open to forming a unique identity in an exciting way:

> Some young individuals will succumb to this crisis in all manner of neurotic, psychotic, or delinquent behavior . . . still others, although suffering and deviating dangerously through what appears to be a prolonged adolescence, eventually come to *contribute an original bit* to an emerging style of life.
>
> (Erikson 1958: 14–15, emphasis added)

James was profoundly influenced by the liberal religious attitude of his father, Henry James Sr., and the budding psychological attitude of his younger brother, Henry James Jr. (expressed in his writing, which broke new ground with its intensely psychological character descriptions). Combining these influences, and with social support, James embodied for the culture the transition from the religious to the psychological attitude.

The stories of James' suffering, as well as Whitman's expressions of hope, are examples of sensitive people who suffer into new ways of thinking and being. They picked up on the unconscious needs of their time, and experienced these needs as Jung's communicative ideas. They experienced the "images" of a new interiority that seeded the growing psychological attitude.

Henderson traces the origin of the psychological attitude to James, who made becoming psychological in his personal and professional life a central concern. Erikson foreshadowed Henderson's view in his interpretation of James' life and its significance for psychology. Stopping short of saying that James actively pursued the development of a psychological attitude or "identity," Erikson noted that for James identity is "something that 'comes upon you' as a recognition, almost as a surprise rather than a something strenuously 'quested' after" (Erikson 1968: 20). However, given the emergent tensions of his time, given the disparity between these tensions and his parent's different responses to them, James also experienced this identity crisis as fearful, which Erikson thinks reflects "the identity of naked and stubborn selfhood so typical for extreme individualism" (Erikson 1968: 153). While very different than the experience of Descartes, James and

Descartes shared the experience of bearing doubt. In James, the indi-vidualism of his time is punctured as his family extends his adolescence without offering answers, which James bears. He is thus forced to seek his own answers, which he does through seeking a new personal identity based on an increasing self-awareness of oneself as a psychological being (Erikson 1969: 19).

Both Henderson and Erikson see in James' life a developmental shift for the culture if not the species, taking human psychological consciousness up a notch. He moved psychological experience from a passive experience to almost being actively sought. In the life of James, Whitman, and many others, we can see what the culture and its public languages were ignoring, which would soon burst forth in revelation. This consolidation of a new identity extended the limits of the political individual, giving rise to the emergence of the psychological person.

In a few sensitive men and women this new identity finally emerges. They suffered and imagined into the new language that would attend to the delight and suffering of others. These people found some way of looking past the dominant language of materialism to create new ways of thinking and being. However, these new voices did not quickly gain moral authority or generational attention. In fact, their language led away from public participation.

The new psychological attitude was not shared widely in public due to its complexity in comparison to the experience of the rugged individual. Although it was expressed in some approaches to the social sciences, it primarily lived within the private spiritualities of a few individuals who resisted the collective materialist norms. These people turned toward the experience of a personal destiny and away from the Puritan attitude that included social responsibility. This began the significant retreat from the public world and into the new private-life spirituality of an internal, private, psychological liberalism.

The divide between public and private identity

In his 1986 book *Identity*, Roy Baumeister describes how a retreat from the public world shows up in the transcendentalist's desire to find destiny in a private life, separated from the "oppressive and mundane conditions of society" (Baumeister 1986: 68). Baumeister cites d'Avenel: "The public life of a people is a very small thing compared to its private life" (Baumeister 1986: 71). This marks a beginning of the conscious divide between public and private experience. A general retreat from the public sphere was initiated by numerous cultural leaders concerned by the callous and inhumane social attitudes that dominated Western cultures. They sought to develop the further implications of the psychological attitude. However, they saw no way to achieve this in the public sphere. Accordingly, they pursued this attitude through their private spiritualities, within which they worked to craft private languages and some shared practices.

By the nineteenth century, interest in a range of spiritualities and philosophies reached a height of clarity in both American transcendentalism and Continental existentialism. In transcendentalism, the person was raised up as a source of truth, poised against society. As Ralph Waldo Emerson wrote in his essay "Self Reliance": "Trust thyself: every heart vibrates to that iron string . . . [and] . . . Society everywhere is in conspiracy against the manhood of every one of its members" (Emerson 1993: 20). In existentialism this same sentiment is expressed by Soren Kierkegaard:

> I have endeavored to express the thought that to employ the category "race" to indicate what it is to be a man, and especially as an indication of the highest attainment, is a misunderstanding and mere paganism, because the race, mankind, differs from an animal race not merely by its general superiority as a race, but by the human characteristic that every single individual within the race . . . is more than the race. For to relate oneself to God is a far higher thing than to be related to the race and through the race to God.
>
> (Copleston 1965: 111)

These expressions of psychological liberalism were given life in an esoteric language appreciated by a small but influential part of the human community. While in opposition to religious institutions, these expressions were still clearly religious – they embodied the renewing potency of the religious attitude. These "spiritual" languages also expressed the psychological face of liberalism seemingly abandoned by political liberals.

However, by the early twentieth century the retreat from the public sphere, celebrated by these and other philosophies, became inculcated in a growing divide between an individual's public and private identities. This divide especially affected the middle class, content to live within the strictures of their private lives. The growing acceptance of this divide led to a loss of awareness of the actual unity between individual and social experience, and grew into its current form as a central ill of modern culture.

One of the earliest descriptions of the withdrawal of the individual from public participation into a "private life" came from Alexis de Tocqueville, a French sociologist describing his experience of the new American culture. Writing in 1845, Tocqueville prophetically described the coming crisis of individualism:

> Individualism is a mature and calm feeling, which disposes each member of the community to sever himself from the masses of his

fellows and to draw apart with his family and his friends, so that after he has thus formed a little circle of his own, he willingly leaves society at large to itself.

(Tocqueville 1945: 98)

While Tocqueville's writing, and that of other social theorists, named the nascent identity crisis, neither they nor anyone else made a connection to existing social attitudes that could transform the "images" Tocqueville experienced into a public language and remedial social actions. Instead, the buoyancy of the emerging industrial age supported a fantasy of unlimited individual agency and freedom, built on a deepening impoverishment of body and soul of the working class, minorities, women, and children – all of which evoked a growing fear in modern culture.

Toward the end of the nineteenth century, the overall experience of the modern world was growing anxiety. The breakdown of traditional community roles and the increase of an impersonal social order led individuals to an experience of being overly exposed. These individuals, told that they were free to create themselves, had little access to healthy emotional expression in a world that overvalued reasoning freedom. The budding political individual was bound in a dilemma.

In the face of these binds, the modern individual became increasingly self-conscious, feeling small in the face of the world. Baumeister traces the adoption of rigid Victorian attitudes and mores to this new self-consciousness. These attitudes helped hide the newly exposed individual behind the stilted patterns of communication and relationship associated with that period (Baumeister 1986: 67). Yet, these patterns also perpetuated and exacerbated the individual's inability to use emotions for assessment, motivation and direction, and connection.

While Tocqueville's perception is itself a prescient "image," it did not move a people who seemed comfortable enough. As Rilke recognized that faith in the future comes through an embodied experience of "strangeness," Tocqueville saw the pitfalls of the retreat into a private life; he felt the future of our culture. Compared with the vision of a "political individual," the psychologically liberal visions of Tocqueville, Emerson, Kierkegaard, and other nineteenth-century thinkers found little traction to support maturation from image to identity to institution. Their voices were not sufficient to redirect their generation's attention toward the inner ills of the culture. They had no distinct method of learning, no learning practice to turn their visions into a new public imagination and language. They had little success connecting their emerging psychological attitude to institutional forms. Thus, they become the voice of the rebellious opposition, embodying a relativistic stage of moral development that rejects conventional morality, but cannot assert an alternative language of the post-conventionality they intuit.

These thinkers recognized the breakdown of community and the emergence of the mass-mind, the impersonal society, and the isolated individual as foreboding signs of trouble, whereas many other thinkers like Karl Marx pursued forms of political liberalism for solutions in the late nineteenth century that solidified the splits between the privatizing individual and the newly formed society. Perhaps this concretization reflects a necessary polarization between the exoteric public language of materialism and the potentially esoteric and renewing private language of psychological liberalism. However, for new experience to rupture the tension, new moral language is needed.

The retreat into private lives led to a profound lack of moral attention, will, and courage, as the middle class attended neither to the suffering of the working class nor ethnic minorities during the farm and labor movements of the late nineteenth century. The plight of these people became acute, as they were increasingly uprooted from their traditional connection to the land. In his book, *A People's History of the United States*, Howard Zinn describes the loss of farm ownership during the late nineteenth century, as small farmers were increasingly squeezed out of their property, having to work instead for the rapidly expanding corporate farms or move to the developing industrial centers (Zinn 2005: 282).

At this time, the externally focused language of political liberalism did not muster enough generational attention to attend to the suffering of the working poor. However, the political alliance between political liberalism and the language of materialism was beginning to break down. This opened an opportunity for greater awareness of social oppression. Yet, significant institutional change did not come from this direction. Rather, it was through the increased suffering of the middle class that a new institution arose. Although able to feed themselves and their families, the middle class became symptomatic due to the stifling conditions of modern culture, experiencing a level of alienation due to the culture's lack of an ethic of care, that is, a lack of moral values.

The rise of modern suffering: the psychological person is born in anguish

Political liberals in the nineteenth and early twentieth centuries did not readily respond to the increasingly privatized and problematized realm of human experience. They seemed to miss the internal level of suffering that paralleled the overtly oppressive external social conditions. However, by the end of the nineteenth century the negative impact of industrial society led to a range of "medical" symptoms, for which the science of the day could not account. People began to appear in the mental institutions and clinics with seemingly untreatable symptoms, and a new language of human suffering had to be articulated. Amidst this anguish appeared the stirrings of a new personal self.

Sigmund Freud and the birth of the institution of psychological liberalism

In the late nineteenth century, medical science struggled to identify the physiological bases for certain "medical" conditions appearing with increasing frequency. Out of this struggle came the possibility that this suffering was "psychologically" and not physically based. This marks a turn toward an "internal" causal agent, which began focusing attention on Wilber's upper-left quadrant, that is, the internal individual.

As a young physician, Sigmund Freud began attending to this suffering, which led him to many new images about human beings that helped address the growing psychological pain. Freud and his community of practitioners dealt directly with the problematic external and overly rational focus of both political liberalism and the social sciences of their time by turning attention inward, toward the unconscious motivations and irrational forces that govern human experience. While Freud primarily articulated an upper-left (individual) language, he also set about creating a lower-left cultural language. Central to Freud's growing understanding of the human being was the notion that we are not essentially rational creatures, but are motivated by unconscious drives and passions. This view radically challenged the public languages of the day and led to the growth of the alternative languages of psychological liberalism.

In this new language, Freud asserted that individuals are primarily motivated by the life and death instincts of "eros" and "thanatos" (Freud 1961: 48–50). Through these instincts the individual was thought to be linked to the world in conflictual and passionate involvement. Through this articulation, Freud reopened the idea of our irrational experience as a central aspect of human motivation, thus initiating a conversation that begins to reintegrate emotion and imagination back into the culture's language as sources of individual and cultural knowledge. This also begins to reintegrate the Enlightenment's hyper-differentiated rational and sensory functions.

Freud's vision helped bring into the culture the emerging psychological liberalism through his public language of psychoanalysis. Through instituting his ideas and practices he began drawing the attention of his generation more actively to the human potential for individual development. While such a vision had earlier manifestations, like the attitude toward self-improvement of women's suffrage, and the ideas of self-development fostered by the transcendentalists and other subcultures, no institutional forms had appeared to explore and extend psychological liberalism.[3] Freud found a way to activate a new "internal" awareness within an individual's experience through his "talking" therapy. Through the tradition of doctor–patient confidentiality, Freud created a semi-public space – a doctor's clinic or office – in which people were invited/expected to express their "taboo" emotions and fantasies. This semi-public space helped challenge political liberalism's deprecation of emotion and interiority, and legitimized the new personal self, born in anguish.

Although the epidemic of psychological symptoms that Freud identified could have been associated with the sociopolitical culture of his time, Freud – embedded in that culture – hypothesized that these ills arose in childhood in relation to the family. Through his study of adult clients, Freud identified the way Victorian attitudes toward children led to severe emotional disturbances not accounted for by the materialistic values of the day. Freud's "private practice" is an example of my Phase Three level of political development in which embodiment practices – in this case, psychotherapy – are used to activate a new internal psychological attitude that supports people becoming psychological. That is, people see how their history affected their present condition, and learn anew about the functioning of emotion and imagination. In the tradition of the Dionysian rites and the Greek tragedies, Freud helped people activate the renewing function of the religious attitude through this new psychological language. While adopting a condemning attitude toward religion, Freud's new language offered people an alternative route to the healing power of religious experience.

Through this new psychological experience of their own irrationality people connected directly to the unconscious. While Martin Luther showed people how to connect directly with God, Freud showed how people could become more whole by connecting directly to the unconscious. To a significant extent, Freud embodied his own revelation, his own new "image" (Phase One). He formed a circle of practitioners and, together, they formed a private language that led to a growing range of healing learning practices (Phases Two and Three). These practices captured the public's imagination, and led to a new public language (Phase Four). The formation of this language extended the medical establishment in such a new direction as to activate a wide range of new vocational and institutional forms (Phase Five, Subphases One and Two).

Freud fathered an introverted psychological liberalism that better accounted for the suffering of people who did not lack material comfort. Freud went so far as to connect his theory of human development to the new science of evolution, thus linking individual development with cultural evolution. However, the fuller implications of this connection got lost in his use of the indistinct concept of instinct. As a result, Freud biologized individual experience, which hobbled his own gifted sense of an emergent language of the cultural sphere. As I described in Chapter 4, as a result of his own limits, and the limits of the times, the connection between individual and cultural experience got lost. Instead, the focus of the growing institution of psychology narrowed to the development of the individual and the familial crises that restricted that development. Due in part to the specialization of medicine and the need for practical treatments for individuals with debilitating symptoms, Freud's theory rightly focuses on the individual outside of a sociopolitical context. However, to the extent that this theory perpetuates, establishes, or condones that separation, developmental theory remains unresponsive to the growing culture of individualism and its symptoms.

The emerging science of psychology focused too intently on the idea that the individual existed independently of a social world. While we can easily imagine the individual independent of a social identity, this act of our imagining is rooted in an existing social construct originating in ideas like tabula rasa. Several centuries after it became part of the culture's public language and imagination, the idea of the autonomous individual became reified – the only view imaginable about the nature of the individual.

The institutional structures of psychological liberalism, in both the universities and the clinics, idolized this reified psychological person. Thus they accepted and brought into their languaging an extreme version of Locke's idea of independence. This reflects a central difficulty of processes of cultural evolution: successful differentiation (Locke's idea of individual independence) risks precluding the next, necessary integrative phase of human development. These calcifying risks of language are expressed by Rudolph Steiner, whose insight about the impact of a new world view foreshadows the understanding of political development developed here: "People generally do not know that a world view or theory will eventually become the social and moral functioning of people . . . generations later; what was only a world view at first develops into actions later" (Steiner 1991: 100).

While bringing to light the internal experience of the individual, psychology also inculcates into its very identity the alienation it seeks to treat. Psychology's pioneers could not see the modern identity as a stage of human development, which was beginning to unravel even as it reached its zenith. As a result, psychological interventions risked exacerbating the isolation, as treatment modalities accepted the public/private split in this identity.

The introverted awareness emerging into the culture through Freud's public language of psychoanalysis limited the connection that could be made between individual development and cultural evolution. Freud did not imagine that the individual could play any significant role in transforming culture. Rather, he thought that the relationship between society and the individual would forever be conflictual. In the midst of his time, such negativity may have been warranted; however, his language perpetuated that pessimism. Freud's attitude toward the individual lasted well into the twentieth century and may largely continue to this day. In addition to the sharp divide between ideas of individual development and cultural evolution, there is something of an "aesthetic attitude" adopted by twentieth-century social sciences to their potential role in the transformation of culture.

Following the positivists' paradigm, which limited their self-image to a passive observation and analysis, many scientists did not attempt to reconnect individual development and cultural evolution. By the early twentieth century, the separation between social and psychological subject matters was well established. Exacerbating this divide, social scientists believed they could use only reasoning and sensory freedom for inquiry. With affect still suspect, social scientists were told, in effect, that their emotional reactions to the suffering in the world could not play a part in their work. Thus, their access to the very foundational capacities they needed to respond to this suffering – compassion, humility, courage, and fierceness – was thwarted. Instead, a passive reasoning freedom would have to suffice.

The political individual partially capitulated to the continued oppression by religion of the individual's experience. While individuals drew from a new trust in reasoning and sensory experience, they lived out the overall deprecating attitude toward their own full experience. This restriction on the humanity of the social scientist crippled the fuller range of inquiry and political initiative to which the social sciences are obligated. In the 1920s, the Frankfurt School of Social Research attempted, and in part succeeded, in making this connection between the political and the psychological. However, as I will show, the faculty at this school was also controlled by the positivists' passive image of the social scientist, which limited their own political development. In the following section we will see the impact of this passivity as we review what may be the most important challenge to the duality between the psychological and social sciences.

The Frankfurt School of Social Research

The Frankfurt School of Social Research was among the first to attempt a bridging of the institutional gap between political and psychological liberalism. The Frankfurt School sought to integrate Freud's understanding of the irrational nature of the individual with a psycho-political understanding of cultural oppression. These efforts led to the founding of the science of political psychology, as it is currently known, as a subbranch of political science. Prior to the research of the Frankfurt School, social theorists had great difficulty imagining how psychology, sociology, and politics could interact to support human growth and freedom. Taking on this challenge, the Frankfurt School tried to unite theory and practice through their work on "praxis" as "self-created action" (Jay 1973: 4).

Beginning as a left-wing response to the successes and failures of the Bolshevik Revolution in Russia and Europe, the Frankfurt School emerged over time as a reappraisal of cultural applications of Marxist theory. Originally focused on the Marxist studies of history and economics, this reappraisal took place in the new light cast by social science inquiry, based in philosophy and psychology. Drawing largely from neo-Hegelian and Freudian approaches to these disciplines, the Frankfurt School became a unique location for exploring the connection between the political and the psychological.

Unlike William James, the faculty at the Frankfurt School did not commit to approaching research as an opportunity to cultivate their own psychological attitude, that is, to use their psychological attitude to form new human capacities. James had the luxury of cultivating the psychological attitude within his private-life experiences, and within his confined identity as a research psychologist. The psychological exploration of religious experience cultivated by James and others was largely an esoteric activity, and the public language it built focused on the individual in isolation from culture. James did not take up the challenge of using psychology to address social ills.

While James broke new ground in understanding the internal experience of the individual, two generations later the faculty of the Frankfurt School sought to reintegrate the individual into a sociopolitical whole. However, they did not base their work on the optimistic images of individual agency available through James' and Dewey's American pragmatism. Instead, they drew from Freud's pessimistic cultural language, which has a more differentiated relationship to the evils of the cultural sphere they sought to alleviate.

The founding faculty of the Frankfurt School – Max Horkheimer, Theodor Adono, and Herbert Marcuse – placed themselves on the fault line between the social sciences and politics. In the face of the intensity of this position, they struggled to create a new role for the social scientist. While the role they found primarily focused on traditional ideas of the social scientist as "researcher" and "educator," they did succeed in creating forms of analysis that offered a new depth of insight into sources of human suffering, such as in their research into prejudice. Unlike Marx, their understanding of prejudice did not focus on social systems but on the individual human personality in the upper quadrants. Combining American empirical methods with the European Frankfurt School's more philosophical interest, this research identified the "authoritarian personality" as a psychological condition that is rooted in, and perpetuates, fascist political systems.

Although a significant contribution, their theories emerged from the dominant idea that the social sciences should limit their political work to social critique. Conforming to the compromise between religious and psychological liberalism, they remained passive scientists, observers producing "objective" work. This equation of passivity with objectivity prevented the Frankfurt School social scientists from developing an image of themselves working on, or working out, their own identity. They did not adopt the attitude of physician heal thyself in the way that James and others did. When examined through Henderson's "cultural attitudes" lens, we see that the faculty's adoption of passive researcher and educator roles was a manifestation of the social, aesthetic, and philosophical attitude. As a result, they did not bring either the active nature of the religious or psychological attitude into their work.

They failed to understand the need to create images of how a social scientist could vocationalize the work of changing political culture; thus, they skipped this essential first subphase of Phase Five of political development, and tried to institute political change through the traditional passive roles of the social scientist. Their image of cultural change derived from an approach to praxis that left out the need for social scientists to draw on a full range of experience to forge a political identity for themselves, and to use that identity – as "political psychologists," "political educators," or "political sociologists" knowledgeable in both "assessment" and "treatment" – to show others how to develop and strengthen their own political identities. While they had some image of a conjoined liberalism, it seems unlikely that they had the necessary learning practices (Phase Three) to activate and sustain their vision (Phase One) as a vocation (Phase Five, Subphase One).

Lacking the ability to translate their social critique into a vocational form of a new type of social scientist, they could only struggle between the poles of political activism and a passive research/education/psychotherapy. Without the guiding hand of affect, they failed to integrate thought and action. Without the ability to integrate thought and action, the tensions within the school could not be contained. Efforts to be both political and psychological became fraught with all the tensions these poles of human experience contain. The faculty brought a potentially renewing tension within the school, but could neither transmute nor contain it. Subsequent ruptures led to Erich Fromm and several other faculty members leaving the school and initiating their own approach to social science inquiry.

From the point of view of the original faculty who stayed, the social scientist provided a critique of modern culture that would be used by the working class or – as it became clear this would not work – the peoples of third world nations to support revolution. This emphasis on critique reflected the domination of reasoning and sensory freedom and lacked awareness of the opportunity to use affect to embody leadership capacities to assess, motivate and direct attention, and to connect.

In the other direction, Fromm and other "post-Freudian" thinkers set out to change the world one person at a time, through psychotherapy (Jay 1973: 103). While identifying some role for affect in healing individual trauma, their acceptance of the increasingly privatized image of psychotherapy fails to account for the severity of the public/private split in identity. This first rupture in the Frankfurt School indicated the difficulty of having an institution maintain its focus simultaneously on personal development and cultural evolution – especially without some learning practice capable of binding the tensions. As I will explore later, a new image of a political psychologist and a transformative political psychology are needed to develop an image of a vocation and a practitioner of that vocation, and a social institution focused on both individual development and cultural evolution.

A second rupture in the Frankfurt School in the late 1960s split students and younger faculty on the one hand, and older faculty on the other. The former opposed the American war in Viet Nam, while the older faculty (like Horkheimer and Adono) felt a kinship with an American establishment that had fought the Nazis in World War II. Both sides of the conflict had a significant body of research to draw on to understand their conflict with the other side. However, neither was able to enter into the conflict with a psychological attitude. This severe generational rupture was paralleled in America during the catastrophes of 1968 (such as the Democratic convention in Chicago), which marked the beginning of the rise of the neoconservative movement with its extreme shift to the political right (documented in the 2004 book *The Right Nation* by Micklethwait and Wooldridge).

These conflicts reflected the extraordinary difficulty that liberals have had when forced to deal with the internal, psychological levels of suffering involved in politics. What is clearly needed is an image of a practitioner who would be capable of entering into these frays in organizations, tackling the crucial task of integrating political and psychological liberalism within effective institutional forms.

Liberalism and cultural evolution: a synopsis

The conflicts on the political left of the 1960s, the struggles between the old and new generations of political organizers, mirror/echo the uncompleted project of the Frankfurt School to integrate political and psychological liberalism. This project successfully brought Freud's essential understanding of humanity's irrational nature into political discourse, replacing the outdated and naive fantasies of the early liberals, as well as the valuable but confused sociopolitical discourse (Marx, etc.) that reduces political failures to sociopolitical oppression by a cultural elite.

Freud and the nascent psychology project unearthed humanity's irrational nature. However, there has been significant divergence about what to do with this information. We are learning to set aside our obsession with rationalism, and have deepened the culture's access to the psychological attitude, but we have not yet learned to use this knowledge to affect culture. Too often, awareness of our irrational nature leads to pessimistic retreat, either through an informed aesthetic attitude or through a quiet resignation to the isolation of modern society and middle class malaise.

When retreat has been avoided, social and political action has yet to integrate the implications of what it means to say that we humans are motivated by irrational forces. Instead, political liberals continue to assume that if we could only find a more rational and coherent way of speaking about the issues as we see them, the electorate will eventually come over to our way of thinking. Unfortunately, social scientists aren't jumping in to help sort out this situation. They continue to imagine themselves as social critics; they too seem to have a naive faith in reasoning our way to freedom.

Viewing the cultural evolution of Western culture through both Graves' developmental lens and an ITP lens, the difficulties that social scientists in the twentieth century experience in transforming culture become more obvious – and we can see history, however haltingly, as a continuous, developmental process. When the psychological and the social remain divided, cultural evolution remains hidden. Only by understanding cultural events as part of a political development process can we see the trans-formations of reasoning, sensory, and affect freedom for what they are: developmental phenomena. As long as scientists use only their thinking and sensing functions – as long as affect is associated with distortion – they have no other way to assert a sense of direction other than through an increas-ingly sterile rationalism, which Lakoff has admitted is the "bane of liberal-ism." This perpetuates a profound pessimism regarding the capacity of the individual to influence cultural evolution. Controlled by medieval notions of individual agency, modern people can only imagine themselves as essentially passive and powerless.

Descartes helped differentiate thinking, and Locke helped differentiate sensing; yet, both imagined that these capacities would only help us to encounter passively a pre-existing external world. While this passivity has released significant individual agency, it has also created a fracture within people where thinking and sensing have been privileged, at the expense of imagining and feeling. Since emotion is responsible for assessment, motiva-tion and direction, and connection, and imagination (whether through the religious or psychological attitude) is a source of new experience, thinking and sensing alone cannot sufficiently activate political development and transform culture.

The positivist's paradigm has midwifed several generations of social scientists who do not know how to use their emotions as part of their work. They remain confused about their role in a world community, accentuating the divide between the public and private spheres. Their uncertainty parallels the ambivalence toward emotions in public shown by the progressive leaders in my research. In both cases, the modern deprecation of emotions, made developmentally necessary by the growth of the political individual, restricts a fuller realization of the liberalizing influence of modern culture. Fortun-ately, there has been a growing confluence between political and psycho-logical institutions, bringing these two liberalizing influences together. The Frankfurt School exemplifies a budding awareness of this task, as well as its difficulty.

Unfortunately, it was not until the late twentieth century that public language began to respond to this condition. This language emerges with an increasingly clear identification of two tears in our experience: first, between our public and private lives, and second, between our hyper-differentiated reasoning freedom and our inability to turn actively toward the development of affect freedom. The first of these tears was recognized in the mid-1980s by Berkeley professor Robert Bellah, and a little later by Harvard professor Michael Sandel, and feminist social theorist Joan Tronto. They recognized how the division between public and private experience destroys our ability to engage in democracy, as few individuals develop a public or political identity (Bellah *et al.* 1985: 43–6; Sandel 1996: 18). While influencing all classes, Sandel notes how the divide between public and private identities distinctly influences the wealthy. He writes that, "more and more, the affluent evacuate public spaces, retreating to privatized communities defined largely by income level" (Sandel 1996: 331).[4]

However, there have been champions over the last century and more who have managed to maintain awareness that individuals need a community to be whole. For example, in 1902 Jane Addams (founder of social work through the Settlement House Movement and a founder of the NAACP) said that "individual needs are common needs, that is, public needs." Addams foreshadowed the public commitment of progressive leaders that carries through to the lives of the progressive leaders of today in my research. Yet Addams and other political liberals are the exception.

Without access to the public function of emotion, the divide between public and private experience remains unbridged. We need affect freedom to activate a public/political identity. While Tronto does not particularly identify affect, she does identify the need for a deeper moral experience, which she associates with Carol Gilligan's idea of an "ethic of care" (Flanagan and Jackson 1993: 70). Tronto asserts that the public/private boundary marginalizes the value of such an ethic. She notes that this ethic has been relegated to the private sphere of subjective, womanly experience in juxtaposition to the masculine, rational public sphere (Tronto 1993: 10).

Tronto's critique of the rationalized public sphere is deepened by Cynthia Burack, who connects a feminist critique of modern culture to the need to have healthy access to human emotions. Burack notes that feminist political thought has successfully expanded our understanding of politics by bringing in psychology to support a fuller understanding of the self. According to Burack, this self is "constituted through connection," which is mediated by emotion (Burack 1994: 8). In her important book *The Problem of the Passions* (1994), she expresses concern that while such thinking is returning attention to the public use of emotion, it still falls short by focusing too intently on the positive emotions involved in connection while setting aside any positive value to "negative" emotions. Burack, like

Samuels, is interested in finding a political use of positive and negative emotions to further our political dialogs.

In Omer's work at the Institute of Imaginal Studies the tasks of the Frankfurt School are taken up and the dilemmas resolved through establishing a praxis that not only integrates the psychological and the political but also integrates the affective and the cognitive within an understanding of human capacities.

In closing

Given how the modern world has so far supported the differentiation of the "autonomous" individual, the task now is to integrate that individual back into a coherent social whole. Without integration, the individual and society suffer from the fragmentation and alienation wrought by differentiation alone. But integration will require developing some new identity – one able to maintain the positive gains of modernity, but also capable of forming complex interdependent relationships in families and communities.

The image of a single human community has existed in many forms since the beginning of time. In fact, it is our first experience. Too often, however, it has been asserted within a tribal mentality that treats human differences as opportunities for domination. The rise of the new psychological consciousness, with its valuation of the individual person, supports the emergence of a willingness to look past tribal differences and to see each person individually. Such sight implies a new moral attitude. By recognizing the value of individual people, the modern individual has helped begin the process of overcoming tribal differences. However, political liberalism has not supported an articulation and institutionalization of a new morality. Instead, it has raised the individual up against the necessary moral capacity that could guide us into a shared future.

It has only been in the last two hundred years that a growing awareness has developed of the way in which autonomy must be balanced within an interdependent field. Throughout the social activism of these centuries we have articulated (if not empowered) images – as language – of our interdependence. At the beginning of this new century and millennium, many cultural leaders and their organizations are working to infuse such imagery with the power necessary to institutionalize the creation of a new psychological and moral type.

Fortunately, in the last two hundred years the hyper-individuality of Western culture has been met by an integrative pull to re-create an experience of community within our diverse and fractured society. This integrative pull also arises from the new psychological consciousness. However, rather than its early focus on the emerging individuality, its current focus is on the activation within the individual of new capacities that bring people back together.

Chapter 11

Emergence of the psychological citizen

Introduction

The story of cultural evolution presented in these first two chapters of Part IV can be used to develop a better understanding of the strengths and limitations of the current movement toward personal and cultural liberty. This story is made up of successive layers of religious, political, and, most recently, psychological liberalism. Unfortunately, this movement has been thwarted by divides within our identities, both as persons and as a culture. As persons our identity fractures along a public/private divide. As a culture this same divide has infiltrated our efforts to institutionalize liberty, as we have split the growing psychological consciousness into – at least – religious, political, and a "private-psychological" form.

The reconciliation of these divides requires developing a public language that can account for these personal and cultural splits. However, in order for this language to have a greater developmental impact than the historical and current language of political liberalism, it must be based on more effective learning practices, ones that account for both social progress and individual development. Unlike the political liberalism of Adams, FDR, or Johnson, this language must account for the first three phases of political development, that is, it must have a vision of political and psychological freedom and responsibility and it must include embodiment practices that guide people and groups through to the development of their own political identities. Otherwise the vision of political liberalism will be reduced to its external manifestation, as has happened to modern political liberalism.

If a public language is articulated that can account for these splits, then it will be able to account for the growth of liberalism through its successive stages and show us the concomitant identities that emerged through each stage. Table 11.1 offers an image that does just that. In Table 11.1 I present a model of the political development of liberalism in Western culture. Through a review of the strengths and limitations of each stage, it becomes easier to imagine the necessary emergent form of liberalism, that is, we can imagine what a new psychological and moral type will look like. At the least, this type would include the strengths of each type while overcoming its limitations.

While the original religious liberalism helped contain the violence released by ritual liberalism, and while it created individuals with the dignity of a personal religiosity, people at this level do not rise above oppressive social roles. While the "political individual" of political liberalism was able to break free of this oppression, its external and short-sighted focus has not brought sufficient human freedom to realize its goal of social progress. While the "psychological person" of a private-psychological liberalism did foster an internal awareness of some depth, it did not know how to return to its community. The psychological person has been steeped in the healing practices of a range of psychotherapies or private spirituality, but has not quite known how to activate an image of citizenship.

Individuals who are embodying the emerging, new psychological and moral type are creating vocational and institutional forms focused simultaneously on individual development and cultural evolution. As a result of writing this book, I am beginning to think of this institutional form as a "public-psychological" liberalism. Further, I will refer to the new type of identity associated with this form as the emergence of the "psychological citizen."

Bringing together the different personalities of the political individual and the psychological person

In the last two chapters I offered a range of descriptions to reflect the evolution of liberalism through its first ritual and religious manifestations, through the religious renewal of the Reformation, into political liberalism and on into the early, private-psychological liberalism of the nineteenth and twentieth centuries. In order to connect this story solidly to the present, in order to articulate images of how it is we will be able to change political culture, and in order to extend liberalism into the future, I will focus my attention on the problematic divide in liberalism between its last two major stages, political and the private-psychological liberalism. Through this attention it is possible to imagine the opportunities for the new "psychological citizen" to engage in learning practices that heal the divide between these two most recent stages of liberalism.

The divide between political and private-psychological liberalism creates two distinct personality types: what I have been calling the "political individual" and the "psychological person." While any effort to create a personality typology risks overgeneralization or the reification of the categories, the value of this approach lies in its ability to help us imagine bridges across the divide.

Political liberalism represents the best of modern individualism, which is expressed through forms of institutions and political identities that are

Table 11.1 Model of the political development of liberalism in Western culture (Drawing on Omer's Imaginal Transformation Praxis)

Dunlap's stages of political development		Prejudice/limitations	Learning practice	Affect transformation	Emergent capacity	Recent manifestation
Institutional form	Individual identity					
Universal liberalism	Religious citizen		Creation of a universal religious community	Affect connects psychological citizens into new institutional forms focused on cultural evolution	Destiny, moral action in the world	Formalized vocations within new institutional forms
Psychological liberalism	Psychological citizen (public)	Struggle to connect through new capacities; risks idiosyncrasy and isolation	Public psychologicalness; attending to liberal prejudices	Affect transmuted into individual capacities moving individual toward unique destiny based on service	Generational attention, public-life affect freedom, morality linked to capacity	Informal, capacity-based vocational forms
Psychological liberalism	Psychological person (private)	Anti-hierarchy, politeness over civility; passivity and depression; internal focus; lacking developmental perspective	Self-development; psychotherapy	Awakening of *private-life* function of emotion	Interiority, private-life affect freedom, moral sensitivity	Middle-class malaise, psychotherapy

Political liberalism	Political individual (egalitarian)	Anti-authority; anti-psychology/process; sole focus on external change; lacking developmental perspective	Political reform, diversity, social change through activism	Necessary shame sublimates selfishness; awareness of the "other"	Reasoning based moral experience	Reform movements of nineteenth and twentieth centuries
Political liberalism	Political individual (libertarian)	Anti-institution; selfish; shortsighted; "freedom from"	Tolerance; revolution; inovation	Fear and guilt repressed in brittle individualism	Reasoning and sensory freedom	Enlightenment, industrial revolution
Religious liberalism	Social roles	Tribalism; intolerance for the "other"; limited internal authority or agency	Ritualized submission to external authority	Fear and guilt used to control emotional impulsivity	Inspiring and controlling images of divine and social order	Reformation
Tribal liberalism	Individual identity	Impulsive, violent	Formation of individual identity	Affect fused w/ imagination → identification w/ numinous god-image	Ritual freedom, rudimentary individual identity	Classical culture
Tribal liberalism	Group identity	No individual identity	Formation of group identity	Elemental forces of nature are represented as affect-laden images	Imagination as source of group will and emergent identity	
Social hierarchy	Mammalian					

oriented toward human freedom. Since its inception, political liberalism has continued to mature its understanding of this freedom to incorporate more advanced egalitarian values that are expressed through a focus on changing the external world. Such changes follow several key themes including: social justice; environmentalism; fair and open political processes; the health, education, and general welfare of children and their families; the adoption of international policies based on a vision of humanity as a whole and not fractured into religious, ethnic, or nationalistic "tribal" groups.

On the other hand there are institutions that focus on the internal, psychological conditions of people for the purpose of healing their suffering and guiding their moral and psychological development. This private-psychological liberalism manifests in the spiritual movements of the nineteenth and twentieth centuries and in psychotherapy in the twentieth century.

While the institutions of political and psychological liberalism focus their liberalizing intent differently, they are both embodiments of the psychological consciousness as it is appearing in Western culture. However, the divergence between the different intents of political and psychological liberalism limits their capacity for collaboration, leaving them vulnerable to the regressive and oppressive cultural forces that work to limit the depth and breadth of the penetration of the psychological consciousness into modern culture.

The personality of the political individual can be characterized as extroverted, using a highly rationalized form of political discourse to attempt to change the public, external structures of society, through a focus on issues. The personality of the psychological person is comparatively introverted. However, it too relies on a highly rationalized form of discourse. Yet, the discourse of the psychological person emphasizes change through a focus on the "internal," private experience of the individual and family. Interestingly enough, like the political individual, the psychological person also focuses on issues – however, with quite a different meaning. The voices of these two liberalisms vary widely. Each has its own unique history, its own story about what it means to be human, care for one another, and how to make necessary changes that would support the work of deepening our humanity. Each has its own language through which distinct theories of change are offered; each of these liberalizing influences also has its own limitation.

The growing criticism of political liberalism identifies how it focuses too intently on making changes in the external structures of society while paying little attention to the inner world of the individual or culture. This inner world has been described as the world of the human soul, the heart of morality, or simply the world of feeling. However, as it is described, this inner world seems to have little place in politics, especially for those political liberals who have borne the brunt of the political scene for too long. Unfortunately, despite their hard work and commitment to structural changes, political individuals have become the chronic voice of the loyal opposition, determined, but unable to gain the audience to found a new voice of a liberal majority. Or if they do rise in power, it seems at best temporary and the result of the conservative's hubris, not their own articulated moral vision, such as in the mid-term US elections of 2006.

Under consideration is the possibility that the political individual needs to connect, both personally and organizationally, with the intent, purpose, and practices of psychological liberalism. However, the limitations of the psychological person make such a connection distasteful. While political liberalism is limited by its extraverted public approach to change, psychological liberalism may be equally hobbled by its introverted approach to change that focuses too intently on an individual's or family's private-life experience. The task seems to be to find or create a new liberalism and a new liberal type, which I am beginning to see as the rise of the "psychological citizen."

Finding one's distinct contribution: the shift to the psychological citizen

The idea that it is possible to set out to form a new psychological and moral type reflects the developmental rhythm of turning passive into active. As we have seen this is a common rhythm of development, whether identified with the child, adult, citizen, or for a people. A second rhythm is also relevant here. Whether described as the rhythmic movement from esoteric to exoteric experience, or more specifically as phases of political development, images appear to people and bring with them new states of consciousness. These images/states are shared and practiced and lead people into continually more developed stages that require a broader and deeper consideration of those around them, as well as freeing them to imagine the future with less fear and more hope and possibility.

Through these rhythms the individual has moved through cycles of outward expansion and inward self-reflection. The first images of individual identity carried with them the numinous power associated with the gods. This led to the emotional self-centeredness of what could be called the "first man" who directed the group's will as their own drive toward conquest. Through their identification with the god-image they created an age of empire. Their burst of differentiating energy, the civilizations they built, and their failures led to an inward cycle of greater self-reflection. Subsequent imagery broke the man–god identification and led to a new religious order based on the manipulation of fear, guilt, a new experience of self-worth, and the responsibilities of service. God now appears as removed and self-contained. Through this stage access to the numinosity of the group's will is controlled though religious doctrine.

In time, the control of the external god leads to rebellion as the outward expanding individual reappears in the rugged individualism of the political individual who gave birth to the modern world. Yet, once again the hubris of expansion led to a growing shame for excess. This next inward cycle led to the emergence of the psychological person who sought development through a private-life spirituality. Yet, this too has limits, including its inability to cope with the external politics of the world. The inwardness of the psychological person leads to a new cycle of outward expression, which is manifesting in the form of the "psychological citizen." However, unlike previous stages of individual development, the psychological citizen is able to maintain a compassionate awareness of the other, while differentiating their own distinctness in the form of new psychological capacities.

Unlike the psychological person, the capacities developed by the psychological citizen are not so much in relation to their private life. Instead, they develop capacities that strengthen their political identities. Here, individual expression is directed toward the developmental needs of the whole. This marks a shift in the rhythmic pattern as the psychological citizen does not lose sight of the whole. They are aware of and focus their attention on the evolution of culture, which turns their passive experience of the future into the active capacity for destiny. Graves' description of the shift from the first to the second tier of consciousness is one good expression of the ability of the psychological citizen to maintain an awareness of themselves without losing sight of the whole. Their focus on their own destiny automatically links them to humanity, for it is their destiny to become more fully human.

For the psychological citizen the impulsivity of the "first man" is channeled through a well developed individuality that seeks their highest level of potential functioning based on individual desire and universal principles. Also, the short-sightedness of the political individual is channeled into a broader awareness of time, historical and teleological. Individual difference and autonomy are viewed through a lens that focuses on the service of the greater possibilities of human development and evolution.

In the formation of the psychological citizen, the affect system goes through distinct changes, specifically around the function of fear and shame. A parallel description can be found in Beck and Cowan's presentation of Graves' thinking about the functioning of emotion at this level. They note how, at "yellow," "compulsions and anxieties" fade as fear is faced. Following Omer's approach to affect, we would conclude that this leads to the maturation of the foundational capacity for courage (Beck and Cowan 2006: 278). With the development of individual courage based in principle, the ability to face problems and arrive at moral solutions becomes more accessible. For example, Martin Luther King inspired many people during the civil rights movement to move toward the psychological citizen as he helped them face the moral and spiritual value of going to jail. He said, "If he puts you in jail, you go into that jail and transform it from a dungeon of shame to a haven of freedom and dignity" (King 1988). Not only did King transform the fears of his followers, but also their experience of shame. These transformations were echoed again and again in my own research with progressive political leaders who spoke of their experience in jail as moments in which they came of age into their political identities.

For the "first man" there is little shame. Later, shame is evoked in order to control emotional impulsivity (religious social roles). But next, shame is repressed in order to break away from the oppression of an external authority (political individual). However, it goes too far in the creed of manifest destiny. Fortunately, shame is reawakened to alert individuals to the harm they do to others and the responsibility to attend to this harm and, generally, to the needs of others (private-psychological person). Unfortunately, at this level no clear public language is articulated to express and direct this shame. Instead, a psychological language of the family is asserted that emphasizes non-judgmentalness. It is not until the psychological citizen's development of an awareness of universal principles that a public language of moral authority re-emerges.

What would a public language that supports the liberalization of our moral experience sound like? Could it reintegrate necessary shame into public practices and institutions in a felt-sense experience? I found the progressive leaders in my research spontaneously addressing these and other similar questions. I will return to their stories in the next section.

In the historical examples in previous chapters we can see the difficulties of articulating a public moral language. In part, the fear and avoidance of authority limited what could be accomplished in the nineteenth and twentieth centuries. This fear causes individuals and groups to associate oppression with hierarchy and thus forces a way of thinking that confuses equality with sameness. This has led to forms of political correctness that fail to acknowledge the differing functional capacities of individuals and groups. As a result, groups and individuals fail to recognize their own developmental advancement and too often try to assert political agendas that are too advanced for the human group in need of clear leadership.

Jimmy Carter, Michael Dukakis, and John Kerry's presidential campaigns all failed to account for the American people's need for enough religious, moral language. Instead, they over-used their reasoning freedom, focusing on political issues, which they employed to express too advanced values and political agendas. They failed to recognize and know what to do with their own advanced political development. Beck and Cowan apply Graves' models to presidential elections, and by way of example claim that "Jimmy Carter's . . . leadership style was arrested at a position one to one-and-a-third of a step beyond where the American people were centered. Ronald Reagan's . . . image was just barely ahead of 'the electorate'" (Beck and Cowan 2006: 126). Awareness of developmental differences may not be the only thing that is needed, but such awareness could not help but enable liberals to engage political culture more consciously.

In order for the psychological citizen to emerge more actively, the disinclination of the psychological person to acknowledge a developmental hierarchy must be challenged. The psychological person must overcome their fears of and prejudices toward authority by working to identify their own distinct capacities, which they will then use to make a unique contribution to the liberalization of culture. This is the task of the psychological citizen.

The fear of authority limits both political and psychological liberals alike. The political individual's identification with rugged individualism may enable them to resist domination, after all "I will bow to no one." Similarly, the psychological person confuses "equality" with "sameness," which has much the same result – after all "Who are you to tell me what to do?" While having healthy intentions – with many positive results – these attitudes limit the ability of both forms of liberalism to move the consciousness of their respective groups to an awareness of the developmental process itself.

Attending to the shyness that both the political individual and the psychological person bring to the issue of a public morality directly addresses the limits of each. In my research with progressive political leaders I had the opportunity to explore these limits. As the conversations unfolded, I witnessed their reticence toward what I came to call "moral speaking." They showed a shyness toward morality in general that typifies their political identities, manifesting the limitations of both the political individual and the psychological person. In their activism they clearly live the lives of political individuals. However, as will become apparent, they also have embodied at least the values of the psychological person. Thus they live with a split in their identity between these two developmental levels.

In addition to their limits I had the chance to meet my own. Through these conversations and through my subsequent writing, I have found many hesitancies and political wounds of my own. Such work has helped me to turn toward the realization of some rudimentary form of identity as a psychological citizen. It has also helped me to see the value experienced by political liberals when they are attended to through some combination of a private/public psychological liberalism. Here are more stories from my work and research with progressive political leaders. In these stories we can see the way in which they embody many or all of the developmental advances and limits described in this and previous chapters.

Stories of progressives and the progressive movement

In a recent meeting with leaders of two liberal political action committees, I became aware of the extent to which they easily fell into a way of speaking that revolved around the two-year election cycle and included concepts like:

"precinct walking," "get out the vote drives," "lawn signs," "fundraising," and other similar phrases that are woven together into community engagement practices, that is, action-oriented meetings. I learned this "political language" in my family in the late 1960s and 1970s, during my father's tenure in the state legislature, and have come to associate it with people willing to sacrifice their time for the good of their communities.

While these political liberals focus externally and seem to have minimal interest in their own internal or emotional experience, they clearly have developed the egalitarian values of the psychological person. This makes them a powerful political force, the people to whom I look to embody the future. However, I also have come to think of their political language as risky and limiting. Listening to their strange yet very familiar language helped me to connect to these liberal leaders. Yet, I realized that their speaking was also rarified, and that few others would be able to understand or enjoy it. This realization has helped me to see how liberal organizers have developed their own language that is effective for the trench work of political organizing, but is too technical to be appealing to people who might, given the right circumstances, be inclined to get involved. This was especially poignant when a new volunteer joined a celebratory gathering that quickly became a political discussion emphasizing strategizing. They did not know how to be more welcoming. If rationalism is the bane of liberalism, as Lakoff claims, then strategizing may be their avoidance of relationship.

While these organizations may represent the morality of the future, their way of speaking and their means of embodiment make it difficult for them to connect to others. Few people could understand, much less enjoy or desire to come back to, meetings in which this political language of liberalism is spoken. When simply viewed from a traditional liberal perspective, their reliance on a technical language leads them to scratch their heads when confronted with the paucity of volunteers they draw, the overwork those few people who do volunteer do, and their difficulty leading their communities in the face of being continually outspent by their conservative counterparts during local, state, and national elections.

When I drew the group's attention to the technicality of its spoken language I used the analogy of boys and men speaking the language of cars, engines, or sports. They found this analogy immediately pleasing and laughed with mild embarrassment and with an appreciative awareness that comes when one's strengths and limitations are being witnessed. Recognizing the limitations of their techno-speak brought relief to this group of liberals, as they imagined using it to help with their significant difficulty in drawing volunteers to their political causes.

Despite the limitations that blunt their moral speaking, notice that these progressives welcomed friendly enough but still critical feedback. They were generally open to my attention. While I had enough of a recognizable political history and could speak their language well enough, they were accepting of the attention of a psychologist. I suspect this reflects the emerging opportunity to create a new psychological citizen. By identifying and further articulating a public language of human transformation that accounts for both individual development and cultural evolution, I am pressing toward the fifth phase of political development, that is, toward the identification of new vocational and institutional forms, which would have as their responsibility the conscious activation of individual development and cultural evolution. However, in this context, it is not the individual's private life that would be the focus of development; rather, it is the development of their political identity for the sake of activating their potential as psychological citizens.

In the remainder of this chapter I will return to the stories of the progressive political leaders in my research. In the course of reading these stories I ask that you look for three things. First, notice the way in which the strengths and limitations of political liberals, as I have been describing, are lived by these men and women; second, see if these stories trigger your own generational attention so that you can see and feel into the way the several centuries old successes and limits of liberalism are currently being played out in these stories; third, notice how they respond to the very simple learning practices and psychological interventions I present.

Liberals' success at forming a public identity and difficulty with emotions

If political liberals represent the modern trend toward liberty, then how are they responsive and unresponsive to the current crises of our culture? For example, based on the last chapter, how do they bridge the gap between an isolated private life and an exhausting public life?

Also, is there a role for a social scientist to engage the public and support a process through which stronger political identities form? If such engagement is possible, what impact would this have on the gulf between political and psychological experience, between interest in social progress and interest in individual development? If the gap between public and private experience can be bridged and if this addresses the gulf between political and psychological experience, what does this have to say about the function of our rational capacities and the role of emotion in our personal and political lives?

I will answer these questions by telling more of the stories elicited in my research with progressive political leaders. These stories show how simple psychological learning practices support political liberals to be able to activate an internal, emotional dimension of their political identity that remains a nascent factor in their ability to more actively transform their experience of the future into the capacity for destiny.

Sacrificing authenticity for a public face

In the course of my research with progressive political leaders I learned that they yearn to share with others a genuineness they came to call their "authentic face," a face surfacing here and there in their day-to-day living, but usually submerged. The authentic face is fragmented. Authenticity is restricted by the climate of public politics which ties into their suffering or what I have come to think of as their various "political wounds." I had the opportunity to look closely at these "political wounds," suffered at the interface between their private and public identities.

Chief among these wounds is the restricted range of affect, which was demonstrated by the masking of their personal experience and emotions in public. This leads to an ambivalent relationship to emotion itself (which is part of what keeps their authentic face submerged). They are especially ambivalent about their shame, but are nevertheless guided in their political intelligence by it. By means of this intelligence, progressive political leaders form their moral experience and activate a capacity for destiny.

The authentic face of progressive activism

The pleasure of good company

In the research group I established an atmosphere of mutual inquiry and supportive attention. As a psychotherapist with a bit of training in facilitating group experience, I created opportunities for new experience to emerge, including how the research participants were able to let down in the group and be themselves; they referred to this experience as being able to show their "authentic face." In the afternoon of Day One the group was invited to reflect on what they had experienced that morning. When given this opportunity they made numerous comments about the time we were spending together, including talking about how, coming into this group, they did not have to bring their "agenda packets." Dave said, "It's rare to be in a situation where we're not having to be strategic." They did not have to think about how they were going to be "read," nor even, as Gillian playfully noted, have to wear their jewelry. She continued, "I felt naked coming here because I did not have to do anything besides just be here."

The research participants continued to express what it was like to be gathered in this group of like-minded leaders without a specific political agenda. Harry reflected, "There is not a lot of time for this kind of sharing and exploring." Frank also enjoyed the new group experience saying, "This has been fun for me because I'm getting to know a bunch of people that I have not known before . . . just to get to know you as people, it's been very inspirational." This was followed by his introspective confession of his own political limitations when he said "I just hate the . . . [political] . . . process and because of that I have not been able to accomplish a lot of things . . . it is so fascinating to see all of you doing it, seemingly enjoying it, and just getting a sense of how that is for you personally."

The relief to be among peers (as opposed to being up before a public they had responsibility toward) was expressed with humor when Frank said, "I just realize that one of the things I like about being here is that I'm not responsible for any of you." This comment brought peals of laughter and was followed by the group cascading into a playful shared fantasy about not wanting to go home, but wanting to stay with me in my home, the location of the first group meeting. Frank started this, saying playfully, "Its cozy in here, we're going to stay," at which everyone laughed long and hard. Harry immediately said, "*And* the food is great!" [group laughter]. This was followed by someone saying, "Give us a glass of wine" [more laughter]. Then I joined in the play saying, "I could probably come up with a bottle or two" [more laughter]. Dave added, "I have a few sleeping bags in the car" [more laughter]. Irene chirped in with, "If I had a pillow."

However, this string of playful comments ended when Sandy said, "We have a lot of responsibilities." She goes on to talk about her responsibilities as an elected official, repeating the word "responsibility" five times in several sentences. She ends with an almost exultant statement, "I . . . I mean, I love it, I . . . I . . . I like to be able to help people." After this interruption of play the expression of the group's satisfaction took a more pragmatic tone as Harry reflected on the potential of the research to help the families of elected officials. He said, "This form of a workshop or variation would be very good for children and spouses of elected officials." Gillian also said, "This is a great time for me to go through something like this with this group, personally it helps me rethink what I'm doing with my life overall."

During the Day Two meeting, Frank was the first one to use the word "authentic." Reflecting on what had been happening in the group he said, "It's getting in touch with that authentic self. And, how much more dynamic and creative would public meetings be if you sitting there as public entities were able to be in touch with that?"

In a similar vein, Dave noticed that, "We are showing up personally here, we're certainly hearing a lot of personal stories. One of the things I walk away from this with is looking at how I show up and how that affects the people around me."

The group attributed their positive experience to the way that they were being "affirmed" by peers. Frank started this line of thinking in his typically open and vulnerable style when he said, "I think one of the things that I see here is how hungry we all are for affirmation. I know I am. I feel a lump coming up in my throat as I talk about it."

Similarly, Sandy said, "I was preparing myself for today [soft, warm, familiar tone in her voice], and that's because of the cool things that happened [here last time]."

Diane also thought that affirmation was important as she said, "I want to agree with affirmation. I think that's the problem, we are hungry for it and in political organizations people do not encourage it."

Toward the end of the second meeting, I asked them what they would like to see this research bring to the progressive community. At this time the phrase "authentic face" was born. Diane expressed hope that the "authenticity" our group had experienced could be extended into the broader progressive community. Diane said, "If groups that work together had discussions like this, maybe people could show an authentic face." In the light of the way the face is the primary site of affect, her choice of words seems very insightful.

In the course of this conversation Gillian said, "I need to learn how to work with those who do not show their authentic face. Or, maybe [we could] show more of who we are personally and publicly [to others]." The authenticity shared during the research meetings was noted by all. Frank referred to our time together as "reflective-time," and "deeper time."

Opportunities for a new *personal* political identity

The current nature of the public/political arena, by reputation in and outside of politics, is largely considered to be insincere. In the course of the research meetings I witnessed the elected officials and other leaders trapped in this cultural form. In the simple setting of this group, and with the minimal support of a trained facilitator, I saw these people emerge from this trap. They live in a limbo between the confines of alienated private identities and an experienced inauthentic public identity. Nowhere can they find a place to have or show fully personal identity integrating their public and privates lives. In this group they eagerly accessed the internal experience of the psychological person.

The research participants had not experienced much support for talking openly about their experience of leading a political life. The typical political life involves a way of giving themselves, which takes a toll and provides little renewal, so authenticity suffers. In our research group, they found relief from this isolation. They were able to take off their political masks among political peers and share in a way that was novel to them. This sharing was essentially healing and transformative and may anticipate successful forms of learning practices through which individuals with political identities find support and growth amongst their peers with the help of psychology.

Particularly interesting was the way that the group had of modulating its growing intimacy and depth. Sandy's interruption of the group play was one example of this. I believe that this was a defensive move she made because she experienced some anxiety about the intimacy that was coming through the playfulness. I also suspect that this intimacy somehow threatened the political identity they were accustomed to, perhaps ending its comfortable isolation. When Sandy says we are "responsible" it is their habitual political identities speaking. Part of them believes that serving the larger purpose requires the sacrifice of the more personal and shared experience they were beginning to have.

I imagine Sandy's political identity as an isolated young girl. She fights off the playfulness because the progressive political identity has been traumatized: it has not gone through a fully successful developmental process. The emergent authentic face of progressive activism is young and inexperienced. It has a wonderful playfulness, but is still restricted by the natural tendency to heroically isolate itself despite its community mindedness. At this time there is little or no identity structure that can balance the harsh public identity with the more feeling private identity. This is the task of the psychological citizen. Such a citizen could help others to turn toward the authenticity of internal experience and to use this "personalness" in their political life.

A "new psychological and moral type": trapped by their burden

According to Samuels, this division between a public, rational world and a private, subjective world has been introjected by the individual into an "intra-personal" space, which defines the individual identity (Samuels 1993: Chapter One). He argues for the necessity of finding within the individual a capacity to bridge this difference, thus treating a social condition by first imagining and then embodying the psychological capacities necessary to respond to this condition. He asks: "In what way is the personal political, and what way is the political personal" (Samuels 1993: 7). The difficulty in bridging this internal gap creates distress as the individual has to withhold their actual experience in order to act "strategically" in juxtaposition to acting "authentically" in the public world. Most Americans cannot bear this internal condition and instead project it outward, blaming their retreat on an indifferent and corrupt political system, rather than seeking their "larger personality" (Mogenson 1992: 162).

In contrast, the research participants, as challenged as they are to maintain their authenticity, have succeeded in making the political personal and bearing the painful results. They do not blame the system as inherently corrupt, or, even if they do, they believe that they can be part of a genuine solution. They embody, at least in part, the larger self with its capacity to imagine and pursue solutions. They recognize the necessity of bearing the weight of a political identity in order to fulfill their obligation as citizens. This obligation clearly brings with it some tension or suffering from having to mask their own personalness as they don the necessary armor of the public sphere. But, in so doing they initiate or found a form of identity that resists the historical trend of individualism that is moving toward a greater valuing of the personal.

In this context, they have achieved the active understanding of identity first described by Erikson. They experience themselves as agents of social change. In effect, they are holding the fabric of a public culture together, keeping it from ripping further, preserving the public integrity necessary for democratic civilization. They are stretched thin over tears in the social fabric that most of the rest of us have abandoned, as we fantasize that our middle-class status will keep us safe from feeling the tear personally. While psychotherapy has eased the middle-class malaise, few of us have turned back to help those at the bottom.

The idea of the "authentic face" represents these political leaders' desire to put down the burdensome aspect of their political identity that they are forced to shoulder in order to participate in the public arena. This desire was fulfilled when they found they could take off the offending public mask in the group. The group's desire to bring forth and share their "authentic face" found support from me as a psychological person, which helped them to find the voice of their "internal" subjective experience. Releasing this internal voice lets the private world of subjective feelings enter the public world of political actions. However, this is taking place within a controlled environment, supported by my own imagery of the possibility of creating a new psychological and moral type. This represents the confluence between political and psychological liberalism operating under the radar of a fully developed public language. Nevertheless, based on Phase Three of my model of political development, we see how certain practicing is taking place which supports the emergence of a new public use of emotion. Watch how this plays out in the subsequent stories.

Political wounds

Taking public wounds personally

While the division between a public and private identity in many moderns leads to the experience of alienation, public participation too brings suffering. Both Diane and Dave told stories of physical suffering or witnessing others' suffering during demonstrations. Diane said, "I've been hurt quite a bit in civil disobedience actions." And Dave said, "I watched three cops take a woman who probably weighed 90 pounds, slam her up against a wall, and repeatedly slam her with their clubs, and she almost died of internal hemorrhaging."

In another story Gillian expressed incredulity toward the effort that progressives put into politics. She said:

Some of us get together and we realize how much we're giving of ourselves [progressives] and we're talking about [other] candidates who do not feel any

of this, but, businesspeople give them $40,000 and say go win an election, and
they're up on the council and they do not *feel* anything, they're just voting the
"right" way.

In another sequence the group shares its dissatisfaction and burn-out with
political meetings as they are currently done. Irene says, "Nobody ever
works together. I guess I'm frustrated even running for [elected office] again
and I just feel like I'm burning out. I just do not need to feel like I'm going
to be shot in the back, literally." As soon as Irene stops speaking Dave
jumps in, "I have a dysfunctional family. I do not need to go to meetings."
    Then Diane adds:

> I'm agreeing with you. I've gone to thousands of meetings and it's a wonder
> that people can do anything. People have power plays, sexism, racist things.
> They do not vision, they work on strategy, they do not form community. It's a
> wonder the Left is doing anything.

Between Day One and Day Two meetings, I came to see their troubled
experience as "political woundings." On Day Two I said:

> We are all wounded politically. Our experience has been ripped into separate
> public and private dimensions . . . most human beings have retreated into a
> private life, and have lost a sense of public participation. I'm getting a lot of
> head nods, you know exactly what I'm talking about.

I then went on to recount specific examples (cited above) from the first
meeting as things I thought related to being "wounded politically." Following this I invited them to share stories of political woundings they had
recently experienced, which prompted several stories from their current
political lives. "Who would like to start?" I said.
    Harry said, "Oh, I'll start, I'm still bleeding. I voted with the more
conservative segment of [elected body] and voted no on a library funding
issue." What happened was, the local political website managed by a close
friend viciously attacked him for that vote:

> She and I [the woman who published the attack] we went out walking
> [without her bringing up the issue] . . . Later when I got home, another
> colleague called me and told me, "You better look at the website." I could not
> believe what I was seeing, it was devastating. So, this issue has cost me, for
> the time being, a very close personal friend. It's something that's not going to
> blow over anytime soon.

This story left the group gasping, in surprise, but also in recognition. Irene pitched in and spoke of how such attacks are a central part of politics, how progressives are always "eating their own," to which Abe added, "I'm not worried about the conservatives criticizing me, I'm worried about the people who are supporting me. That's where you're going to get your most vicious attacks."

Irene's story followed. She told of suffering a public verbal attack that she described as "personal . . . ugly . . . the worst in ten years." Here are her words:

> This last Wednesday night somebody got up and viciously attacked me at a public meeting. And I knew for 15 months that I was the targeted candidate, by the pro-growth group, they want me out. I've cost them tens of millions of dollars. They hate me.

She goes on to describe how she responded to this attack:

> I just sat up and . . . made sure I was the first [elected official] to respond. As I was speaking my voice was fairly strong, but it was starting to break . . . and then I said that I needed a five-minute break and I just had to walk out and compose myself because I was really going to cry. You do not really want to cry in public, because politicians never cry in public.

Opening their "woundedness"

These leaders do not experience much support to talk openly about their political wounds. However, when given the opportunity, they are willing to vulnerably share these wounds at some depth. In our two meetings they found it relieving to be able to set aside their public faces, in the context of a supportive small group of peers, not simply in private retreat. For, in their private lives their families and friends often were caught up to some extent in their sacrifices and could not necessarily provide them with such support. Also, families and friends have not necessarily developed their own political identities such that they could be peers and offer peer support to these leaders.

While the group did not overtly embrace the notion that the progressive movement could be moved forward through their tending to their political wounds, in fact, these wounds were tended to and healing was experienced. While I had hoped this would be possible, I did not know how it would happen or if it would happen until it did. It seems that we were all learning the potential of bringing psychology and politics together with the intent of transformation. This took place with a mixture of relief and pleasure as we came to experience the common thread of our suffering within our political wounds.

Physical harm and betrayal were types of woundings. However, the wound that garnered the most common attention was from having to wear the public mask, and bear attacks in which they were treated impersonally, as only the mask, without humanity, and disregarding crucial, private-life experiences such as friendship. The repression of personal/subjective experience, represented by the need to wear this public mask, was a group-level wound that the group successfully began to heal. In this group the progressives learned that it is possible to draw meaningfully from their emotions, contrary to hundreds of years or more of cultural deprecation of this emotionality.

Harry's story reflects another group wound, that is, the expectation that attacks will come from within the progressive movement. That these internal attacks are considered normal, to be expected, shows an acceptance of traumatic experience and little faith that it could be any different, that there could be healing. This wound reflects how the progressive movement, in Diane's words, does not "vision" or "form community." This leaves them having to be, in Dave's words, "strategic," wondering how they are going to be "read" instead of tending to their own and each other's wounds.

A new language and a new identity: speaking about work and healing

According to Kerlinger: "Liberalism is a set of political, economic, religious, educational, and other social beliefs that emphasizes . . . secular rationality and rational approaches to social problems" (Kerlinger 1984: 15). Following Bellah, we can speak of this "favoring" of rationality as an aspect of the "voice" or "language" of liberalism.

Progressive leaders learn to speak what Habermas refers to as a "technical language" of social progress rather than an "emancipatory language" that would work to rebuild community and inspire political leadership and participation through a deeper expression of and concern for human need (Matustik 2001: 45). Their technical language limits their ability to think of political events as events with psychological consequences or meaning, that is, it is difficult to think in terms of political wounds when you're stuck on political issues.

A consequential political identity can, however, graft the liberal's technical/rational language to a psychological language of internal, personal experience. Samuels thinks that this talking across the outer world and inner world divide is at best difficult and at worst silly sounding. He says: "The language of the heart (inner world language) and the language of politics (outer world language) have become so separate that to mingle them sounds like embarrassing wooly-headedness" (Samuels 2001: 10).

Yet, Samuels is determined to bridge this gap by creating a new "hybrid language" that makes psychology a part of a new definition of politics (Samuels 2001: 13). He adds: "Future generations will be much better than we are at providing what is missing and speaking the new hybrid language of politics and transformation that is being born" (Samuels 2001: 13).

Part of what is currently confusing is the general lack of differentiation in our language and experience between personal and private experience. In the research meetings it became clear that the leaders were living a difference between these two that is difficult to talk about. Is it something emergent? It is clear that they do take their political experience personally and so are quite ready and motivated to work on the "new language," though they may not actually do it without prompting from the psychological side. It seems to me that they have the potential to model a new type of *civic personality*; but they need the help of a transformative political psychologist.

To fulfill what Samuels calls the "psychological need to be political," individuals need to work on their "political self." In politics, healing will take place as the Left learns to "set its subjectivity free in the political world" and as it pays "more attention to the psychological development of [its] members" (Samuels 1993: 55). According to Samuels, without attending to the psychology of the progressive movement, the "New Left" movement of the 1960s ignored "human needs" and, as well, did not know what to do with the power drives that emerge in political meetings. Samuels echoes Diane's comments about power dynamics in groups when he writes:

> There was total denial of the . . . all-too-human power struggles that were going on, as the leaders sat around for hours discussing what to paint on the banners to be held up outside of car plants.
>
> (Samuels 2001: 25)

The political development of progressivism, and thus liberalism, requires a wedding between its current technical language and a language of tears. Good-hearted people feel forced to wear an inauthentic face in public, one that cannot cry. They continue to move "forward," pretending they are not hurt, when they clearly are. Attending to our political wounds will help bridge political and psychological liberalism. Central to this ministration is the task of drawing on the wisdom of psychological liberalism, its attention to personal experience, without getting caught up in its problematic perpetuation of the private/public split in identity. In the last story from my research I draw attention to the personal, subjective, and emotional experience of the progressive leaders in a way that would seem to fit the bill. I stay focused on their public/political identity and attend to, minister to, their experience. As a result, a larger awareness of the value of their emotional experience begins to emerge.

Affect freedom, shame, and political identity

Shared feelings, especially shame, lead to questions about moral speaking

In addition to what I have already presented, three particular but related experiences surfaced in my research meetings. These are:

1   Reaching toward affect freedom, from within political identity.
2   Shame within political identity.
3   The will to express morality within the political sphere.

I will present each of these and then draw out possible meanings within these connections.

During the first meeting I was excited by the degree of vulnerability shared by the research participants. Between meetings, as I began transcribing and analyzing the first day's audio and video recordings, I noticed the ambivalent attitude shown by the participants toward their subjective experience of emotion. On the one hand they spoke of hiding their subjectivity, but on the other hand, when it appeared in the group, it was deeply valued.

Abe spoke of the way he withholds his personal experience as a political official. He said, "When you're sitting on the other side, the side that all the elected officials are, you do not reveal much about yourself. You get very guarded about that."

Similarly, Irene ended her story about being attacked at the public meeting by saying, "You really do not want to cry in public, because politicians never cry in public."

Sandy explains her emotional experience as a public official somewhat apologetically, saying, "I've been known to be a little emotional . . . not sobbing or something, at public meetings." In contrast to this hesitancy to show their personal experience in public, the leaders were able to express personal feelings in the group.

Diane expressed surprise and enjoyment toward hearing what she called the "electeds" in the group showing feeling. Speaking to the group she said, "It's interesting to see the emotion in this room. I'm going 'wooh, you're humans' [group laughter]. It's nice to see you cry, to boot [expressing amazement] you have emotions!" [more group laughter].

After personal experiences were shared the group was invited to reflect on its own experience of being together. Harry did this saying, "There's not a lot of time for this kind of sharing and exploring." He said, "[Typically] we do not get to say to each other, 'how does that make you feel? Why do you feel that way?'"

Sandy said, "I feel comfortable in the group . . . I get emotional because I'm passionate." Frank responds to Sandy saying, "And when you're emotional I appreciate that, that's who you are, and it came out of a place of passion which I really appreciate in people . . . that's refreshing to me."

However, the group did not simply spend its time in the mutual appreciation that has been caricatured as "feel-good" psychology. Instead the following discussion, which came around to being about the difficulty of speaking morally in public, emerged. We had watched a 20-minute Martin Luther King video at the beginning of the first meeting. Abe spoke of being wrapped up in grief (he grieved the loss of King) but of also feeling "envy, I really envy his moral clarity and his spirituality. And [pause, head nod down and to the side, body sags away from the group], let's go on to someone else." When I went back to him a little later Abe continued:

> I envy Martin Luther King his spirituality, for being able to [speak morally in public] and I do not know that you can do that in public life, it's difficult to do that. When you're sitting on the side that all the elected officials are, you do not reveal much about yourself. You get very guarded about that. When I'm talking about affordable housing I make intellectual arguments, I make policy arguments, I do not say it's morally our obligation to provide this housing.

Frank and Dave subsequently compared themselves to King and found themselves wanting. Frank said, "Why cannot I rise to that level?" Dave said, "Why am I not being as true to the cause as he was? I'm feeling fearful of being uncommitted." Harry observed that his community "studiously avoids moral questions."

Immediately following these statements a long exchange took place about the difficulties of making moral arguments in public. It moved back and forth between expressions of doubt about the validity of making such statements in public, and statements of its necessity. On the one hand, doubt was expressed by Abe who says, "People have their own moral compass. I'm confident of mine and very reticent to criticize others." Similarly, Gillian notes a public official who "pushes her morals on other people publicly, I respect people who do *not* do that." On the other hand, making moral arguments did receive more than just marginal support. Regarding Abe's comment about affordable housing, Harry said, "On that particular issue I do not have a problem looking at the audience and saying, 'We're doing the right thing.'" Frank added, "When it becomes a moral imperative, that's different from a specifically religious perspective. And, we struggle with it in public, and I feel that right now, so, so much." The conversation drifts back and forth between emotions and morality and Harry returns to the topic of showing emotions in public:

> People crave it and want it, and that's part of the growth process, to maybe get more into it and deliver. I do not feel like the public would be opposed to

my showing more emotion. I think it would be beneficial and I think that they react to someone like Martin Luther King because it fills a need.

Dave swings it back again:

> I think there is a difference between pushing morality and showing moral conviction. I mean you say showing emotions, I think it's about showing moral conviction, it's about modeling personally – he [King] was embodying it. I think there's a distinction between pushing a personal moral agenda vs. appealing to everyone's aspiration or most people's. There's a difference here and I do not know how to name the difference.

Sandy joins in:

> I hate, I personally do not like to do the morality thing because I, I do not know if it's my place to talk about morality. It's about all of us communicating and letting us be who we are and then trying to make collective decisions. I do not know if that makes any sense.

Abe also struggled to make sense of both his lack of emotionality and lack of being able to speak morally:

> I'm a math person. I have a hard time with touching my own emotions. I'm used to analyzing things. I can analyze public policy until the cows come home, but I think I'm starting to struggle with this, "how to speak from" . . . we talked about this last time, how to speak from your morals. How you convince people that you're right and they're wrong?

On Day Two, following my interpretation of the "political wound" and their subsequent stories about these wounds, I offered the following second interpretation. I began by briefly introducing Jung's idea of the "collective unconscious" and then read from a poster paper where I had written the Jung quote cited earlier in Chapter 3:

> Those factors which are suppressed by the prevailing views or attitudes in the life of a society gradually accumulate in the collective unconscious and activate its contents. Certain individuals gifted with particularly strong intuition then become aware of the changes going on in it and translate these changes into communicable ideas . . . if the translation of the unconscious into a communicable language proves successful; it has a redeeming effect . . . form[ing] a new source of power.
>
> (Jung 1919: 314–15)

Next, I told them that this new power comes from emotion. I added, "So it's just no wonder that there's 'no crying in public', because that would be releasing power." I added this Jung quote:

> To gain possession of the energy [from the collective unconscious], he [a person] must make the emotional state the basis or starting point of the procedure. He must make himself as conscious as possible of the mood he is in, sinking himself in it without reserve . . . The whole procedure is a kind of enrichment and clarification of the *affect*, whereby the affect and its contents are brought nearer to consciousness . . . This is the beginning of the transcendent function.
>
> (Jung 1957a: 82, emphasis added)

I went on to say:

> [Emotional capacities] are significantly oppressed in the political sphere which leads to the repression of the full range of our experience . . . I believe the most severely repressed emotion in our country is shame. We seem to be in many ways a shameless people. Unfortunately, this severely retards or degrades our experience of moral integrity. And this creates a vicious circle, we retreat into individual, private lives, shamelessly oppressing the world's people and consuming the world's resources. Shame is so severely repressed that we can barely speak the word. However, individuals within the progressive movement have maintained their experience of necessary shame and because of that have been able to maintain their experience of being a citizen as well as their moral integrity.

Then I went on to cite several excerpts from the first meeting as examples of their expression of "necessary shame." I characterized comments of Dave's as expressing our culture's shame. He had spoken of the injustices of that time and of "wanting to yell and cry." The other examples I gave entered into personal expressions of shame. Evelyn had said, "I just . . . [feel] . . . immense shame for our history, I just realize it again and again and again." Frank spoke of feeling "regret" and "guilt" for not playing a larger role in the 1960s peace movement. Sandy, tearing up and sounding quite vulnerable, spoke of her own political trials describing them as "horrible."

Irene, speaking about her family's financial gain in the 1950s in the construction materials trade, said:

> The Korean War was going on . . . and all of a sudden we went from hamburger to prime rib, and I just did not get it! And all of a sudden we were rich . . . God! We had money! It was great, and then as I got older I just

started . . . [to realize] . . . I wondered if the money came because people were being killed.

In relation to why she got involved in politics, Gillian said, "I think the shame I felt was for the environmental degradation I saw." Here, the implication is that we should feel ashamed for how we treat the environment. Similarly, Diane tied in shame with her dissatisfaction with political meetings. She said, "I think that people are ashamed by being real in meetings." She adds, "I found that over the years, people are not real. They are embarrassed by their emotions. They are ashamed about their comments; they are ashamed to comment on other people's comments."

The group's response to this new interpretation was mixed. Harry simply said, "I'm not big on shame. I'll think about it to see if there is something about motivational factors that I associated with shame." Several other participants "tried on" the word shame, and found some surface area where they connect to it. Sandy associated shame with other people's failings, particularly how other elected officials do not prepare by doing the background work on different political issues, that is, they do not "do their homework." But she saw embarrassment as the relevant emotion, not shame. Listen to her wrestle with this:

In regard to shame . . . To me it's more, I would be embarrassed about the decisions that I'm making if I did not do my homework. It's not shame, maybe it's shameful, but I feel embarrassed for others when they do not do that . . . I said it was embarrassment not necessarily shame. And, not my embarrassment, but embarrassment for them.

Irene said: "I was raised with a certain amount of shame. We never used the word moral, we always just assumed that you never kneeled to God, you always stood right there. To be present right there, it's really inside your heart." She goes on to finish, "I understand what you're talking about the word shame. Not even in my vocabulary." (Sandy had seemed to feel similarly about the word "moral," or what she referred to as doing the "moral thing.")

Chances for affect freedom: bearing shame and asserting moral authority

These progressive leaders suffer from cultural norms that repress important subjective capacities. For example, a full range of emotion is repressed in making informed political decisions. Affect freedom would draw from the biological and psychosocial function of the affect system to help determine moral experience, take effective political action, and support fulfilling connections to others regarding moral issues. The political use of affect freedom comes out of an individual's ability to know what subjective, emotional experience they are having in relation to a political issue or situation. Reflexive use of this experience motivates political participation. It also increases the acuity of moral experience while motivating moral action.

The restriction on the public display of emotion, such as crying, is only one symptom of this restricted affect freedom. Greater freedom was experienced by the leaders as they tapped into the fuller range of emotion/ authenticity. Also, given the chance to imagine such freedom, they made connections to their political life and to the progressive movement. However, when such freedom seemed to point toward the inclusion of shame, one of the darkest emotions, they stumbled on this path to freedom. Also, as they began to use the group experience to expand their range of affect freedom, they were confronted with one of the most serious limitations facing liberals, that is, their struggle with asserting moral authority.

There is a cultural expectation that elected officials, and other leaders in the public eye, will not be "personal" in their political roles. By contrast, in traditional cultures the personal experience of leaders is sought out and contains cultural and moral knowledge. Today, this personal experience of leaders is not viewed as a source of knowledge; in fact, it is viewed as something to be studiously avoided, especially in political settings. The taboo regarding emotional experience may be particularly strong in progressives, given their inclination to identify with rational means. The rational and objective dimensions of political experience are what are considered "legitimate" (Samuels 2001: 5). In the context of our group, the individuals found new sources of legitimacy.

As the group's natural inclination toward expressing and valuing the emotion emerged, the research began to transform the research participants. A reconsideration of the taboo against subjective experience was implicit in how they naturally enjoyed, valued, and began to follow the trail of their emotions. In fact, this often happens in individual psychotherapy and group therapy; it is just that, in this case, it happened in a group exploring their political identities.

They naturally fell toward trusting the intrinsic worth of their emotions. On the one hand, "politicians never cry in public;" on the other hand, progressive leaders, in the right setting, are able to drop into their feelings and allow these to guide them toward a refreshing intimacy with one another.[1] This intimacy was based on a shared depth, but also included delight. They were pleased and affirmed, and grew in their willingness to look on darker things with one another. There were many times in the group experience when individuals shared their darkness. However, when it came to calling it shame, they were reluctant. Only once, before we took up the issue specifically, was the actual word used by a participant telling their story.

Evelyn, the group's 80-plus-year-old member, showed enough presence of mind to be able to actually name shame as one of the shared feelings we had after watching the King video. Shame was naturally evoked in the face of his sacrifice, legacy, and the prejudice of our communities that he exposed. Evelyn was not as caught up in the liberal taboo against shame. Others felt it, but would not name it. Remember Abe's naming of "grief" and "envy" but not shame? However, as he spoke his body slumped to the side and away from the group. This is an aversion response associated with shame. Measuring himself against the image of King, he was ashamed, he found himself lacking. Similarly, Frank's expression of "regret," and "guilt," as well as Dave's expression of "fear," were overtly named feelings, but only partially capturing their experience of not measuring up. Implied by their statements is the hidden feeling of shame.

In Irene's story about how her family gained financially during the Korean War, we can also see her showing but not showing, or showing but not naming, her shame. Her tones were upbeat, expressing some incredulousness. However, analyzing the tones and the words together it seems to be an expression of shame. "Hamburger to prime rib, and I just did not get it . . . all of a sudden . . . we were rich!" This comment of Irene's shows the development of her political awareness and political sensitivity. She goes on to link shame with moral experience.

When I interpreted their experience as expressions of shame some were able to try this on while others struggled with it. Sandy struggled. She imagined elected officials feeling embarrassment for not doing their homework, not shame. Her efforts to reduce their clear failure from shame to embarrassment, while splitting hairs with phrases like "not shame, maybe it's shameful," shows that she is in some bind around the word shame. This bind is connected to the liberal's fear of moralizing and their efforts to steer away from any moralizing language as well as steer away from shame (which is a primary affect involved in moral experience). Despite their bodily reactions they tried to maintain moral neutrality.

This limitation is part of the American repression of shame, but a particularly liberal version, in which necessary shame is largely felt and the necessary actions implied by the shame are largely taken. They feel shame and they act on it but they do not necessarily say what is going on as they do it. "Moral speaking" is not yet a necessity. Shame repression limits the articulation that would aid the liberal's political leadership. Shame, in its connection to morality, has somehow become taboo for the liberal. Michael Lerner expressed this dilemma quite well when he wrote: "The Democratic Party is filled with people who are involved precisely because they have moral and spiritual sensitivity, even if they are reluctant to label it as such" (Lerner 2006: 27). Reverend Wallis writes similarly saying: "The Democrats should be much more willing to use moral and religious language" (Wallis 2005: 10).

In taking up the question of "moral speaking," the group's discussion reflected the conflict between the liberal language of progressivism, in its judgment-free inclinations, and the actual lived experience of these leaders (who seemed to clearly live by high moral standards). In their burgeoning experience and in the ambitions they express is the desire for a new capacity that rests somewhere between an articulated and embodied morality, suggesting their intuitive recognition of the tasks of Phases Two and Three of the political development of their political identities. Also, their discussion implies that this new capacity will require some degree of affect freedom, as Harry recognizes that the public may "crave" more emotionality from a leader who is "showing more emotion."

However, Dave seems confused as he tries to leave emotion out of the equation, in favor of an idea of embodiment. He seems further confused as he wants this idea of embodiment to be distinct from "pushing morality" with words (i.e., he seems to be contrasting embodiment and speaking). Clearly he is sensitive to the risks of moralizing, but he seems to risk sacrificing not only emotions, but also the voice, in his idea of embodiment. This evokes an image of a noble savage, stoic, mute, and too vulnerable to colonial catastrophe. In Dave's resistance to emotion and pushing morals is the progressive's fear of both subjectivity and moralizing, that is, both emotion and speech become suspect. The progressives sacrifice the opportunity that comes with moral authority in their fear of falling into the trap of pushiness or lack of authenticity (characteristics of the conservative's moralizing).

Sandy said, "I do not do the morality thing," and Irene said, "I was raised with a certain [small] amount of shame . . . We never used the word moral." They resist both shame and moralizing. Included in Irene's outlook is an ideological resistance to bowing to God. Similarly, Sandy resists any external authority as she focuses on "letting us be who we are," and believes that someone who moralizes takes away that identity. However, their fear of moralizing can be contrasted with the group's recognition that King was a great leader and that his strength came from asserting his personal sense of right and wrong without seeming to limit anyone's choices.

King stands directly in the way of their isolation and moral relativism. He turns out to be a sort of political shaman, capable of asserting morality without moralizing. Regardless, King's second-tier political identity really bothered these progressives. They felt envious and ashamed, and inspired – each in a unique way. They recognized his higher state of political development, without calling it such, and envied/admired it. They had some idea of what it was they envied, but were a bit tongue-tied about it, just as they were in their own estimation, by comparison with King, tongue-tied when it came to speaking in strong moral terms. The group wrestles with the image of King as someone of superior development. As they wrestle, they identify specific capacities involved in this development, including the capacity to *articulate* moral positions based on moral principles and *embody* these principles in a lived presence. Embodied articulation uses shame and other emotions to move people; this is part of affect freedom and reflects the second and third phase of political development.

Abe so much wants to be able to move people. Yet, he does not know how. Instead, he talks about being very "very guarded," and laments that in public he can only make "intellectual arguments," not moral statements. Abe envies King's spirit and has no felt access to it. The progressive's dilemma hangs over him, inhibiting his leadership and his freedom. Abe finds himself restricted to speaking a narrow, intellectual language that is dissatisfying. A broader expression, to him, is lost. Similarly, Sandy says, "I hate, I personally do not like to do the morality thing." She backpedals away from strong affect, moving from the full force of "hate" to the easier "do not like." Here, she minimizes her own "personal" experience, implying that it might not be true exactly because it is only her personal experience. Once again, we see her identification with the belief that individual, subjective experience is inherently flawed and limited and that "hate" is, perhaps, "bad" or politically incorrect. While tempering hate is crucial to society, the liberal's disidentification with strong affect is suspect. Could it be that they over-identify with fear, also one of the affects – specifically fear of moralizing?

Resistance to strong affect can be seen in Sandy's earlier reduction of shame to embarrassment of hate to dislike, and her dislike for making moral assertions in favor of the liberal's adopted rational approach of "open communication." Remember she ended saying, "I do not know if that makes any sense." The fact that she is not sure her speaking "makes any sense" supports the conclusion that she, at least, is dissatisfied with what she is able to say. Clearly, there is little cohering satisfaction for her in speaking these ways.

Again, there's a connection here to the larger issue of speech difficulties suffered by liberals/progressives and the way these difficulties are linked to restricted affect freedom. For both Abe and Sandy the issue of morality leaves them at least a little inarticulate, and struggling to effectively identify, share, and be directed by their own emotional experience. The speech difficulty here is a very good example of the tension experienced at the shift from the psychological person to the psychological citizen. Fortunately, the solution is not far away. As they spend time together they begin to trigger off of each other and move in the right direction. For they begin to recognize the passionate solution in each other, if not in themselves. This is the "emergent" task of the group.

Political transformation: responding to the liberal's fear of moral speaking

The ambivalent attitude that these progressives have toward their subjective/emotional experience is potentially evidence of a pattern of repression within the progressive movement and liberalism more broadly. Liberals have been shaped by cultural forces that limit their identity, its possible range of actions and what liberals can and cannot say. A pattern of repression in liberalism is to be found in relation to shame and morality.

Prior to the research meetings I had not focused attention on the connection between shame and morality. I too have lived in the liberal haze around these crucial experiences. After the meetings I went back to both Erikson and the affect literature and discovered for myself the way shame and morality arise together in early childhood and the way they are then linked in the psychosocial development of the adult. Erikson notes that effective parenting supports the child to balance the experience of self and other, through appropriate feeling of shame (Erikson 1968: 110–14). Through a balance of shame and autonomy, children learn the value of shared experience. At this stage they are learning to connect to a social world, as represented by the family. Its laws provide for the child's first experience of "judiciousness" (Erikson 1982: 47). Erikson notes how the institutional level of this stage of development takes place as adult individuals continue to balance shame and individual freedom. Accordingly, we could say that shame not only functions for the child – by which they internalize cultural mores – but also functions for the individual in society – for the citizen – in this same way.

Taking it a step further, we can associate Abe and Sandy's condition with a failure to complete this early stage of development within their political identity. For the child, failure to integrate necessary shame restricts autonomy and will and leads to compulsivity. For Abe and Sandy, failure to draw on the shame they feel and assert moral authority constricts their political development. Thus, at an institutional or political level they are playing out the failure to be "judicious" and, instead, getting caught in what Erikson calls "legalisms" (Erikson 1982: 48). Erikson's description of "legalism" is actions that are "now too lenient and now too strict [and] is the bureaucratic counterpart to individual compulsivity" (Erikson 1982: 48). Notice the parallel between Abe's self-description as "technical" and Erikson's description of "legalism." Both have an overly formal quality with Abe's "technical" language being comparable to what is called "legalese," as another form of legalism.

This parallels the reduction of traditional voices of authority to expert systems speaking in their own technical languages. It also connects to Samuel's and Lakoff's sense of the liberal's over-reliance on rationalism. However, what Erikson is adding is the understanding that this is a *failure of development*. In this case, it is a failure in the development of the political identity of liberals.

Here, the political correctness of the psychological person protects them from using their emotions publicly, which is what King did as he asserted himself, his emotions, and moral values. King's advanced political development enabled him to rise out of the political correctness of the pack and risk becoming a target. The courage necessary is profound as King's assassination makes all too clear. Following this line of thought we can say that the exposure of the group to the King video evoked an ideal image to which they all aspire. It showed them a "higher" level of political development. However, this image was not experienced as pleasant or friendly, but as frightening and shame and envy evoking. King's embodied, articulated second tier public language (my political development Phases One to Four) ruptures their technical speech compromises. It sliced through their limited affect freedom, exposing them to a range of unprocessed affect including envy, fear, guilt, grief, and shame. Exposure to these affects evoked creative and painful moments in our group. They saw King's freedom as unattainable.

As they shared their pain, the natural relief that comes with what Omer calls the "creative transgression of taboo" moved them past their hidden shame and the paralysis of legalisms (Omer 2005: 32). The experience of communal purpose transcends private identity and it is that (the communal) on which "political transformation" can focus. Political transformation does not focus, per se, on the reintegration of repressed experience into an individual's private-life identity. Instead, the release of repressed experience led to moments of affect freedom, which vitalizes the political/communal identity, moving it toward riskier expressions of integrity through its impassioned moral speaking.

In effect the research views the political wounds of these leaders as sites of repressed affect that, if effectively attended to, coalesce as new forms of political identity at higher stages of political development. By doing this "therapeutic" work, there is benefit to the individual's private identity. However, the primary focus is on the political identity and political development of the individuals and group. These political identities are viewed as the primary vehicle for social change. They provide the opportunity for the progressive movement to move forward. By following Erikson's theory of psychohistory, in which individual identity is conceived of as a potential source of humanity's future, we can think of the efforts to heal the progressive's political wounds as an effort to release their own future and liberalism's future contribution to American politics. Released "future" activates destiny.

Thinking of their resistance to the word "shame," as a subpersonality, figure, or, as a character, we could then say that the "character" of their political identity is concerned or fearful of judgment. Thinking about their difficulty with the word "morality," we could say that the "character" of their political identity is sensitive to the risks of moralizing. The image of the liberal's character that begins to appear is that of someone wounded who is hesitant to assert moral authority publicly for fear of more suffering, including the possibilities of bodily injury and even death.

Here, I am beginning to imagine a liberal political identity that is afraid of death. This fear restricts the liberals' affect freedom and keeps them functioning at a level of political identity below their own ideals. But when confronted with images of King, they are reminded of their ideals and naturally feel ashamed for being afraid of sacrificing even further than they already have, possibly even facing death. While making significant sacrifices compared to most Americans, they know that they are capable of more, they know that more is necessary. In the video I showed, King said, "A man who is not willing to die for something is a man who does not know what life is for" (King 1988). However, built into the language of liberalism is a type of "soft-heartedness" that keeps us from rallying too loudly, from asserting the type of moral authority they see in King, which did get him killed.

Instead they fall into the trap of moral relativism, claiming that "people have their own moral compass . . . I'm confident of mine and very reticent to criticize others." And saying "I hate, I personally do not like to do *the moral thing* because I, I do not know if it's my place to talk about morality." In both these statements moral relativism is asserted.

By dampening the affect system and reducing hate to dislike, the liberal is able to avoid making statements that might bring the wrath of the political right and the guns that come with its fringes (I felt myself hesitate to put this last phrase in print; is this my own self-protective liberalism?). Does this reflect a very deep-seated ambivalence about political participation? On the one hand, the participants all place themselves in harm's way, in one way or another, and bear significant political wounds. On the other hand, they simultaneously retreat from making potentially horrifying or ultimate sacrifices. This retreat is built into the moral relativism of their language. This stage is captured in the phrase "To thy own self be true." This is an advance over the earlier stage in which morality is based on group norms. Yet, it also reveals this group's limited ability to articulate and embody moral reasoning that applies more broadly to society. "Inability" may be too strong, though, given the insight and strength they brought to the research meetings.

Nevertheless, when viewed through my model of political development, they neither have the embodiment nor articulation practices needed to activate the public imagination and bring to life a public language once vivified by King. If we consider these limitations built into the liberal's language to be a function of the traumas that liberals have witnessed and suffered, then we can look at the research meetings as an example of a form of "political transformation" that helped them with their soft-heartedness that comes from moral relativism.

By guiding the progressives through a process that therapeutically activated the "group level trauma" built into their language of liberalism, the research was able to support them to find a degree of the affect freedom achieved by religious and political leaders like Gandhi, Martin Luther, and

Martin Luther King. In effect, this research attempted to make more conscious or more active the naturally occurring processes that aid the political development of their political identities.

Following Erikson's theory of how at one time individual identity came upon "chosen" people and now is something that can be "sought out," we can say that the research actively takes up seeking the developmental constituents of political identities. It supports this movement psychologically, as it awakens the psychological attitude and moves it further toward being a conscious psychological capacity. Accordingly, it is possible to begin to imagine what process of political development these progressives will need to go through to "become the change," as Gandhi said. Through this process of activating the further development of their political identities they will develop into the type of politicians capable of realizing their vision of a just and sustainable society.

Summary

Progressive political leaders embody one possible image of a necessary healing of what Samuels and Bellah refer to as the divide between public and private experience and what Omer refers to as the "privatization of experience" (Omer 1990). Their embodiment offers one way of being that is necessary for a fuller experience of citizenship, one in which the "psychological need to be political" is not repressed (Samuels 2001: 30). They are living it; however, they do not know what they have. In the course of my research we traced the different sides of their embodied being.

Underneath a public persona there is an "authentic face" that they have difficulty finding. When attended to in a group of peers these leaders were able to drop this mask. As they found their authentic face it was clear that it was wounded, a wound that appeared at the interface between their private and political identities. However, the fact that they bore this wound reveals their capacity to make politics personal. Their attitude toward their own emotional experience was not as psychological as would benefit them and their cause. Instead it was problematized by cultural attitudes toward emotion. They learned to withhold their emotional experience in public, especially negative emotions like anger, shame, and displays of hurt such as crying. This was part of what we recognized as a group and explored. The group experienced the pleasure of shared emotion and realized its importance in forming the depth of their political experience. Yet, it became more complicated as the issue of shame was turned to – perhaps the most repressed emotion in American culture. The progressive leaders were capable of expressing and exhibiting shame without necessarily being able to identify that that is what they are feeling. In all, exploration of shame and other subjective emotional states led us to discuss morality.

While shame has the function of raising moral experience, it was never-theless resisted. Exploration of the shame experience evoked reflection and conversation about morality. These progressives felt the risks of moralizing, but also felt the necessity for it. This evoked ambivalence, fear, and left them dissatisfied with what they could say and ultimately who they were. This reflected their restricted language of political liberalism, especially their overidentification with social progress.

To the degree that political liberalism remains entrenched in an anti-moral mode of speaking, Sandel's moral neutrality, liberals will have great difficulty developing the political voice necessary to help other Americans overcome repressed shame and account for their shamelessness. To the extent that political liberalism is adverse to the actual function of emotions, its strengths of moral vision will have to be couched in forms of techno-speak.

The moral neutrality of liberalism seems successful as a way of protecting its speakers from rising to positions of social conscience where they would be visible and vulnerable. As long as they do not try to assert moral authority, they will not have to run the risk of drawing fire from the political and religious right. However, given their already significant current sacri-fices, no wonder they buy into moral relativity. Perhaps when more of us risk moral speaking, guiding the moral experience of our culture will have more support.

When this understanding is applied to the research group we see that they actually began to find a way out of the binding language of political liberalism. The voice of psychological liberalism appeals to them, especially when it is applied to their experience of being political and not left to fester in an isolating language of our private lives; like me, they may intuit the opportunities for creating a new psychological citizen.

Remember in Chapter 3 the way they connected shame with power, anger, and sensuality/sexuality. This burst the rational language of liberal-ism and led them to a wider and deeper experience of affect freedom. Affect freedom is an emergent capacity through which individuals overcome cul-turally repressed emotional experiences in order to have available the full biological/emotional/cultural ability to, for one thing, move in the political world and make moral judgments and take moral actions. This, in turn, opens the individual to the capacity for destiny as another, distinct, emer-gent human capacity. These emergent capacities can become active, and can be effectively organized in a group context.

Because of the degree of repressed shame in American culture, the will-ingness to express and exhibit a shame experience is a central part of the "activation of destiny" for Americans. These progressive leaders have suc-cessfully lived more openly with their shame and, therefore, have achieved a personal strength displayed in the sacrifices they make to maintain their political identities. When an individual or group turns toward shame and releases its repression by facing moral necessities, their passionate soul may open, enabling them to develop the capacity for destiny. For the progressive political activists in this group the "capacity for destiny" catalyzed their political identities, enabling them to identify their personhood with the future of the world, as psychological citizens.

The learnings in this research begin to show the opportunities to create a range of learning practices that bind the twin intents of political and psychological liberalism, thus releasing a new capacity for destiny that combines interest in social progress with interest in personal development.

Based upon these practices an emancipatory language is emerging and being used that can capture the public imagination and be vocationalized. Through a process of professionalization, a transformative political psychologist takes responsibility for creating new institutional forms whose goal is to bring into culture those emergent capacities that are needed by the time, starting with a broader and deeper embodiment of the psychological attitude, which leads to unique psychological capacities.

Part V

Practices of a political psychologist

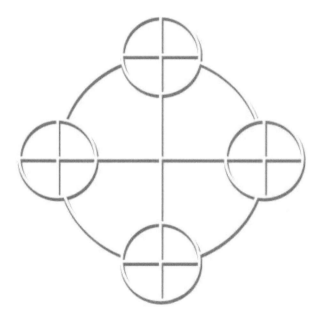

Chapter 12

Envisioning a transformative political psychologist

Summary and introduction

With ITP as a foundation for further thinking and action, we can adopt the premise that individual development and cultural evolution are not separate phenomena, but are twin dimensions of a single process of *human transformation*. Further, we are currently in a phase of transformation that is increasingly focused on the opportunities for the individual to take up a position as a creator of culture.

In order to become creators of culture, people need to find their own unique contribution while learning to speak in the new language of a "public-psychological" liberalism. Speakers of this language are becoming psychological citizens; they are a new moral type. They embody capacities, foundational and emergent, that bridge their own unique sensitivities, talents, and suffering, and the needs of our time. The realization of the life of the psychological citizen marks a significant transformation of our relationship to affect.

At the level of religious liberalism, emotional impulsivity is repressed using fear and guilt. At the level of the private-psychological liberalism, selfish and short-sighted individuality is sublimated through an awakening of healthy shame. At the level of the public-psychological liberalism, the developmental shift is not marked by either the repression or sublimation of affect, rather it is transmuted into foundational and emergent capacities. Psychological citizens functioning at this developmental level focus their attention on their devotion to, and willingness to sacrifice for, the good of humanity. They use their newly realized capacities to create and serve a range of learning organizations, the purpose of which is to pursue cultural evolution.

The life of the psychological citizen is based on their conscious use of their sensitivities and suffering, turning these into talents in order to activate the capacity for destiny, which is nothing fancy. Destiny is simply a human capacity that emerges when the threads of a person's personal development intertwine with the evolutionary needs of their times. This intertwining transforms their passively felt experience of the future into an active shaping of that future. This marks the transformation from a passive, private-psychological liberalism to an active, public-psychological liberalism, from the tension between the political individual and the psychological person into the embodied public dynamism of the psychological citizen.

Seeking one's destiny is no longer the pursuit of rarified religious initiates or exceptional cultural leaders, but is actively sought by a range of progressive leaders within our communities. As my research shows, these leaders have come to recognize their capacity to be cultural creators and have found some experience of personal/political transformation through the pursuit of this capacity. However, these leaders are limited by the political liberal's focus on the external world and have a mixed relationship with the transformative potential of their affect systems, as emotion has not been wholly embraced for its culturally transformative value. This difficulty in embracing the public, transformative use of emotion reflects a divide within our culture, as the institutions that are coming around to understanding this identity-shaping function of affect have focused too intently on its private-life application.

While progressive political leaders are inexperienced with and have some resistance to the psychological dimension of their own advanced consciousness, they are also open to the ministrations and guidance that are possible when facilitated by someone with psychological training. This reflects an emergent potential lying between the institutions of political and psychological liberalism. As the masculine focus of the political liberal receives the feminine-focused ministrations of the private-psychological liberal new things start to happen.

In this chapter I will discuss the opportunities to birth a new active psychological citizen that are possible when political and private-psychological liberalisms come together. I have been imagining this as the activation of Phase Five of my model of political development, that is, the opportunity to vocationalize and institutionalize the emerging psychological citizen within a new institutional form of a "public-psychological" liberalism.

New methods for a new type of cultural practitioner

Implied by the approach taken in this writing is an understanding of the role of the individual in bringing new knowledge into the world (Erikson, Jung, Dewey, Thomas Kuhn, etc.). Through my own theorizing I bring these ideas together within a theory of political development. This theory is not strictly about political experience, rather it identifies a "political" dimension to the culture's process of acquiring new knowledge as well as the increasing role of the individual in that process.

Central to political development is an understanding of how new knowledge begins within a creative experience of an individual or group and makes its way into wider circles of application through developmental rhythms such as the motion between esoteric rupture and exoteric consolidation and the rhythm of moving from passive to active. Included in political development is the step in the cycle in which individuals and groups seek to change political culture through embodiment practices that bring a new cultural ethic into the world. While these practices appear historically as part of whatever particular new consciousness is emerging, currently there is a movement to vocationalize the very process of creating embodiment practices, regardless of any particular state of consciousness that is trying to be embodied. This reflects the active phase of a public-psychological liberalism, one that focuses more directly on human transformation.

For example, there is a growing recognition of the need for a new type of practitioner who could help individuals and groups to identify their distinct capabilities as part of finding their destiny. The need for such practitioners has been identified by Omer as "ritual specialists" and "cultural leaders" (Omer 2003: 40), or as "gap specialists" or "cultural coaches" (Inglis and Steele 2005: 42), and by myself as "transformative political psychologist." I suspect many other names for such cultural change specialists have also been coined.

Within science there has always been some line from idea to discussion, to testing, to general application, to institution shaping. However, when the subject matter is human transformation, the process of scientific inquiry becomes very complex. For example, to what extent would a theorist or group of social scientists and cultural practitioners/leaders apply the research to themselves as part of their testing and verification process?

The idea of self-experimentation is not new; there is quite a history of such self-exploration in psychology ranging from the original work of Wilhelm Wundt and Edward Titchner in their exploration of human sensory experience, to the consciousness experiments of William James, or even to the problematic work of the self-proclaimed New-Age introspectionist, Timothy Leary. While the excesses of Leary and others might seem to limit interest in scientific exploration of human transformation, it is more likely that the limitation of the political individual, its fear of cultivating an internal psychological consciousness, inhibits the scientific exploration of human transformation. As this limitation is institutionalized within science as part of the positivist's paradigm, reasoning and sensory freedom are celebrated within a limiting passivity. Outside of science, this passivity also infects political individuals in their own passive, neutral relationship to moral speaking.

As a result of the passivity of science and the neutrality of political and private liberalisms, the conscious transformations of the self have been hidden away in a private-life psychotherapy or in esoteric spiritual practices. In the wake of this modern passivity, much of the use of the self in science and politics has been dismissed; individual "subjectivity" continues to be viewed as problematic. Fortunately, there has been a significant resurgence in the social sciences that is reconsidering the value of "subjectivity" in the process of good science. Numerous researchers have been developing alternative methodologies that emphasize the positive role of the researcher's subjectivity in the development of good science. Peter Reason and John Heron's articulation of this idea is expressed in their concept of "critical subjectivity" (Heron and Reason 1997: 180). Other social scientists also support an expanded role for subjectivity in good science such as in Omer's "Imaginal Inquiry" (Omer 2006). James Holstein and Jaber Gubrium consider the use of the researcher's experience in social science interviewing (Gubrium and Holstein 1995), and Kathryn Kohler-Riessman examines "narrative analysis" (Riessman 1993).

In the context of a conjoined practice focusing on individual development and cultural evolution, the role of the subject could be unusually interesting. For example, would the validity of such research depend on the success of the research's own political development? How would such "development" be validated? Would the researchers take on the task of creating developmental practices that would be applicable to different groups of people and, if so, what groups?

Returning to the interesting work of Inglis and Steele, they argue that it would be the function of "cultural coaches" to "actively stimulate and support the emergence of *complexity intelligence* in our society" and that these coaches would need to be trained in processes of human development and the "*designing of public process*," analogous to the private process of psychotherapy, in order to "support the transformation of dysfunctional societal issues" (Inglis and Steele 2005: 37, emphasis added). In my own work I make a parallel distinction between my clinical and political work or between my "private" and "public" practices.

Following Inglis and Steele, Omer, and others, it is clear that a number of practitioners have taken up the call to become such agents of social change, and at least a few of them are attempting to form themselves into psychological citizens. In many groups a range of learning practices is used to embody the values associated with their vision of what it means to be human. They are combining interest in self-development with interest in political change.

Some are not so concerned with identifying their work with the social sciences; not all need to work through those institutional structures. Others are actively addressing the questions about their relationship to the social sciences, which supports the opportunity to integrate their work within the bodies of research and institutional forms that already exist. Asking and answering questions about researcher participation and the generalizability of research results is a necessary part of any research that focuses on the expanded understanding of human transformation that is emerging through numerous formal and informal research projects and other cultural activities.

The opportunities to participate in cultural evolution for the social scientist exist in many different forms. My own particular interest lies in the opportunity to combine formal scientific inquiry with community engagement. This creates opportunities to extend the institutionalization of an active, public-psychological liberalism within a new field of transformative political psychology for a new vocation of a transformative political psychologist to support the emergence of the psychological citizen.

A *new* type of political psychologist for a *new* political psychology

Political psychology

We need a new type of political psychologist in order to activate the political development of individuals, groups, and of ourselves as a people. In a brief conversation with Andrew Samuels I asked him if he would consider himself a "political psychologist." He responded by saying that he had worked as a "political consultant" (Andrew Samuels, personal communication, 19 June 2006). I suspect that the rubric "political consultant" is more practical and self-explanatory than the opaque idea of a "political psychologist." I suspect that Samuels' adoption of this title reflects a practicality that stems in part from the difficulty of being identified with the vague but intriguing notion of a "political psychologist." I also suspect that Samuels may not see the extent to which he is opening a new field of inquiry, that is, a new political psychology. However, in order to fulfill its potential, this field will need to distinguish itself from political psychology as it is currently conceived and institutionalized.

The field of political psychology is already established as a subfield of political science, which traces its beginning, for one, to the creative work of the Frankfurt School of Social Research. Current-day political psychology draws from the research accomplished by the Frankfurt faculty and has taken up the work of analyzing human motivation as it relates to political leadership, and the sociopolitical relations between people and groups. However, it does little to consider the political development of people or the role that a "political psychologist" could play in supporting or accelerating that political development.

What strikes me as a "miss" of the current field of political psychology is the lack of attention it pays to the opportunities and necessities for political psychologists to "work on" their own political development as part of their work. Like the founding faculty at the Frankfurt School, they follow the idea of social scientist as researcher or educator. They do not follow dictum in Luke's gospel of "physician, heal thyself," which many, including William James, have lived to our great benefit.

In clinical psychology the psychologist follows this ethic in order to be capable of helping others. However, no such ethic seems to be established in political psychology. I suspect that this reflects the current field's lack of interest in integrating a "clinical," "developmental," or "transformative" dimension into its range of functioning. Instead, it has a decidedly analytic disposition, which, according to at least one political psychologist, Fred Alford, does not seek to bring about change, having "no solutions," rather only to provide understanding (Alford 2002: 195). Here, the distinction between the educator and the therapist is stark.

This lack of a "clinical" dimension to political psychology parallels the Frankfurt School's problematic adoption of a passive relationship to human transformation, and its retreat into a decidedly analytic or even aesthetic attitude. While Eric Fromm's move into individual development through psychotherapy is no better, at least within the discipline of psychotherapy the role of the therapist has begun to overcome passivity.

In political psychology some interest in the subjective nature of the individual has appeared, which is promising. In the last few years political psychologists, like University of New York professor Leonie Huddy, have shown a particular interest in the "subjective" dimension of human experience that is so crucial to the therapist and would be central to any effort to focus on the political development of citizens (Huddy 2001: 130).

In my own research, I reflected on the current field of political psychology's approach to social science as overly rational and passive, reflecting the positivist's paradigm that perpetuates a problematic separation between thought and affect in relation to human inquiry and its institutionalization in science. Reintegrating affect and thought, analysis and intervention, theory and practice, brings two disparate pieces of the social sciences back together within some yet articulated vision of praxis. Central to this new idea of praxis is the ethic of the political psychologist working on the political development of their own political identity. Bringing in the idea of "physician, heal thyself," a new type of political psychologist would lead through their own political development.

A new type of political psychologist

In my use of the idea of a transformative political psychologist, I refer to "practitioners" who take on the task of engaging in a "public" or "political" practice. This idea parallels the attitude in clinical psychology in which "clinical" practitioners engaged in clinical work as "private" practices. In their "private" practices clinicians attend to the development of themselves as what I have called a "psychological person." In this respect many clinical training programs are often both educational and, if you will, healing. They often expect trainees to engage in their own psychotherapy. Accordingly, a transformative political psychologist would be expected to work on the political development of their political identities in order to realize their destiny as a "psychological citizen."

Going further, this would lead to a transformative political psychology whose mission would be to create or renew political culture through the cultivation of *cultural leadership* for the purpose of guiding the emergent strands of personal development and cultural evolution; for, it is a society's political culture that influences its willingness and ability to develop and evolve. By focusing attention on creating cultural leadership, a transformative political psychologist recognizes the reciprocal relationship between personal development and cultural evolution. This relationship is nowhere more intimate than in leadership, for a leader's development or transformation coincides with the development or transformation of society. As Erik Erikson's description of the lives of Mahatma Gandhi and Martin Luther shows, cultural leadership necessitates a "blending," of individual development and cultural evolution. Omer's ITP offers theory and practices that support such a blending.

In the context of this broad understanding of cultural I would suggest that psychology, particularly a transformative political psychology, is a discipline in which the benefits of a "political consultant" such as Samuels could be further vocationalized and then institutionalized. Psychology may be a discipline that can work effectively with the types of foundational and emergent capacities that the human species is currently differentiating in such a way as to direct the activation of these capacities toward consistent acts of cultural leadership. In this context, psychology might be considered more than one of the social sciences, and certainly more than it has been imagined to be in its clinical identity. Psychology may be the institutional form currently embodying a passive, private-psychological liberalism, but this cannot be assumed to be what psychology is or is meant to be. The further institutionalization of psychological liberalism likely requires turning toward the political and toward an active, public-psychological liberalism. The efforts of the Frankfurt School and more recently the Institute of Imaginal Studies to bring together political and private-psychological liberalism have paved the way.

Uniting the transformative intent of clinical psychology with the analytical intent of political science could be realized within a *transformative political psychology*. One of the primary purposes of such a field or discipline would be the education and training of psychologists who would focus their attention simultaneously on the present and historical processes of cultural evolution and on the present and historical processes of individual development. Through this focus such psychologists would not only be able to attend to and ease the unique suffering of individuals and groups, but would also be able to support the emergence of the unique psychological and moral capacities called for by the time, within the political identity of a psychological citizen.

Working within a transformative political psychology it would be possible to identify those emergent capacities that the culture or species is currently differentiating. The cultivation of these capacities would take place – is taking place – through the identification and use of learning practices that combine the best educational, healing, and community engagement practices drawn from political and psychological liberalism. This process of cultivation would activate within the population a generally higher level of political development, thus constellating a response to the gap that Kegan notes between what we know and who we are on the one side and the actual world in which we live on the other side.

These learning practices have three primary orientations including: *educational, community engagement*, and *healing* (attending to human suffering). Additionally, each of these orientations embraces a range of foci. Educational practices include: public outreach, research, and the development of degree programs in transformative political psychology. Community engagement practices include: political consultation, community advocacy, and coalition building and organizing. Healing practices include: working with the suffering within individuals and small groups, particularly their political wounds, and leadership training.

While any one learning practice may draw from more than one of these orientations, existing "social change" groups tend to draw much more heavily from one of these three orientations than from the others. Typically, groups who engage in one have some aversion to at least one of the others. Healing practices appear to be the most difficult to engage in. Under consideration is the possibility that such aversions reflect deep divides within the culture between individual and social experience and between internal and external approaches to human transformation. These divides can be addressed through the use of effective learning practices that turn our attention to all quadrants of human transformation.

If we adopt the goal of transforming political culture, then how is it that a political psychologist would set about completing that task? I suggest that through the use of learning practices individuals and groups are able to evoke new states or stages of political development in themselves and more widely in other social contexts.

The use of learning practices

Three types of learning practices

Through the development of a new range of learning organizations we are in a position to bring together informal approaches to both personal development and cultural evolution and formalize the task: that is, we are in a position to go from a passive, informal approach to human transformation to an active approach to this goal. Following Inglis and Steele, the goal is to

design "public processes" that "support the emergence of complexity intelligence" (Inglis and Steele 2005: 37). Following Omer, the goal is to create
"rituals" that heal "cultural traumas" and cultivate broad foundational
human capacities (Omer 2005: 30–33). Following Wilber, the goal is to create
transformative practices that integrate our current stage of development with
our advancement to higher stages. I have used the phrase "learning practices" in this same way. A "learning practice" could be just about anything
that supports either or both individual development or cultural evolution. In
this section I will draw attention to three types of learning practices that I
have found to be of interest to theorists and practitioners working the edge
between individual development and cultural evolution.

Practices that support individual development could be any repeated
activity that a mother adopts to teach her child about herself and the world.
The relationship between mother and child is governed by what Erikson
describes as "ritualizations," which reflect to the child what is good about
its nature and support it to be able to attend both to the world and to
others (Erikson 1982: 44). Learning practices extend past childhood to
encompass adolescence and adulthood. Through the life cycle we engage in
developmental tasks that bring opportunities for service and self-mastery.

Practices that support cultural evolution apply to groups, communities,
and whole peoples and can be thought of in terms of traditional cultural
practices from those that manage hygiene to tool making and using practices, to religious rituals, elections, or secular programs of education.

Both explicitly and implicitly, learning practices contribute to personal
development and to cultural evolution. In order to establish a framework
that works on both, I distinguish between *healing*, *educational*, and *community engagement* learning practices. These distinctions are not meant to
be inclusive, rather they are simply practical and come out of my own
education and experience.

It has been my experience that efforts to address human difficulties tend
to emphasize one of these and too often exclude the others: that is, educational practices tend to exclude healing practices and community engagement practices, healing practices can exclude practices of education and
community engagement, and community engagement practices too often
skip the other two. I know that there are exceptions to this limitation.

For example, there are numerous efforts by liberal thinkers, like Lakoff,
who want to focus on identifying and articulating the values that drive left-
leaning agendas – I caricaturize their stance as that of the "educator."
Their emphasis suggests a model of change that focuses on understanding.
While valuable, I find such thinkers do not seem to be interested in attending to their own or other's distinct suffering. They do not factor issues of
"healing" into their approach to either individual development or cultural
evolution. Instead, they focus on understanding, perhaps overidentifying
with reasoning freedom.

The stance of the educator can be juxtaposed with that of other thinkers who are more interested in attending to suffering than to understanding. This second group can be characterized as the stance of the "therapist." While not adverse to understanding, some therapists limit their interest to the suffering of the individual person. Or, if they combine healing and understanding their efforts focus on an individual's private-life development and not on either their public identity or on cultural evolution.

Both the stance of educator and therapist can be compared to the stance of the "activist" or "organizer," who has minimal interest in healing suffering, but definitely has an interest in understanding. However, I have noticed that the stance of the activist is so focused on the trench work of politics in a daily or election-cycle-focused way that their pursuit of understanding is limited to understanding issues, not values, not the larger context of human history, not issues of their own or their culture's evolution, and certainly not suffering. Or, if they are attentive to suffering, it is within the traditional liberal approach of imagining community and governmental programs that address suffering like poverty, racism, illiteracy, etc.

In my own experience, if these three stances are openly distinguished from one another then not one of them can be thought of, or asserted, as holding all of the answers. While more examples or definitions of each would help, my brief characterizations need to suffice for the moment. Noteworthy in my current description is the absence of the idea of "religious" learning practices. Despite the training I received in my graduate program, covering the importance of and practical experience with religious practices, I have yet to find a way to sufficiently integrate this into my thinking and actions. I view this as both a personal limitation and I suspect it reflects other cultural limitations that I participate in, which need attention. Perhaps this limitation of mine reflects a general resistance of both political and psychological liberalism to the necessities of religious liberalism.

Following the evolution of Western culture laid out in Chapter 9, I am all but certain that learning practices begin in human culture within religious liberalism and become "religious" practices. Accordingly, I suspect that some larger synthesis or reconciliation is needed to reintegrate the value of such practices without either evoking the current fears of the abuses of religious institutions and religious leaders or repeating those abuses.

I conceive of this writing as, itself, an "educational" learning practice that has as its purpose to direct the reader toward the types of practices which would change them into the type of person our age needs. In particular, we can begin imagining the tasks for each "type," that is, the task for "educators," "therapists," and "activists" in their service to one another and to the progressive movement.

For *educators* the job would be to create learning practices for therapists, activists, and other citizens that activate advanced states of political development through the pursuit of an *understanding* of theories of human development and evolution.

For *therapists* the job would be to activate advanced states of political development in educators, activists, and other citizens by creating learning practices that ease, attend to, or *heal the suffering* intrinsic in failed, truncated, or simply difficult development.

For *activists* the job would be to receive the ministrations of educators and therapists in order to advance their own political development and to have this development carry over into their community work. While this may seem passive, it is these progressive political leaders who have been holding the fort and simply need to be supported to continue doing what they do, though with some adjustment for the broader context of their own political development. Further, activists could also help activate more advanced states of political development in educators, therapists, and other citizens by supporting them to come out into the public eye in their own communities, perhaps by creating public forums for their learning practices.

Educators, therapists, and activists alike can develop learning practices that pursue understanding, healing, and community engagement, all with the intent of working on their political development. The concept of political development not only provides a context for individuals and groups to work on their own "development" while engaging their communities, but it also supports consideration of the larger evolutionary context through which solutions to human ills can be pursued.

Author and social activist Bill Moyer asserts the importance for activists to identify the developmental context for their work. He identifies that the task for current progressive groups is to "develop an analysis that shows that the problems we are addressing are caused by the modern era itself and can only be ultimately solved by a new era that includes the next developmental step for humanity" (Moyer 2001: 195).

The transformation to a new "developmental step" need not be thought of as abstract or problematically "New Agey" or too overtly psychological, but can be thought of as an essential ingredient to the future effectiveness of community organizing that begins, according to Moyer, with the needed development of political activists themselves (Moyer 2001: 195–7).

Following Samuels and Moyer, we can argue that there is a need and an opportunity for activists to come together with educators and therapists in order to forge some hybrid professional and/or civic identity and language. Such an identity might attempt to "work out" – using the language of the therapist – their "issues" with their own political development by establishing learning practices that combine the best of the educator, therapist, and activist's intent. I conceive such an identity as that of the psychological citizen.

Learning practices and conflict

Through the development of learning practices, people and communities form collaborative bonds that contain and direct necessary conflict. Necessary conflict is at the heart of a vital democracy and must be distinguished from polarizing conflicts that perpetuate hostility and maintain destructive power relations and structures. Learning practices can focus attention on the concerns and suffering of people and groups as well as the unfortunate polarization that our concerns and suffering evoke in others. When used within a context that bridges the interests of political and psychological liberalism, learning practices are developed within a "small group" format as a way to explore their development and use. Within that format the learning practices can be used as follows:

- To identify a group's concerns and suffering as well as any evoked polarizations within that group or between groups.
- To identify the different perspectives within individual and group conflicts.
- To explore the distinct experiences within that conflict as it is perceived, felt, and thought about by the members of the working group.
- To identify remedies to the polarization that activate the group's capacities to address their own concerns and suffering and move them toward increased self-care and community engagement.

Through this approach I have found that the original experience of polarized conflict is transformed. Previously entrenched positions within groups and conflicts identified by groups become less calcified. Individual and group experience (sensitivities, talents, and unique suffering) is transformed into an expanded range of perceptions and capacities that inform group experience and activate leadership within the group. Increased group leadership emerges as group members are supported to imagine, embody, articulate, speak in public about, and form vocational and institutional directions for their work with the goal of forming a humane future for their communities. Within the context described, conflict is consciously attended to. It becomes part of the developmental rhythm, and moves from being passively suffered to being actively pursued. Consciously pursued conflict enables people to attend to differences, which activates human transformation.

Short- and long-term strategies for the development of learning practices

Learning practices have a wide range of practical applicability. On a short-run basis, learning practices are used in public forums to engage in immediate political debate within a community. Such short-term practices include expanded ways of engaging in politics for the benefit of moving progressive values to the forefront of a community's awareness and rooting political decisions in these values. Additionally, short-term learning practices include the identification, support, and election of candidates for public office who have progressive values and who support a progressive political agenda or platform.

Learning practices are also longer term, emphasizing the political maturation of individuals and community groups over time. These practices are not conceived nor implemented with the intention of having an immediate impact on current political agendas, realities, or circumstances. Such long-term practices emphasize the education and healing of individuals and community groups in order to support the realization of their political potential.

Unlike traditional psychotherapy, long-term learning practices do not focus on an individual's or group's private-life suffering. Instead, these learning practices recognize that individuals suffer in relation to their experience of having a public or political identity. While traditional political groups successfully channel this suffering into concrete political action, long-term learning practices focus on the political development of individuals and groups by attending directly to their prejudices and thus their suffering in order to heal and channel it into the development of foundational and emergent human capacities. I will return to discuss what I see to be specific prejudices of the progressive movement in the next chapter.

When viewed from a short-term perspective, that is, from the basis of traditional political liberalism, learning practices may seem indirect or indulgent. However, when balanced with short-term practices, long-term practices enhance the mutuality or collaborative potential between individuals, within groups, and between community groups. They address what the progressive leaders in my research saw as a limitation of progressive groups, that is, the chronic focus on strategizing and the lack of community building. Additionally, by focusing on attending to suffering in their public lives, long-term practices accelerate the political development of individuals and groups by supporting the emergence of the capacities called for by the current political situations.

There are an unlimited number of potential learning practices that roughly combine educational, community engagement, healing, and religious intents. The work I did with the progressive political leaders in my research is indicative of simple practices that have had significant results. Each group situation is unique and calls for its own learning practice.

Selecting effective learning practices depends on the individuals and groups involved, particularly the training, expertise, and capacities of the leaders or facilitators of the groups. It also depends on the intent of a group. The learning practices in this and the next chapter should be led by individuals trained in a range of facilitative skills and should already have some reasonably well-developed sense of their own political identity. How-ever, with that said, there is a need for innovation and people and groups can explore their own developmental ranges as long as careful attention is directed toward voluntary participation, respect, and remembering that it is time to direct ourselves toward community engagement. The endless pro-cessing of so-called self-help groups is to be studiously avoided.

Earlier in 2007, I had the good fortune to participate with a group of people to create for ourselves a workbook based on David Korten's (2006) book, *The Great Turning: From Empire to Earth Community*. Working with this group helped me to imagine more closely the specific practices that would be needed to put Korten's, my own, and other thinkers' work into practice.

Embodying and practicing generational attention

In this section and most of the rest of the chapter I will pursue a distinct approach to learning practices that specifically comes out of my interest in supporting groups to activate the capacity for generational attention. While these practices could be used for other purposes, I am using them in relation to the complex task of supporting people and groups to activate, sustain, and extend their capacity to understand and act on the needs of our current times.

I will introduce three learning practices that focus on the development of *generational attention*. These practices support the development of emo-tional awareness and thus also activate some level of *affect freedom*. However, they are not specifically focused as healing practices, and so they do not directly attend to our suffering or the activation of that capacity. One of the distinct facets of generational attention is the way in which it can shape a person's relationship to history, that is, they can imagine their own and their people's history developmentally. This supports the shift from the political and a private-psychological liberalism to a "public-psychological" liberalism.[1]

The capacity for generational attention does not simply activate a thoughtful consideration of personal and cultural strands of experience; rather, it supports acts of passionate engagement that bring together the personal and cultural as an experienced unity or confluence. As a person or a people activate their capacity for generational attention they are able to more effectively attend to the problematic divides within their generation's experience: that is, they attend to the developmental and evolutionary dilemmas of their time. Accordingly, generational attention supports us to focus attention on our personal connection to a problem – thus creating the opportunity to heal ourselves – but it also enables us to attend to the severity and historical depth of the problem for the people of our time.

In our time, generational attention is helping us to focus on the artificial separation between cognition and affect. This is the task of the psychological citizen as it needs to redeem the political individual's deprecation of emotion while shifting attention toward the articulation of a public language of psychological liberalism. The emerging capacity for generational attention has two distinct aspects or dimensions, cognitive and affective. Without either of these dimensions, generational attention cannot be said to have been successfully activated. Activating and integrating the *cognitive aspects* of generational attention requires:

- an interest in and knowledge of human history
- an interest in and knowledge of human development as applied to self and others
- some – at least rudimentary – interest in and knowledge of the confluence between the first two.

Someone developing this capacity would need to be versed in significant theories of human development, evolution, political theory, cultural history, and other relevant sources of knowledge.

With this knowledge a psychological citizen would be able to contextualize conflict from a cultural evolutionary awareness that enables them to integrate individual, cultural, and species history. This context supports coherent thinking about effective political interventions and initiatives. However, thought is not sufficient to understand the context of conflict. It is also necessary to be able to respond to what Omer calls the "cultural trauma" associated with the conflicts, which requires the cultivation of the affective aspect of generational attention (Omer 2005: 30–33).

Development of the *affective aspects* of generational attention requires individuals to learn to focus on their own pain, suffering, and the corresponding unconscious patterns of behavior that restrict personal development. Generational attention also requires focusing on the pain, suffering, and unconscious patterns that restrict the cultural evolution of their time.

Samuels identifies how political consultants could draw from the psychotherapist's knowledge of how they, the therapists, use their own experience as a "countertransference" response to a client to identify what type of intervention might be called for in a political or cultural setting (Samuels 1993: 31; 2001: 159–61). Similarly, Omer identifies how cultural leaders can use their own experience to "transmute how they are personally affected by the culture into creative action that midwives the future" (Omer 2005: 30–33).

When applied to the actions of a psychological citizen, attention to emotions, as rooted in the functioning of the affect system, supports the capacity for objective discernment of personal, group, and community dynamics. Additionally, the full functioning of the affect system enables this citizen to motivate others by transmuting their own affective experience into political truth and leadership.

Without a coherent understanding of the role of affect to discern personal and political truths and to motivate cohesive efforts for social and political change, there can be no institutional center for the liberalization of culture. In effect, the translation of theory into practice is made too difficult with political institutions facing outward toward the world, risking ignoring the development of the people within their own organizations. Similarly, traditional psychological institutions face inward, risking ignoring the larger social forces that are shaping the lives of the practitioners they train and their clients. This outward–inward split parallels a similar split within all of us moderns between thinking and feeling.

Central to the development of generational attention is a reintegration of a cultural split between thought and feeling. As I described in Chapters 9 and 10, this split is a function of a distinct stage of cultural evolution that may have been utterly necessary, but its continued domination limits our prospects for the future. In order to describe the capacity for generational attention and the way it accounts for the problematic separation between thought and feeling, I will digress briefly and tell another small piece of my own story. Through this story I show how several of Henderson's "cultural attitudes" work together and reveal the unique opportunity to reconsider the historical and present functioning of human thought and feeling.

The divide between thinking and feeling

Over the last 25 years I have been developing my own capacity for generational attention. Originally motivated by a "political attitude" (a form of Henderson's "social attitude"), I was raised as a political liberal, believing that individual people have the power and responsibility to initiate liberal social changes. As I described in Chapter 2, this identity broke down, which enabled me to attend to my own private-life suffering, drawing from the wisdom of an introverted, private-psychological liberalism.

In combination with rudimentary experiences of religious feeling, I was able to combine my external political focus with an internal psychological focus that helped me to imagine that, as a people, we have a potential to realize a *divine future*, a future in which our experience of the sacred is brought to greater life through the relief of human poverty and our attention to our own transformative nature. This religious feeling of being a part of something larger, what Pierre Teilhard described as a "sense of the species," combined with my political attitude and kept me from abandoning politics (Teilhard 1963: 197).

While I was not politically active for more than two decades I never was satisfied with my psychological improvements. In fact, I felt that my personal development was always incomplete, no matter how much I was able to resolve my psychological condition. Over my twenties and thirties I honed my religious feeling into a modest religious attitude that helped me to integrate my therapy experience with a felt sense of the suffering of my time. I similarly cultivated a philosophical attitude, which enabled me to think coherently about this suffering. Like Henderson notes, this philosophical attitude helped me to connect my personal thoughts and feelings to human history and contemporary events, thus grounding feeling in thought and actuality. As a result, I have some experience of the kairos of our time that I am bringing to bear in this writing.

More specifically, in response to the psychological and religious feeling evoked through my crises, I pursued a study of human cultural and evolutionary history. As part of that study I came across the late nineteenth century writings of Wilhelm Dilthey of the influential Southwestern German school of the emerging social sciences who sought to create a "human science" capable of understanding human consciousness from the broadest possible context (Polkinghorne 1983: 24–32).

Social theorist George Steiner acknowledges Dilthey as the first social scientist to recognize the historically relative nature of thought. For Dilthey each act of understanding "is itself involved in history, in a relativity of perspective" (Steiner 1976: 249). Implied by this understanding is some experience of the notion that thought develops. Dilthey's insight became the basis for his concept of "historical consciousness," which he used to reconcile previously contradictory philosophical, scientific, and religious systems by viewing them as parts of disparately pieced human history, each containing aspects of truth relevant to their time (Meyerhoff 1959: 37).

Steiner recognizes the importance of Dilthey's contribution, but also recognizes the need to expand the "cognitive" focus of historical consciousness to include an "affective" dimension. Steiner refers to the work of Nicolai Hartmann whose idea of "retrospective empathy" begins to show the way in which history was also something that was experienced emotionally (Steiner 1976: 249). Here, *feeling history* is an awkward expression that attempts to capture the way in which "understanding" is linked to the affects. However, the awkwardness is symptomatic of a modern impoverishment of the idea of affect separated out from thought. More recent research in affect theory as well as more recent studies in Buddhism suggest that thought and feeling cannot be so divided (Goleman 2003: 134).

Implied by this turn of thought is the notion that, when conjoined, feeling and understanding become an empathetic feeling state that knows history. The integration of thought and feeling is a dimension of generational attention. It leads to the recognition of the unity of personal development and cultural evolution. By implication, the rupture between thought and feeling not only disrupts the functioning of individuals but also of institutions.

Integrating thought and feeling: focusing outward/inward in organizations

As a result of the rupture between thinking and feeling, organizations devoted to either political or psychological change have a great deal of difficulty in connecting thinking about social problems to motivating themselves and others to actively participate in community engagement learning practice. The struggle that results from the divisions between thought and feeling and between thought and motivation are in effect the same divide and end up perpetuating the separation between personal development and cultural evolution.

Like their orienting institutions, political individuals end up problematically pointed outward and psychological persons confusedly pointed inward. Individuals without awareness of their own emotional suffering retreat into a public world and forgo the personal renewal possible through healing practices; whereas, individuals without awareness of the larger connections to their communities and to their humanity retreat into their private lives, forgoing the collective renewal that is possible through public participation. A new psychological and moral type can balance this split orientation from within the identity of the psychological citizen.

The activation of generational attention supports the recognition of longstanding patterns of human suffering and the potential for personal development and cultural evolution. Again, such "recognition" is not simply a matter of perception or understanding, in their traditional passive sense, but rather to recognize the means to see, feel, know, and act reflexively in order to support the transformation of a person's, their group's, and their community's current suffering.

Through the activation of generational attention a thoughtful consideration of history evokes passionate engagement. Through this engagement, awareness focuses simultaneously on personal development and cultural evolution. Once activated, generational attention supports human development as it enables individuals and groups to integrate history at personal, generational, and cross-generational levels both cognitively and emotionally. Accordingly, generational attention integrates both the educational and healing needs of a person within the context of their community, while placing the person and their community within a larger historical context.

In the context of a conjoined concept of history and development, generational attention is a fuller capacity than what can be provided by just a "political" capacity. Through generational attention individuals and groups are able to focus their attention on different dimensions of history for the purpose of social justice, etc., while attending to the personal and political wounds, and the passions that live within their experience.

Attending to these wounds, and the prejudices that hold them in place, releases the passion needed to renew ourselves and our community. This requires a collaboration between the individual's and the group's cognitive and emotional experience such that knowledge of history can be combined with an empathetic awareness that enables the political wound to be healed, transformed, which supports the individual or group to be able to renew or revive their political hope and have the power to contribute to a new shape for political culture. Generational attention arises when individuals:

- learn how to tell their "political histories," how they are similar and different than others in their communities
- learn how to tell our generation's political stories and listen to the political stories of other generations
- learn about the larger historical trends, as described in Chapters 9 and 10, that are actively shaping our current circumstances, in order to imagine the scale upon which we are trying to transform ourselves.

The activation of these three levels of generational attention takes place through a range of learning practices, with Chapters 9 and 10 as examples of the third level. In the next section I will provide examples of the first two types. Through these practices we can renew our experience of our political values and remember who we are.

Generational attention

Telling our personal political histories

David Korten, author of *When Corporations Ruled the World* (2001) and *The Great Turning: From Empire to Earth Community* (2006), asks us to "find your own stories, share them with others in your own words and in the manner true to your experience" (Korten 2006: 237). By finding our own stories we can become what Korten calls the "storytellers of a new era" (Korten 2006: 237):

> Compelling, unifying stories that speak to the potentials of the mature human consciousness are essential to the work of birthing Earth Community, and progressive movements should give substantial priority to the development and sharing of those stories.
>
> (Korten 2006: 250)

Korten's insight into the importance of story follows a view of social science research that is drawing forward the importance of story that originated in the "earth community" values of earlier human societies. In this context stories are more than fictitious events meant to entertain: they are sources of identity and faith. Through learning to tell our own story and the story of our times we can activate the faith that we can change political culture, reflecting my Phase Four of political development – the development of a public language that captures the public's imagination. The goal of such a language is to support a more developed, fuller, relationship to the future.

In order to change the culture we need to have the confidence that our actions can make a difference. Such faith in our own agency emerges as we learn, heal, and actively engage in our communities. This activation of faith supports the images of a new, mutual political future.

In the learning practice that follows, participants are invited to recount their experience of being political as a way of addressing the extent to which our experience of being political has been repressed. Following Samuels, there is a growing interest in reawakening our political awareness by exploring our original experiences of becoming political. Groups currently using this practice find themselves enjoying each other's company, having insights into their political identities, and generally recommitting to their political values and to political activism.

According to Samuels, we inherit much of our politics from our family, through osmosis, conversation, debate, or rebellion (Samuels 2001: 28). Experiences in the family give rise to rudimentary social feelings, including compassion, courage, shame, which begin our social thinking and our moral experience, such as with the experience of injustice. People also come into their "political history" or "political myth" through "their class, ethnic, religious, and national backgrounds – not forgetting the crucial questions of their sex and sexual orientation" (Samuels 2001: 28). Each of these plays a role in forming our political identities.

By adding sociopolitical factors into our thinking about the development of the person we are able to consider the effects that political events have on an individual's development. Samuels refers to this as "the political history of the person" (1993: 53). By focusing on this history we can also discuss the repression of the person's "political potential" or "political energy" (Samuels 1993: 56–73). Samuels' identification of political potential enables him to ask questions about the need for the individual to have avenues to express its political energy:

> If a culture does not allow a flowering of political potential to occur and express itself and the political self to flourish, then that culture loses one of the most productive avenues for personal growth and individuation. The individual loses out as well as the prospects for transformation and healing of psychopathology within political systems.
>
> (Samuels 1993: 58)

According to Erikson, we also come to form a political identity, or not, through our identification with role models. In effect, through role models we come to have a sense of the importance and possibility of politics. Through our interactions with role models we determine if we see any future in politics for ourselves; if we can see such a future for ourselves – as voter, activist, or leader – we are said to have formed a political identity.

According to Samuels, other influences on our political identity include both generational issues like Viet Nam and the assignations of cultural leaders, and an innate politicalness which some possess. Individuals can have either more or less of this than their families, peers, or culture (Samuels 2001: 28).

Exploring our "political selves," our "political identities," or exploring our "political energy" can be invaluable. Through such an exploration we challenge the current cultural limits to our ability to bring our full personal experience to political conversation. Often political conversation is too dry, technical, or issue oriented without being personal. These conversations can be frustrating and leave us feeling helpless or argumentative. Sometimes this leaves us with only our private lives to discuss with our neighbors, friends, or family as politics often becomes taboo.

We have all experienced the personal pleasure that comes from sharing our private-life stories. Those who are in one of the helping professions may have found how sharing such stories can be transformative, as an individual is able to passionately tell their story and come to find many reasons for previously unstoried experiences that support an emergence of the capacities of courage, compassion, and humility. Would such transformations also be possible through telling our public/political stories? Certainly, the stories told by the participants in my research would support this idea.

The following learning practice uses political stories to recreate a common experience of public space in which our private and public lives are given the chance to come together. Through some of the following questions we can support each other to find out just how personal our experience of politics really is.

Telling our political stories

In my work as a transformative political psychologist I have led workshops in which I use story to support the cohesion of political groups and to help the group's members connect more personally to politics. During this learning practice I ask individuals to break up into groups of two to four and tell a story about one of their earliest memories of politics, of political awareness or action. Any of the following questions can be used to facilitate this practice. I draw them from Samuels' splendid book, *Politics on the Couch*, in which he describes his own group practices which he refers to as "political clinics" (Samuels 2001: 162).

FAMILY

- What did you learn about politics from being in your family?
- How has your family experience informed your current experience of politics today?

- What is your first political memory?
- When did you become aware that there is a political system with competing approaches?

POLITICS AND YOUR HISTORY

- What experiences shaped your current political thinking or ideology?
- What experiences did you have that influenced your desire and willingness to participate in politics?

After asking these and other questions in the smaller group, I invite the larger group to re-form and reflect on what they have gone through. In order to help them integrate their experience I use questions like these:

REFLECTIONS ON THE PRACTICE

- What is it like to tell your story and listen to the stories of others?
- What emotions did you go through in telling your story and listening to the story of others?
- Are there any common themes in our stories: what do we hold in common?
- What is distinct about your own story and what distinctly do you bring to this group?
- If your politicalness could be said to have a direction, what is that direction?

In his own work Samuels has had very interesting results. Through his political clinics Samuels has found that people are more political than they think they are; know more about politics than they realized; have been more politically informed than they thought; that recalling their memories often brings people to tears and may be either cathartic or traumatizing; have a stronger commitment to politics than they knew.

Samuels also notes how it takes time for a participant's relationship to politics to emerge and that they come from "private, secret 'countertransference' reactions everyone has to what is going on in the political world," which leads to the likelihood that such responses to politics are repressed, having no "ready outlet, since they are all too often dismissed as 'subjective'" (Samuels 2001; 162). Samuels suspects that people fear that "their secret responses to politics would not pass muster in everyday political discourse" (Samuels 2001: 163). Once again, we see the split between the external and rational focus of the political individual and the internal, emotional reality of the psychological person. Certainly, through such "political clinics" these can be brought closer together.

In my own experience with this workshop format I have found results similar to Samuels. Particularly noteworthy has been the way that the politics of a time affects people differently, such as when one workshop participant retold the story of being a refugee during the Viet Nam war. His story moved the whole group and created room for his profound difference to be acknowledged by a group of people who already knew and loved him. The tears and passion from this workshop were inspiring to me.

In the following learning practice the focus shifts from telling our personal stories, and connecting them to the events of our time, to linking these stories to a number of generational patterns including: identifying the distinct coming-of-age events of a given generation, and noticing patterns of personality that both parallel and shape the political events of the time. One of the most powerful dimensions of this workshop experience has been the way in which, starting with the oldest generation and moving toward the youngest, it becomes possible to see patterns of successful and halted development that each generation has typically suffered in isolation.

Telling our generations' political stories

At the beginning of this chapter I proposed the idea that "individual development and cultural evolution are not separate phenomena, but are twin dimensions of a single process of human transformation." Also, in Chapter 2 I suggested that both generational attention and destiny are emergent capacities that are responses to the multiple political and identity crises of our time. Implied by these ideas is the notion that our identities emerge on the basis of the needs of our time. Whatever our unique sensitivities are, and whatever way in which we suffer, supports us to turn our sensitivities into talents or capacities that are responses to this suffering.

If there is such a connection between identity and the kairos, then why is it that we experience them to be so separate? In part, it may be due to the extent to which identity formation is new and is still largely passively engaged in. Erikson describes the process of identity formation as largely unconscious, enabling the individual to move from mother to the world:

> This process is . . . unconscious except where inner conditions and outer circumstances combined to aggravate a painful, or elated, "identity-consciousness" . . . at its best it is a process of increasing differentiation . . . it becomes ever more inclusive as the individual grows aware of a widening circle of others significant to him, from the maternal person to "mankind."
>
> (Erikson 1968: 23)

Passively engaged identity formation is also influenced by the particular phase of cultural evolution, that is, the phase of the differentiation of the "political individual." During this most recent phase the repression of guilt and fear has actually broken us away from the "sense of the species," in Teilhard's words, which would enable us to experience the immediacy between our own process of identity formation and the formation of our times.

In the first generational attention learning practice, "telling our political stories," participants began experiencing a reconnection between themselves and the world as telling their own and listening to each other's stories helped them to experience the connections between their private lives and the stories of their times. These were healing stories. Erikson too notes this connection:

> We cannot separate personal growth and communal change, nor can we separate the identity crisis in individual life and contemporary crises in historical development because the two help to define each other and are truly relative to each other.
>
> (Erikson 1968: 23)

Central to this practice is a welcoming attitude toward the emotions that had become privatized and led to isolation. In psychotherapy and in the political workshops I do, people get in touch with the grief and shame that lies just under the surface of the modern, political individual, thus giving birth – in anguish – to the psychological person. However, the political workshops seem also to be able to get underneath the way isolation continues within this new, psychological person, as much twentieth-century psychotherapy has proven.

The learning practices created for these political workshops do not attend simply to the participants' private lives: it is to the life of each participant as a *citizen* that attention is drawn. In these practices the public function of affect is restored as participants are given the chance to connect their emotions not only to the events of their private lives but also to their public, political identities.

Extending the practice of telling our political stories, this next learning practice reawakens the emotional and imaginative life between generations. At the level of traditional culture people ritualize and celebrate their shared experience, which builds connections, maintains culture, and sometimes can create new culture. At the level of modernity, the political individual has lost much of this capacity. Unfortunately, the private-life focus of the psychological person has not whole-heartedly responded to this loss. Fortunately, some return to a public religiosity is helping to re-create such rituals, consciously, thus moving from a passive to an active phase of development and evolution.

The following learning practice is derived from the ground-breaking work of Ken White of the Praxis Tank for Progressives. In a salon developed for the Praxis Tank, White successfully brought together several social science theories that reflect on both the developmental levels of cultural evolution and the distinct developmental tasks of each generation. White initiated this salon by bringing together individuals representing four generations, which he described as the "silent," "boomers," "gen-x," and the "millennials." At first these members of each generation were invited to gather into their four groups and asked to find the "coming-of-age stories" unique to the characteristics and experiences of their particular generation. These stories focused on commonalities that marked each generation, regardless of political affiliation, class, gender, or other common differentiators. Then White asked each generation, starting with the eldest, to tell their story in the larger group. Cascading from one generation to the next, these stories created a profound weave among people and generations. As the stories unfolded the group experienced a seamless consistency amidst the significant disparity.

Lastly, White initiated an integrative conversation that focused on the distinct opportunities for each generation to identify the contribution they have to make to enable a transformation of political culture. Much emphasis was placed on the need to guide, serve, or support the rising generations, with an eye on the unique place, responsibilities, and capacities of the millennial generation. The group agreed that attention on this upcoming generation can help all of us identify and support our unique contributions to their potential to lead us into an as-yet unimagined future.

In this salon a learning practice was created that extended the wisdom of Samuels' telling our political histories. Moving from the budding awareness of the connection between our unique private-life and public-political histories, this practice creates a conscious awareness of the crucial connection between generations. While conservatives have maintained this awareness in numerous ways, such as the valuable traditions of church and community, liberals have allowed multigenerational connections to be ruptured. Instead of relying on meaningful connections between people, liberals have relied on reason to connect the past to the future. I cited Patrick Garry in Chapter 4, defining political liberalism as an ideology that connects the "past with the future by interpreting the past and using it to guide the future" (Garry 1992: 3). We now know that such reasoning freedom is not enough. Re-creating a healthy connection between past and future requires some larger awareness that includes affect freedom.

Through telling the stories of each generation we are able to explore our sensitivities and suffering in order to reconnect to the larger stories of our culture and to overcome the powerlessness that comes with isolation. Through our sensitivities and suffering we find our distinct contribution and find how this contribution fits with that of others, other people and the people from the surrounding generations.

In this learning practice we see the extent to which it is possible to activate an awareness of political identity at generational levels that supports greater political awareness, hope, and political agency. In fact, the agency activated is not simply individual, but begins to once again become communal. More than the positive shared experience of purpose manifest in political organizations with common ideological affiliations, it is possible to reconnect more broadly to being human, to Teilhard's "sense of the species," which begins to provide us with a shared experience of the future. It creates an experience of the future in a way that would seem to be activating some rudimentary capacity for destiny.

In these first two learning practices I have approached the development of generational attention from the lived experience of the individual and begun to build successive layers of history, starting with our own experience and moving to identify with our own and surrounding generations. In Part IV, Chapters 9 and 10, I previewed the third learning practice oriented to activate generational attention at the level of culture. While barebones, this story supports an active consideration of our mutual cultural history, its political story, political wounds, and invites us to identify the unique role, destiny, to which we can all aspire in our quest for individual development and cultural evolution.

By learning to tell the larger story of the evolution of our culture we have the opportunity to explore the continuities as well as the failures of this process. Drawing from truth, caring, and accountability practices, this telling of our larger story can help us to connect to other cultures as we can reflect on our contribution to cultural liberty, and on the harm our culture has propagated. Similarly, telling this larger story can help us contextualize the current work of our generation, and of each of us as unique individuals. In all, the cultivation of generational attention requires all three practices: individual, generational, and cultural.

These learning practices are responsive to cultural trauma while attending to "cultural shame about the defeats, failures, and loses of the past. In doing so we come to realize the wisdom of failure." These learning practices "activate our cultural memory, reversing the collective forgetting that cultural trauma induces" (Omer 2005: 33).

In the following chapter I will move more concretely by offering several other learning practices that I have used in my work with educational and political groups. These practices are helping me to vocationalize and imagine the institutional forms that will be needed to bring political and psychological liberalism closer together in order to activate our psychological citizenship.

Chapter 13

Attending to the prejudices of liberalism

Introduction

In this chapter I will synthesize the discussion about the learning practices that are designed to activate generational attention with the major themes of this book including: the developmental history of Western culture, the role of affect in the future activation of the political identity of political and psychological liberals, and a critique of the current liberal political identity, that is, what I call the prejudices of progressivism. The purpose of this synthesis is to continue articulating a new form of liberalism that I have been referring to as a public-psychological liberalism.

The function of a public-psychological liberalism is to develop these and other learning practices in order to identify and heal the personal and cultural traumas that restrict our access to liberty. Central to this new liberalism is an awareness that recognizes the uncertainty of the future. What Descartes began through his radical doubt we must continue as we try to bridge the gap between the complexities of our current world and our capacities to respond to that world. We cannot afford the repressive certainty of religions, nor can we invest in the political individual's naive idea of social progress. Instead, we are in a position to activate a new liberalism based on the recognition of the opportunity to become psychological citizens who participate in their own development and in culture's evolution.

In the face of the unknown environmental consequences of the industrial culture it is important to be willing to openly face the future with humility and a truthful uncertainly. It is from this attitude of not knowing that the liberal's rational hubris can be transformed. Speaking openly about what we don't know is a form of a healing learning practice that helps open the future. Once we have learned to accept and openly share how little we really know about the future, we can "step into the future" together, which also is a valuable practice. Stepping into the future involves learning how to create new forms of public space within a group for the purposes of creating a shared experience of the future. Unlike traditional visioning processes, this learning practice does not focus on imagining possible futures; rather, the focus is on learning to enter into the shared emotional and imaginal states that activate the emergent capacities which opening futures requires, that is, the capacity for destiny.

The three learning practices in the last chapter and three others introduced in this chapter (*attending to our prejudices*, *not knowing*, and *stepping into the future*) will begin to provide a shape for the type of public-psychological practice that activating the future requires. This practice will be based on an understanding of the need to address human suffering from both political and psychological perspectives at the level of culture.

Imagining the future

In Chapters 9 and 10 I introduced a learning practice designed to activate generational attention at the level of culture (which could also be discussed as the level of *civilization*). In Chapter 12 I filled in two learning practices designed to activate generational attention at the earlier personal and generational levels. As individuals and groups use these practices, in relation to their political identities and histories, an *experience of the future* often follows. This takes place through a natural activation of the imagination.

I suspect that the activation of these three levels of generational attention is intrinsically renewing, thus bringing out the natural function of the imagination to lead us into the future. These practices address the way in which the future is repressed as we have been cut off from history at personal, generational, and cultural levels. Without a public or "political" identity that is activated by telling our political histories, without an awareness of our generation's uniqueness and a similar awareness of the distinct positions of those generations immediately around us, without an understanding of the larger context of cultural evolution, we have, following Pierre Teilhard, no sense of the species and thus no imagination for the future (Teilhard 1963: 197).

Engaging generational attention prepares the way for individuals and groups to identify their distinct sensitivities, talents, and suffering. Through identifying these dimensions of our experience, the future begins to appear as a bodily "strangeness," which is the context for the emergence of the *capacity for destiny*. By activating generational attention at these levels the capacity for destiny emerges. However, this also requires attending to affect, both in the form of suffering and in the form of emergent capacity. In earlier chapters I told stories about the political wounds suffered by progressive leaders. Besides showing their political wounds, these stories showed the healing and catalyzing effect that is possible when a group is supported psychologically, that is, when their political identities are supported by facilitation emerging from the new "public-psychological" form of liberalism.

These stories also support a growing understanding of the extent to which the human affect system has been disenfranchised as a source of objective experience for both the individual and the culture. More specifically, for both liberal social scientists and liberal political leaders, emotions are problematic. They are experienced, suffered, and set aside. They have not become a central enough player in either scientific or political discourse. They do not become an intrinsic part of the identity of the political leader or the social scientist – we do not know how to use them for what they are for.

Through the institutions of a private-psychological liberalism, particularly developmental and clinical psychologies, there is a movement to reintegrate and extend affect as a source of trustworthy experience, at least within the individual's private life. This movement has largely relied on increasingly convergent theories of the individual as a human being focused on what Robert Kegan calls "meaning-making" (Kegan 1982: 1–12). However, a more recent discipline, affect science, drawing from its own traditional ethological roots in Charles Darwin and more recently in the work of Silvan Tomkins, has caused a renaissance in understanding of the objective function of affect, which has prepared the way for a range of studies exploring the public function of affect.

The idea that affect functions publicly, and that this functioning is not intrinsically irrational, but is in fact intelligent, is new. While the history of this idea can be tracked into the roots of a range of thinkers, the cultural aversion to trust emotion is deeply embedded in our heritage. Up to this point, I have traced the deprecation of emotion to the "original oppression" of the individual by culture, that is, the idea that culture oppresses the unique experience of the individual. While this idea is central to this writing, it is important to reflect on the way in which original oppression is also necessary.

A review of the last 150 years of research exploring the history of human consciousness reveals a growing awareness of the way in which individual experience is differentiated in relation to culturally oppressive forces. Through the interaction between a collective culture, rooted in our mammalian, tribal, and environmental experience, a unique individual experience begins to become trustworthy. Over thousands of years the individual gains increasing levels of self-awareness and earns the respect of the collective as a source of trustworthy cultural experience. Accordingly, the oppression of individual experience is only shed as the individual works their subjectivity and becomes a source of objectivity. As I noted earlier, in Chapter 6, Jung reflects on this point as he brings subjectivity and objectivity back together and opposes both to collectivity.

Accordingly, emotions need to be worked to become increasingly trustworthy sources of experience. Simply put, affect develops. Based on this idea, we can view the emergence of *affect freedom* as an essential capacity that is beginning to support a reconciliation of the function of emotions at religious, political, and psychological levels. As I have described, restricting the cultural validity of emotions supports the cultural freedom (reasoning and sensory freedom) of the modern human, breaking out of the religious collectivity and into the freedom of the political individual. However, the downside of this act of differentiation is the difficulty in reintegrating emotions into some necessary private and public function.

At the level of the political individual, emotions become marginalized and associated with other marginalized dimensions of Western culture, such as the realm of the feminine, the home, and an individual's private life. In contrast, the public world is associated with thinking and with sensing, to the extent that these capacities are used for short-term gain through the objectification and manipulation of nature and others. As a result of this differentiation, and lack of subsequent integration, individuals are forced to retreat from the public world as they have no way of connecting to it, because connection is a function of emotion. Further, those who do find a way of connecting are forced to use the available language of materialism, and, at best, political liberalism.

In order to extend the valuable developments of the modern world, affect must be reintegrated into the public sphere as a source of cultural knowledge, but not by regressing to using emotion for oppressive control of people through the manipulation of fear and guilt. We cannot go back to the external authority of a narrowly conceived paternal image of social order. Rather, the reintegration of affect is taking place through both the feminine assertion of egalitarian values and a new masculine assertion of moral authority, based in these values. This confluence between the nonjudgmental approach of the mother, through a private-psychological liberalism, and a new moral approach of the father, through a public-psychological liberalism, offers a path to human freedom founded in the new moral and psychological type of the psychological citizen.

Reintegrating the mother's use of emotion to care with the father's use of emotion to assert accountability creates a private and public context for the maturation of the human affect system, which will activate a range of capacities, foundational and emergent. This new use of emotion is based on the capacity for affect freedom. Affect freedom changes our relationship to the future as it brings together the best of political liberalism – interest in social progress – with the best of psychological liberalism – interest in individual development. However, the development of this capacity will require facing the differences between these two institutions. In particular, I look to the institution of psychological liberalism to learn to attend to the suffering of political liberals in order to support their political identities and to activate their political development. This would require a new institution of a "public" psychological liberalism, which I currently identify as a transformative political psychology.

Combining affect science with the emerging public focus of a transformative political psychology will enable us to establish learning practices to activate and embody emergent and foundational capacities. Through the recognition of the affective basis of these crucial human capacities, we can learn to use emotion more effectively in private and public, which connects emotional, moral, and political development.

One of the crucial functions of a public-psychological liberalism would be to support political liberals to grow their organizations, support their membership, and to care for and strengthen their political identities. Such a task will require addressing their strengths and limitations, which I have had the opportunity to encounter first hand. In my current work with liberal/progressive groups I have experienced the difficulty in creating this new liberalism as I have worked to apply my clinical training to their experience. It turns out to be difficult to integrate political liberalism with a traditional private-psychological liberalism. Facing this difficulty seems to require that I learn to identify and openly discuss the many strengths and limitations of both of these two languages and identity types. Such openness is clearly a prerequisite of any effort to create a new vocational and institutional form, the task of the last phase of political development.

In this writing I have identified the bridging of these two liberalisms as the task for a transformative political psychologist. Such a practitioner is responsible for creating the necessary learning practices that would lead to conjoined forms of public practices that would be the basis of a new public-psychological liberalism. Such an institutional form would need to find a way of accounting for the strengths and limitations of all previous liberalisms. Of particular importance will be the way in which a new public-psychological liberalism would address what I have come to see as the prejudices of the current progressive movement.

Attending to our prejudices

The progressive movement is the latest constellation of the voice of political tolerance, social justice, diversity, and ecological sanity. It rises up in the wake of the latest failures of late twentieth-century liberalism. These failures have been chronicled by many over the last decade and need not be discussed here in detail. Broadly speaking the divides between the liberalisms, between the religious and the political, and between the political and the psychological, haunt us and hobble our future.

In response to these failures people and groups with egalitarian values are rallying around the progressive banner in hopes of continuing the fight for justice, freedom, and other core universal principles. In order for this movement to outgrow the failures of its previous incarnations they will need to work through their prejudices.

In this section I will present a learning practice that I have designed based on my assessment of the prejudices of progressive groups. I refer to this practice as: "attending to our prejudices." It has the following goals:

1   Expose individuals and groups working on their political development to the range of prejudices they may act on or need to work with to transform political culture.

2   Introduce practical structures which support the development of their ability to engage their own and others' prejudices "reflexively."[1]

3   Prepare individuals and groups to be able to engage in healing practices that respond to the "political wounds" that underlie all human prejudices.

The topic of progressive prejudices could be introduced into any gathering, whether the groups were ongoing or not. However, unless a group has a history of working together psychologically, with the support of effective facilitation, I suspect that such an introduction would need to be approached as an educational learning practice, thus postponing the third goal of creating a healing learning practice. However, even as an educational practice, it may be difficult to refrain from moving toward healings, as I have found that asserting an understanding of another's or a group's prejudice is very evocative, which I attribute to the immediacy of the wound within the prejudice.

In working with groups I have simply introduced the topic of progressive prejudices, which is sufficient to get the group reflecting on the topic. Initially, it has been valuable to identify the traditionally acknowledged prejudices such as classism, racism, sexism, and others. Once acknowledged, the facilitator of this learning practice asks the group to temporarily set those aside. This is and of itself is evocative, for the risk of minimizing the depth and insidious influence of these prejudices is substantial. They truly need our ongoing attention to find their subtle manifestation in each of us and in all social and political groups. However, in my work with progressive leaders and groups I have come to identify a range of other prejudices that significantly undermine the effectiveness of the progressive movement, particularly as they remain unnamed and unexplored.

Raising the issue of prejudice outside of those already identified evokes resistance and is, itself, a move toward a public-psychological liberalism. It challenges the problematic autonomy claims of both the political individual (i.e., "who are you to . . .?") and the psychological person (i.e., "you can't say that, it's judgmental"). By challenging these distortions, a public-psychological liberalism attempts to return to Western culture images of the good father. Such images have been hard to come by in the wake of the severe harm done by men, but also by a failure to associate a good deal of that harm to the necessary sacrifices of earlier stages of cultural evolution.

Teasing out the difference between these two is one of the primary tasks of a language of a new public-psychological liberalism. This will require the use of the foundational capacities of fierceness, compassion, courage, and humility as well as the emergent capacities of generational attention and affect freedom. These capacities will enable us to create truth, caring, and accountability practices to attend to the cultural traumas suffered by women, children, and minorities at the hands of men. However, the suffering of men, whether caused by other men, women, or the original oppression of culture itself, will also need attention. Offering this attention is the responsibility of the psychological citizen.

A public-psychological liberalism will tell a new story of our culture for the purpose of honesty, healing, and integrity. Only then will we release the repression of the future and open our collective capacity for destiny. Attending to such repression begins as we turn toward our prejudices.

In ongoing groups with effective facilitation it is possible to attend to the suffering in which all prejudices are rooted. Through conversation it is possible to help individuals and groups to consider a range of prejudices that reflect the developmental issues stemming from the oppressiveness of religious social roles, the rebellion of the political individual, and the retreat and isolation of the psychological person. Through a presentation of these possible prejudices, individuals and groups can be supported by relatively simple healing practices that focus on good listening and an exploration of the emotional nature of these prejudices.

In the following sections I describe five primary prejudices I have encountered in my work with politically progressive individuals and groups, and attempt to offer a sense of direction through which the progressive movement could become more self-fathering in order to overcome these prejudices. I am sure that there are other prejudices that I have missed. Also, I do not intend to suggest that all progressive groups are hobbled by these prejudices; rather, in my work I have found these prejudices to live in such groups in an unreflective way that leads me to suspect that it is a broader condition of the progressive movement.

The prejudice against religion

The first prejudice that I find the progressive movement to be at risk from indulging in and being hobbled by is the prejudice against religion. Progressives are at risk for basing their understanding of religion on preconceptions that have little basis in science, in the best sense of "science." While the institutionalization of the religious experiences of cultural leaders such as Mohammad, Jesus, or Martin Luther has led to severe abuses on the part of their so-called followers, it is both unjust and untruthful to attribute those failures to "religion." It is too simple an equation to associate these failures with the nature of religions or the experience of the religious. These failures are more accurately attributable to the difficulties that the human species has with any process of institutionalization, whether political, educational, commercial, or religious.

While the term "spiritual" is being used to identify a personal relation to the divine or to sacred experience, the wider adoption of this term bypasses the need to integrate the history of religious institutions in our culture, their shames and their triumphs. We have mistaken the personalization of religious experience with its privatization. Further, the privatization of our religiosity implied by the term "spiritual" has not created the public conversation that is necessary to evoke the public and moral function of religion.

However, many religious leaders like Michael Lerner and Jim Wallis are currently satisfied with the term "spiritual." They are working expediently to bring together a "religious/spiritual left" made up of secular, spiritual, and religious people and organizations centered around egalitarian values. While in the short run such alliances are absolutely necessary, even urgently needed, it is also necessary to understand the actual historical circumstances that led to the rupture within Western culture between our religiosity and the rise of secular humanism. Pursuing this understanding is part of the practice that will heal the historical and continued suffering that this rupture has caused. Seeding future conversations, this rupture might be understandable by viewing it through the lens of the theories of human development and cultural evolution presented in this book.

For example, using Lawrence Kohlberg's theory of moral development, it might be worth looking at the anti-religious sentiment, emerging out of the nineteenth century, as a growing moral sensitivity to the limitations of the authoritarianism of the religious institutions of the time. This sensitivity reflects a stage in which morality is considered relative, inviting the non-judgmental mothering attitude of the private-psychological liberalism. Staying with Kohlberg, this is thought to be an "in-between stage" between a morality determined by one's social group and a morality of universal principles. The value of this stage is reflected in the way in which individuals become able to question the authoritarian approach to morality and social organization that emphasizes external authority.

Individuals at the stage of a private-psychological liberalism have worked to establish an "internal" locus of authority that supports their growing moral sensitivity. Through this sensitivity these individuals are able to recognize the value of diverse cultural groups, generally overcoming the "tribal" distinctions between cultural groups, which also applies to overcoming traditional cultural prejudices of all sorts including racial and gender based prejudices. However, despite the significant moral advancement of this stage, it risks a relativity of moral values that has accidentally supported the twentieth-century retreat into a private-life spirituality and the domination of the public moral conversation by regressive individuals and political groups.

The prejudice against hierarchy

In *The Great Turning: From Empire to Earth Community* (2006), David Korten cites Albert Einstein's observation that "no problem can be solved from the same level of consciousness that created it" (Korten 2006: 239). In fact, resolving our current political problems requires stepping outside of our current ways of thinking, the ones that created these problems, and into what Einstein referred to as the "next highest level" (Gellert 2001: xiv). Unfortunately, this idea of higher and lower levels of consciousness has always been a problem for progressives. In fact, progressives continually act fearfully in relation to the hierarchical assertions that are part of the reality of higher and lower levels of consciousness. This fear shapes their identities and leaves them prejudiced against hierarchy.

Without spending too much time on this issue here, for it has been discussed at length by Wilber in his books, including *A Brief History of Everything* (2000), it is important to say that it seems likely that the future of the progressive movement will depend, in part, on developing a clear political philosophy, language, or understanding of their fear of hierarchy and the way this leads to impoverished, prejudiced thinking and actions. In brief, we can understand this prejudice in relation to the progressive's inability to distinguish between what Wilber calls "dominator hierarchies" and "natural hierarchies" (Wilber 2000: 24–6). According to Wilber, recognition of the threat of dominator hierarchies shows a sensitivity to the abuse of power.

Wilber notes how dominator hierarchies can cause suffering on many levels. He uses the examples of the way that cancerous cells dominate a body, the way a "fascist dictator dominates a social system, or a repressive ego dominates the organism" (Wilber 2000: 25). In each of these contexts, domination destroys the health of the organism, social system, or the integrity of an individual's identity.

This sensitivity to the misuse or abuse of power or authority represents a comparatively high level of moral development. However, there are risks that manifest at this level of development. Specifically, following the same vein described in the previous section, progressives tend to become wary of any assertion of hierarchy or moral authority. This fear is rooted in a sensitivity to the misuse of hierarchical thinking: thinking that asserts false moral arguments in order to maintain domination.

As a result, a fear of moralizing leads to the adoption of a rigid stance of moral relativism. Once this stance hardens, rises above questioning, progressives have, in effect, abandoned their own developmental advancement. In effect progressives abandon their own well-earned moral authority, leading them to have difficulty with moral speaking, as the stories of the progressive leaders in Chapter 11 demonstrate.

When fear of moralizing and hierarchy controls progressive thinking and speaking, progressives either fail to recognize and assert their own moral authority or they go so far as to dismiss all "development" as a means of resisting all domination. That is to say that the progressive movement may be one of the most morally developed political philosophies available; but because of their fear of hierarchy, they may short-circuit their political effectiveness by denying the possibility of advanced moral development.

Confronting this prejudice requires attending to the individual and group political wounds that the prejudice is rooted in. By approaching the suffering implied by this prejudice it may be possible to create a "public space" in which a more rational and emotional dialog could eventually be possible for progressives. However, as much as progressives are defended against rational dialog in relation to these prejudices, they are equally or even more ferociously defended against the use of any practice that might offer freedom from the fears and other emotional sufferings that are at the root of their prejudices. This becomes the catch-22 that makes the progressive identity partially impermeable to change. I refer to this as the prejudice against process.

The prejudice against process

In my work with progressive political leaders and groups I have come to notice the difficulty progressives have with growing organizations, specifically with drawing volunteers and with consensus building. One leader compared her efforts to move an organization in a coordinated direction with "herding cats." While this difficulty can be accurately attributed to a number of different variables, including the nature of working with little money against well-financed political opponents or against embedded community interests, it also reflects progressives' issues with authority. Because progressives are not naturally inclined to submit to external authorities there is a struggle in their organizations to find other ways of making decisions and establishing lines of authority. This is a side effect of the resistance to hierarchy as the egalitarian values system has turned its back on forms of external authority, but may not yet have found other objective sources of authority.

The natural way through this difficulty is for groups to attempt to work out new methods for decision making, group coordination, and lines of authority. However, progressive groups are also inclined to desire to be "action oriented," that is, focused on doing political work in their communities. This makes it difficult to focus their attention on their own internal process (many progressive communities and groups have made significant progress on this issue).

The necessary process work that such groups engage in may reflect the natural difficulties of moving from Kohlberg's stage of moral relativity, with its emphasis on everyone's opinion needing to be heard, valued, considered, to a higher level of moral and organizational development that identifies which voices are to be trusted, followed at any given time, while maintaining an open process that is inclusive. Unfortunately, but for some good reasons, this necessary process work has proven to be very difficult –

sometimes impossible. For example, in speaking with progressive leaders and in my own experiences in progressive groups, there is a lot of wariness about what it takes to form egalitarian decision-making processes. Three factors seem to limit the progressive's willingness to form such decision-making processes. First, our recent cultural history is rooted in decision making through external authority; second, the development of alternative methods is arduous and overwhelming; third, the extroverted, action orientation of progressives has made it difficult for them to value the internal exploration of self that is often necessary to find other trustworthy means for group decision making, such as the potential objectivity of their own subjective experience.

The prejudice against science

The progressive's prejudice against science is one of the more interesting or at least most mischievous to talk about. On the surface one might think that this is impossible. In fact, progressive liberals, progressive democrats, and just progressives are fond of using this argument themselves against the neoconservatives who have been having their way with America for the last one or two generations. Thus, to accuse them of this same misdeed implies a hypocrisy that will likely be resisted requiring me to offer irrefutable proof – but would that be enough?

While progressives are fond of science, their understanding of it is limited to those sciences that provide them with information that fits the world view they have already constructed. They are comfortable with scientific information that addresses global warming, the connection between crime and a child's environment, and are especially fond of science that links the personality of conservatives to narrow mindedness, prejudice, and fear. Unfortunately, they are less interested in science that addresses their own psychological limitations or that suggests that the conservative world view has at least some coherence, as Lakoff has so clearly shown. More specifically, they have a significant resistance to any science that suggests that people are innately religious, that the world is organized into natural hierarchies, or that human beings could aspire to higher states of consciousness as a necessary part of their political work. More specifically still, they are resistant to a science that identifies their prejudices and links these to their limited political effectiveness. While painful, facing our fear of the religious and hierarchy will bring us closer together and help us to courageously engage others to change political culture.

Lastly, progressives seem to have a hard time surrendering or sharing their authority in relation to areas of political concern to social scientists. In all, it would seem that the progressives' issues with external authority not only make their internal organizational work difficult, but also limit their ability to recognize authority in other points of view. This is nowhere more apparent than in the progressive's relationship to the science of psychology.

The prejudice against psychology

While psychology is a science, I am treating the progressive's prejudice of it as a separate category. The progressive's prejudice against psychology is a special case. Not only do all of the above prejudices against science and process apply here, but progressive politics has a particularly negative relationship to psychology. While some progressive political organizations are successfully adapting psychological thinking and processing to their organizational work, there is still resistance to imagining that psychology could have anything useful to say about the progressive's political effectiveness.

Addressing these prejudices

In order to address this prejudice against psychology, I have drawn attention to the limitations of clinical psychology, shown how it is a product of its time and can overcome its limitations by aspiring to take its clinical skills out into the public (Molad 2001: 98). Central to the task of "going public," that is, creating a public-psychological liberalism, is learning how to use emotions as key players in public process. Whether fearful of process, psychology, or emotions, political progressives have every reason to be nervous about how they spend their precious time organizing. A vast majority of political organizing at the community and state level is still accomplished by volunteers – as it should be. However, as my many hours in meetings indicated, there is too much to do, by too few, who already spend too much time in meetings. This may be the primary dilemma of the progressive movement: too many meetings, attended by too few of the same people. No wonder they are shy about any turn toward psychology, process, or emotions. Despite this problem, I suspect there is a direction, if not an answer.

Learning practices as tools for a psychological citizen

Following Lakoff, we can say that political liberals focus too intently on political issues. Lakoff argues that this reflects their overidentification with rationalism. He would have us work more actively on framing our "issues" in terms of values, at least to recapture the common vision and the public language that liberals lost when they turned their back on traditional religions. While I am grateful for Lakoff's identification of the need to "frame" our values in a clear public language, his approach does not seem to account for the possibility that we need to do more than just present what we already know in new, and better, ways. Perhaps, I am misreading

Lakoff or focusing on a different part of the elephant. Regardless, I want us to consider that we do not already have the answers that we need and that by focusing on how we frame issues we risk the liberal's hubris of thinking that we are the rational ones and we already have the right answers. In fact, we do not have near enough answers to the questions we need to be asking.

Many times in this book I refer to Dewey's statement that we need a "new psychological and moral type." Using this quote as a launching point, I have asserted that we need to create a new type of psychological citizen and a new form of public-psychological liberalism. Key to the work of this citizen and its supporting institution is attending to the difficulties in redirecting the attention of political liberals toward their own internal experience. In the next section I will introduce a learning practice that I use to support political liberals to turn attention toward what they do not yet know, that is, toward the strangeness that holds the future.

Not knowing

In order to move beyond the limitations of their prejudices and the hubris of any thoughts that we already have the answers, liberals need to balance their external, overtly political focus with an interest in human development. The hybrid language that this book is helping to articulate is intended to be, at least a little, attractive to political liberals as it recognizes their political goals and efforts as key forms of cultural leadership in the work to establish a sustainable global culture. However, I still am asserting that political liberals will need to meet psychological liberals part way and find an interest in their own development. Interest in development is a primary defining feature of a new public-psychological liberalism and a defining trait of the psychological citizen.

In order to begin activating a new liberalism, political liberals will need to turn their attention away from an exclusive external focus on social ills and winning elections. Whether we win or lose elections, we need to evolve. Through evolution we can define the conversation and determine what the political issues are that warrant our attention.

In the groups that I have been working with shifting attention toward development is a difficult task. It seems to bring right to the fore some fear of the unknown. I encountered this fear in numerous situations in political groups during which I found the group's attention to pull away from what they did not know and to focus on what they already knew and to then launch into dwelling on self-praise or dwelling on strategizing community engagement practices that seek to use what they already know.

In order for a group to embrace or even consider incorporating a public-psychological liberalism into its identity, it will need to learn about the importance of exploring what is not already known. As a psychotherapist I am constantly supporting my clients to expand their ability to consider what they do not yet know. This is difficult for any of us, not just for liberals. In order to begin the exploration of what is unknown, a group must set out to develop the capacity for "negative capability" (Omer 1990). This capacity, identified in the early nineteenth century by the poet John Keats, requires developing the willingness and capacity to face/experience the unknown. This is much more difficult than one would suspect. The inclination to know is wonderful and insidious at the same time. However, to the extent that we are identified with knowing we cannot go through the process of moving from a revelatory image to new identities and new institutions – remember the challenge faced by Descartes.

In order to go through the five phases of political development we need to be able to give up knowing. This attitude of "not knowing" will be required in order to avoid premature closure of our relationship to the future. Negative capability is experienced in wide-ranging ways that have been described by poets and mystics as both inspiring and frightening. Remember my favorite Rilke poem, cited here for the last time:

> You must give birth to your images
> They are the future waiting to be born.
> Fear not the strangeness you feel
> *The future must enter into you long before it happens*
> Just wait for the birth, for the hour of new clarity.
>
> (Rilke 2007, emphasis added)

In this poem Rilke simply identifies that higher states of consciousness may be experienced as "strange." In another poem, beginning his famous *Duino Elegies*, Rilke goes further to speak of the terror that can be evoked by the "unknowns" of higher consciousness:

> If I did cry out, who would hear me through the Angel
> Orders? And suppose one of them suddenly
> Pulled me to his heart: I'd dissolve beside
> His stronger existence. For beauty's nothing
> But the start of terror we can just manage to bear,
> And we're fascinated by it because it serenely
> scorns to destroy us. Every angel is terrifying.
>
> (Hammer and Jaeger 1991: 21)

In these introductory lines to Rilke's famous *Duino Elegies*, begun in 1912, we see the inference of the extreme difficulty that approaching higher consciousness can bring and the clear necessity of being willing to live on the edge of not knowing, where beauty and terror meet, where we risk some dissolution of identity in order for a greater identity to emerge.

This same edge is described in depth psychology as clinicians have trained themselves to approach the unconscious and to bear its *numinosity*. Following Jung, many depth psychologists have recognized the way that psychotherapy can help the person awaken to their own path of development through an engagement with the unconscious. Jung identified the way that the unconscious is both historical and oriented toward the future. He writes: "The unconscious has a Janus-face: on one side its contents point back to a preconscious, prehistoric world of instinct, while on the other side it potentially anticipates the future" (Jung 1939: 279).

Through the shift from a private to a public psychological liberalism groups can learn to bear the discomfort they feel as they attempt to follow each other's sensibilities, talents, and sufferings. I have introduced this practice to groups simply by sharing what I don't know that I wish I knew. Sometimes seeding this practice is enough, even when focused on the brasstacks of organizing, people often recognize the value of vulnerably turning toward what we do not know but need to learn.

However, too often this turn is resisted. When the turn toward what we don't know is resisted, often the group is in need of either direct leadership or an indirect coyote move to draw the group toward the edge of the unknown. Once when a group was engaged in a type of "group think," in which I experienced them to be stuck in a cycle of asserting what they already knew without really listening to each other, I simply asked if the group would be willing to take five minutes to speak about what it is that they did not know. This disrupted the group to such an extent that by the next meeting several members had quit and several others were very excited by the new direction.

I think this group's falling out was along the political/psychological liberalism divide. The political individuals who were focused externally could not bear the strangeness of attending to not knowing, their identity precluded shifting inward to the psychological person, which is required prior to shifting back outward to the psychological citizen. My intervention focused on the developmental edge of the group, which revealed to me the extent to which including an internal dimension to our political identities is painful. As I described in Chapter 10. the psychological person is born in anguish.

After the falling out, some month or so later, this same group experienced hesitancy toward the unknown. However, this time the group's developmental "center of gravity" was higher and found a way of entering into this learning practice that brought a solemn kindness and vulnerability to our sharing as we spent some time speaking openly about our fears and our shames about what we do not know about ourselves or the future. Engaging in this learning practice moved the group toward attending to its prejudices and traumas.

Attending to prejudice and trauma leaves room for something new to emerge in the experience of each individual and in the group as a whole.

While any one of us or the group may have significant expertise or may have already developed significant capacities, it is important to note the extent to which the new consciousness, what David Korton calls the "Earth Community consciousness," is in the process of emerging. Earth Community consciousness is – at least in part – new, and thus unknown.

Speaking from the future

I have used this next and last learning practice in several different groups with interesting results. In one group I planned to use this next practice but somehow spontaneously found myself initiating the "not-knowing" practice first. I think this was a lucky turn of events because the not-knowing practice helped the group "empty out," which supported the spontaneous sharing that transpired next.

In this next practice a group is invited into the "future" as people sit in a circle and begin "speaking from the future." This practice, one of many within Imaginal Transformation Praxis, uncovers the way in which the future has been repressed through the privatization of experience and the alienation between affect and cognition. Omer identifies this as a symptom of modernity, which clearly parallels the political individual's deprecation of affect (Omer 1990: 49).

Initially a group can be prepared for this practice by reading Rilke's poem. Using this poem, a facilitator can set the stage by asserting that when next we speak the year is ____ (five or more years into the future). As the group begins to "speak" from that year people typically will share private-life events and sometimes what is going on in the world. When a group has previously been focusing on the external circumstances in the world it can make the shift toward the "public" future.

As the group's "future speaking" unfolds, the facilitator can attend to the limitations in the group's ability to speak from the future. Often these limitations will appear in members being simply unable to put themselves in the future. This limitation comes through when they say things like "the future might . . . ," or "I will either be a policeman or a school teacher," rather than saying "I am a . . . ." Omer identifies such resistance to future speaking as a failure of imagination, which is a symptom of the repression of the future.

Similarly, people might not be able to speak in detail, might not be able to speak passionately, or might be inclined to speak only of an idealized future. All of these limitations reveal weaknesses in the individual's affect system, imagination, and relationship to the future. Fortunately, each time that I have done this practice one or two individuals are able to show a greater vulnerability in their "speaking," thus showing the group the potential affect freedom and imagination that, in effect, begin to release the repression of the future.

It has been my experience that when someone enters into the future with hope, open fear, and clear and specific fantasies/images about the events that are taking place in the future as well as their own personal role in those events, a group's intimacy deepens and its passionate nature begins to be activated. While I was using a different learning practice in my research (see Chapter 3), remember Frank's vulnerable and passionate sharing and how it led to greater personal sharing by the others and how this catalyzed their political identities. By bringing a group toward their "future speaking," a facilitator can begin to address the repressed fears and hopes that conservatives do not seem to attend to and liberals repress through their reduction of the fear to forms of issue-oriented rational speak.

Concluding thoughts regarding learning practices

In this chapter I have added three new learning practices to the three meant to activate generational attention introduced in the last chapter. Activating generational attention, turning toward our prejudices, turning toward not knowing, and the future, are practices that provide a rough idea of what can be done in a group to activate foundational and emergent capacities in relation to a group's and its individuals' political identities.

These practices are not inclusive, they are illustrative. They offer a scaffolding. There are numerous other practices that would fall somewhere within the divisions between community engagement, educational, healing, and religious practices. They represent one of the central activities that a transformative political psychologist would use in their professional work. Besides these public/clinical/therapeutic learning practices, a transformative political psychologist would also engage in the traditional range of social science activities: teaching, research, consulting. However, central to their identity is the awareness that they are working to become the change they wish to see in the world. They are working on their own political development for the purpose of strengthening their own political identity. Lastly, this image of the political psychologist is a transformation of the nineteenth- and twentieth-century idea of the social scientist.

The twenty-first century political psychologist, and the social scientist in general, recognizes that the primary function of science is to support the resolution of human problems through their own development, that is, through their development as psychological citizens. Accordingly, this political psychologist is actively pursuing their own affect freedom because this is the primary function being differentiated by the species, at least in Western culture, as a trustworthy source of individual and cultural knowledge.

Central to the practice of a transformative political psychologist is the recognition that politics and the future of humanity cannot be left to others. The political psychologist must play an active role as a psychological citizen, both externally and internally, both politically and psychologically. The political psychologist cannot simply be a neutral observer and analyzer of cultural events. This was one of the mistakes of the Frankfurt School for Social Research. In this context, the political psychologist must learn to model the emerging capacities needed by the culture. This modeling requires finding the future within their own experience – as Erikson's *new capacities*, as Jung's *communicable ideas*, or as Rilke's *strangeness* – and take responsibility for finding ways of activating it within the attention of a generation.

Within our own generation the task is clearly for the political psychologist to learn to model affect freedom in order to support a return to a sense of the species. In this content, a sense of the species means that we need to return to and extend our experience of being human. More specifically, attending to being human means learning how affect functions – to assess, motivate/direct, and connect. Once attended to, affect activates and turns a generation's attention toward the necessities of our time, a task that neither George Bush nor John Kerry had the affect freedom to do.

As political psychologists, by any name, learn to activate their affect freedom it will be possible to turn a generation's attention and release the repression of the future. This will activate the capacity for destiny. Central to the activation of these capacities is the need to recognize the extent to which we suffer from what I call political wounds, or what Omer calls *cultural traumas*. Recognizing this suffering, that is intrinsic to our experience, to our very identity, is a prerequisite to the renewal of liberalism and to the development of a new institution of a public-psychological liberalism.

Following Max Horkheimer and Theodor Adono, the first generation Frankfurt School faculty who initiated the first institutional effort to bring political and psychological liberalism together, we need to learn the extent to which the modern identity is not whole, is not complete. According to these thinkers, the belief that the individual personality is complete and simply needs to be supported through psychotherapy fails to recognize the extent to which it is a historical construct built upon thousands of years of cultural transformations and oppression. While these men did not fully know what to do with this insight, it did help them to set a standard that subsequent generations of psychotherapists have neglected. If we assume this historically constructed nature of identity, then we will need to find both a theoretical structure to account for it and a plan of action that would enable us to support its "treatment," that is, its further transformation.

In the last chapter I will present two theoretical perspectives that I view as essential to the task of accounting for and transforming the historically situated human identity and core to the formation of a transformational political psychology. Drawing from the important work of Omer and San Francisco Jungian Tom Singer, it is possible to create a language of human suffering that supports our efforts to bring treatment or transformative practices for this suffering. Central to this language is a new understanding of political affinities, conservatism and liberalism, that is based on the development of the affect system.

Chapter 14

A public psychological liberalism

Futurity is the necessary condition of ethical being.

(George Steiner)

Thomas Singer's unifying vision of individual and cultural suffering

In order to fully develop a theory that supports the transformation of the individual and society simultaneously, it is important to account not only for the creative processes through which individuals can become more differentiated, but also to account for the severe destructive patterns that groups and nations fall into and in which individuals get catastrophically caught up. In their theory of "the cultural complex" Sam Kimbles and Thomas Singer shed light on a cultural dimension of human experience that may be largely responsible for much human suffering (Kimbles and Singer 2004: 1).

In the introduction to their book, *The Cultural Complex*, Kimbles and Singer discuss the need to understand how to bring together the cultural differences that lead to the conflicts that tear us apart. They identify the likelihood that such an understanding can be gained by looking at the "autonomus processes in the collective and individual psyche that organize themselves as cultural complexes" as the source of the conflicts that tear us apart (Kimbles and Singer 2004: 1). Singer and Kimbles' interest in drawing attention to cultural complexes has as its purpose helping us to develop "an enhanced capacity to see more objectively the shadow of the group in its cultural complexes" (Kimbles and Singer 2004: 4).

Following Jung, Singer and Kimbles address the way in which individual experience and identity are rooted in group or "collective" experiences that have an ancient history that continues to influence individuals in the present. According to these authors, Jung's recognition that such a collective level influences the life of the individual has yet to be systematically applied to groups. Instead, Jung's own analyses emphasize the broadest sense of the meaning of collectivity in his idea of the archetypes.

Samuels speculates that Jung's theory of the archetypes is rooted in the individual's and group's experience of affect (Kimbles 2004: 199). Accordingly, affect – as group emotion – may play a central role in the harm that happens between individuals, groups, and nations. Singer unites the idea of cultural complex and affect when he speaks of what happens when a group's cultural complexes are activated. He writes: "When these complexes are triggered all of the emotion of the personal and archetypal realm gets channeled through group life in its experience" (Singer 2004: 20). He describes the way in which complexes evoke "powerful moods and repetitive behaviors," and how opposed to change they are as they "resist our most heroic efforts at consciousness, and they tend to collect experience that confirms their pre-existing view of the world" (Singer 2004: 20).

Linking the intractability of group volatility to Donald Kalsched's theory of individual trauma, Singer notes the way that groups defend themselves in much the same way as individuals suffering from severe trauma (Singer 2004: 17). Kalsched describes the way the psyche of such individuals splinters into a "daimonic defense system" (Singer 2004: 18) with one part attacking anyone coming close from the outside and another part attacking inward, where the "personal spirit" of the traumatized individual hides. This leaves the individual without healthy ego strength, reducing them to a shell-like "false self" (Singer 2004: 18). Because genuine ego strength is diverted into these attacking forces, individuals' private and public life become passive, struggling to know how to love, to be a citizen, trapped in consumer glory.

According to Singer, this outward–inward defense structure also exists for groups, whether small or made up of larger populations. He recognizes the way in which the actions of distinct groups are analogous to the actions of traumatized individuals. Singer asks, "what if this highly schematized outline of the psyche's response to trauma applies as much to a group's response to trauma as it does to the individual's?" (Singer 2004: 18). See the way Singer is indirectly addressing the gulf between individual and cultural experience? He notes that such a traumatized group can have a history of acting out its injury politically, that is, through acts of revenge and defiance, spanning generations or millennia (Singer 2004: 19). Further, the traumatization of the group is internalized by the individual within a group.

Whether identified within the religious extremism of the Middle East, our own religious fundamentalism, or simply within the reactivity of a political group, right or left, each group casts a shadow, that is, has its unreflective history which is embodied – to some extent – by any individual who identifies with that group. When not attended to, these histories perpetuate a people's fears and hatreds, enabling them to project their fears and shames as prejudices.

If a goal of a political psychology of the future is to learn how to treat group and individual traumatization simultaneously, then the affect associated with each would need to be the subject matter of effective learning practices. The learning practices offered so far in Chapters 12 and 13 support individuals and groups to identify such traumatizations and to learn to attend to them through the cultivation of foundational and emergent capacities, particularly affect freedom.

Cultural trauma and the collaborative self

If we think of affect freedom as an emergent capacity for both individual and culture, then we can view its realization as a form of treatment for individual and group traumatization. Following Omer this requires exploring the link between learning and conflict. Omer links learning with conflict and states that "learning through conflict requires that we contend with affect" (Omer 1990: 315). Accordingly, he views collaboration as a capacity that can support us to engage in emotionally aware conflict, for the purpose of learning. Implied by Omer's thought is a receptive attitude toward conflict and affect as a means of breaking out of privatized lives and regaining a public life as a citizen.

For Omer, attending to cultural traumas can take place deliberately as individuals and groups participate in transformative practices that cultivate the emergence and consolidation of human capacities. According to Omer, a "capacity" is "a distinct dimension of human development and human evolution that delineates a specific potential for responding to a domain of life experience" (Omer 2006). Notice the way in which his definition of "capacity" bridges the divide between development and evolution. Through the transmuting of affect these capacities become central to the life of the psychological citizen, who Omer characterizes as embodying a collaborative self.

Applying Singer, Omer, Samuels, and my own thinking to the current realities of politics creates opportunities to begin imagining the tasks that would be involved in addressing the current polarizations.

The work ahead: conservative and liberal responses to trauma

In his book *The Plural Psyche*, Samuels describes two distinct types of morality that are deeply rooted in the human psyche: "original morality" and "moral imagination" (Samuels 1989: 195). Applying Samuels' understanding of these two types of morality to politics we can loosely view the tension between them as analogous to the tension between conservatives and liberals. Here, "original morality" is *conservative* and associated with "original sin" (Samuels 1989: 194). Original morality is prone to black and white thinking and is morality "'by the book,' correct, stolid and safe, reliable" (Samuels 1989: 196). But, in its self-certainty, it leads to catastrophic results, whereas moral imagination is *liberal* and is capable of flexibility, ingenuity, and forgiveness. However, when used alone it is ungrounded, lacking conviction, and, as we shall see, too fearful (Samuels 1989: 196). In effect, current political process polarizes along this moral axis. In my research, the liberal's evasiveness appeared as a hesitancy to speak in moral terms. Instead there was a retreat into the troubled techno-speak of rational liberalism.

Following my earlier description of the difference in personality type between conservatives and liberals, we can say that individuals also polarize along this morality axis, psychologically. Accordingly, some individuals are liberals and some are conservatives and, by implication, polarizing in either direction is problematic, leading to rigidity in the conservative and rigidity in the liberal (i.e., the liberal's rigidity appearing as a chronic lack of groundedness). Of course, as I am discovering for myself, most of us are awkward combinations of both liberalism and conservatism.

Implicit in Samuels' analysis is a form of generational attention that can be further differentiated by connecting it to Kalsched's theory of trauma and Horkheimer and Adono's view of the modern personality. Horkheimer and Adono's view of the modern personality as a historical construct built upon thousands of years of cultural transformations and oppression can be better understood when viewed from Kalsched's trauma model. Based on this model, we can say that the personality of the modern individual has been traumatized and that this trauma is expressed in its passive consumer glory.

When the two forms of morality create political polarizations, dividing into conservatism and liberalism, you could say that they are creating the current ineffectual citizen with their false self, with conservatives taking the outwardly attacking stance and liberals taking the inwardly attacking stance. The outwardly attacking "conservative" voice points a contemptuous, blaming finger at outside sources – and toward liberals – while an inwardly attacking "liberal" voice points a fearful, blaming finger inward, toward American culture – and toward conservatives. This result of traumatization creates a cultural malaise or depression that keeps at bay an essential dialog between conservatives and liberals or between original morality and moral imagination. According to Samuels, what is required is some piercing of the depression and an active reclaiming of the dialogue through a positive use of aggression, not to be mistaken for violence. Samuels writes: "Just as in sexuality and spirituality, the transformation of aggressive fantasy tends to be in the *general* direction of its opposite: creativity and moral imagination – toward forgiveness" (Samuels 1989: 210).

In depression, the depressed person or culture is locked into believing that the world's or their own evils are insurmountable, thus the simultaneous inward and outward attack, making healthy aggression unavailable. In depression, the freedom of the moral imagination is temporarily lost. What regains this freedom is some positive assertion of aggression. Here is where Sandy's retreat from the word "hate" and the word "love" to "dislike" and "like" suggests the liberal's depression and inability to activate enough affect freedom to move through the liberal malaise (see Chapter 11).

In my research both Abe and Sandy need to be told a new story about the role of affect in their political identities: that way Abe could overcome being a "math person" and Sandy could risk a more active use of her passions. My telling them this new story would be one of the practices that would help them to cultivate their own generational attention. This would give them purchase over liberalism's overly rational attitude and support them to begin experimenting with a fuller range of affect freedom, which would help them to gain access to levels of political observation and action available through the heightened perceptiveness and motivation of affect freedom.

This could support the creation of a revitalized liberalism that could more effectively challenge the rigidified original morality of the conservatives: what Sandel refers to as the cultivation of necessary "civic identities" and I am referring to as the political identity of the psychological citizen (Sandel 1996: 338). In this context, a transformative political psychologist could offer psychological explanations for social events, without reducing them to overly clinical descriptions. For example, by combining Samuels', Singer's, and Kalsched's work the ensuing analysis is possible.

Following these psychologists, we could say that the conservative's response to trauma, say the bombing of the Pentagon and the World Trade Center on 11 September 2001, is to indulge in black and white thinking, as George Bush's immediate response focused on the Muslim extremists' "evil" and their hatred of American "freedom" suggests. Here, we may have original morality acting without a necessary connection to moral imagination. However, the peace movement's "liberal" response may be similarly problematic. While the conservative finger points outward, the liberal finger points inward. While the liberal's assertion that we have significant responsibility for the hatred felt toward America is valid and warrants attention, it seems equally necessary to point to the crippling conditions in many totalitarian societies, in which human rights have yet to gather much support, and the importance of not turning a blind eye to their situation.

Using the ideas of these three thinkers, and others, it seems possible to conceive of chronic political conflicts as trauma responses. If we assume that both conservatives and liberals are protecting their own experience of "personal spirit," then I can imagine a transformative political psychologist's responsibility would be to support either or both sides to learn to move vulnerability toward their personal spirit, while minimizing the polarizing influence of their demonic defense system. Practices involved in this disarming process would, at least initially, work to create an atmosphere of trust, understanding, and playfulness. But it would also require the cultivation of affect freedom and its necessary struggles with moral experience.

This image begins to sound too idealistic, even to my ears. Nevertheless, in the meetings with my research participants and other groups, such a disarming process did take place. Once an emotionally open space was created they were quite willing to disarm. Perhaps it is unrealistic to imagine that such a process could take place on any significant scale between conservatives and liberals. Nevertheless, once the trauma theory is adopted in relation to these two modern political identities, supporting more openness in relation to the fearfully protected "personal spirit" is a primary path of transformation. Further, by pursuing this path, if only with one of the two groups, it is likely that the transformation of that group would change the political dialog more generally, for the better. And, a larger transformative practice between stalwart opponents could be pursued as well.

Supported with this understanding, it is possible to interpret events that took place during the research meetings in a way that shows how the progressives may suffer from a form of Samuels' "cultural depression" that is not linked, per se, to their individual or private experience, but rather is linked to their identification with liberalism. Applying generational attention, we can begin to see the way that political identities carry with them their own psychopolitical history. That is to say that liberalism, as one form of historical political identity, is one way in which political relations have shaped the culture's affect system. The depression suffered by progressive leaders reflects both a strength and weakness of the liberal's soul. Liberals are strong as they are vulnerable to the necessary depression evoked by a modern world spinning largely without intelligent and humane control. Liberals are weak, perhaps, as they repress fear with a defensive posture that uses an overly rationalized rhetoric. I will discuss this repressed fear in more detail shortly.

The transformative political psychologist's response to liberalism, their own affect experience, would be a countertransference response through which they use their emotions to metabolize the history of a group and begin to imagine and initiate the practices needed to transform it. The learning practices I have been developing are a bare beginning. They come out of my immediate experience as I use my imagination and emotional responses to political change groups to draw attention to a group's developmental limitations and opportunities. Attending to these groups includes turning toward the political wounds of each individual and the group as a whole. While rudimentary, the response from these groups indicates that some transformation is taking place.

In my research group with progressive leaders and in subsequent political change groups, transformation manifests in the way in which participants are turning toward disarming in front of one another and toward an open exploration of their political identities. This is revealing a "youthfulness" that, again, did not seem particular to anyone's individual or private identity, but revealed the "personal spirit of liberalism" in its youthful and wounded quality. In my research group, this youthfulness came through when Abe, at one point, physically withdrew or "wilted" when he expressed his grief and envy to the group. It came through in Sandy's fearful retreat from the strong affects of "love" and "hate" to the more depressed choices of "like" and "dislike." It also came through in the tender vulnerability expressed by several when they told stories of their political wounds. Simultaneously, it came though in the way they came to joke, tease, and generally be playful with one another. Frank's claim that "we're going to stay" (in the researcher's home) was the most poignant moment, as it implied that he had found a "good enough father" to finally protect liberalism's "personal spirit."

However, remember that the cascade-into-play, initiated by Frank, was interrupted by Sandy who rained on the spontaneous picnic when she said, "We have a lot of responsibilities." Here, Sandy's comment interrupts the vulnerable child mode, that is, the group's revealing its personal spirit. She reminds them that the virtue of service lies in accepting responsibility and drawing value from serving, and not from playfulness or mutual pleasure. In this situation it seems that Sandy is acting as the group's "daimonic defense system," keeping them from moving toward the healing found in the re-emergence of their personal spirit and instead toward finding satisfaction in a zealous, isolating overwork. Here, the potential of the group – found in these moments of play and later in expressions of passion – is hobbled by its use of the liberal technical language that limits moral expression and fosters isolation in a false self.

This false self may be safer, less vulnerable, but it fearfully keeps the research participants, and possibly most liberals, locked into the rugged individualism of the political individual. Isolated liberals do not foster interdependence, or enough moral courage to overcome their fears about taking more political risks. Nor do isolated, overly rational liberals inspire enough passion to awaken others to build a movement that would have enough political and psychological support to overcome their basic fear of being attacked by the political right. This reminds me of what Sandy said when she was doing a role play as Martin Luther King. She said, "You must awaken the dead in leaders and you must awaken the dead in the masses." In this role play Sandy steps past the passion-restricting limits of liberalism for a moment, and shows she really does understand (at least via her imagination) the need to cut through to an underneath place, where we can once again inspire and awaken others. She cuts through to where affect freedom offers connection and motivation.

Looked at broadly, from the perspective of generational attention, we can begin speaking more directly about the liberal's affect system, or their general level of affect freedom. Given that identity is to some large extent affect-shaped by history, we begin breaking out of the limited perception of most twentieth-century psychology by discussing the extent to which individual identity is shaped by its historical milieu. While an obvious statement, it has not been sufficiently worked in either psychology or in politics.

I would argue that both the research participants and many others I have encountered in various groups since are afraid of becoming stronger politically, for the use of such strength would put them more in harm's way. They are also afraid of their shame, for if they follow their shame they would be even more politically engaged. Given the sacrifices that many already make in order to maintain a public/political identity, it is not at all surprising that they are afraid of making a larger commitment. While Dave said, "I'm feeling fearful of being uncommitted" it seems likely that he may have actually felt ashamed of being uncommitted and fearful of being more committed as well as fearful of his shame – if he attended to the shame he would make a more frightening, deeper commitment to politics.

This analysis begins to show a likely connection between fear and shame in these research participants, and probably in liberalism more generally. The appearance of these fears was not predicted and they were unexpected. However, their appearance seems quite significant. Based on this analysis, I note that these fears seem quite rational at the level of their private, individual identities. Though, however rational they are, they also seem quite developmentally "young." By participating in the language, history, and affect system of liberalism, the leaders expose their own private vulnerabilities. When compared to the larger liberal political identity with its history of courage, sacrifice, and political success, they feel small. Despite making more sacrifices than most of the rest of us Americans, they feel smallness as they set themselves beside King, John Kennedy, and others. However, I suspect that this experience of smallness is not limited to their private/personal identities, but also reflects a way they are connected to the protected "personal spirit" of liberalism. Despite its long history of sacrifices and successes, political liberalism too is young. It has a mere few hundred years, in its current incarnation, of shaping the historically ancient affect system of Western culture. And my research participants have joined their identity to this lineage.

They each participate in this powerful political/historical identity and embody its courage; but they also embody its fearfulness. They protect themselves and they protect liberalism itself. Both are protected from opening to fear as they engage in the rational, liberal techno-speak that maintains isolation and precludes vulnerability. Here, the liberal seems afraid of their shame – the higher commitment it implies – and ashamed of their fear – the youthful vulnerability it implies. Perhaps this last sentence is diagnostic of a primary bind that the liberal's affect system is in. A 2003 "Doonesbury" cartoon captures this condition as a politically "conservative" character (Mark's male companion) admonishes his "liberal" friend (Mark) who he

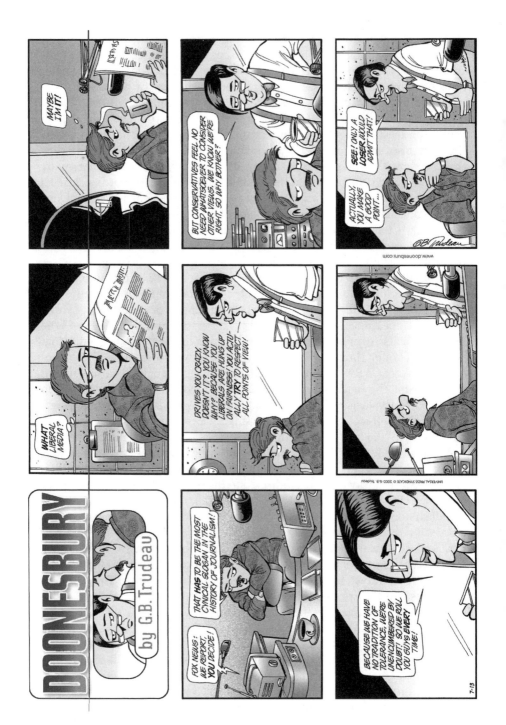

sees as bound up by liberalism's history of "tolerance" (Trudeau 2003). Whereas, he notes, he – and conservatives generally – have no such history and are "free" to pursue their own private agendas. In this cartoon the conservative's shameless nature is portrayed simultaneously with the liberal's self-doubting fearfulness. While the value of tolerance cannot be reduced to a fearfulness, simply by having tolerance as a value the liberal sets up an ego ideal that opens them to shame and its implied necessary activism, which, in turn, they modulate by being frightened of what they will have to do to live up to the shame's implied moral standards.

Here, the liberal response to the modern trauma is lived in the specific shape taken by the liberal's affect system. This shape has its own repressions and vitalities. In the way that liberals may repress fear, they may need to be supported to rise to the task of challenging conservatives on their own turf.

Overcoming fear and shame in the modern world

It is difficult for me to imagine premodern culture. As noted by Baumeister, it had a degree of solidity, of community. However, given the opportunity, people fled its constraints. Over the next several centuries most people retreated as far as possible into a private world. This retreat is responsible for leaving the public sphere without sufficient resources to maintain democracy. Overcoming the fear and shame of the modern world requires that we return to the public sphere, but from within a new psychological and moral type, as a psychological citizen.

As we activate and apply our generational attention to this problem we can look for ways of getting people more involved in the public sphere. Viewing the retreat as a trauma response requires that we find ways of supporting people to overcome both their fear and their shame (and other repressed affects). Fear and shame can be seen as being in system with one another, as two faces of the same response to modernity.

The relationship between repressed fear and repressed shame came to my attention during my research with progressive political leaders when I read a *Newsweek* magazine article in which the author cites democratic politico Julian Bond. Bond succinctly and insightfully captured the relationship between repressed fear and shame when he responded to a question about why the democrats were wiped out in the 2002 elections. He says, "In the competition between the shameless and the spineless, the shameless win every time" (Cose 2002: 47).

In this comment Bond exhibits a form of generational attention, which captures the problematic relationship between repressed shame and repressed fear and crystallized for me the mutual system that fear and shame are in. His insight supports us to begin to speak of the way in which political culture and political identity fracture around failed affect development. In this context, conservatism can tentatively be identified as that form of political identity and organization that develops when shame is repressed. Con-comitantly, liberalism might be identified is that form of political identity and organization that develops when fear is repressed, especially as I have noted a fear of shame.

This analysis begins to shape the current conversation about the political, moral, and psychological identity of people and political movements in relationship to the development of their affect system. Thinking in terms of the way that individual and political cultures are shaped by repressed affect may offer a possible new way of considering the problem of evil (i.e., as a problem of repressed, unintegrated affect).

When applied to the issues of affect development faced by my research participants, we can say that they were profoundly influenced by King, for he clearly spoke the liberal language, but at a new "pitch." He rose above the liberal's repressed fear as he extolled his fledgling movement that anyone who did not have something for which they would be willing to die could not really be alive (King 1988). Several days before he was shot, King anticipated, if not foretold, his own fate (or chosen destiny) when he spoke of not being afraid of dying and telling his audience that he might not make it with them to the promised land but that they would make it for he "had been to the mountain top and seen the promised land" (King 1988). Here is the capacity for destiny incarnate.

Willingness to risk death would slow the liberal's retreat into moral relativity, further accelerating its political development. Fear of death seems to restrict the liberal's fuller use of affect freedom and the moral speaking that would come out of it. Based on this analysis, and supported by learning practices, one could say that transformative political psychologists could support liberals to embody more courage to enact their visions of the future, to activate their emergent capacity for destiny. Courage to face shame transmutes the shame at not being able to live up to one's political ideals into the destiny of one who does something to live up to them. This makes the capacity for destiny a function of an evolving affect system supporting the confluence between private and public identities. Remember participant Diane's exalted moment when her dead Jewish ancestors applauded her as she was arrested and jailed for civil disobedience. Remember King extolling his followers with the following passionate statement, "If he puts you in jail, you go into that jail and transform it from a dungeon of shame to a haven of freedom and dignity" (King 1988). Like Omer, King also knew that shame led to dignity and, as I am discovering, to destiny. As Omer has stated "shame makes us human" and "shame is being's call to belonging" (Omer 2006).

Concluding reflections

Culture shapes the affect system of its people. This power is both liberal-izing and oppressive. To the extent to which people pursue a conscious relationship with affect, affect freedom relives this original oppression of culture. As a culture becomes more complex, different groups within the culture come to represent different dimensions or phases of the relationship between oppression and liberty. For example, in Chapter 9 I described the way culture differentiates through the esoteric/exoteric developmental rhythm. The esoteric phase ruptures existing cultural and individual identities, leading to an exoteric phase during which the emergent new identities are consolidated.

Conservatives and liberals are one recent and powerful manifestation of this developmental rhythm. However, unlike efforts to find a "post-partisan" approach to politics, the developmental rhythm between conservatives and liberals is not a wrestling match between developmental equals. Unlike the nonjudgmental mothering language of the psychological person, there is a new father language emerging that risks addressing the difference of political ideology in terms of a developmental hierarchy.

This new language of a public-psychological liberalism raises questions about the maturity of political ideologies. Following Kohlberg and others, greater maturity requires acceptance of a widening public sphere in which all individuals are considered worthy, no one group considered other. However, this psychological thinking about politics is new and difficult. While liberals certainly would seem to embrace the value of the diversity and egalitarianism of the psychological liberalism of the last two centuries, their resistance to the further implications of a public language of political psychology limits their capacity to assert a moral agenda.

As Samuels rightly worries: "It would be tragic if the most psychologically minded politicians were to turn out to be conservative leaders" (Samuels 2001: 19). Here is the bind. While liberals would seem to be more developed politically – they attend to issues of diversity and equality – they may not recognize the way the wind of the liberalization of culture is passing though the psychological. Here we return to the central thesis of this book – cultural evolution is transpiring through a process of becoming more psychological.

In just the last one or two hundred years this psychologicalness has intensified into a semi-conscious psychological attitude that has created a new internally focused identity. Through this identity we are learning to respect anew the function and enjoyment of our emotions. They help us to assess our relation to the world, they motivate us and direct our attention, and through these emotions we connect to others. The future of the liberalization of culture depends on recognizing and actively participating in cultural evolution in this psychological manner.

While our rational mind is powerful and has helped us gain great freedoms from the restrictions of nature and the oppression of culture, its heroic identity, known here as the "political individual," is too brittle, failing to grasp the importance of our irrational, emotional intelligence. Through the relatively new "psychological person" many have come to value a new internal identity that has emerged through spiritual reflection and psychotherapy within our private lives. Within both spiritual and psychotherapeutic practices, the depth of our internal experience has been explored and we have come to know it to some significant extent. However, Dewey would not accept the psychological person as the new psychological and moral type he has called for and asked us to seek. There is a profound need for the psychological person to go outside and return to the public sphere.

If we accept that the task is to return to the public sphere, thus reversing the direction of liberalization from that initiated in the early nineteenth century by the transcendentalists and others, then we will need to adapt practices that extend what we have learned in our spiritual and psychological practices back out into the public. Whether through religion or politics, we are in a position to create a range of learning practices that extend the more developed egalitarian languages of political and private-psychological liberalism to a public-psychological liberalism.

In this book I have introduced a few of these practices based on the idea that the goal of such practice is to activate increasingly advanced stages of development through the realization of capacities. These capacities are both foundational and emergent. Following and adding to Omer's Imaginal Transformation Praxis, foundational capacities are activated as mourning practices transmute grief into compassion and grace; as accountability practices transmute shame into humility, dignity, and the capacity for destiny; as conflict resolution practices transmute anger into fierceness and devotion; and as intimacy and encouragement practices transmute fear into courage and faith in the future. However, foundational capacities are not enough. Our current human situation requires that we form a new psychological and moral type, one capable of transforming the relatively new "psychological person" into a "psychological citizen." The founding of this type requires the activation of capacities unique to this time in human history.

While there are likely to be numerous emergent capacities that we need to identify and aspire to embody, through my research I have identified three primary capacities: *generational attention*, *affect freedom*, and the *capacity for destiny*. Through appropriate learning practices these capacities are being activated. While the goal is to activate psychological citizenship broadly, there is a narrower immediate need to initiate a variety of cultural practitioners. Fortunately, this need is currently being fulfilled by numerous people whose informal efforts to transform political culture are becoming more formally organized. This represents the latest shift in the developmental rhythm of going from a passive process to the active pursuit of such new vocational roles.

The new vocational roles that are being identified support the emergence of the psychological citizen. As cultural coaches, ritual specialists, or transformative political psychologists we are recognizing the need to transform political culture by simultaneously engaging in individual development and cultural evolution. These new, formalized vocational roles will need to be supported by emergent institutional forms, which have as their purpose the institutionalization of cultural evolution.

Whether as an institutional form, a new vocation, or simply in the life of a new psychological citizen, all new emerging learning practices are rooted in a devotion to the principles of truth, caring, and accountability. Based upon these principles we are learning to focus simultaneously on education, community engagement, and healing. Through such focused attention our prejudices are checked and the underlying political wounds are attended to. As we attend to this suffering we activate our passionate faith in ourselves, connect to one another as friends and citizens, and embody the emergent capacities called for by our time. Through the activation of these capacities we renew liberalism and awaken once again our faith in the future.

Notes

1 The liberal's emotional body opens our faith in the future

1 Typically, the word "religiosity" refers to an exaggerated religiousness. That will not be my meaning. At the risk of foolishly attempting to change the meaning of a word, I find it necessary to have a word that refers simultaneously to a person's innate "religiousness" and their experience of being religious. While the word "spiritual" might suffice in the long run for my meaning, I balk at that word. I find the use of the word "spiritual" to imply something too private and not open to public conversation, nor open to the need to forage a new public "religiosity." Fortunately, in his book *God's Politics* I found Reverend Jim Wallis to be using the word in the manner I am also using. Wallis writes: "We are all guilty of succumbing to a diminished *religiosity* that is characterized by privatized belief systems" (Wallis 2005: 36, emphasis added). Here, the goal is to create a new public religiosity.

2 Through generational attention individuals and groups are able to sort through the relevant issues of their time and work effectively to understand, heal, and activate a community's political energy. The development of this capacity combines the best of religious, political, and psychological liberalism as it does not privilege political change or psychological healing over one another. Through generational attention, it is understood that emancipatory transformation requires both the structural changes sought in politics and the developmental changes sought in psychotherapy. Further, this capacity holds these transformations within the larger religious or spiritual context that is fundamental to human nature.

3 "Affect" is the biological dimension of emotion; it refers to the existence of a distinct "affect system" that functions in all mammals.

4 A brief aside – this discussion of emotions may evoke concern that, especially given that I am a psychologist, my focus on emotions will be indulgent. This concern would be especially relevant if I did not acknowledge the limitations of traditional psychotherapy, particularly the way that historically it has narrowly, though beneficially, limited its focus to helping individuals integrate the healthy functioning of emotions in their private life, while neglecting the public function of emotions. This book is about capacities like generational attention and affect freedom, which are emerging at this time in human history in response to our *public needs* and the role that emotions play in the activation of these emergent capacities.

2 Transforming the felt sense of the future into the capacity for destiny

1 Original oppression refers to the way in which culture misuses force in its efforts to direct or control individuals and becomes oppressive: that is, it damages individuals through the use of physical force or destructive social norms that are communicated through its institutions, social conventions, and familial structures. I think of this impact as one of the first impacts of culture on the individual, and thus I have named it "original" oppression.

Original oppression is quite distinct from the way a culture successfully supports individuals to sublimate their instinctive drives, impulsivity, and emotionality. This term parallels Herbert Marcuse's concept of "surplus repression," though my own term is embedded in a developmental perspective and supports a distinction between the positive developmental relationship between individuals and culture and the negative oppressive relationship between the two (Marcuse 1955: 35).

2 This statement is balanced by Pierre Teilhard who writes: "The discredit into which faith in progress has so rapidly fallen . . . is partially explained by the habitual illusion which causes all new movements to believe at their birth that the object [social progress], whose appearance draws them on, is within hand's reach and can be grasped within the space of a generation" (Teilhard 1969: 174).

3 Accordingly, during these years of psychotherapy, I pursued an introverted path by studying philosophy with the guidance of my professor Stanley V. McDaniel at Sonoma State University in California. Stanley V. McDaniel studied with Donald Piatt, a former student of John Dewey's, and Abraham Kaplan, an articulate interpreter of Deweyan Pragmatism, at the University of California at Los Angeles in the 1950s. From Stan I learned to consider human suffering within a broad existential and anthropological context that helped me to view humanity as a whole for the first time, and to realize that we are still evolving and, in fact, have a higher destiny.

3 Stories of political destiny

1 If the separation between self and world is simply a developmental step away from an externalized authority, that is, the original oppression of tribal religious culture, then the current task may be to locate a source of internal and yet *mutual* authority. This idea of mutual authority first occurred to me when I was 23 and had just purchased a red bumper sticker with white letters proclaiming QUESTION AUTHORITY. Later, I began reflecting on that message and I realized that we needed a second bumper sticker that announced the need to *CREATE AUTHORITY*. I never got around to making such a sign. I suspect that 26 years later it is now time.

5 The variety of uses of the idea of development

1 In effect, increases in complexity and in the differentiation of the functioning of the individual were viewed quite narrowly. For example, in political anthropology, "action theory," which drew from the German sociologist Max Weber, reduced the individual to their efforts to acquire power. According to action theory, individuals are goal oriented, and adopt "manipulative strateg(ies)," for the purpose of "maneuvering," and "decision making" in order to determine relationships on the basis of dominance and subordination (Lewellen 1983: 102).

This view is echoed by social conflict theory which discusses cultural evolution in terms of "competition between human groups" (Corning 2005: 246).

In its efforts to describe the complexity of tribal or nation-state interactions, political anthropology and other social sciences do not seem to consider looking at culture in terms of a developmental process over time. Instead, the use of the word development is limited to its meaning "appearing" such as when social tension leads to the "development of a 'crisis'" (Lewellen 1983: 103).

2 Jane Loevinger encourages a reconsideration of the recapitulation theory.

7 Political development and emotion

1 Samuels is hesitant to speak of political development in terms of stages of "higher" and "lower" development. Given the abuse of hierarchical thinking, Samuels' hesitance is well founded. However, based on research completed in the last 40 years, there are models of development that account for the abuses of what are referred to as "dominator hierarchies" as distinct from "natural hierarchies" (Wilber 2000: 24–6).

9 A new story of liberalism

1 Whether the theory of cultural evolution articulated in this and the next chapter applies cross-culturally is not addressed in this writing. My interest is in humanizing and liberalizing Western culture.

2 As Cornford notes, because there is no real *individuality* at this point, it is difficult to describe whose affect system or imagination is being activated. Is it the individual's or the group's? For convenience, I will simply speak of the group's collective affective and imaginal experiences.

3 According to Cornford, enthusiasm is a state in which "god enters into his group" and ecstasy is "man rising out of, and above, the prison of his individuality and loses himself in the common life of the whole, becoming 'immortal' and 'divine'" (Cornford 1912: 112).

4 It was not until second-generation psychologists in the early twentieth century that a direct study of children helped found better developmental theory.

10 The advent of psychological liberalism

1 Gellert notes that while Adams' understanding of human psychology was limited by today's standards, particularly his understanding of the extent and depth of the human shadow and its origins in collective experience, his introspective awareness recognized the perils to genuine freedom released by Jefferson's reading of the psychology of the time.

2 Adams seems to have been aware of what Jung would later characterize as the power drive of the unconscious or *shadow*. What institutional form could we look for to reintegrate the external focus of political liberalism with the internal focus of a personal religiosity? Following Henderson, depth psychology – for one – and particularly the work of Jung can help us imagine the necessary institutional structures. Such structures would bring more social meat to the bones of the psychological attitude. However, the gap between political and psychological liberalism must be more fully understood in order to distinguish between our current vision of psychology as one of the "social sciences" or as "clinical psychology," and a vision of psychology as an institutional form capable of

taking the *psychological consciousness* (its intensification in the *psychological attitude*), and making it into a *psychological capacity* that forges a public language binding political and psychological liberalism.

3 As I write this I am considering whether this makes Freud the father of a truly psychological liberalism. I suspect so.

4 The affluent class's retreat from public participation breaks from an earlier tradition of service, leaving a void of role models for public participation. According to Pastorino, without role models with whom to identify, political identity development remains "defused" (Pastorino *et al.* 1997: 574). The retreat of the affluent impoverishes the images of democratic participation needed by a community's children. The ensuing crisis of the isolated individual separates a privileged private life from the needs of a community, which makes it very difficult to awaken a larger sense of community purpose.

11 Emergence of the psychological citizen

1 One has only to remember Democratic presidential candidate Edmund Muskie, who cried when his wife was attacked during the New Hampshire primary, and how that undermined his presidential bid.

12 A transformative political psychologist

1 I suspect that cultural leaders throughout human history have had some rudimentary experience of generational attention, which allows them to be aware of a connection between their own experience, including basic sensory and perceptual experiences, and an active image of their people as a whole. Through this experience, cultural leaders are able to activate an increasingly personal relationship with the unconscious, and thus provide the rudiments for them to attend to their own personal development. While the phenomenon of "personal" development may be extremely rudimentary in the earliest human settings, over time the experience of a leader is a focal point for the differentiation of personal experience, and thus the locus for emerging cultural evolution.

13 Attending to the prejudices of liberalism

1 Following Omer, I identify "reflexivity" as a crucial capacity emerging at this time in human history. The capacity for reflexivity integrates affect, cognition, and relationship, enabling individuals and groups to transform their relatively passive ability for "self-reflection" into an *active* affect-laden capacity.

According to Omer, reflexivity is the "capacity to engage and be aware of those *imaginal structures* that shape and constitute experience." Imaginal structures are themselves patterns of unconscious individual and group activity which Omer describes as: "assemblies of sensory, affective, and cognitive aspects of experience constellated into images; they both mediate and constitute experience. The specifics of an imaginal structure are determined by an interaction of personal, cultural, and archetypal influences" (Omer 2006).

Reflexivity supports an active process of working with these unconscious patterns in order to identify and transform the personal, political, and cultural wounds that are at the root of problematic identifications with these patterns. Attention to these wounds is necessary for a group's intent upon changing political culture through their own political development.

References

Adono, T.W. (1982) *The Authoritarian Personality*, New York: Norton.

Alford, F. (2002) 'Group psychology is the state of nature', in K. Monroe (ed.) *Political Psychology*, Mahwah, NJ: Lawrence Erlbaum Associates, Inc.

Atlas, J. (2005) 'Out of the past: what anti-poverty groups can learn from the American Legion', *Tikkun*, September/October: 40.

Bai, M. (2005) 'The story of how the Democrats learned to tell stories again', *New York Times Magazine*, 17 July: 40.

Barrows, A. and Macy, J. (1996) *Rilke's Book of Hows*, New York: Riverhead.

Baumeister, R. (1986) *Identity: Cultural Change and the Struggle for Self*, New York: Oxford University Press.

Beardsley, M. (1960) *The European Philosophers: From Descartes to Nietzsche*, New York: Random House.

Beck, D. and Cowan, C. (2006) *Spiral Dynamics: Mastering Values, Leadership, and Change*, Oxford: Blackwell.

Beebe, J. (1995) *Integrity in Depth*, New York: Fromm.

Bellah, R., Madsen, R., Sullivan, W., Swidler, A. and Tipton, S. (1985) *Habits of the Heart*, Berkeley: University of California Press.

Bentley, A. and Dewey, J. (1960) *Knowing and the Known*, Beacon Hill: Beacon Press.

Bottomore, T. (1984) *The Frankfurt School*, London: Tavistock Publications.

Brown, L. (ed.) (1973) *The New Shorter Oxford English Dictionary*, Oxford: Clarendon Press.

Burack, C. (1994) *The Problem of the Passions: Feminism, Psychoanalysis, and Social Theory*, New York: New York University Press.

Buxton, C. (1985) *Points of View in the Modern History of Psychology*, Orlando: Academic Press.

Clark, L. and Watson, D. (1994) 'Distinguishing functional from dysfunctional affective responses', in P. Ekman and R. Davidson (eds) *The Nature of Emotion*, New York: Oxford University Press.

Copleston, F. (1965) *A History of Philosophy*, vol. 7, part II, Garden City: Image Books.

Cornford, F.M. (1912) *From Religion to Philosophy*, Atlantic Highlands: Humanities Press.

Corning, P. (2005) *Nature's Magic: Synergy in Evolution and the Fate of Humankind*, Cambridge: Cambridge University Press.

Cose, E. (2002) 'The voice that nobody heard', *Newsweek*, 140, 21: 47.

Crane, W. (1980) *Theories of Development: Concepts and Applications*, New Jersey: Prentice Hall.

Dewey, J. (1925) *Experience and Nature*, New York: Dover.

—— (1929a) *Individualism Old and New*, New York: Capricorn.

—— (1929b) *Liberalism and Social Action*, New York: Capricorn.

—— (1929c) *The Quest for Certainty: A Study of the Relation of Knowledge and Action*, New York: Minton, Balach.

—— (1931) *Philosophy and Civilization*, New York: Minton, Balach.

—— (1935) *Liberalism and Social Action*, New York: G.P. Putnam & Sons.

—— (1938) *Logic the Theory of Inquiry*, New York: Holt, Rinehart, and Winston.

—— (1949) *Knowing and the Known*, Boston: Beacon Press.

Dunlap, P.T. (2003) 'Destiny as capacity: the transformation of political identity in human development', unpublished Ph.D. Psych. dissertation, Institute of Imaginal Studies.

—— (2004) 'Embodying destiny through shame and fear', paper presented at San Francisco Jung Institute Conference on American Soul and the Body Politic, San Francisco, October.

Eliot, T.S. (1943) *Four Quartets*, New York: Harcourt, Brace.

Emerson, R.W. (1993) *Self-Reliance and Other Essays*, New York: Dover.

Erikson, E. (1958) *Young Man Luther*, New York: Norton.

—— (1968) *Identity Youth and Crisis*, New York: Norton.

—— (1969) *Gandhi's Truth*, New York: Norton.

—— (1974) *Dimensions of a New Identity*, New York: Norton.

—— (1980) *Identity and the Life Cycle*, New York: Norton.

—— (1982) *The Life Cycle Completed*, New York: Norton.

Faigan, G. (1990) *The Artist's Complete Guide to Facial Expressions*, New York: Watson-Guptill.

Flanagan, O. and Jackson, K. (1993) 'Justice, care, and gender: the Kohlberg–Gilligan debate revisited', in M.J. Larrabee (ed.) *An Ethic of Care*, New York: Routledge.

Fosha, D. (2000) *The Transforming Power of Affect*, New York: Basic Books.

Freud, S. (1961) *Civilization and its Discontents*. New York: Norton.

Friedman, G. (1981) *The Political Philosophy of the Frankfurt School*, London: Cornell University Press.

Gandhi, M. Quote from online posting. www.thinkexist.com (accessed July 15 2007).

Garry, P. (1992) *Liberalism and American Identity*, Kent: Kent State University Press.

Gellert, M. (2001) *The Fate of America*, Dulles: Potomac Books.

Goleman, D. (2003) *Destructive Emotions*, New York: Bantam Books.

Graves, C. Quote from online posting. www.clarewgraves.com (accessed July 26 2007).

Henderson, J. (1984) *Cultural Attitudes in Psychological Perspective*, Toronto: Inner City Books.

Heron, J. and Reason, P. (1997) 'A participatory inquiry paradigm', *Qualitative Inquiry*, 3, 3: 274–294.

Holstein, G. and Gubrium, J. (1995) 'The active interview', *Qualitative Research Methods Series*, 37.

Huddy, L. (2001) 'From social to political identity: a critical examination of social identity theory', *Political Psychology*, 22, 1: 127–155.

Hunt, M. (1993) *The Story of Psychology*, New York: Random House.

Inglis, J. and Steele, M. (2005) 'Complexity intelligence and cultural coaching: navigating the gap between our societal challenges and our capacities', *Integral Review*, 1.

Jaworski, J. (1996) *Synchronicity the Inner Path to Leadership*, San Francisco: Berret-Koehler.

Jay, M. (1973) *The Dialectical Imagination*, Boston: Little, Brown.

Jaynes, J. (1976) *The Origin of Consciousness in the Breakdown of the Bicameral Mind*, Boston: Houghton Mifflin.

Johnson, S. (1996) *The Practice of Emotionally Focused Marital Therapy*, Florence: Brunner/Mazel.

Joyce, J. (1916) *Portrait of a Young Artist*, New York: Colonial Press.

Jung, C. (1919) 'The psychological foundation of beliefs in spirits', *Collected Works*, vol. 8, part V, Princeton: University of Princeton Press.

—— (1927) 'The structure of the psyche', *Collected Works*, vol. 8, part III, Princeton: University of Princeton Press.

—— (1928) 'On psychic energy', *Collected Works*, vol. 8, part I, Princeton: University of Princeton Press.

—— (1931) 'Basic postulates of analytical psychology', *Collected Works*, vol. 8, part V, Princeton: University of Princeton Press.

—— (1939) 'Conscious, unconscious, and individuation', *Collected Works*, vol. 9.i, part VI, Princeton: University of Princeton Press.

—— (1957a) 'The transcendent function', *Collected Works*, vol. 8, part I, Princeton: University of Princeton Press.

—— (1957b) 'The undiscovered self', *Collected Works*, vol. 10, part IV, Princeton: University of Princeton Press.

—— (1971) *Psychological Types in Collected Works*, vol. 6, Princeton: University of Princeton Press.

Kalsched, D. (1996) *The Inner World of Trauma*, London: Routledge.

Kaplin, J. (1980) *Walt Whitman: A Life*, New York: Simon and Schuster.

Keats, J. (1817) Definition of "negative capability". Online posting. www.Wikipedia.com (accessed July 15 2007).

Kegan, R. (1982) *The Evolving Self*, Cambridge: Harvard University Press.

—— (1994) *In Over Our Heads*, Cambridge: Harvard University Press.

Kerlinger, F. (1984) *Liberalism and Conservatism: the Nature and Structure of Social Attitudes*, Mahwah, NJ: Lawrence Erlbaum Associates, Inc.

Kimbles, S. (2004) 'A cultural complex operating in the overlap of clinical and cultural space', in S. Kimbles and T. Singer (eds) *The Cultural Complex*, New York: Brunner-Routledge.

Kimbles, S. and Singer, T. (eds) (2004) *The Cultural Complex*, New York: Brunner-Routledge.

King, M.L., Jr. (1988) The Speeches Collection of Martin Luther King, Jr., MPI Home Video, ISBN# 1-55607-009-8.

King, R. (1972) *The Party of Eros*, Chapel Hill: University of Northern Carolina Press.

Kohlberg, L. (1981) *The Philosophy of Moral Development*, vol. 1, San Francisco: Harper & Row.

Korten, D. (2001) *When Corporations Ruled the World*, 2nd edn, Bloomfield, CT: Kumarian Press.

—— (2006) *The Great Turning: From Empire to Earth Community*, San Francisco: Berrett-Koehler.

Kuhn, T. (1970) *The Structure of Scientific Revolutions*, Chicago: University of Chicago Press.

Lakoff, G. (1996) *Moral Politics*, Chicago: University of Chicago Press.

—— (2004) *Don't Think of an Elephant*, White River Junction: Chelsea Green.

Lerner, M. (2006) *The Left Hand of God*, New York: HarperCollins.

Lewellen, T. (1983) *Political Anthropology*, Westport, CT: Bergin and Garvey Press.

Loevinger, J. (1976) *Ego Development: Concepts and Theories*, San Francisco: Jossey-Bass.

McDaniel, Stanley V., *Transtantric Metaphilosophy: a New Direction in East-West Synthesis*, Privately published, 1998. Available from the author, 1055 W. College Ave. #273, Santa Rosa CA USA 95401.

Macy, J. (1991) *World as Lover, World as Self*, Berkeley: Parallax Press.

Marcus, J. and Tarr, Z. (eds) (1984) *Foundations of the Frankfurt School of Social Research*, New Brunswick: Transaction Books.

Marcuse, H. (1955) *Eros and Civilization*, Boston: Beacon Press.

Matustik, M. (2001) *Jurgen Habermas: A Philosophical-Political Profile*, New York: Rowman and Littlefield.

May, R. (1981) *Freedom and Destiny*, New York: Norton.

Meyerhoff, H. (ed.) (1959) *The Philosophy of History in Our Time*, Garden City/New York: Doubleday.

Micklethwait, J. and Wooldridge, A. (2004) *The Right Nation*, New York: Penguin Books.

Mogenson, G. (1992) 'The erotics of blame', *Journal of Analytical Psychology*, 37: 153–171.

Molad, G. (2001) 'On presenting one's case: embracing trauma and the dialogue between analysts', *The Psychoanalytic Review*, 88, 1: 95–111.

Moyer, B. (2001) *Doing Democracy*, Gabriola Island: New Society Publishers.

Nathanson, D. (1992) *Shame and Pride: Affect, Sex, and the Birth of the Self*, New York: Norton.

Omer, A. (1990) 'Experience and Otherness: on the undermining of learning in educational organizations', Brandeis University.

—— (2003) 'Between Columbine and the Twin Towers: fundamentalist culture as a failure of imagination', *Revision*, 26, 2: 37–40.

—— (2005) 'The spacious center: leadership and the creative transformation of culture', *Shift: At the Frontiers of Consciousness*, 6: 30–33.

—— (2006) *Selected Concepts from Imaginal Transformative Praxis*, Petuluna CA: Institute of Imaginal Studies.

Orren, K. and Skowronek, S. (2004) *The Search for American Political Development*, Cambridge: Cambridge University Press.

Outhwaite, W. (1998) 'Jurgen Habermas', in R. Stones (ed.) *Key Sociological Thinkers*, New York: New York University Press.

Partridge, E. (ed.) (1959) *Origins: A Short Etymological Dictionary of Modern English*, 2nd edn, New York: Macmillan.

Pastorino, E., Dunham, R., Kidwell, J., Bacho, R. and Lamborn, S. (1997) 'Domain-specific gender comparisons in identity development among college youths: ideology and relationships', *Adolescence*, 32, 127: 559–577.

Piaget, J. (1962) *Play, Dreams and Imitation in Childhood*, New York: Norton.

Polkinghorne, D. (1983) *Methodology for the Human Sciences*, Albany: State University of New York Press.

Prager, K. (1986) 'Identity development, age, and college experience in women', *Journal of Genetic Psychology*, 147, 1: 31–36.

Pye, L. (1966) *Aspects of Political Development*, Boston/Toronto: Little, Brown.

Rawls, J. (1996) *Political Liberalism*, New York: Columbia University Press.

Riessman, C.K. (1993) 'Narrative analysis', *Qualitative Research Methods Series*, 30.

Rilke, R. (1991) *The Duino Elegies*, trans. L. Hammer and S. Jaeger. Old Chapman: Sachem Press.

—— (1996) *Rilke's Book of Hours: Love Poems to God*, trans. A. Barrows and J. Macy, New York: Riverhead.

—— Quote from online posting. http://www.learningful.com (accessed July 15 2007).

Samuels, A. (1989) *The Plural Psyche*, London: Routledge.

—— (1993) *The Political Psyche*, London: Routledge.

—— (2001) *Politics on the Couch*, London: Profile Books.

Sandel, M. (1996) *Democracy's Discontent*, Cambridge: Harvard University Press.

Santayana, G. (1968) *The Birth of Reason and Other Essays*, New York: Columbia University Press.

Satel, S. and Sommers, C. (2005) *One Nation Under Therapy*, New York: St. Martin's Press.

Scherer, K. (1994) 'Evidence for both universality and cultural specificity of emotion elicitation', in P. Ekman and R. Davidson (eds) *The Nature of Emotion*, New York: Oxford University Press.

Singer, T. (2004) 'The cultural complex and archetypal defenses of the group spirit', in S. Kimbles and T. Singer (eds) *The Cultural Complex*, New York: Brunner-Routledge.

Smith, M.B. (1994) 'Selfhood at risk', *American Psychologist*, May.

Sommers, C. and Satel, S. (2005) *One Nation Under Therapy*, New York: St. Martin's Press.

Sonnert, G. and Commons, M.L. (1994) 'Society and the highest stages of moral development', *Politics and the Individual*, 4, 1: 31–55.

Steiner, G. (1976) *After Babel*, New York: Oxford University Press.

Steiner, R. (1991) *Social Issues*, New York: Anthroposophic Press.

Tarnas, R. (1991) *The Passion of the Western Mind*, New York: Ballentine Books.

Teilhard, P. (1963) *The Activation of Energy*, New York: Harcourt Brace.

—— (1969) *Human Energy*, New York: Harcourt Brace.

Tocqueville, A.D. (1945) *Democracy in America*, vol. 2, New York: Alfred Knopf.

Tronto, J. (1993) *Moral Boundaries: A Political Argument for an Ethic of Care*, New York: Routledge.

Trudeau, G. (2003) 'Doonesbury', *The Press Democrat*, 13 July.

Varange, V. (F.P. Yockey) (1962) *Imperium: The Philosophy of History and Politics*, Costa Mesa: Noontide Press.

Wallis, J. (2005) *God's Politics*, New York: HarperCollins.

Walsh, D. (1997) *The Growth of the Liberal Soul*, Columbia: University of Missouri Press.

Wilber, K. (1995) *Sex, Ecology and Spirituality*, Boston: Shambhala.

—— (2000) *A Brief History of Everything*, Boston: Shambhala.

—— (2001) *A Theory of Everything*, Boston: Shambhala.

—— (2006) 'What we are, that we see. Part 1: Response to some recent criticism in a Wild West fashion', Online posting. KenWilber.com blog. (accessed July 7 2006).

Will, G. (2005) 'Today's therapeutic culture', *The Press Democrat*, 21 April.

Zinn, H. (2005) *A People's History of the United States*, New York: HarperCollins.

Index

Page entries for headings with subheadings refer to general aspects of that topic
Page entries in **bold** refer to figures/diagrams
Page entries for personal names are subdivided (where necessary) according to the ideas/discourse of that person.